INTERACTIVE PROCESSES IN READING

Edited by

ALAN M. LESGOLD
CHARLES A. PERFETTI
University of Pittsburgh

 LAWRENCE ERLBAUM ASSOCIATES, PUBLISHERS

1981   Hillsdale, New Jersey

Lawrence Erlbaum Associates, Inc., Publishers
365 Broadway
Hillsdale, New Jersey 07642

Library of Congress Cataloging in Publication Data

Main entry under title:

Interactive processes in reading.

Proceedings of a conference held at the Learning
Research and Development Center, University of Pittsburgh,
in Sept. 1979.
Includes bibliographies and index.
1. Reading, Psychology of. I. Lesgold, Alan M.
II. Perfetti, Charles A.
BF456.R2I54   428.4'01'9   80-21048
ISBN 0-89859-079-5

Printed in the United States of America

Contents

Preface

Huey (1908) remarked that to understand reading would entail descriptions of some of "the most intricate workings of the human mind [p. 6]." Whereas research on these intricacies has focused on analysis of component processes in isolation, there has been widespread acknowledgment that some account must be taken of the interaction of these components. Interest in process interaction has been stimulated especially by the publication of Rumelhart's (1977) paper, "Toward an Interactive Model of Reading." In addition, there is an increased sophistication in approaches to language understanding generally, quite aside from reading itself. Work on text structure and knowledge structure has progressed to the point that descriptions of word recognition and reading comprehension can build upon accounts of the structures contained in texts and of the accumulated knowledge of the reader. Moreover, there is growing interest in the sources of individual differences in reading skill. As we begin to take fuller account of reading process interactions, it seems likely that our understanding of reading disability will be modified. It was against this background that the idea of a conference on interactive reading suggested itself. This volume is the edited proceedings of that conference, which was held at the Learning Research and Development Center of the University of Pittsburgh in September 1979.

As plans for the conference on interactive processes developed, we had several opportunities to consider which issues we thought most important to address. One of our more palatable lists is shown in Fig. 1. The idea for this list originated in an after-hours discussion at some distant meeting of the American Educational Research Association (perhaps in Toronto). Present at this conference were Lin-

BILL OF FARE OF THE READING RESTAURANT

BEFORE DINNER, COCKTAILS IN THE BOTTOM-UP ROOM

- Data-driven Daiquiri
- Working Memory Wallbanger
- Gibson (Distinctive Features with a Twist)
- Gin and Phonics
- Rumelhart and Coke
- Lesgold Wasser
- Slow Decay Fizz
- Limited-Capacity Zombie (Limit 5 ± 2 per customer)

APPETIZERS

- Raw Graphemes on the half-shell
- Processes à la Maison
- Kintsch Lorraine
- Terrine d'Accesses Lexical
- Fresh Saccades (in Season)

Above served with Phonological Recoding, $1.25 extra

ENTREES

Pasta

- Fettucini Alfonetica (A variation on the classic dish that tastes like it sounds)
- Lexical Linguine in Grapheme Sauce (al dente, of course)
- Lasagne LaBerge (layers of homemade automaticity)

From the Sea

- Macrostructures Marinara (for large appetites)
- Deep Fried Orthographies Leonardo (Old Yugoslavian Recipe)
- Semantic Networks stuffed with Schemata (If ordered 24 hours in advance, fresh scripts can be substituted for schemata)
- Fresh Texts Sauteed in Propositions (Texts flown fresh daily from Colorado Mountain Streams)

Meat and Fowl

- Context Kiev (a traditional favorite of slow decoders)
- Miscue Tripe à la Mode (the dish of National Holidays in Reading Land)
- Decoders of Beef with Dyslexia Tips
- Rack of Syntax with Boiled Parsers
- On-Line Processes au Just (appealing to the eye as well as the palate)

Above served with sight word salad, and choice of blended graphemes. pseudowords au gratin, and mashed knowledge structures

FOR DESSERT

- Longitudinal Loquats in heavy syrup
- Kolers Upside Down Cake
- Fresh Fonemes of the Season
- Petit Foregrounders
- Contextualist Custard
- Graphic Surprise

After dinner, visit the Top-Down Room featuring entertainment by the Semantic Distractors.

Visit us for Sunday Brunch, featuring such favorites as Eggs Dialect, Orthographic Irregularity Prune Danish, etc.

viii

nea Ehri and Rod Barron, in addition to the two of us; however, the final Bill of Fare shown in Fig. 1 is solely the responsibility of the editors.

The outcome of the conference is the set of chapters presented in this book. A few of the chapters are substantially different from the presentations made at the conference; however, most closely reflect them. We decided against formal discussion chapters, though many of the chapters have been modified in response to the lively informal discussion at the conference.

The 15 chapters share a number of common issues. These include the role of contextual influences on lexical access, specific models of lexical access and word pronunciation, speech and visual processes in reading, the role of knowledge in comprehension, and sources of skill difference and skill development.

The first two chapters, by Levy and by Rumelhart and McClelland, set out theoretical considerations relevant for interactive models. Levy (Chap. 1) discusses a number of methodological and pretheoretical issues raised by an interactive-processes framework, and Rumelhart and McClelland (Chap. 2) present a detailed account of an interactive model and apply it to the problem of identifying words.

Issues of speech processing in reading are dealt with by Glushko, Katz and Feldman, Baddeley and Lewis, Levy, Barron, and Lesgold and Curtis. Baddeley and Lewis (Chap. 5) discuss an important distinction between two aspects of speech processes in reading—the acoustic "inner voice" and the articulatory "loop." They argue that neither plays a critical role in reading, although the latter may play a memory support role under some conditions. Questions of orthographic structure in lexical access are addressed by Katz and Feldman, by Glushko, and by Barron. Katz and Feldman (Chap. 4) provide a framework for dealing with phonological and visual codes for words and word parts, especially syllables, emphasizing an important role for phonological coding. They report experiments with bi-alphabetic Serbo-Croatian subjects as well as with English-speaking subjects. Whereas Katz and Feldman point to the rule-governed nature of orthography and its relation to a phonological level, Glushko (Chap. 3) takes a quite different approach to the lexicon. He argues, with support from several experiments, that the rules relating spelling to sound are unnecessary to describe how ordinary reading and pseudoword-reading work. Mechanisms for pronouncing words and pseudowords depend on access to a lexicon in which words are organized into neighborhoods according to the graphemes that they share. Barron's chapter (12), which is focused on individual differences, relies on Glushko's neighborhood model to account for his reader ability differences in lexical decision tasks.

A focal concern of an interactive framework is the influence of syntactic and semantic constraints in text on word identification. This issue is discussed by Danks and Hill, McConkie and Zola, Carpenter and Just, Stanovich, Perfetti and Roth, and Frederiksen. The wide range of experimental tasks reported in these chapters testifies to the importance and pervasiveness of contextual influences, but also suggests that they are not yet well understood. Thus, Danks and Hill (Chap. 6) demonstrate that influences of context on oral reading are quite large, and McConkie and Zola (Chap. 7) report that the durations and locations of eye fixations are not as much influenced by a word's predictability as one might expect. Also using eye movement data, Carpenter and Just (Chap. 8) develop a multicomponent model to account for accumulated eye fixation durations. Their model assigns a significant role to properties of text structure as well as to properties of words and sentences. Perfetti and Roth (Chap. 11) use comparisons of word vocalization latency in different contexts to support their analysis of contextual effects on word identification and their suggestion that less skilled readers are more dependent on context. Frederiksen (Chap. 14) also uses this measure in research that suggests a more complex picture of context effects. Stanovich (Chap. 10) provides an account of two distinct contextual mechanisms that may help account for the effects of facilitative and nonfacilitative contexts in tasks of identification. He suggests that an automatic, attention-free process may precede a nonautomatic, conscious expectancy.

An emphasis on comprehension, beyond word identification, is present in the chapter by Bisanz and Voss, as well as the one by Carpenter and Just. Bisanz and Voss (Chap. 9) argue that knowledge relevant to understanding stories and other texts will affect comprehension. They demonstrate that knowledge concerning character motivation is important for superficially straightforward children's stories, and they suggest developmental aspects of such knowledge. They also point out that individual differences in specific knowledge, as opposed to general verbal abilities, have profound effects on components of reading comprehension.

Individual differences in reading skill are addressed by a number of authors. In addition to Bisanz and Voss, who stress specific knowledge differences, questions of the source of reading disability are discussed by Katz and Feldman, by Stanovich, and by Lesgold and Curtis and are a primary focus of Perfetti and Roth, Barron, and Frederiksen. Lesgold and Curtis (Chap. 13) report some results of an in-progress longitudinal study of beginning reading. They suggest that among beginning readers, there are differences in general reading achievement that are related to differences in tasks involving significant phonological components. An important feature of their work is that they can tie performance on information-processing tasks to progress through a reading curriculum. The implication of phonological sources of reading skill difference in beginning readers is mirrored by Barron for older children (Grades 5 and 6) and, in part, by Frederiksen for teenagers.

Barron (Chap. 12) suggests that a phonographic strategy, using phonological information to access the contents of a lexical entry, is characteristic of skilled readers but not of less skilled readers, and he offers some possible explanations for this relationship. Perfetti and Roth (Chap. 11) present an activation model for word identification and demonstrate that rapid activation based on lower-level features is characterized by slower activation and a corresponding greater influence of context. They also point out that less skilled readers are less able to use context in some conditions. This latter point is one of many problems identified by Frederiksen for older readers. He concludes that more able readers, who are skilled at decoding, in context reduce their reliance on lower-level decoding. In addition, Frederiksen reports data on representative tasks at the word level, the discourse level, and the sentence integration level, and he argues that differences in the efficiency of component processes are found at all these levels.

The final chapter (15), by Lesgold and Perfetti (not presented at the conference), discusses theoretical and methodological considerations that are implied by taking seriously the possibilities of interactive processes.

We wish to acknowledge the participation of those who increased the quality of interactive processes at the conference without making formal presentations: These include Isabel Beck, Elizabeth Gallistel, Henry Halff, Thomas Hogaboam, Michael Masson, Richard Olsen, Linda Sala, Margaret Schadler, and Phyllis Weaver, as well as a number of our faculty and student colleagues from the University of Pittsburgh and Carnegie–Mellon University. We are especially appreciative of the efforts of Patricia Graw in arranging the conference and in helping with many conference and book-related matters. We also thank Gail (Yaksic) Kratt for her assistance during the conference, and we gratefully acknowledge the important editorial assistance of Margaret (Lechowicz) Lazzari in preparing this volume.

We greatly appreciate the support this project received from the National Institute of Education and from Robert Glaser and Lauren Resnick, the Co-Directors of the Learning Research and Development Center.

Charles Perfetti

Alan Lesgold

REFERENCES

Huey, E. B. *The psychology and pedagogy of reading.* New York: Macmillan, 1908. (Republished by M.I.T. Press, Cambridge, Mass., 1968.)

Rumelhart, David E. Toward an interactive model of reading. In Stanislav Dornic (Ed.), *Attention and performance VI.* Hillsdale, N.J.: Lawrence Erlbaum Associates, 1977.

1 Interactive Processing During Reading

Betty Ann Levy
McMaster University

The study of reading has enjoyed recent advances both in the development of theory and in the accumulation of important data. This chapter attempts to highlight these advances while pointing to areas needing further clarification. The first section outlines the basic assumptions of serial versus interactive models of reading. Assumptions needing refinement are discussed. The second section consists of a review of studies on context effects from different paradigms. The aim here is to show the variety of ways in which context influences stimulus analysis. Finally, the third section reviews some of my own research on a vocal suppression effect. The idea again is to show the flexibility of processing that must be captured by any adequate model of reading.

WHAT IS ASSUMED IN AN INTERACTIVE MODEL OF READING?

A few years ago disenchantment with serial-stage models led some theorists to postulate more flexible conceptualizations in which to capture the richness of human reading skills. Models of interactive processing, heavily influenced by work on artificial intelligence seemed to offer a clear alternative to the "bottom-up" processing models then available in the literature. Though differing in important ways, most serial-stage models of reading shared some critical features (e.g., Gough, 1972; LaBerge & Samuels, 1974). Essentially, the visual signals were transmitted from visual analyzers to phonemic analyzers (optional in some models; e.g., LaBerge & Samuels) and finally to the semantic system. Signals were analyzed through these stages *successively*. The output from the earlier

1

stage acted as a *data base* for the subsequent stage, and this was the main form of integration or data accumulation across stages.

It was to offer an alternative to these serial-stage assumptions that interactive processing models were formulated. In one of the more detailed descriptions of interactive processing during reading, Rumelhart (1977) suggested an information-processing system consisting of several knowledge sources, each operating independently but all in parallel. These knowledge sources were processors at different levels of linguistic representation, including feature, letter, letter-cluster, lexical, syntactic, and semantic levels. The outputs from each of these knowledge sources were hypotheses or best guesses from the data available at that level. These hypotheses were transferred to a central device (message center) where they could be viewed by all other knowledge sources, thus being available as evidence for or against hypotheses at other levels. Comprehension of a message was attained when the accumulated evidence most strongly supported one particular hypothesis. Three basic differences in assumptions between the serial and the interactive approaches, then, were: (1) sequential versus parallel analyses at different knowledge levels; (2) the output from each level acted as a data base for only the next stage in serial models, but acted as a data base for all knowledge levels in the interactive model; and (3) comprehension referred to reaching the semantic level in the serial model, but it referred to the best ''guess'' based on evidence from multiple sources in the interactive model.

Although on the surface the assumptions of interactive processing look straightforward, they are in fact complex and may have led to some confusion as to what such models predict in experimental tasks. Rumelhart (1977) originally conceptualized the integration of hypotheses from different knowledge sources in terms of a mathematical model of hypothesis evaluation. The dependencies among knowledge sources stemmed from the support relationships for hypotheses contained in the message center. A particular hypothesis gained support from other hypotheses at the same level but also from hypotheses from other knowledge sources that were consistent with the view in question. For example, a hypothesis for *the* at the lexical level could be supported by a hypothesis for *th* at the letter-cluster level, as well as by the expectation of a determiner at the syntactic level. Rumelhart suggested that the overall strength for any hypothesis could be calculated by determining two components: (1) the strength of direct evidence coming largely from analyses of the stimulus input or the bottom-up processing; and (2) the contextual support coming from the same and higher levels, indicating largely the amount of top-down support. Total strength was determined by a multiplicative relationship between these feature-based and contextually based components.

It appears, then, that one should expect dependencies among the knowledge sources, since they support each other's processing, but it is not clear how these dependencies are manifested during processing. Specifically, how does a strongly supported hypothesis at one level influence the processing at other knowledge sources? One possibility is that the influence occurs at the stage of data integration only. That is, each processor continues to analyze independently and uses the message center information only to decide when to terminate processing. There is perhaps a threshold strength for determining when comprehension of the message is achieved. Threshold or comprehension could be achieved through strong top-down support, with only weak bottom-up support or vice-versa, so long as the total strength was above some value. The point here is that the *nature* of data accumulation within a knowledge source is unaffected by the message center information, but the total *amount* of processing could change if other levels have strongly supported hypotheses. For example, if semantic constraints were strong, less supporting evidence from the data-driven levels would be required before a comprehension threshold would be reached. This is a rather passive view of data integration where the nature of evidence accumulation is unaltered by other available information.

A more active view of interactive processing might suggest that message center information is used to modify the activity of individual processors. That is, when a particular hypothesis has strong outside support, the analyzers of a particular knowledge source may now actively change their own processing, either to seek confirming evidence for that view or to accept that view and therefore fail to analyze infomation they would otherwise have tested. For example, the nature of feature analysis may change if upper-level analyzers strongly support *bat* as opposed to *hat*. The feature analyzers may actively "search for" relevant distinctive features rather than analyzing for all features, or if semantic context makes a particular stimulus highly predictable, the feature analyzers may fail to read that stimulus. Since interactive processing is often viewed as the reading equivalent of "we see what we expect to see," this view is not untenable. The form of the "interactiveness" here is a change in the nature of processing at a particular level, when outside views are available.

Simply having knowledge about the total strength of hypotheses within the message center does not really indicate how this evidence affects the individual analyzers. Do they use this information only at the integration level to determine termination of processing, or do these strength values lead to modification in the use of individual analyzers during subsequent processing?

As evidence accumulates showing contextual effects early in processing, it becomes more critical for us to specify the mechanisms involved in producing process interactions. At the level of experimentation, support for interactive processing is sometimes claimed when a *statistical* interaction is obtained between data level and contextual level variables. Such statistical interactions do not necessarily clarify the nature of the process interactions involved. Following additive factors logic, such statistical interactions would be taken to indicate that the experimental variables affect the same *stage* of processing. Separating stage theory from interactive processing theory explanations of such statistical interactions requires clearer specification of the mechanisms involved in interactive theories.

This point is highlighted by recent advances in model development. Massaro (1977) offered convincing arguments against an interactive approach and suggested a serial-stage model to explain data believed to necessitate an interactive interpretation. Massaro's most damning criticism of the interactive approach was that it is based on computer models that possess fewer limitations on processing or memory capacity. Human information processors have marked limitations in both processing and memory capacity, thus violating assumptions of the interactive framework. In order to allow data accumulation over time, in the manner outlined by Rumelhart, information at all knowledge levels must be continuously available. Yet there is evidence that visual feature information has a short lifetime in iconic storage and could not be replenished without frequent regressive eye movements (each of which overwrites prior feature information as one moves along a line of print). There is also memory data indicating that different levels of processing have different memorial life spans, and peripheral information can only be maintained through rehearsal (Craik & Tulving, 1975). This, of course, requires directing processing resources to a particular level, and it is unclear that capacity is available to maintain all knowledge sources simultaneously. An enormous memory load would be encountered in reading even short passages. Massaro, therefore, argues that data availability cannot be continuous at all levels; it must be accumulated in stages to relieve the information overload.

Massaro then suggested a modified serial-stage model, where the "stages" do not act strictly sequentially. Rather, as soon as data from the earlier stage arrive, processing at the later stage begins. Thus the stages overlap in time, allowing for contextual influences on word recognition. While sharing many features with interactive models, Massaro's model integrates lower featural and orthographic information, which then combines with syntactic and semantic constraints. Thus the model cannot accept the assumption that lower-level processes are modified by higher-level constraints. Although it is not clear that this interpretation was intended in Rumelhart's models, it has been embraced by others using an interactive perspective (e.g., Marslen-Wilson & Welsh, 1978).

A major issue, then, is whether "interactiveness" stems strictly from simultaneous processes or whether successive processes could also be involved. Critical to this choice may be the specification of the manner in which higher-level processes influence lower-level processes. Certainly, interesting possibilities are now being explored. Notably, McClelland's (1978) model suggesting cascading processes that run in parallel, but with different times needed to reach completion, seems worthy of study.

Though we have covered some distance in showing the early occurrence of contextual interactions, the current interactive models need elaboration to handle the complex effects described in the literature. The next section of the chapter outlines some of these context effects often taken to indicate interactive processing.

CONTEXT EFFECTS: EVIDENCE FOR INTERACTIVE PROCESSING?

Context effects have been observed in lexical decision tasks, in studies of phoneme monitoring, during listening, and in work on memory for prose. The main findings are now briefly summarized, with the aim of documenting the many forms such contextual influences can take.

Lexical Decision

Semantic priming effects in lexical decision tasks have provided a useful analytical tool for exploring mechanisms involved in semantic processing during recognition. Semantic priming refers to the facilitation observed in the reaction time required to make a word–nonword judgment when the target word (e.g., *doctor*) is preceded by an associatively related word (e.g., *nurse*), compared to when it is preceded by an unrelated word (e.g., *butter*). Meyer, Schvaneveldt, and Ruddy (1975) concluded that semantic priming represented a contextual influence early in word processing when they found that the magnitude of the priming effect was enhanced using a degraded, rather than a clear, stimulus presentation. Following additive factors logic, Meyer et al. decided that this stimulus quality × context interaction indicated that these variables affected the same stage of processing. Since stimulus degradation affects grapheme encoding, they concluded that context also affected this early grapheme-encoding stage of processing.

Initially, semantic priming was believed to involve only one mechanism, but further experimentation suggested that several kinds of priming may exist. One form is a fast-acting, automatic semantic activation that leads to facilitation, but there is also a slower, attention-demanding process that can produce facilitation for expected words and inhibition for unexpected words (e.g., Becker, 1976; Fischler, 1977; Fischler & Goodman, 1978; Neely, 1977). An interesting finding related to the automatic form of priming is that this facilitation can occur (and indeed may be optimally obtained) when subjects are not consciously aware of the priming stimulus (Fischler & Goodman, 1978; Marcel, 1976).

An important generalization of these semantic priming effects was to the case of sentence primes. Schuberth and Eimas (1977) used both congruous and incongruous sentence frames as primes to the target words used in a lexical decision task. Both facilitation for congruous contexts and inhibition for incongruous contexts were observed. The picture for sentence processing is not this simple, however, as illustrated by three further studies of sentence-priming effects. Fischler and Bloom (1979) studied sentence contexts used as primes for highly predictable targets, for congruent but unlikely targets, and for anomalous targets (i.e., words not congruent with the context). They found inhibition for words anomalous to the context primes, but significant facilitation occurred only for the most predictable target for each contextual prime. This narrow range of facilitation was not under conscious control, and it was not related to the larger inhibition effect. Two mechanisms appeared to be involved—one that provided automatic facilitation to the most predictable targets only, and the other, more controlled inhibitory process for words not consistent with the contextual primes.

However, Kleiman (1980) tested conditions similar to those used by Fischler and Bloom but uncovered a broader range of facilitative effects. Kleiman varied both the relatedness of the prime to the target response and the degree to which the prime plus target formed an acceptable sentence. His targets were: (1) best completions or the most predictable target response to that prime; (2) targets associatively related to the best completion but that were unlikely to be generated as responses themselves; and (3) unrelated targets. The related and unrelated targets varied (high, medium, low) in the degree to which the target plus prime formed an acceptable sentence. Like Fischler and Bloom, Kleiman found large facilitative effects for best completions, but he also found some facilitation for words related to best completion and for words that formed acceptable completions to sentences. Further, those two forms of facilitation were independent and additive. That is, related words were responded to faster, even if they formed anomalous sentences with the prime, and words that formed acceptable sentences with the prime were responded to faster, even if the target word was not associatively related to the best completion; and both effects could occur together. Kleiman suggested a more complex model for contextual facilitation. This included automatic spreading activation to account for the best completion and related prime results (consistent with Fischler & Bloom's view), as well as a schematic component whereby sentence frames act as schemata with variable constraints. Concepts in a sentence frame constrain the words that can fill that frame by spreading activation to acceptable completions.

The picture of how context affects word recognition, then, is neither straightforward nor simple. There is reasonably good consensus that best completions and maybe words associatively related to best completions are automatically activated by sentence contexts. There also is some evidence for broader-range context effects, in that Kleiman finds facilitation for words that form acceptable completions to sentences even when these words would not be the generated responses. Further, Stanovich and West (Stanovich & West, 1979; West & Stanovich, 1978) found that young children showed facilitation for targets congruous with the sentence frames and inhibition for words incongruous with these frames. Adults showed only the facilitation effect under normal reading conditions, but when the stimulus conditions were degraded, the inhibition effect for incongruous words then appeared. A temporal analysis indicated that the facilitation effect occurred very rapidly, but the inhibition effect needed time to develop. Stanovich (see Chapter 10 in this volume for details) has related his facilitation and inhibition results to the Posner and Snyder (1975) distinction between conscious and automatic processing.

Of particular interest to the issue of interactive processing is the Stanovich and West (1979) stimulus degradation effect for adult readers. They found inhibition for incongruous primes only if the stimulus was difficult to read. They argued that this was because word recognition is normally very rapid for adult readers and that there is insufficient time available for the inhibitory effects to develop. If reading is made difficult, as in the degraded stimulus case, processing is slowed down, and the inhibitory effect of context can be observed. This interpretation of a context × stimulus quality interaction invites comparison with the earlier interpretation of the interaction given by Meyer, Schvaneveldt, and Ruddy. These two explanations highlight the interpretive problem in addressing a statistical interaction involving context. When context interacts with a stimulus quality variable, does that mean that context is acting on the same early stage of encoding being influenced by the stimulus quality variable, or does it mean that stimulus quality variations require changes in the use of the processing system? Stanovich and West (1979) speculated: "An interactive model thus leaves open the possibility that higher level processes could actually compensate for deficiencies in lower level processes" (P. 84). An example of such compensation is that slower word recognition (for young children or with degraded stimuli) may be compensated for by more reliance on top-down or contextual constraints. Thus interactiveness between contextual and stimulus effects is viewed as changes in the nature of processing, though it is not clear whether this means a difference in the nature of stimulus analyses themselves or a change in the dependence on stimulus information before reaching a comprehension threshold.

Several important points should be noted from this lexical decision literature. Even in this simple situation, there is more than one way in which context affects word processing. First, there is a rapid automatic facilitation for highly predictable words. This could be the purest form of predictive reading and may be explained in terms of less, or different, stimulus processing when context highly constrains the lexical alternatives. Second, there is the slower, more conscious form of contextual influence, whereby words not consistent with prior wording are inhibited whereas those consistent with prior context are more easily processed. This form of context effect looks more like a data integration than a data prediction effect and could be due to the ease of organizing new with past information.

Further, Stanovich and West have provided an interesting explanation of stimulus quality × context interactions. The stimulus variables and contextual variables both affect the speed of processing, and the work of both McClelland (1978) and Perfetti and Roth (this volume) indicates that the speed of processes may prove important in understanding reading phenomena. This and the earlier automatic versus attentional forms of context effect put an emphasis on processing capacity requirements—another area that needs clarification in existing interactive models. Finally, a note of caution has been sounded by Stanovich and West and clearly echoed by Broadbent and Broadbent (in press) concerning our understanding of how stimulus clarity affects processing. Effects due to the nature of the stimulus display characteristics deserve future attention, since they may offer insight into the nature of processing changes due to contextual constraint. Most interactive models, as currently formulated, seem to offer limited guidance in understanding the variety of contextual influences seen even in this simple paradigm.

Phoneme Monitoring

Phoneme-monitoring tasks have also been used to question how prior context constrains the processing of words. In the case of ambiguous words, one can ask whether a bias in the context will lead to disambiguating a particular target word, so that it is no more difficult to comprehend than an unambiguous word. Foss and Jenkins (1973) found that a prior contextual bias toward one interpretation of an ambiguous word did not make the ambiguous word easier to recognize. They suggested that disambiguation followed lexical access of the multiple meanings of ambiguous items. Thus context did not affect processing by *predicting* a particular lexical interpretation; it affected processing by constraining the choice among the multiply processed meanings at a later decision stage. However, Swinney and Hake (1976) showed that if the prior context *strongly* predicts only one possible interpretation of an ambiguous word, then that word is as easily understood as an unambiguous word. Again, as in the lexical decision task, there appear to be two effects of prior context: (1) an early processing constraint for best completions to sentence frames; and (2) a later constraint imposed at the decision phase when the bias constrains the possible alternatives but does not strongly indicate only one possible lexical interpretation.

A further question has also been studied using a phoneme-monitoring technique—namely, how top-down and bottom-up processes interact during processing. Morton and Long (1976) found that initial phonemes were detected faster if the target word was very predictable from the prior sentence context. Their argument was that prior sentence context facilitated rapid lexical access for an expected word and that this rapid lexical access allowed subjects to bypass prior stimulus analysis. They took their findings as support for the claim that phoneme identification occurred after the word had been recognized. Newman and Dell (1978), on the other hand, found that a similar-sounding phoneme in the word prior to the critical phoneme slowed detection time and led to error. If constituent phoneme identification follows word identification, it is difficult to see how a constituent of a prior word could lead to phonemic confusion in the target-word analysis. In a subsequent article, Dell and Newman (1980) showed that predictability of the target word from the sentence context had no influence on performance if the stimulus environment was nonconfusing. However, when similar phonemes led to confusability in the feature analysis, performance was determined by the word's predictability, as found by Morton and Long. There was a disjunctive rather than an additive effect; that is, the system seemed to operate either top-down or bottom-up.

It is tempting to equate Dell and Newman's confusable environment manipulation with the degraded stimulus conditions used by Stanovich and West in the lexical decision task. Both manipulations slowed down stimulus processing, and then one observed a larger effect of contextual constraint. Again, we might be observing a change in processing strategy so that processing resources are reallocated to the domain providing the best hypotheses. Another possibility is that all analyses proceeded in parallel but the decision process was determined by the best source of information. One might expect that the computations of the message center would be confused by the conflicting evidence from the signal domain in the Dell and Newman study, and although the cognitive constraint would help to alleviate this problem, some slowing of decision times should be observed. This did not occur, instead a complete trade-off or processing change was observed. As in the lexical decision literature, then, several forms of contextual influence can be observed. Both predictive and later decision effects occur, and the system seems able to move from a top-down to a bottm-up processing bias at the whim of task demands.

Listening Studies

Some of the most interesting work on the interaction of contextual and stimulus factors comes from studies on mispronunciation during listening, reported by Cole and by Marslen-Wilson and their collaborators. Cole and his co-workers (Cole & Jakimik, 1978, 1980) asked subjects to detect mispronunciations while listening to passages and then varied the syntactic and semantic constraints in the context preceding the mispronounced word. The influence of top-down processes could be observed in that mispronunciations were detected faster and more frequently in words related to the theme of the passage. It appeared that thematic constraints led to predictions about the upcoming word, which then led to faster rejection of the stimulus if it did not verify that view. Similar syntactic constraints were observed in that prior context determined whether "carko" would be heard as a mispronunciation of "car go" or as "cargo."

Interestingly, for both types of constraints, the mispronunciations were detected faster when they appeared in a later syllable rather than the first syllable. Here Cole and Jakimik argued that later syllables are more predictable than first syllables because they are constrained both by the top-down factors and by analyses of the first syllable. Thus mismatches of the input with the very specifically predicted syllable will be easily detected. Cole clearly views perception as a product of both top-down and bottom-up constraints, with subjects predicting what will occur in the stimulus array. Cole's data are quite compatible with Massaro's model in that the top-down constraints are maximal after some feature analysis and at the word recognition stage. However, Cole's view differs from Massaro's in that the nature of stimulus processing is altered by contextual constraints in Cole's explanation, but not in Massaro's. The syllable effect seems to be compatible with an interactive and a serial-stage model (at least as Massaro sees serial processing).

Marslen-Wilson also used mispronunciations in a listening task, but he asked some subjects to shadow the passage (i.e., repeat it back exactly) rather than detect the errors. His measure was fluent restorations of the mispronunciations— that is, rapid responses of the correct pronunciation to the mispronounced word. Fluent restorations appear to be subjects' perception of what is expected, rather than what is actually said. Marslen-Wilson and Welsh (1978) find evidence for bottom-up constraints in that large deviations (three features) are better detected than small deviations (one feature). However, they also find an interesting inter-action between the syllable in which the mispronunciation occurs and the con-textual constraint. Mispronunciations in the third syllable are more often restored than mispronunciations in the first syllable if the prior context strongly predicts the mispronounced word. If prior context places little constraint on that word, then syllable of the mispronunciation does not affect the probability of restoration. It is again as if a combination of strong top-down constraint, plus confirming evi-dence from the first syllable, leads to a prediction of what will follow, so that the third syllable is heard as what is expected rather than what is actually said.

Comparison of Cole's data with Marslen-Wilson's data leads to an apparent dilemma. The combined top-down plus first-syllable constraint leads to *better detection* of third-syllable mispronunciations (Cole's work) and also to *more* fluent *restorations,* or misperceptions of what is actually said (Marslen-Wilson's data). How can the same constraints lead to better and also worse perception of the stimulus content? Again, flexibility to adapt to the task demands is indicated. Cole's subjects were attempting to detect errors and were thus listening carefully for signal deviations, which then were more perceptible when they deviated from a specific expectation. Thus better detection occurred when the system was geared to detect mismatches. Marslen-Wilson's subjects, on the other hand, were not made aware of the presence of mispronounced words in the text and were encouraged to attend mainly to meaning so that they could answer later com-prehension questions. Their instructions emphasized content, not form. Then the combined constraints seem to have led subjects to predict the remainder of the word and thus not fully process the entire word, so third-syllable errors were restored. Thus the same combined top-down and bottom-up constraints could lead to better signal detection in one task and worse signal detection in the other task, optimally fitting the purposes of both experiments. Should these results be seen as a flexibility to modify the use of the available processors, or does each processor proceed unaltered by the outside constraint but with processing terminated earlier by a later decision process?

Reading Prose Passages

Although no reading equivalents to the listening studies have yet been reported, some interesting beginnings have been made. Intuition alone indicates that there is interplay of stimulus and contextual factors during reading. Consider the case of typing and spelling errors in your own manuscripts versus those in students' essays. Whereas most of us find it very difficult to spot errors in manuscripts we have just written, we also have trouble comprehending student works because the typing and spelling errors are so distracting. Why are we so stimulus bound in one case and so prone to missing errors in the other? A possible explanation is that the cognitive constraints on our own writing are so great that we require minimal stimulus analysis to verify what is on the page. Thus full stimulus analysis is not carried out, and we miss the physical errors. With student essays, constraints on our semantic system are often all too low, so the focus is on stimulus analysis, leading to easy detection of physical errors. These sorts of everyday experiences with stimulus error detection and restorations point to the worth of further work in this area of reading. Since visual signals are not temporal, as in the listening case, we may find a different use of processes in the reading and listening domains.

Drewnowski and Healy (1977) have provided evidence for stimulus-contextual interplay in a series of studies asking subjects to detect function words (*and, the*). The common function words were frequently missed when placed in appropriate contextual settings, suggesting that they had become unitized with the nouns. However, such detection errors could be offset by making the syntactic environment inappropriate or by disrupting the visual display by using mixed-case typing. It appeared that top-down constraints, plus verification from undisrupted syntactic and visual feature analyses, were needed to cause the function word errors. That is, only if both bottom-up and top-down constraints led to strong predictability was the stimulus display not fully analyzed, giving rise to the detection misses.

Schindler (1978) demonstrated flexibility in this effect of prose context on word detection. He found that when a target letter was embedded in a content word, it was better detected in prose than in scrambled contexts. When, however, the letter was embedded in a function word, then prose context made it more difficult to detect the letter compared to the scrambled case. Thus again the same cognitive constraint led to better and to worse detection. In this case a likely explanation is that prose structure focused the subjects' processing on content words, leading to incomplete processing of function words. Thus letters in content words were better processed, whereas letters in function words were missed.

Again, stimulus analysis seems to be altered by the contextual constraints, and considerable flexibility in use of processors to suit task demands was indicated.

Using more naturalistic reading situations, two further studies have examined the relationship between higher constraints and stimulus processing. Danks, Fears, Bohn, and Hill (1978) studied disruptions in oral reading when lexical, syntactic, semantic, and factual distortions occurred, and they examined the temporal patterning of these disruptions. Lexical distortions caused their reading disruptions earlier than syntactic and semantic distortions, which in turn had their effects earlier than factual inconsistencies. The temporal patterning of syntactic and semantic effects was the same, and the effects were additive in that when both types of distortions occurred, the disruption in reading was larger and occurred earlier. The picture laid out here is one of parallel processors with different time characteristics. The levels extend to textual information-spanning phrases and sentences. One interesting point is that restorations occurred in the Danks et al. data. When *injury* was the error substituted for *injured,* subjects read the word as *injured* but then paused as if a low-level check now indicated the perceptual error. The more spatial nature of reading may thus allow full analyses at all levels, leading to less reliance on the predictability of language, particularly if subjects are aware that stimulus errors are present in the text.

Mitchell and Green (1978) also found little evidence for predictive reading when measuring reading speed. They reasoned that if top-down constraints increase as one goes through a sentence, then reading speed should increase toward the end of the sentence where predictability is greatest. This did not occur. In fact, they found no evidence indicating that greater semantic or syntactic predictability led to increases in reading rate. Word frequency and number of characters in the display were determining variables. Though difficult passages took longer to read than easy passages, this was explicable in terms of ease with which new information could be integrated with, not predicted from, the preceding text. The picture here is of subjects actively trying to understand the message, with facilitation for congruity, but with no obvious automatic priming or predictability leading to less stimulus analysis to speed up the reading rate. Perhaps with natural passages, words are rarely so constrained as to be utterly predictable, and semantic constraints may be more useful for aiding integration of new ideas with past knowledge rather than for predicting these new ideas. (Chapters 10, 8, and 7 in this volume by Stanovich, by Carpenter and Just, and by McConkie and Zola, respectively, are relevant to this issue.) A look through these reading studies reveals that there appear to be some situations where reading is predictive and where processing might change because of contextual constraint, but there are also contextual facilitation effects that could be viewed as integrative, where decision criteria may be affected. As pointed out in the first section, either form could be made compatible with an interactive processing perspective.

One possibility that has been explored is that processing demands may lead the subject to use available processors differently. This suggestion was manifested in one form in studies by Kolers (1975, 1976). He suggested that as readers become more skilled, control of visual analyses is under automatic control, so that the skilled reader's attention is focused largely on the meaning of the message. Unskilled reading, however, requires conscious analysis of the superficial visual aspects. In a series of experiments producing skilled and unskilled reading by asking subjects to read normal versus geometrically transformed text, Kolers reported the counterintuitive finding that less skilled reading led to better memory for the passage. This was supposedly due to the more extensive analyses conducted in the unskilled condition. These findings are not compatible with a view of independent analyzers whose joint evidence determines performance. All levels of analyses should be optimal under normal reading conditions, so that the parallel analyses should give better performance under normal than transformed conditions. Rather, a change in the degree of peripheral analyses is indicated when one goes from skilled to less skilled forms of reading.

Another explanation, however, comes from Craik and Lockhart's (1972) suggestion that memory reflects the encoding operations carried out during processing. Events processed to a deeper semantic level will show enhanced memorability. The better performance for unskilled reading reported by Kolers might reflect greater semantic involvement in decoding the transformed text, rather than more extensive processing of the visual signals per se. This point was nicely illustrated by Masson and Sala (1978). They argued that the transformations led subjects to use syntactic and semantic constraints in the sentence to help determine the identity of the sentence words. That is, rather than greater attention to the visual characteristics, Masson and Sala argued that the transformations led to greater attention to the semantic and syntactic constraints. The better memory in the transformed case than in the normal case, then, reflected the greater semantic involvement in decoding the input. To demonstrate the validity of this claim, Masson and Sala showed that the transformation benefit was as great for paraphrases of the original text as for verbatim repetitions—thus emphasizing semantic, not word, processing. Furthermore, inducing additional semantic analyses, with a sentence continuation task, enhanced retention for normal reading to the level of transformed reading but had no additional benefit for the transformed text. The transformed text appeared to have already benefited from a full semantic analysis. Masson and Sala, then, argued that word recognition is jointly determined by the stimulus array and the higher constraints.

Sala and Masson (1978) extended this work in an attempt to relate automatic versus attentional processing notions to the interactive processing framework. They examined the relationship between memory for wording, for typography, and for meaning over 7 days to determine whether these components were represented and forgotten in a dependent fashion. From the proportion of correct recognitions, it appeared that wording and typography were forgotten more rapidly than meaning, suggesting that these information sources were represented independently in memory. However, memory for meaning was better if expressed in verbatim rather than paraphrase form, even after 7 days, suggesting some interdependence of exact wording and meaning in the memory trace. Masson and Sala explained this discrepancy in terms of consciously accessible traces versus traces that influence behavior even though they cannot be consciously accessed. The idea was that surface information may be automatically processed and may then not be accessible to consciousness. Meaning, on the other hand, is processed in a controlled fashion and therefore can be brought to bear on recognition. By this analysis, the processing demands (automatic versus controlled) may determine whether the different levels appear to operate in independent or interdependent fashion. This is an interesting speculation that bears further investigation.

This review of context effects, as found in a variety of paradigms, points to the conclusion that context may influence processing in a variety of ways. That is, there is no single form of contextual effects. In tightly constrained situations, sentence contexts that strongly predict a particular word seem to spread activation automatically to that word and perhaps to its close associates as well. This is seen for best and related completions in lexical decision work and in the strong bias effect in disambiguating words. Whether these rapid, automatic forms of contextual facilitation influence an early stage of processing or have their influence on the integration process is unclear. The mechanism needed to explain broader contextual effects is also unclear. In some experiments, context seems to facilitate problem solving in the sense that it aids in determining the nature of the visual array (degraded stimuli, stimulus transformations, or acoustically confusable arrays). This effect may be expressed as a complete shift from bottom-up to top-down processing (Dell & Newman, 1980), or as an interaction such that contextual effects are larger for degraded stimuli (Meyer et al., 1975; Stanovich & West, 1979). There is also evidence that several forms of contextual facilitation may occur in parallel (Broadbent & Broadbent, in press; Kleiman, 1980). Finally, the flexibility of use of contextual information can be seen in the case where the same constraints can lead to better error detection (Cole & Jakimik, 1978, 1980) and also to more error restorations (or detection misses; Marslen-Wilson & Welsh, 1978). Clearly, context effects are found in a variety of tasks, but they do not take the same form either across paradigms or even within a paradigm. The weakness of most current models is that they are not specific enough in describing mechanisms that could determine this range of processing flexibility, such that the model could predict the nature of experimental outcomes from knowledge of stimulus characteristics, cognitive constraints, and total processing demand.

VOCAL SUPPRESSION AND CONTEXT EFFECTS

My own research has also indicated a need for a considerable degree of processing flexibility. Several years ago I became interested in the use of phonemic processing during reading. Was subvocal speech just a bad habit, or did it provide information useful to the reading process? This interest has led me to a general concern for the nature of stimulus-contextual interactions. In my earlier studies (Levy, 1975, 1977) we asked subjects to count while they read or listened to sentences. The counting activity was used to prevent subjects from vocalizing the sentence words as they read or listened. Following the successive presentation of three sentences, subjects decided whether a test sentence was identical to or changed from one of the preceding three. Changes could be lexical (i.e., synonym substitutions that changed a word but left meaning intact) or semantic (i.e., subject–object reversals that preserved syntax and wording but altered the sentence meaning). Both types of change occurred randomly among test sentences identical to those presented. For both lexical and semantic changes, detection rates were substantially lower if subjects counted rather than read silently. Practiced subjects did not show a decrement due to counting while listening (rather than reading), though unpracticed subjects showed some lesser detection decrement.

The original interpretation offered for these results was that sentence wording was maintained in short-term memory until comprehension of the entire word string had occurred. Since short-term memory appeared to be a phonemic system and since visual memory was rather transient, recoding of visually presented words was necessary to make them acceptable to short-term memory. Counting disrupted this phonemic recoding, so that visually presented sentences could not be maintained until comprehension occurred. For listening, on the other hand, the auditory input was more compatible with the phonemic code of short-term memory, so speech recoding was not necessary for auditorily presented sentences. By this view, then, comprehension followed word processing, and since visual word processing was interrupted by vocal suppression (counting), comprehension was also hindered. Similar results and conclusions were presented by Kleiman (1975).

Subsequent work, however, indicated that this notion was too simple—the processing was too sequential to account for top-down or contextual effects. There is also reason to question whether the vocal suppression decrement is entirely due to speech-specific interference. I briefly summarize attempts to evaluate the speech specificity of the suppression decrement. Then I review studies of its interaction with contextual manipulations and next describe a study that more directly examined stimulus-contextual interaction during text processing.

Speech Specificity

My original interpretation of the effects of vocal suppression followed from work in short-term memory. There it had been shown that repetitious counting eliminated acoustic confusions for visually presented words (Murray, 1968; Peterson & Johnson, 1971) and substantially reduced visual recall while having no effect on auditory recall (Levy, 1971). Since the decrements were only for visual language, and phonemic processing seemed to be eliminated, the decrement appeared to be localized in the phonemic recoding process for visual language. Indeed, since counting was a repetitious act that required little effort or attention, as evidenced by the fact that it didn't affect listening performance, I argued that a differential effort account could not explain the visual memory decrement.

However, Baron (1976), following Norman and Bobrow's (1975) notion of data- versus resource-limited processing, argued that listening might simply be easier than reading, even for identical material. Therefore, for listening, sufficient processing capacity was available to handle both the counting and memory tasks, whereas for reading, counting competed with the memory task for the available processing capacity, and a performance decrement resulted. He concluded that whereas the reading curves were resource limited, the listening curves were not. This argument is difficult to counter since we have few available indices of the amount of processing capacity used in a task. There is no theoretical reason to argue that listening is easier than reading, and since performance for listening and reading was equivalent for all but the final sentence in our studies, there was no empirical suggestion that listening was an easier modality. A simple effort notion, then, has difficulty handling the specific visual decrement when other indices show equivalence of performance in the two modalities.

However, the effort notion has some intuitive appeal; after all, we are more practiced at listening, since it is a skill easily acquired early in life by children, whereas reading is a difficult skill and is acquired later in life. We therefore attempted to find ways to manipulate the effort required by the suppression task in order to see if effort played a critical role in the visual decrement. Briefly, we have found: (1) Extended practice does not lead to a decrease in the magnitude of the suppression decrement, as might be expected when subjects become more skilled at both tasks; (2) giving subjects control of the presentation rate so that they can adjust their reading speed to provide enough resources to cope with both tasks is unsuccessful; they choose to speed up rather than slow down their reading rate while counting, even though this strategy leads to a large decrement in retention; and (3) when the presentation rate was slowed down so that subjects had more than a full second to read each content word, the magnitude of the decrement tended to increase rather than decrease. In fact, in the extreme case (i.e., when the final sentence had just been seen for 6 seconds), where detection performance was highest, the suppression decrement was greatest. It is difficult to use an effort explanation when the easiest case shows the largest decrement. In summary, then, all correlates of effort that we have studied have failed to influence the magnitude of the suppression decrement.

While these experiments failed to support an effort interpretation, they also failed to provide any direct evidence for the speech-specific interference view. Michael Withey, a graduate student in my laboratory, was able to show that humming (vocal but nonverbal) caused less decrement than counting (vocal and verbal), but one could argue that humming is easier (requires less processing capacity) than counting and that is why it causes less decrement. We therefore attempted to devise a nonverbal equivalent to counting. To this end, we compared two suppression tasks: (1) rhythmical counting 1,2,3—1,2; 1,2,3—1,2; etc.; and (2) rhythmical tapping 1,2,3,—1,2; 1,2,3—1,2; etc. Subjects were given practice on the tapping task until they did not have to count out the rhythm but could tap it out quite fluently. The idea was to have equivalent subsidiary tasks in a verbal and a nonverbal domain. The detection paradigm was exactly like that used in earlier studies. Essentially, three unrelated sentences were presented successively for 3 seconds each, followed immediately by a test sentence. Subjects simply indicated whether the test sentence was identical to or changed from one of the preceding three. All sentences conformed to the grammar: article, adjective, noun, verb ($=ed$), article, adjective, noun. Changes were either lexical or semantic, as described earlier. For example, if the original sentence was *The fat boy kicked the helpless donkey,* a lexical change would be *The fat lad kicked the helpless donkey,* and a semantic change would be *The fat donkey kicked the helpless boy.*

Subjects participated in two sessions. In one session the sentences were presented visually, and in the other they were presented auditorily. Within each session, one-third of the sentences were attended to silently, one-third while counting, and one-third while tapping. Appropriate counterbalancing ensured that materials were identical in all conditions across subjects. Our interest, then, was in whether the verbal task (counting) would cause a greater decrement than the nonverbal task (tapping), and whether these effects would be modality specific.

Figures 1.1 and 1.2 display the relevant data. "Sentence position" refers to whether the first, second, or third sentence in the set was the tested one. To calculate d' values, false alarms were defined as the probability of responding "changed" to identical tests, whereas hits were correct detections of the lexical and semantic changes. Without going into detail for all effects, let me summarize the data relevant to the present case. The main effects of task type and modality were both significant ($p < .01$), and their interaction was of borderline significance ($p < .10$). Subsequent analyses indicated that in the auditory modality, neither suppression task caused a significant decrement in semantic detection, but both cause a decrement in lexical detection ($p < .05$). The magnitude of these decrements was equivalent for counting and tapping. In the visual modality, on the other hand, both semantic detection and lexical detection were hindered by counting ($p < .001$ in both cases), as well as by tapping ($p < .01$, $p < .05$, respectively). The magnitude of the decrement was greater for counting than for tapping for lexical detection ($p < .01$), but this difference was not significant for semantic detection (largely because of the Position 1 reversal).

The auditory data are not unlike our earlier auditory data for unpracticed subjects (Levy, 1975). A small decrement occurs, but in this study we have further shown that the "verbalness" of the task does not seem to matter. Clearly,

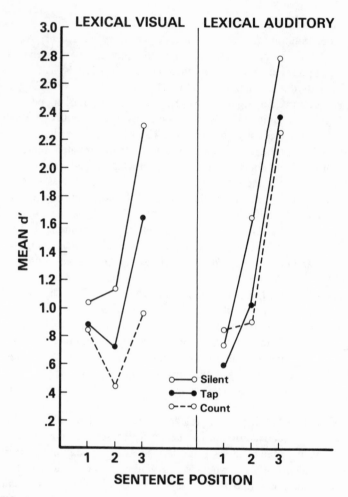

FIG. 1.1. Lexical detection for verbal and nonverbal concurrent tasks in the visual and auditory modalities.

subsidiary tasks do tax processing capacity somewhat even in this simple situation, and the decrement resulting is not speech specific. The visual results are less clear. Again there is a general loss due to any subsidiary task, but there is also greater loss if the task is verbal. It appears reasonable to conclude that both processing capacity and speech encoding are related to the suppression phenomenon, but this begs the question of how they are both involved. Other data give some indication of the possible relationship. Using a more complex task than our own, Margolin and Wolford (1979) failed to find modality specificity when speech recoding was suppressed by counting. Further, in studies where we have extended the size of our passages to seven rather than three sentences, we find suppression decrements of equivalent magnitude in the two modalities. It now

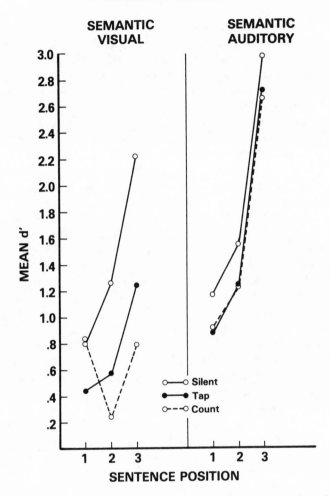

FIG. 1.2. Semantic detection for verbal and nonverbal concurrent tasks in the visual and auditory modalities.

appears that increasing the task demands will lead to a suppression decrement for both forms of language processing. Although this general decrement may be entirely due to a general resource limitation, I favor the position that when processing resources are taxed, subjects fall back on speech recoding to maintain the stimulus input for both modalities. This line of reasoning is pursued after discussing some work on context effects.

Context Effects

Whereas the data collected on unrelated sentences were consistent with a sequential short-term memory account of sentence processing, this picture changed considerably when we moved to the study of thematic passages. Our interest here was in whether thematic constraints would lead to less reliance on speech processing (i.e., we were searching for a suppression × context interaction). If interactive processing allows for compensatory relationships among levels of analysis, then it seems reasonable to suppose that reliance on word-holding mechanisms might be lessened when thematic structure allows incoming words to be easily integrated with the contents of semantic memory. If counting interferes with these word-holding mechanisms, as we had postulated, one would expect less decrement due to vocal suppression for thematic than for unrelated passages, since subjects could rely on thematic processes in the former case.

To evaluate this hypothesis, seven-sentence passages were constructed, each sentence conforming to the seven-word sentence frame described earlier. Minor changes were made in a few filler (nontested) sentences to make the paragraph more syntactically natural. Each passage was given a title reflecting its central idea, and subjects were instructed to relate the seven sentences together so that the whole set would be more memorable. A second group of subjects received matched unrelated sets. For these sets the test sentence for each paragraph was kept in its position but the six surrounding context sentences were shuffled randomly across paragraphs. No two sentences from the same paragraph occurred in an unrelated control set, and for each unrelated set, no obvious thematic relationship existed among its seven sentences. Subjects were simply instructed to learn all seven sentences, and of course no titles were given to the unrelated sets. For unrelated and thematic passages, the sentences were presented on index cards at a rate of one sentence per 2 seconds. Half of the passages were read silently and half while counting by both thematic and unrelated subjects.

Two types of tests were used (described in detail in Levy 1978a, 1978b): (1) lexical and semantic tests as described earlier; and (2) paraphrase tests, where two words were altered in each test sentence. For one version of these paraphrase tests, the word substitutes were synonyms, so that meaning was unaltered; whereas for the other version, unrelated substitutions were used, thus altering the meaning. Subjects in the paraphrase groups were told that the sentence wording would always be changed and their task was to decide whether the word changes altered or paraphrased the meaning of the original sentence. In summary, then, there were four main groups of subjects—two who read thematically related paragraphs, and two who read unrelated control sets. One of each of the thematic and unrelated groups received lexical and semantic tests, whereas the other groups received paraphrase tests.

In fact the paraphrase groups were used to test an explanation of the lexical and semantic outcomes. In the lexical-semantic groups, changed and identical tests occurred randomly, so that subjects never knew in advance whether the wording or the meaning might be altered. An optimal strategy in this case is to maintain wording in memory on all occasions. Since we were interested in whether comprehension could occur without reliance on word-processing mechanisms, we wanted a task where memory for wording would not be required. The paraphrase test, then, is a situation where word memory cannot aid performance, since wording is changed on every test. Subjects must decide whether the meaning remains unaltered despite the wording changes.

Whereas the lexical-semantic results have been found in two experiments (Levy, 1977, Exp. 3; 1978a), the paraphrase test was only used for the 1978 study. Figure 1.3 presents the summary findings from the 1978 report. For the lexical measure, there was a large decrement in detection for the suppression conditions, but thematicity had no effect on performance at all. This result could be explained in that general meaning could not aid in choosing between synonyms, both being consistent with the theme. Clearly, meaning did not facilitate word processing here. For the semantic measure, there was a main effect of thematicity (detection being better for thematic passages) and a main effect of suppression (counting being worse than silent reading), but no interaction of these two variables ($F < 1$). It appeared that meaning and wording made independent contributions to detection. We argued that this was because subject-object reversals could be detected in two ways: (1) by noting an order reversal of the lexical items, and (2) by noting a change in the meaning of the sentence. These wording and semantic components could operate in parallel, thus explaining the two main effects, with no interaction. For the paraphrase measure, on the other hand, only a semantic representation should have been maintained, so only the thematicity effect was expected. The results confirmed the prediction: No

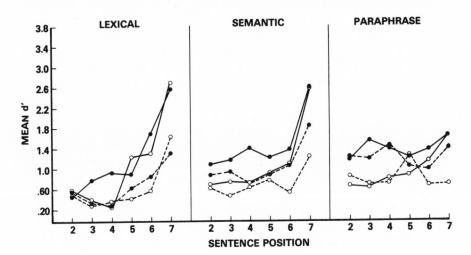

FIG. 1.3. Lexical, semantic, and paraphrase detection for thematic and unrelated passages, read silently or while counting. ●——● Thematic-Silent; ●---● Thematic-Suppressed; ○---○ Unrelated-Silent; ○---○ Unrelated-Suppressed (after Levy 1978a).

suppression decrement occurred for the paraphrase detection, but semantic altera-
tions were better detected in thematic than in unrelated passages.

To handle these results, I suggested that meaning could be analyzed without
extensive use of speech-recoding mechanisms, and that these mechanisms were
used only when word identity could provide useful information (e.g., when word
memory is tested, in cases of comprehending reversible sentences, or when the
processing load is excessive). The independent effects result obtained in the
lexical-semantic task argued against the sequential, short-term memory explanation described earlier. If wording acted as the data base used for integration and
comprehension mechanisms, then disrupting that data base with counting should
have led to a decrease in semantic processing, as evidenced by a smaller effect of
thematicity under suppression conditions. This did not occur, but neither was
there a larger thematic effect for suppressed conditions, as might have been
expected from the interactive processing view. One might have predicted that
when thematic constraints were high, word processing would be facilitated or
relied on less, and thus the suppression decrement would be offset by thematicity. Although the obtained result is consistent with the notion of independent
analyzers, no trade-off between stimulus and contextual processing was observed.

To pursue this question further, we decided to look at the context-suppression
relationship in audition, since some interactive processing effects with prose
passages had already been observed in that modality. At this point in time, we
made several modifications in our procedure that, with hindsight, appear to be
important. *First,* on rereading our paragraphs for recording, we decided that they
were linguistically quite strained, since all seven sentences in each passage
conformed rather closely to the same seven-word sentence syntax. We decided to
relax the syntactic constraints on the context sentences, so that these seven-word
sentences now were written in a variety of syntactic arrangements. The total
effect was to make the passages sound more like natural stories (see example in
Table 1.1). They were recorded starting with a title, followed by 2 seconds of
silence, followed by the sentences, presented at a rate of one every three seconds
and read with natural emphasis and intonation (i.e., as if the speaker was telling a
story). The unrelated passages were constructed as in the earlier studies and were
recorded at the same rate, but they were read as if the speaker was reading
unrelated sentences. The same lexical-semantic and paraphrase test groups were
used again. That is, the same four-group design was used again, with the same
instructions for thematic and unrelated groups. The test sentences were presented
visually on index cards. No time limit was placed on responding, though a
response was to be given on every trial.

Second, since we had altered the passages, we decided to run four parallel
reading groups so that the auditory and visual results could be compared. The
second change, then, was in the visual display system. Since we had acquired a
microcomputer, we decided to display our visual passages on its scope. Not only

TABLE 1.1
An Example of a Thematic Passage and Test Changes

Fun on Christmas Morning

The Christmas tree brightened up the corner.
The cuckoo clock struck the eighth hour.
Eagerly the family descended the staircase.
Torn wrapping paper littered the whole floor.
And excited laughter filled the entire room.
The happy children hugged their pleased parents.
And warm cheer lit their bright faces.

The happy youngsters hugged their pleased parents (lexical change)
The happy parents hugged their pleased children. (semantic change)
The happy youngsters hugged their contented parents. (paraphrase yes)
The happy sisters hugged their exasperated parents. (paraphrase no)

---

was the presentation smoother and easier to read on the scope than from index cards but subjects seemed more motivated to concentrate on the task. Since they controlled passage initiation, they felt in control of the computer, a motivator that spanned the four ½-hour sessions!

Although these two changes seemed unimportant, they may explain the results obtained in this study. Figure 1.4 displays the visual data and Fig. 1.5, the auditory data. Comparison of Figs. 1.3 and 1.4 will indicate that performance levels for both lexical and semantic detection were somewhat higher in this

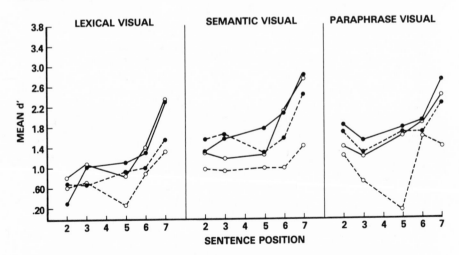

FIG. 1.4. Lexical, semantic, and paraphrase detection for thematic and unrelated passages, read silently or while counting. ●——● Thematic–Silent; ●---● Thematic–Suppressed; ○---○ Unrelated–Silent; ○---○ Unrelated–Suppressed.

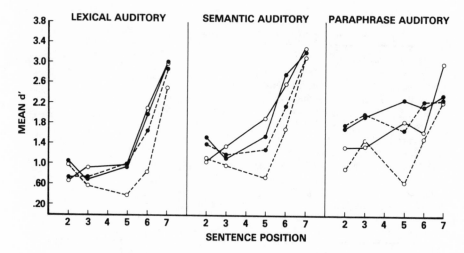

FIG. 1.5.   Lexical, semantic, and paraphrase detection for thematic and unrelated passages, heard silently or while counting. ●——● Thematic-Silent; ●---● Thematic-Suppressed; ○——○ Unrelated-Silent; ○---○ Unrelated-Suppressed.

experiment than for the earlier data. This may be due to the better display, more motivated subjects, or slower presentation rate. The analysis of variance results for the lexical-semantic task were very clear (all p's $< .01$), with no other effects approaching significance. Overall, thematic passages led to better performance than unrelated passages; lexical detection was worse than semantic detection; auditory performance was better than visual, but mainly over the final sentence positions; counting led to worse detection than silent reading (or listening), particularly for the last sentences; and memory improved from the first to the last sentence. The only other significant effect was the suppression $\times$ thematicity interaction. The relevant means (d's) were: thematic–silent 1.66, thematic–suppressed 1.46, unrelated–silent 1.63, unrelated–suppressed 1.10.

These data are markedly different from the earlier data in two respects: (1) Whereas thematicity affected only semantic detection in the earlier study, the thematicity effect appeared for both lexical and semantic detection here; (2) in this study suppression and thematicity acted in an interactive fashion for both modalities. The form of the interaction here is of interest. For silent reading there was little effect due to meaningfulness; whereas the thematic facilitation was quite marked for the suppression groups, with thematicity essentially eliminating the suppression decrement. The form of this result resembled the stimulus quality $\times$ context interaction described by Stanovich and West, where the contextual facilitation was larger for noisy stimuli. Perhaps one should view counting as another means of slowing down processing, thus leading to greater reliance on contextual facilitation.

It is unclear why thematicity did not aid silent reading here as in the earlier study. Perhaps the highly motivated subjects semantically organized the unrelated as well as the related sentences, accounting for the higher performance levels in this study. Counting may have prevented organizational activity for subjects reading unrelated sentences, whereas thematic structure facilitated semantic processing for subjects reading related sentence sets. It is clear from the paraphrase data that subjects in this experiment were attempting to read for meaning. Modality of input had no influence on paraphrase detection, but both thematicity and suppression did, showing the same form of interaction as in the lexical-semantic task. The relevant means d's were: thematic–silent 2.00, thematic–suppressed 1.85, unrelated–silent 1.84, unrelated–suppressed 1.18. Although for this measure, there was a thematic superiority even during silent reading, the effect is markedly larger for the suppressed conditions. Since word memory is not emphasized in the paraphrase test, the interactive effects observed here may represent greater reliance on semantic processing when the stimulus input is "noisy". Counting might then be viewed as another means of slowing down stimulus analysis, and the interaction with context is analogous to that seen with noisy stimuli by Stanovich and West.

Although the overall picture regarding the context × suppression relationship is unclear, one point should be noted. All of the measures within each study acted consistently, suggesting that the differences are due to variable changes across studies, not just to random variation. That is, the first study showed no interactive trade-off for any measure, whereas the present study finds this compensatory relationship for all measures. The situation is uncomfortable in that we don't know which variables are critical in obtaining the compensatory relationship. Since our context manipulation is reliant on subjects choosing to organize the sentences thematically, the paradigm is open to strategy effects. But two things seem clear: (1) The sequential short-term memory model that we originally advocated cannot handle either the independent main effects observed in the first studies or the compensatory effects observed in the final study, since then the thematic effect should be less evident when the stimulus analysis is hindered by counting; and (2) subjects seem to be flexible in how they use context in the face of additional processing demands. This flexibility may be related to the nature of the context manipulation, the stimulus display characteristics, or the motivation of the subjects. Although all of the effects described could be handled by the interactive processing notions, we have as yet little understanding of the factors underlying the varied performance observed in this rather simple paradigm. Current models offer little assistance in understanding the flexible use of parallel analyzers.

Stimulus Quality, Context, and Processing Capacity

In considering both the speech specificity and the contextual studies, it is clear that processing resource limitations, as well as encoding flexibility, must be included in a complete explanation of the suppression effect. When dealing with the earlier three-sentence task, where the processing load was minimal, a speech-recoding interpretation of the suppression decrement seemed reasonable. The greater effect in the visual than in the auditory modality and the greater decrement for counting than for tapping suggested that some form of speech-specific encoding was disrupted for visual language processing. However, even in this simple task, and to a much larger extent in the paragraph task, another component was also present, and this appeared to cause a more general processing deficit.

On considering how the earlier findings might be generalized to a real reading task, the following considerations arose. Rarely will one have such a light reading load as was used in our studies; passages tend to be much longer and not so predictable in form as those we used. Though memory is not stressed, comprehension requires memory for events occurring throughout the passage. When might one fall back on verbal processing during reading? Intuition suggests two occasions when one finds oneself vocalizing while reading: (1) when the message is very complex (i.e., the cognitive constraints are low), and we struggle to understand the total message; (2) when the visual signals are fuzzy, such as when one reads small or smudged print (a poor Xerox, for example). In this case, saying the words seems to make them clearer. In both cases more processing resources are required, and these resources are often manifested in some form of active verbal processing. This is not unique to the visual domain. Auditory correlates might be such situations as when you are trying to communicate with a foreign speaker of English whose accent is marked, or when listening to a taped interview recorded with background "noise." These noisy signal cases may well be situations where signal analyses are slowed down, as discussed by Stanovich and West, and thus should provide fertile soil for finding compensatory interactions in real comprehension tasks.

F. I. M. Craik (University of Toronto) and I attempted to operationalize these notions. The experiment I describe is a first, rather simple attempt at finding an interaction between signal clarity and cognitive constraint—mostly to illustrate that with real passages, the straightforward predictions are not easily realized. We chose 16 easy and 16 difficult passages. Each passage was 350 ± 10 words in length and was reasonably linearly structured (i.e., an argument or description was systematically unfolded). The easy passages were taken from the intermediate levels of a reading series (SRA Individualized Reading Skills Program) and consisted of descriptive passages on a variety of topics. The difficult passages were chosen from advanced-level psychology textbooks on a variety of topics (thus ensuring that no introductory psychology subject would already know the material). The difficult passages were largely expositions, consisting of main ideas and supporting evidence. See Tables 1.2 and 1.3 for examples of the passages used.

The easy and difficult passages were randomly divided into two sets, each containing 8 easy and 8 difficult passages. Half of the subjects read each of the two sets, thus generalizing our results over stimulus materials. Each subject

TABLE 1.2

An Example of the Easy Passages Used and of the Comprehension Questions

There is probably no other mountain where the mountaineer is exposed to greater danger than on Kanchenjunga, for not only has he ice avalanches to contend with, but uncertain weather as well. The huge annual precipitation of snow on Kanchenjunga is a disadvantage, for it plasters itself on the mountain and fills every hollow with clinging masses of ice. Because of this snow that is ever building up, plus the tug of gravity, these icy masses move downwards to join the main glaciers which they feed.

The most striking property of Himalayan glacier ice as found in the Kanchenjunga district is its plasticity. This results in several differences in the general characteristics of glaciers here as compared to glaciers in the Alps or other temperate or cold regions. In the Himalayas, owing to a far greater range between day and night temperatures, and the fact that the sun is almost directly overhead at noon, snow is changed into pure ice nearer the surface than it is in the Alps. Thus, instead of a flaky intermediate stage, snow is converted almost straight away into glacier ice, and ice tougher and more rubbery than that found in most Alpine districts.

The hanging glaciers of Kanchenjunga are very much "alive", and the speed of their downward movement, owing to the huge annual snowfall, is considerably greater than that of similar hanging glaciers in the Alps. Also, these hanging glaciers are frequently of enormous thickness, and walls of ice 600 to 1,000 feet high decorate the sides of Kanchenjunga. Were hanging glaciers of this size in the Alps, there would be great avalanches, but they would not be nearly so great as those that occur on Kanchenjunga. The reason is that the ice, owing to its brittleness, would break away more often, and there would be many avalanches, but none of a magnitude comparable to those that fall from Kanchenjunga. On Kanchenjunga the ice walls bend farther over the edge of precipices before breaking off, and when at last the ice is no longer able to withstand the internal stresses set up by unstable equilibrium, it cracks, and a huge avalanche occurs.

Questions:

Macro 1—What is a striking property of the glaciers in the Himalayas and why is this?

Macro 2—Why are the avalanches so large in the Kanchenjunga region?

Micro 1—How high can walls of glaciers be?

Micro 2—Besides avalanches, what other dangers do mountaineers in the Kanchenjunga region face?

Lexical —The hanging glaciers of Kanchenjunga are very much _____ and the speed of their _____ movement, owing to the huge _____ _____, is considerably greater than that of similar hanging glaciers in the Alps.

served in four 1-hour sessions on successive days. Each day the subjects read 4 passages—2 easy and 2 difficult—randomly arranged. On each of the 4 days, subjects read under different conditions; on 2 days subjects read silently, and on 2 days they read aloud (order counterbalanced). For 1 silent and 1 aloud day, subjects read the passages from slides in clear focus, whereas on each of the other days, they read from fuzzy slides. The fuzzy slides were our attempt to slow down reading rate by putting noise in the signal. Since subjects varied in the degree of fuzziness required to slow down their reading, a rough criterion was devised for deciding on the degree of fuzziness used. In a pretest each subject read 2 passages aloud (from the same sources), and the mean reading time was recorded. To meet our criterion the fuzzy presentation had to slow down reading rate by at least another 30 seconds, but with no increase in error rate. The fuzziness was produced by sheets of clear plastic wrapping over the projector lens. This filter made the entire page fuzzy but did not blot out parts of words differentially. Subjects were to read every word in both clear and fuzzy conditions, the difference being in the time required to do so.

The experiment, then, was a three-way factorial—clear or noisy visual displays, easy or difficult passages, for subjects reading aloud or silently. We used both silent and aloud reading because subjects might use different strategies under these two conditions. Our basic hypothesis was that the noise would cause less disruption in comprehension of easy than difficult passages. That is, we hoped for some compensatory relationship such that noisy passages would enhance the easy–difficult effect. This might be more true for silent than aloud reading, since subjects may adopt more flexible strategies for silent reading (even though the instructions emphasized reading every word).

Comprehension was tested in a variety of ways. First, we took reading times per passage in order to evaluate the effects of our variables on on-line comprehension (i.e., reading times acted as a measure of ease of processing the stimulus input). Then, to measure final comprehension, we used several types of test: (1) First, subjects attempted to free recall as much of the passages as possible in as close to the same words as possible; however, it was stressed that any ideas from the passages, irrespective of memory for wording or order, should be written down; (2) after the free recall, subjects were asked to summarize in a sentence or two the main ideas or message of that passage; (3) finally, subjects were asked a series of five questions. Two of these questions asked about main or macro ideas from the passage; two asked about details or micro ideas; and one was a lexical test asking subjects to fill in missing words. These questions were asked and answered orally, whereas the first two tests required written answers. No time pressure was placed on any testing phase. Illustrations of the questions can be found in Tables 1.2 and 1.3.

The data reported are for the reading times (and errors) and the questions, since analyses of the other data have been hindered by the difficulty in finding reliable summary measures. Reading times are means per passage for the various conditions. Reading errors could only be collected for the aloud conditions. In order to score the answers for the five questions, a system was constructed that allotted a score of 1 for each main point, for a perfect answer as we saw it. The number of points possible therefore varies across questions and across passages. The data are consequently expressed in proportions and analyzed by analysis of variance, with full awareness of the possible statistical violations. However, the effects are so clear-cut that we choose to use a summary statistic to represent the data. A point to note is that all passages, and therefore all questions with their scoring schemes, are equally represented in all conditions over an experimental replication. The data are for 19 subjects who represent two complete replications, plus 3 subjects in an incomplete replication.

TABLE 1.3

An Example of the Difficult Passages Used and of the Comprehension Questions

According to tradition, prematurity is caused by some imprudent act on the part of the mother. This "imprudence" was supposed to be too strenuous physical exertion, being emotionally disturbed, drinking, or smoking. Today it is believed, though not actually proved, that prematurity comes either from uterine crowding or from some glandular imbalance in the mother's body.

Prematurity is more common in multiple births than in singletons. This would suggest that when the combined size of twins, triplets, or other multiple births reaches a point where the uterine walls can expand no further, they are discharged from the uterus ahead of schedule.

Prematurity is more common when mothers suffer from prolonged stress than when they experience only the normal amount of emotional disturbance during the pregnancy period. Prolonged stress is always accompanied by glandular disturbance of minor or major seriousness. This affects the glands that are directly involved in procreation and causes them to start up the uterine contractions that dislodge the fetus from its attachment to the uterine wall before it is ready for postnatal life.

The tradition belief that smoking by the mother causes prematurity has been substantiated to some extent by studies of the relationship between excessive smoking of the mother and prematurity of her baby. In one study it was reported that prematurity was about twice as great for smokers as for nonsmokers, and the number of premature births increased as the number of cigarettes smoked per day by the mother increased. Among mothers who smoked over 31 cigarettes a day, for example, there was 33.33 percent of the premature births in the group studied.

Interpreted on face value, this would suggest that a serious cause of prematurity is cigarette smoking. Looking under the surface, one sees the relationship between heavy smoking and emotional tension. Women who smoke excessively do so generally because of stress, just as is true of those who drink excessively. Smoking, per se, may have nothing to do with prematurity. Instead, prematurity may be caused by glandular conditions brought about by prolonged emotional stress, of which smoking is only an outward manifestation.

Questions:

Macro 1—What factors cause premature births?

Macro 2—How could one interpret the relationship between smoking and premature births?

Micro 1—What is the evidence that uterine crowding leads to increases in premature deliveries?

Micro 2—How could stress cause prematurity?

Lexical—Looking under the surface, one sees the relationship between _____ _____ and _____ _____.

Figure 1.6 shows the mean reading times for each condition for the silent and aloud subjects. Error rates were very low (for aloud readers): 1.5% for clear–easy, 1.3% for clear–difficult, 2.5% for noisy–easy, and 2.6% for noisy–difficult. Clearly, time–accuracy trade-off will not account for the comprehension results that are presented. As Fig. 1.6 shows, noisy passages slowed down reading time, and difficult passages required more reading time than easy passages for both silent and aloud readers ($p < .001$ in both cases). The effects were statistically independent (interaction term $F < 1$). The only other effect was that silent reading took less time than reading aloud ($p < .001$). Both manipulations, signal clarity and semantic complexity, were effective in determining performance, but there is no trace of an interactive trade-off in on-line comprehension. Signal noise was not less disruptive for easily read passages.

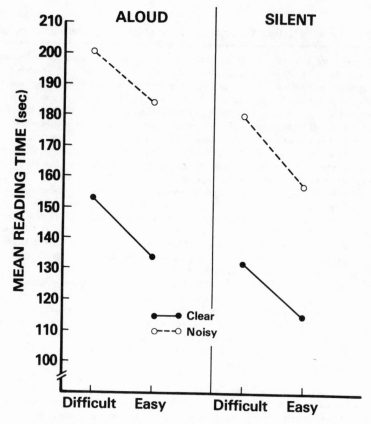

FIG. 1.6. Mean reading times in seconds for difficult and easy passages presented clearly and with noise.

Given these results from on-line processing, one might have expected parallel effects in the later comprehension questions. Figures 1.7 and 1.8 illustrate the memory data for silent and aloud readers, respectively. A surprising outcome is that reading the noisy signals, which slowed down processing considerably, did not influence later memory for any level of questioning. Analyses of variance for each type of question indicated large effects of the ease–difficulty variable ($p < .001$ in all cases), but with no other effects approaching statistical significance. Unlike Kohler's finding with transformed text, the later comprehension measure here does not reflect the difficulty of initial processing, as measured by reading times. These results may indicate an important feature of final comprehension—namely, that it reflects the goodness of the semantic representation and not the number or ease of analyses by which this was obtained. In the present experiment, the later memory tests may have necessitated semantic analysis even for normal reading conditions, so that no additional semantic

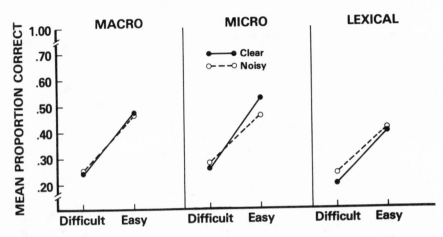

FIG. 1.7.   Mean proportion correct responses to comprehension questions for silent readers.

benefit was gained when the signal was made difficult to read. Since clarity of presentation also did not affect the lexical measure, either wording is part of the final representation, or, more likely, knowing the message content allows equivalent reconstruction of wording for noisy and clear presentations.

The experiment I have just described was designed as a straightforward test for the interaction between semantic constraint and stimulus clarity. Clearly, that interaction was absent both in the reading-time data and in later memory for the passages. Rather, as in our earlier studies of vocal suppression, we have found evidence for independent effects from the semantic and stimulus analyses under

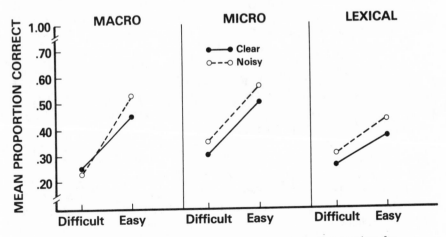

FIG. 1.8.   Mean proportion correct responses to comprehension questions for aloud readers.

conditions that, on the surface, looked ideal for obtaining compensatory processing. One could argue, of course, that this experiment did not encourage interactive processing, since subjects were told to read all words, not just to scan the passages, even in the noisy conditions. Also the present paragraphs were not highly predictive, in the sense that specific words could not be predicted from the context. However, the sentences were more easily integrated with one another in the easy case than in the difficult one. It is possible that if the passages had been highly constrained so that words were predictable from the context, and if subjects had been permitted to engage in speed–accuracy trade-off (i.e., scanning), then the sought-for interaction would have been obtained. One must, however, then question the generality of interactiveness in normal reading tasks. In this sense, our data agree with those of Mitchell and Green (1978), who also failed to find predictive effects when natural passages were read, even though there was an easy–difficult effect that could best be explained by the ease of integrating the new and old knowledge. The present study, then, offers two notes of caution: (1) Reading-time measures seem to reflect the difficulty of comprehension, rather than just the final state of comprehension, as measured by later memory tests. Memory tests cannot be taken to reflect all aspects of on-line processing; they seem instead to reflect largely the degree of semantic integration obtained during processing; (2) The occurrence of compensatory interaction between semantic and stimulus levels of processing may be limited to a narrow range of reading tasks. Clearly, possible limitations in generality deserve further exploration.

Taken together, the experiments I have described are incompatible with early stage models of reading that suggested that the output from word-processing analyses provided the data base from which later semantic-interpretative processes worked. In both the studies on speech suppression and the study with noisy signals, causing difficulty in the stimulus analysis in no way restricted the amount of semantic processing performed. The systems worked independently (early suppression studies and the noise study) or interactively (final suppression study). The questions we must pursue, then, concern the conditions that lead to differential use of various levels of analyses. What mechanisms determine when a task will be treated in a strictly top-down or a strictly bottom-up fashion or when an interactive outcome will be obtained? In the literature reviewed in the first section of the chapter, we saw instances of context leading to all three outcomes. In my own data, both independent and interactive effects were obtained. In all instances the stimulus conditions, semantic constraints, and processing requirements that move the system from one state to another are undefined. The rules or decision processes involved in data integration across levels of analyses must be specified before an interactive model can be predictive. To date, considerable progress has been made in documenting the existence of relationships between stimulus variables and contextual constraints, but the nature of that interface is still unclear. Although the parallel processing notions under discussion offer a convenient umbrella for describing many effects, it is not clear that our understanding of the mechanisms of interaction would allow us to predict specific outcomes in a large number of experimental tasks.

ACKNOWLEDGMENTS

This research was supported by Grant A7657 from the National Research Council of Canada. I am grateful to Mrs. Catherine Mamer and Mrs. Deborah Richter for their assistance in collecting and analyzing data and to Drs. F. I. M. Craik, G. Kleiman, and G. Logan for their critical reading of the manuscript.

REFERENCES

Baron, J. Mechanisms for pronouncing printed words: Use and acquisition. In D. LaBerge & S. J. Samuels (Eds.), *Basic processes in reading: Perception and comprehension.* Hillsdale, N.J.: Lawrence Erlbaum Associates, 1976.

Becker, C. A. Allocation of attention during visual word recognition. *Journal of Experimental Psychology: Human Perception and Performance,* 1976, *2,* 556–566.

Broadbent, D. E., & Broadbent, M. H. P. Priming and the passive/active model of word recognition. In R. S. Nickerson (Ed.), *Attention and performance VIII.* Hillsdale, N.J.: Lawrence Erlbaum Associates, in preparation.

Cole, R. A., & Jakimik, J. Understanding speech: How words are heard. In G. Underwood (Ed.), *Strategies of information processing.* New York: Academic Press, 1978.

Cole, R. A., & Jakimik, J. A model of speech perception. In R. Cole (Ed.), *Perception and production of fluent speech.* Hillsdale, N.J.: Lawrence Erlbaum Associates, 1980.

Craik, F. I. M., & Lockhart, R. S. Levels of processing: A framework for memory research. *Journal of Verbal Learning and Verbal Behavior,* 1972, *11,* 671–684.

Craik, F. I. M., & Tulving, E. Depth of processing and the retention of words in episodic memory. *Journal of Experimental Psychology: General,* 1975, *104,* 268–294.

Danks, J. H., Fears, R., Bohn, L., & Hill, G. O. *Comprehension processes in oral reading.* Paper presented at Psychonomic Society meeting, San Antonio, Texas, 1978.

Dell, G. S., & Newman, J. E. Detecting phonemes in fluent speech. *Journal of Verbal Learning and Verbal Behavior,* 1980, *19,* 608–623.

Drewnowski, A., & Healy, A. F. Detection errors on *the* and *and*: Evidence for reading units larger than the word. *Memory & Cognition,* 1977, *5,* 636–647.

Fischler, I. Associative facilitation without expectancy in a lexical decision task. *Journal of Experimental Psychology: Human Perception and Performance,* 1977, *3,* 18–26.

Fischler, I., & Bloom, P. A. Automatic and attentional processes in the effects of sentence contexts on word recognition. *Journal of Verbal Learning and Verbal Behavior,* 1979, *18,* 1–20.

Fischler, I., & Goodman, G. O. Latency of associative activation in memory. *Journal of Experimental Psychology: Human Perception and Performance,* 1978, *4,* 455–470.

Foss, D. J., & Jenkins, C. M. Some effects of context on the comprehension of ambiguous sentences. *Journal of Verbal Learning and Verbal Behavior,* 1973, *12,* 577–589.

Gough, P. B. One second of reading. In J. F. Kavanagh & I. G. Mattingly (Eds.), *Language by ear and by eye: The relationships between speech and reading.* Cambridge: MIT Press, 1972.

Kleiman, G. M. Speech recoding in reading. *Journal of Verbal Learning and Verbal Behavior,* 1975, *14,* 323–339.

Kleiman, G. M. Sentence frame contexts and lexical decisions: Sentence acceptability and word-relatedness effects. *Memory & Cognition*, 1980, *8*, 336–344.

Kolers, P. A. Memorial consequences of automatized encoding. *Journal of Experimental Psychology: Human Learning and Memory*, 1975, *1*, 689–701.

Kolers, P. A. Reading a year later. *Journal of Experimental Psychology: Human Learning and Memory*, 1976, *2*, 554–565.

LaBerge, D., & Samuels, S. J. Toward a theory of automatic information processing in reading. *Cognitive Psychology*, 1974, *6*, 293–323.

Levy, B. A. Role of articulation in auditory and visual short-term memory. *Journal of Verbal Learning and Verbal Behavior*, 1971, *10*, 123–132.

Levy, B. A. Vocalization and suppression effects in sentence memory. *Journal of Verbal Learning and Verbal Behavior*, 1975, *14*, 304–316.

Levy, B. A. Reading: Speech and meaning processes. *Journal of Verbal Learning and Verbal Behavior*, 1977, *16*, 623–638.

Levy, B. A. Speech analysis during sentence processing: Reading and listening. *Visible Language*, 1978, *XII*, 81–101. (a)

Levy, B. A. Speech processing during reading. In A. M. Lesgold, J. W. Pellegrino, S. D. Fokkema, & R. Glaser (Eds.), *Cognitive psychology and instruction*. New York: Plenum, 1978. (b)

Marcel, A. J. *Unconscious reading: Experiments on people who do not know that they are reading.* Paper given to the British Association for the Advancement of Science, 1976.

Margolin, C. M., & Wolford, G. *Speech recoding and reading: A failure to replicate.* Paper presented at the Eastern Psychological Association, 1979.

Marslen-Wilson, W. D., & Welsh, A. Processing interactions and lexical access during word recognition in continuous speech. *Cognitive Psychology*, 1978, *10*, 29–63.

Massaro, D. W. *Reading and listening* (Tech. Rep. No. 423). Madison Wisconsin Research and Development Center for Cognitive Learning, 1977.

Masson, M. E. J., & Sala, L. S. Interactive processes in sentence comprehension and recognition. *Cognitive Psychology*, 1978, *10*, 244–270.

McClelland, J. L. *On the time relations of mental processes: A framework for analyzing processes in cascade* (Chip Report No. 77). San Diego: Center for Information Processing, University of California, San Diego, 1978.

Meyer, D. E., Schvaneveldt, R. W., & Ruddy, N. G. Foci of contextual effects in word recognition. In P. Rabbit & S. Dornic (Eds.), *Attention and performance V*. New York: Academic Press, 1975.

Mitchell, D. C., & Green, D. W. The effects of context and content on immediate processing in reading. *Quarterly Journal of Experimental Psychology*, 1978, *30*, 609–636.

Morton, J., & Long, J. Effects of word transition probability on phoneme identification. *Journal of Verbal Learning and Verbal Behavior*, 1976, *15*, 43–52.

Murray, D. J. Articulation and acoustic confusability in short-term memory. *Journal of Experimental Psychology*, 1968, *78*, 679–684.

Neely, J. H. Semantic priming and retrieval from lexical memory: Roles of inhibitionless spreading activation and limited-capacity attention. *Journal of Experimental Psychology: General*, 1977, *106*, 226–254.

Newman, J. E., & Dell, G. S. The phonological nature of phoneme monitoring: A critique of some ambiguity studies. *Journal of Verbal Learning and Verbal Behavior*, 1978, *17*, 359–374.

Norman, D. A., & Bobrow, D. G. On data-limited and resource-limited processes. *Cognitive Psychology*, 1975, *7*, 44–64.

Peterson, L. R., & Johnson, S. F. Some effects of minimizing articulation on short-term retention. *Journal of Verbal Learning and Verbal Behavior*, 1971, *10*, 346–354.

Posner, M. I., & Snyder, C. R. R. Facilitation and inhibition in the processing of signals. In P. Rabbitt & S. Dornic (Eds.), *Attention and performance V*. New York: Academic Press, 1975.

Rumelhart, D. E. Toward an interactive model of reading. In S. Dornic & P. Rabbitt (Eds.), *Attention and performance VI*. Hillsdale, N.J.: Lawrence Erlbaum Associates, 1977.

Sala, L. S., & Masson, M. J. *Top-downing upside down sentences*. Paper presented at the Psychonomic Society Meeting, San Antonio, Texas, 1978.

Schindler, R. M. The effects of prose context on visual search for letters. *Memory & Cognition*, 1978, *6*, 124–130.

Schuberth, R. E., & Eimas, P. D. Effects of context on the classification of words and nonwords. *Journal of Experimental Psychology: Human Perception and Performance*, 1977, *3*, 27–36.

Stanovich, K. E., & West, R. F. Mechanisms of sentence context effects in reading: Automatic activation and conscious attention. *Memory & Cognition*, 1979, *7*, 77–85.

Swinney, D. A., & Hake, D. T. Effects of prior context upon lexical access during sentence comprehension. *Journal of Verbal Learning and Verbal Behavior*, 1976, *15*, 681–689.

West, R. F., & Stanovich, K. E. Automatic contextual facilitation in readers of three ages. *Child Development*, 1978, *49*, 717–727.

2 Interactive Processing Through Spreading Activation

David E. Rumelhart and James L. McClelland
Program in Cognitive Science
University of California, San Diego

A central issue in the development of a model of the reading process is the way the context in which a linguistic element is found affects the way that element is processed and ultimately interpreted. Rumelhart (1977) proposed a very general model, dubbed an *interactive model,* of the reading process that was designed to explicate the role of context during reading. In brief, an interactive model is one in which data-driven, bottom-up processing combines with top-down, conceptually driven processing to cooperatively determine the most likely interpretation of the input. Roughly speaking, processing in an interactive model of reading proceeds in the following way: The reader begins with a set of expectations about what information is likely to be available through visual input. These expectations, or initial hypotheses, are based on our knowledge of the structure of letters, words, phrases, sentences, and larger pieces of discourse, including nonlinguistic aspects of the current contextual situation. As visual information from the page begins to become available, it strengthens those hypotheses that are consistent with the input and weakens those that are inconsistent. The stronger hypotheses, in turn, make even more specific predictions about the information available in the visual input. To the degree that these hypotheses are confirmed, they are further strengthened, and the processing is facilitated.

Interactive processing is thus a form of cooperative processing in which knowledge at all levels of abstraction can come into play in the process of reading and comprehension. In earlier work on this topic, Rumelhart (1977) proposed a processing mechanism of this general sort. The mechanism was very general and suffered from a lack of direct connection to an empirical base and a related lack of specificity of exactly how the brain might actually carry out such complex computations. In this chapter (and the more complete descriptions of McClelland

& Rumelhart, 1980; and Rumelhart & McClelland, 1980), we have attempted to propose a mechanism that is both closely tied to an empirical data base and that is sufficiently specific to compare the results of computer simulations of the model with the empirical data.

Clearly, it is premature to develop a model of the kind of specificity we are proposing for the entire reading process. We have attempted to make a step in that direction by developing a model in which knowledge about words plays a central role in the perception of sequences of letters, which may or may not form familiar words. There is a large amount of literature on this topic, so there are a large number of important findings to constrain our theorizing. We view this domain as a kind of testing ground for the general question of how contextual information and general knowledge guide processing, but also as a testing ground in which we can get firm empirical predictions. We begin by reviewing some of the findings that we take as central to the area of word perception, and in so doing, we begin to suggest the outlines of an interactive model that can account for them.

SOME IMPORTANT FACTS ABOUT WORD PERCEPTION

Study of the perception of letters in words goes back a very long time in psychology, to the early research of Cattell (1886) and others (see Huey [1908] for a review). Most of these early experiments demonstrated that words could be perceived under conditions that were not sufficient to allow accurate perception of all the letters. In the late 1940s and 1950s, researchers in the "new look" in perception focused attention on the fact that more frequent words could be perceived more accurately than less frequent words at a given exposure level and could be perceived at lower exposure levels (Howes & Solomon, 1951). In addition, the important discovery was made that letters were perceived more accurately in nonwords that conformed to some of the statistical properties of words than in nonwords that did not (Miller, Bruner, & Postman, 1954).

Although these phenomena are consistent with the view that perception of the letters in words (and nonwords) is not merely a matter of independent perception of unrelated elements, it was possible to interpret them in terms of postperceptual guessing or forgetting processes. A large number of unrelated letters might pose a memory load that would limit accuracy of identification, even if all the letters were actually perceived correctly. And, it was argued, knowledge about what makes a word in English could allow subjects to *guess* imperfectly perceived letters in words more accurately than letters in unrelated strings.

In 1969, Reicher introduced a procedure that controls for these "nonperceptual" interpretations of the classic findings in word perception. In this procedure, the subject views a target item, followed by a mask, and is then given a pair of alternative letters, either of which might have been presented. For example, if the item *WORD* is shown, the subject might be tested with a choice between *D* and *K*. On another trial, a nonword such as *ORWD* might be shown, followed by a choice, as before, between *D* and *K*. Subjects were more accurate in their choices when the item formed a word, even though the context letters really do not provide any clue as to which of the two letters, *D* or *K*, should be correct. Thus, the fact that the letters formed a word seemed to permit the subject to perceive more information relevant to a discrimination between the letters in the word. The possibility that postperceptual forgetting processes were responsible for the effect was eliminated by the fact that Reicher obtained a word advantage not only over letters in four-letter nonwords but also over letters presented in isolation.

Reicher's experiment has stimulated a large body of research, and his method has become the method of choice for studying the role of word contexts in facilitating perception of letters. For this reason, results obtained using this paradigm have been the primary focus of our modeling effort, although we do have occasion to note a few findings, which have been obtained using the classical whole report technique, that are consistent with our model.

The literature provides several important clues to the processes at work in word perception that have been central to the development of our model. One central finding is the fact that it is not necessary for words to be presented in a familiar visual form to produce a perceptual advantage over sequences of unrelated letters. McClelland (1976) found that the advantage of words over unrelated letters could be obtained using mixed upper- and lower-case type. Adams (1979) reproduced this result using stimuli in which the upper- and lowercase letters differed widely in size, so that the visual configuration was quite unfamiliar indeed. Mixing upper- and lowercase type does have a disruptive effect, and it appears to apply equally well to both words and nonwords when both types of stimuli are tested at comparable performance levels (Adams, 1979). These results suggest that an adequate model of word perception cannot rely (at least not exclusively) on recognition of familiar shapes of words to account for superior perception compared to unrelated letter strings. It would seem that it is knowledge of the arrangement of letters in familiar words that facilitates their perception rather than knowledge about their exact visual form.

But how is this possible? If word knowledge specifies what letters co-occur in words, then it seems to follow that word knowledge must be applied to the results of letter perception. But at the same time, the results of Reicher's experiment seem to show that letter perception is facilitated by word context. It seems like we are trying to have it both ways.

The paradox can be resolved if we observe that the process of letter identification need not be complete, exhaustive, or accessible to report before partial results of letter processing begin to interact with our knowledge about words (Massaro, 1975; McClelland, 1976). Perhaps what word knowledge does is allow us to reinforce partial, preattentive activations of letters that are consistent with words in our vocabulary (Rumelhart, 1977). Suppose the presentation of a display produces activations of letters consistent with the display and that these in turn produce activations of words consistent with the letters. These activations, in turn, produce feedback to the letters, reinforcing the activations of letters consistent with the activated words (Adams, 1979). An illustration of this conception is presented in Fig. 2.1.

A second important clue to the process of word perception comes from the finding that the stimulus need not in fact even be a word to produce facilitation compared to unrelated letters or single letters. A large number of studies using Reicher's procedure have shown that the word advantage over unrelated letters extends to pronounceable nonwords as well as words (e.g., Baron & Thurston, 1973; Spoehr & Smith, 1975), and one study has obtained a large and reliable

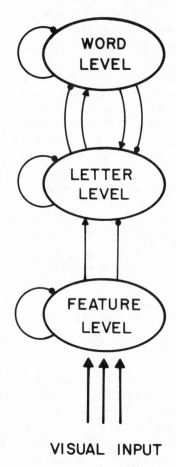

VISUAL INPUT

FIG.2.1   Sketch of the interactive activation model of word perception.

advantage of pseudowords compared to single letters (McClelland & Johnston, 1977).

One view that has often been taken concerning these findings holds that knowledge specific to words is not directly used in word perception. Instead, it is assumed that perceptual processing relies on a set of orthographic or phonological rules or on a parsing process that constructs representations of words and pseudowords in like manner (Spoehr & Smith, 1975), prior to a postperceptual lexical access process. It appears, however, that such a mechanism could not be the whole story, since in many experiments an advantage for words over pronounceable nonwords is obtained (Manelis, 1974; McClelland, 1976), even if it is not always statistically reliable (MeClelland & Johnston, 1977; Spoehr & Smith, 1975). Although attempts have been made to explain these differences away on the basis of possible orthographic and/or pronounceability differences between words and nonwords (Massaro, Venezky, & Taylor, 1979), the word–pseudoword difference does raise the possibility that word knowledge plays a sizable role in the perceptual processing of words. On the basis of this finding, McClelland and Johnston (1977) argued for two mechanisms—one in which familiar words were recognized, and a second in which representations of pronounceable strings are constructed. Similarly, Adams (1979) suggested that the words and nonwords both had an advantage over unrelated letter strings because of excitatory interactions between frequently co-occurring letters, whereas words had an advantage over regular nonwords because of feedback, as already mentioned.

Would it be possible to get by with a model that makes use of knowledge of specific words only? Recent work on the process of constructing pronunciations of pseudowords (Glushko, Chap. 3, this volume) suggested to us that it might. Glushko has shown that when constructing pronunciations of both words and nonwords, our knowledge of the pronunciations of specific words similar to the target word seems to influence the time and accuracy of our responding. On the basis of these findings, he has suggested that pronunciations of novel pseudowords are synthesized out of activations of pronunciations of the words that are similar to the target. In other words, we know how to pronounce *REAT* because we know how to pronounce words with similar spellings. These words, if partially activated in the process of perceiving *REAT*, would then produce partial activation of their corresponding phonological codes, which could then be synthesized to produce a pronunciation.

Much the same thing could be happening in the perception of pseudowords. Perhaps the presentation of a string like *REAT* produces partial activations of words with closely related spellings (for example, *HEAT, REST,* and *READ,* among others). These partial activations could then produce feedback to letter activations, just as in the case where an actual word stimulus is shown.

Thus, instead of explaining the perception of words and pseudowords in terms of a single mechanism that relies on orthographic or phonological knowledge, it might be possible to explain the perception of both words and pseudowords on the basis of a single mechanism that relies solely on knowledge of specific words. Feedback from activations of specific words could reinforce activations of letters that happened to spell words, as well as activations of letters in strings that appeared to be close in spelling to some words. If, however, the string is a sequence of random unrelated letters (e.g., *OMTP*), it may not be similar enough in spelling to any words to generate much feedback.

There is one more finding that has played a central role in the development of our thinking. This is the fact that the perceptual advantage of words over non-words is greatly affected by the details of the visual conditions used. In particular, two sorts of visual conditions have been widely studied. In one, the target display itself is either very dim or very brief or both, and is followed either by no mask or a simple light mask. These conditions characterize most of the early work (pre-1970) on word perception, as well as a few more recent studies (e.g., Juola, Leavitt, & Choe, 1974; Rumelhart & Siple, 1974). Under these conditions, it seems reasonable to imagine that performance is limited largely by the quality of the information that can be extracted from the visual display. Large advantages for words over nonwords are obtained in these experiments, but only when a free-report measure of performance is used (Rumelhart & Siple, 1974; Smith, 1969); similar results are obtained for items presented in peripheral vision (Bouwhuis, 1979). When a forced-choice task is used, as in the Reicher procedure, there is only a slight advantage for single letters compared to letters in words, and the word advantage over nonwords is quite small (Johnston & McClelland, 1973; Juola, Leavitt, & Choe, 1974; Massaro & Klitzke, 1979). In contrast, when the target display is a bright, clear, high-contrast presentation of the word but is followed quite quickly by a high-contrast patterned mask, large advantages for words and pseudowords compared to single-letter and unrelated letter stimuli are observed.

A variety of different interpretations have been offered for the dependence of the word advantage on masking. One possibility is that the fact that the stimulus is a word makes it possible to maintain activations of a representation capturing the information in the display longer than would otherwise be the case, thereby increasing the chance that the subject would have sufficient time to translate the activated representation into a form suitable for overt report. The feedback mechanism we have been describing might have just such an effect. That is, feedback from activations of words could keep the representations of the letters active longer in the face of masking than would otherwise be the case. In no-mask conditions, this feedback would tend to reinforce possible letters that are consistent with the words that the subject knows but would tend to reinforce all the letters consistent with both the subject's knowledge of words and the visual information that he or she has managed to extract from the display. Qualitatively, then, we would expect the subject to pick a set of letters that form a word or a pronounceable nonword if asked to give a whole report. But he or she should not show much of an advantage in discriminating between word (or pronounceable nonword) possibilities left open by information successfully extracted from the stimulus.

To summarize, the major findings we have reviewed thus far seem to be compatible with a model in which partial, preattentive activations of letters give rise to activations of words, which in turn produce feedback reinforcing the letter activations. We now review the model we have worked out to achieve this result. More detail is available in McClelland and Rumelhart (1980).

THE MODEL

We have already shown the general conception of the model in schematic form in Fig. 2.1. Perception is assumed to consist of a series of interacting levels, each level communicating with those immediately above and below it. In general, of course, a given level may have more than one level immediately above or below it, but for simplicity we now consider the case in which there is a linear ordering of levels. We have assumed that communication proceeds through a spreading activation mechanism in which activation at one level "spreads" to neighboring levels. Furthermore, we have assumed that the communication can consist of both excitatory and inhibitory messages. Excitatory messages increase the activation level of their recipients, and inhibitory messages decrease the activation level of their recipients. The arrows in the diagram represent excitatory connections, and the circular ends of the connections represent inhibitory connections. The intralevel inhibitory relationships represent a kind of lateral inhibitory relationship in which certain units at the same level compete. Thus, for example, since a string of four letters can be interpreted as, at most, one four-letter word, the various possible words mutually inhibit one another and in that way compete as possible interpretations of the string.

Although we assume that there are many levels that might be important in reading and perception in general and that the interactions among these levels are important for many phenomena, we have found that we can account for many of the major phenomena in word perception by considering only the interactions between "letter-level" and "word-level" elements. Thus, we have elaborated the model only on these two levels, have assumed that the other levels merely generate input into these levels, and have ignored the feedback that may occur between word and letter levels and any other levels of the system.

Specific Assumptions

For every relevant unit in the system there is an entity called a *node*. There is a node for each word, and there is a node for each letter in each position. The word nodes are located at the word level, and the letter nodes are located at the letter level. Each node has connections to a number of other nodes. The set of nodes to which a node connects are called its *neighbors*. Each connection is two-way and may be either excitatory or inhibitory.

Connections occur both within levels and between adjacent levels. Connections within the "word level" are mutually inhibitory since only one word can occur at any one place at any one time. Connections between the word level and letter level may be either inhibitory or excitatory depending on whether or not the letter is a part of the word in the appropriate letter position. The set of nodes with excitatory connections to a given node are its excitatory neighbors, whereas the set of nodes with inhibitory connections to a given node are its inhibitory neighbors. A subset of the neighbors of the letter *t* are illustrated in Fig. 2.2.

Each node has a momentary level of activation associated with it. This level of activation is a real number bounded between a maximum or ceiling level and a minimum or floor level. Any node with a positive degree of activation is said to be *active*. In the absence of inputs from its neighbors, all nodes are assumed to decay back to an inactive state—that is, to an activation value at or below zero. This resting level may differ from node to node and corresponds to a kind of a

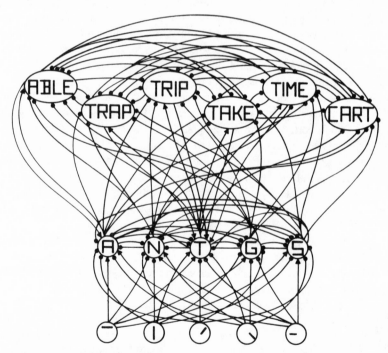

FIG. 2.2   A few of the neighbors of the letter *t*, in the first position in a word, and some of their interconnections. Excitatory connections are represented by arrows ending with points, and inhibitory connections are represented by arrows ending with dots.

priori bias (Broadbent, 1967), which might be affected by frequency of activation of the node over the long term.

When the neighbors of a node are active, they influence the activation of the node by either excitation or inhibition, depending on their relation to the node. These excitatory and inhibitory influences combine by a simple weighted average to yield a net input to the unit, which may be either excitatory (greater than 0) or inhibitory. Note that inactive nodes have no influence on their neighbors; only nodes in an active state have any effects, either excitatory or inhibitory.

The net input to a node drives the activation of the node up or down depending on whether it is positive or negative. The degree of the effect of the input on the node is modulated by the node's current activity level to keep the input to the node from driving it beyond its maximum and minimum values (Grossberg, 1978). The new value of the activation of a node at a given instant in time is equal to the value at the previous instant, minus the decay, plus the influence determined by the activations of its neighbors at the previous instant in time.

Upon presentation of a stimulus, a set of featural inputs are assumed to be made available to the system. For simplicity, the model assumes that the input consist of letters written in the font used by Rumelhart and Siple (1974) and shown in Fig. 2.3. During each moment in time, each feature has some probability less than or equal to 1 of being detected if it has not been detected already. Upon being detected, the feature begins sending activation to all letter-level nodes that contain that feature. All letter-level nodes that do not contain the extracted feature are inhibited. The probability of detection and the rate at which

FIG. 2.3. The features used to construct the letters and the letters themselves (from Rumelhart & Siple, 1974).

the feature excites or inhibits the relevant letter nodes are assumed to depend on the clarity of the visual display.

Presentation of a new display following an old one results in the probabilistic extraction of the set of features present in the new display. These features, when extracted, replace the old ones in corresponding positions. Thus, the presentation of an *O* following the *R* described earlier would result in the replacement of detected features already described with their opposites.

The Operation of the Model

Now consider what happens when an input reaches the system. Assume that all prior inputs have had an opportunity to decay, that the entire system is in its quiescent state, and that each node is at its resting level. The presentation of a stimulus initiates a chain in which certain features are extracted and excitatory and inhibitory pressures begin to act upon the letter-level nodes. The activation levels of certain of the letter nodes are pushed above their resting levels. Others receive predominantly inhibitory inputs and are pushed below their resting levels. These letter nodes, in turn, will begin to send activation to those word-level nodes of which they are a part and inhibit those word nodes with which they are not consistent. In addition, the various letter-level nodes attempt to suppress each other, with the strongest ones getting the upper hand. As word-level nodes become active, they in turn compete with one another and send excitation and inhibition back down to the letter-level nodes. If the input features are close to those for one particular set of letters and those letters are consistent with those forming a particular word, the positive feedback in the system will work to converge rapidly on the appropriate letter set and word. If not, they will compete with each other; and perhaps no single letter set nor single word will get enough activation to dominate the others, and their inhibitory relationships might strangle each other. The details of the process are greatly affected by the values of various parameters of the model. Some of these effects are described in McClelland and Rumelhart (1980).

Simulations

Though the basic ideas of the model are simple, its behavior is quite complex and cannot be understood without actually "running" it. We have been able to do this by simulating the performance of the model using a computer. To do this, we have had to make several simplifying assumptions. First, the simulation of the model operates in discrete time slices or ticks, updating the activations of all the nodes in the system once each cycle, on the basis of the values on the previous cycle. We have endeavored to keep the time slices "thin" enough so that the model's behavior is continuous for all intents and purposes.

Second, we have assumed that the weight of the excitatory and inhibitory effects of one node on another depend only on the levels at which the nodes are located. In other words, the strengths of the connections between all letter nodes and all word nodes of which they are part are assumed to be the same, independent of the identity of the words.

Finally, these simulations have been restricted to four-letter words. We have equipped our simulation with knowledge of 1179 four-letter words occurring at least two times per million in the Kucera and Francis word count (1967). Plurals, inflected forms, and occasional unfamiliar entries arising from apparent sampling flukes, acronyms, abbreviations, and proper nouns have been excluded.

An Example.   For the purposes of this example, imagine that the visual display illustrated in Fig. 2.4 has been presented dimly to a subject on a CRT. In the first letter position, the letter *W* has been dimly presented. In the second letter position, the letter *O* has been dimly presented. In the third position, the letter *R* has been dimly presented. In the final position, only those features consistent with both the letter *K* and the letter *R* have been presented, and there is a blotch or something obscuring the features that would distinguish between these two possibilities. We wish now to chart the activity of the system resulting from this presentation. Figure 2.5 shows the time course of the activations for selected nodes at the word and letter levels.

At the word level, we have charted the activity levels of the nodes for the words *WORK, WORD, WEAR,* and *WEAK.* Note first that the word *WORK* is the only word in the lexicon consistent with the presented information. As a result, its activation level is the highest and reaches a value of .8 through the first 40 time cycles. (The maximum and minimum activation values are set at 1.0 and −.2, respectively.) The word *WORD* is consistent with the bulk of the informa-

FIG. 2.4.   A hypothetical display presented to a subject in an experiment on word perception.

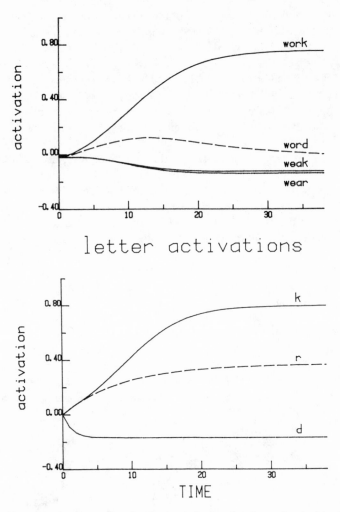

FIG. 2.5.   The time course of activations of selected nodes at the word level (upper panel) and letter level (lower panel) after onset of the display shown in Fig. 2.4.

tion presented and, as a result, first rises and later—as a result of competition with *WORK*—is pushed back down to (and below) its resting level. The words *WEAR* and *WEAK* are consistent with the information presented in the first and fourth letter positions, but inconsistent with the information in the second and third letter positions. Thus, the activation levels of these words drop to a rather low level, but not as low as the activation levels of words such as *GILL*, which contain *nothing* in common with the presented information. Although not shown in the figure, these words attain activation levels of about $-.20$ rather quickly and retain them throughout. Note that *WEAR* and *WEAK* are equally consistent with the presented information and thus drop together for the first nine or so time units. At this point, however, top-down information has determined that the correct final letter is K and not R. As a result, the word *WEAK* "becomes" more similar to the input than the word *WEAR* and, as a result, begins to gain a slight advantage over *WEAR*. This result occurs in the model because as the word *WORK* gains in activation level, it feeds back down to the letter level to strengthen the K differentially over the R. This strengthened K and weakened R in turn feed back into the word level and strengthen words ending in K and weaken those ending in R.

Now consider the activity at the letter level. Here we have plotted the activation levels of the letters D, R, and K. Note that at the start, the information clearly disconfirmed the existence of a D in the fourth position, and thus, the activation level of the D node decreased quickly to near its minimum value. However, the bottom-up information from the feature level supported both a K and an R in the fourth position. Thus, the activation level for each of these nodes rose slowly. These activation levels, along with those for W, O, and R, pushed the activation level of *WORK* above zero, and it began to feed back; by about Time Cycle 4, it was beginning to push the K above the R (*WORR* is not a word). Note that this separation occurred just before the words *WEAK* and *WEAR* separate. It is this feedback that causes them to separate. Ultimately, the R reaches a level well below that of K, where it remains, and the K pushes toward a .8 activation level. Note that in our simulations, we have adopted the simplifying assumption that there is no word-to-letter inhibition and no intraletter inhibition. Thus, K and R both coexist at moderately high levels—the R fed only from the bottom up, and the K fed from both the bottom up and the top down.

This example shows how our model permits relatively weak and ambiguous bottom-up information to be reinforced and enhanced by top-down processes. Here we have a very simple mechanism capable of parallel cooperative processing of words.

On Making Responses

One of the more problematic aspects of a model such as this one is a specification of how these relatively complex patterns of activity might be related to the content of percepts and the sorts of response probabilities we observe in experiments. The model assumes that the percept corresponds to a temporal integration of the pattern of activation over all the nodes. The integration process is assumed to occur slowly enough that very brief activations may come and go without necessarily entering perceptual experience or being accessible for purposes of responding; the longer an activation lasts, the more likely it is to be reportable.

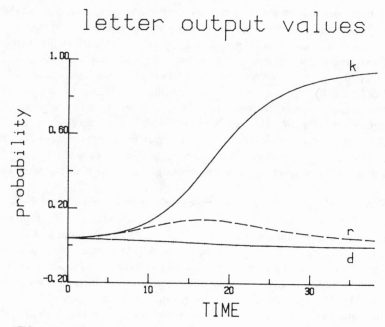

FIG. 2.6.   "Output values" for the letters *R, K,* and *D* after presentation of the display shown in Fig. 2.4.

Specifically, we think of the response strength in the sense of Luce's choice model (Luce, 1959)—as being an exponential function of the activation of the relevant node averaged over the immediately preceding time interval. Following Luce's formulation, we assume that the probability of a response dependent on a particular node at a given level is equal to the ratio of the strength of that node, divided by the sum of the strengths of all other relevant nodes (e.g., nodes for letters in the same letter positions).

   With regard to the previous example, it is useful to look at the "output values" for the letter nodes *R, K,* and *D*. Figure 2.6 shows the output values for these simulations. The output value for a particular letter at a particular time is the probability that the letter would be selected as the output or response if the response were selected at the given time. As intended, these output values grow somewhat more slowly than the values of the letter activations themselves, but eventually come to reflect the activations of the letter nodes as they reach and hold their asymptotic values.

APPLICATIONS OF THE MODEL TO THE LITERATURE

The model we have described turns out to provide a good account for a wide range of phenomena in the literature on word perception (McClelland, 1980). In this chapter, we lack the space to consider all the experiments that the model can account for in detail. What we do instead is try to illustrate a few of the major features of the model's operation, in accounting for some of the most important facts.

The Word Advantage and Its Dependence on Masking

As mentioned previously, it is commonly observed that subjects are able to report the letters in a dim, degraded, or parafoveal presentation of a word more accurately than letters in unpronounceable nonwords. However, there is very little advantage for letters in words compared to nonwords under these conditions if Reicher's forced-choice test is used. Under these conditions, it is assumed that performance is limited quite simply by the quality of information that the subject has extracted from the display, and the information extraction process is not affected by feedback from the word level. What is affected is the probability of choosing particular letters that are compatible with the extracted visual information.

When the target is presented clearly but followed by a postdisplay mask, a large advantage for forced-choice performance on letters in words over single letters or letters in unpronounceable nonwords is obtained. Under these conditions, we assume that the target presentation results in complete feature extraction in all conditions, and performance is limited by the time available for encoding the activations produced by the presentation of the target before they are wiped out by the mask. The role of the word level is to provide feedback activations to the letter level that have the effect of increasing the strength of the activations of the correct letters at the letter level, thereby increasing the probability of correct encoding.

Figure 2.7 illustrates the behavior of the model in two trials of an experiment under this type of visual conditions. The target is the word *READ* in one case and the single letter *E* in the other. When *READ* is shown, the nodes for the letter *E* and all the other letters begin to get active soon after target presentation. These activations in turn activate the node for *READ,* which produces feedback, reinforcing the activation in the case where the *E* is presented in the context of the word. The mask drives down the activations quickly, but the area under the activation function is considerably larger in the case of the *E* in *READ* than in the case of the *E* alone. The result is that the probability of encoding the correct letter reaches a higher peak for the letters in *READ* than for the letter *E* alone. Note that as time goes on, the probability of encoding the correct letter drops back to chance. Thus, it is necessary to invoke the encoding process at the right time in order to ensure optimal performance. In applying the model to data, we assume that the subject learns when to "read out" as a result of practice in the task.

Perception of Pronounceable Nonwords

The mechanism just described is capable of producing facilitation for letters in nonwords as well as in words so long as the nonwords are similar to several

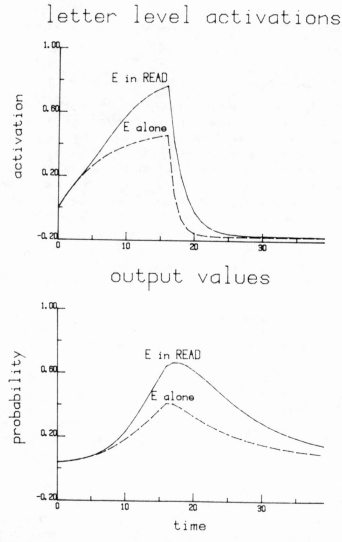

FIG. 2.7.   The upper curve shows activation functions for the letter E in isolation and in the word *READ* under conditions of distinct target presentation followed by a distinct posttarget mask. The lower panel shows the output functions for the corresponding conditions.

words. The reason is that the presentation of a nonword similar to words results in activation of the nodes for the similar words, and these nodes then produce feedback, reinforcing the activation of the nodes for the letters. Of course, no actual word will reinforce the nodes for all the letters. However, if several words share one subset of letters in common and several others share other subsets, then all the letters in the word can receive facilitation. For example, consider the pronounceable nonword *MAVE*. This item shares its last three letters with nine words, the first and the last two letters with one word, and the first two and the last letter with eight more words. All these words receive partial activation from the presentation of *MAVE,* and therefore, all the letters in *MAVE* receive some feedback reinforcing their activation. For this reason, the letters in *MAVE* will have a greater chance of being correctly encoded than the same letters in isolation.

There are now two papers in the literature showing that perception of letters in pronounceable nonwords is facilitated—compared to perception of letters in unrelated letter strings—only if the subject is aware that the list of stimuli may contain pronounceable nonwords. Interestingly enough, the facilitation for letters in words does not depend on expectation in this way. So, for example, if subjects expect nonwords, there is an advantage for letters in words, but not for letters in pronounceable nonwords. In fact, if they expect only words, there is an advantage for letters in words over pronounceable and unpronounceable nonwords and no advantage for pronounceable nonwords (Carr, Davidson, & Hawkins, 1978).

At first glance these results seem to suggest that there is one mechanism for the perception of words that is automatic, and a different mechanism for the perception of pronounceable nonwords that is only brought into play when pronounceable nonwords are expected. However, our model provides a very different type of account. We assume that the result depends on the ratio of excitation to inhibition in the influence of activations at the letter level on activations at the word level. Consider, first, the case where the inhibition is three times as strong as the excitation. In such a case, the presentation of four letters that have three letters in common with some word will have no effect on the perceptibility of the word. For example, presentation of *MAVE* will not result in the activation of any words. The reason is that the excitatory effect of the three letters that are compatible with a particular word would be canceled by the inhibitory effect of the fourth letter. So with high letter–word inhibition (relative to excitation), *MAVE* would produce no activations at the word level and no feedback-reinforcing activations at the letter level. But if the item is actually a familiar word (say, *CAVE*), the node for *CAVE* will receive strong activation because all four letters would excite the node and none would inhibit it. Thus, high letter–word inhibition will result in facilitation for letters in words but not for letters in nonwords.

Now consider again the case in which the letter–word inhibition is low relative to letter–word excitation. This is actually the case we considered initially when considering the partial activations of words that might result from the presentation of the nonword *MAVE*. Of course, such partial activations will also occur in cases where a word is actually shown. However, in this case, the node for the word shown still gets considerably more excitation than the nodes for other words. And because there is competition among nodes at the word level, the nodes for words with only three letters in common with the word shown are kept from becoming strongly active. Thus, the node for the word shown is the major determinant of the amount of feedback whether the letter-to-word inhibition is low or high.

The Flexibility of the Perceptual System

One of the intriguing aspects of the literature on word perception has been that different results are often obtained in experiments that are superficially quite similar. What we see in the experiments already discussed is evidence that both the visual conditions of stimulus presentation and the expectations of the subject for what types of materials will be shown are important determinants of perceptual performance. The model nicely captures these effects. The model, like the human subject, behaves in different ways under different conditions, where the conditions include both the characteristics of the inputs to the system and the settings of various parameters in the system itself.

Other Effects in the Literature

There are a number of other phenomena in the literature that we have been able to account for with our model. One of these comes from an examination of the effects of intraword constraints on forced-choice performance by Johnston (1978). Johnston found that the letter *S* is no more easily seen in *SHIP* than in *SINK*, even though the context in the first case is consistent with (that is, forms a word with) only 3 possible letters, whereas the context in the latter case is consistent with 12 to 14, depending on what is counted as a word. Johnston used only words in the experiment, so we would expect that the subjects would have adopted a high value of letter–word inhibition. The visual conditions were like the distinct target/patterned mask conditions in which the word advantage over single letters is obtained. Under these conditions, only the nodes for the letters actually shown receive net excitation on the basis of stimulus input, and only the node for the single word containing all the active letters receives net excitation from the output of the active letters. Under these circumstances, the number of words quite similar to the target is irrelevant, because none of the corresponding nodes receive any net excitation. Thus, under the distinct target/patterned mask conditions of the Johnston study, the model produces no constraint effect either.

When a lower value of letter–word inhibition is adopted, the matter becomes more complicated. Under these circumstances, words that share three letters in common with the target do receive some activation, and as a result they compete with the target word. The more such words there are, the less active the node for the target word becomes, and therefore the less feedback there is to reinforce activations at the letter level. Thus, highly constraining contexts, in which few words share the same three context letters with the target, produce less word-level interference than weakly constraining contexts, and therefore these items have a very slight advantage (a 1% difference in a simulation of accuracy differences in forced-choice responding). The reason is twofold. First, the node for the letter shown dominates the activation at the word level, and the weak activations of competing words have rather little effect. Second, there tend to be several words that share three letters with the target word including the critical letter. For example, in the case of *SINK,* there are words like *SANK, SILK, SING,* etc. Such words, when they become partially active, actually reinforce the activation of the critical letter and thereby help to dilute the effects of the words that have the three noncritical letters in common with the target.

Constraints do make a difference in the model when the input is degraded so that multiple-letter possibilities are partially activated by the input features. This is especially true if the response the subject must make is to identify what word is shown. Given incomplete feature input, relatively unique words—words sharing three letters in common with few other words—stand a greater chance of being uniquely compatible with the extracted features than words that have three letters in common with a large number of other words. For words that are themselves frequent, uniqueness is not so important, since such words tend to dominate the response of the system if other words are partially activated anyway. But for infrequent words, uniqueness is quite important, since it increases the likelihood that the correct node will be the one that is most compatible with the features extracted. When the node for a word that is more frequent than the word shown is as compatible with the extracted features as the actual word shown, the word shown tends to lose out to the more frequent word. Thus, the model has the following property: With degraded input, uniqueness is important for low-frequency words but not for high-frequency words. This characteristic of the model has been observed experimentally by Broadbent and Gregory (1968).

Another recent finding (Johnston & McClelland, in press) is that the word advantage over single letters is greatly reduced when the patterned mask contains letters rather than non-letter-patterned elements. Johnston & McClelland (in press) found a large word advantage with nonletter masks, but a much smaller advantage when the mask was made of letters. It did not matter whether or not the letters spelled a word.

In our model, this result comes about only in cases where the input is strong and of very high quality, so that the effect of feedback from the word level is to increase the persistence rather than the height of the activation function. The benefit for letters in words under these circumstances is due to the longer time available for readout of the activations at the letter level, when feedback causes them to persist for a longer time. The reason why the presence of letters in the mask reduces the word advantage is that the letters in the mask quickly produce activations of their own, which interfere with the readout process (recall that the probability of correct readout depends on the strength of the correct node, divided by the sums of the strengths of the other nodes). Letters in the mask only have a very slight effect on performance of single-letter trials because the activations of the target letters are already wiped out by the mask by the time the activations of nodes for the letters in the mask have a chance to affect readout. In essence, the idea is that in the case of words, there is still something left for the mask letters to interfere with, but this is not so (or, rather, is so to a very limited extent) in the case of single letters.

In order to get the model to behave this way, we found it was necessary to restrict the inhibitory effect of the mask on active letter representations while making the excitatory effect of the mask letters on the nodes for the letters in the mask quite strong. It was only in this way that we were able to keep the mask from wiping out the old activations long enough to let the new ones due to the letters in the mask have an effect.

Context Enhancement Effects

In addition to accounting for all the findings already discussed, we have applied the model to a new set of findings that we call "context enhancement effects" (Rumelhart & McClelland, 1980). We briefly describe these effects, then consider how the model can account for them.

The basic idea of these studies is to use Reicher's forced-choice procedure to study how the information that subjects are given about the context of a target letter influences the identification of the target. To do this, the durations of the context and of the target letters are varied separately. For example, in our first experiment, the context could be turned on at various times—before, simultaneously with, or after the target letter. In this experiment, the target and mask letters were turned off together and replaced with a patterned mask. Figure 2.8 shows the results of this first study. What we see is that the accuracy of performance in identifying the target letter depends on the duration of the context. When the context is on 1.67 times as long as the target, performance in identifying the target is 15% more accurate than when the context is on only .33 times as long as the target, even though the target is on for the same amount of time in all cases. Thus, the longer the context information is available to the subject, the more accurately he or she can perceive a target letter in that context. Of course, since we used the Reicher procedure, it is not possible to attribute the effect simply to an influence of the context in helping the subject guess the target letter.

Our model has little difficulty in accounting for these results. The reason is that the longer the context is on, the more it contributes to the activation of the node for the whole word and the more this node, in turn, produces feedback reinforcing the correct alternative. Of course, if the context is on before the target letter, it tends to produce feedback exciting the node for the incorrect alternative as well, but because of the strong bottom-up inhibition from the feature to the letter level, the presentation of the target letter quickly nullifies such effects.

In a long series of experiments, we discovered several other important facts about these contextual enhancement effects. First, we demonstrated that the

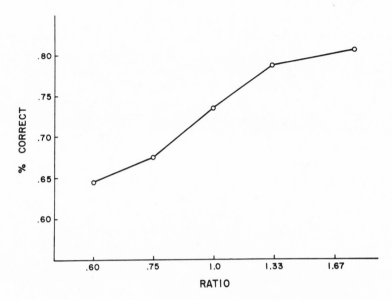

FIG. 2.8.   Effect of context duration on probability correct forced choice on a critical target letter.

effect could not be obtained if the context consisted of three randomly chosen digits instead of the letters of a word. Second, we demonstrated that the effect was stronger if the extra context information preceded rather than followed the target letter. The effect of presenting the context early versus late was particularly strong for letters in the middle positions. Third, we carried out a complete factorial experiment, independently varying the duration of each of the four letters and the position of the letter tested. In this study, we were able to determine how much extra information about the letter in one position tended to facilitate perception of the letter in each other position. In general, the result was that the effect of extra information was greatest when it occurred in a position adjacent to the target letter.

The model accounts for all these effects, although additional assumptions are necessary to account for the fact that the internal letters benefit more from context than the external ones. The fact that completely unrelated context fails to produce facilitation is expected because completely unrelated context would fail to activate any higher-order nodes containing the target and the context, and thus would not afford any increase in feedback (or, for that matter, any feedback at all). The fact that the context must come earlier to be of much use also falls out of the simulations. Indeed, the model tends to overpredict the magnitude of this effect somewhat. The reason is that under the conditions assumed to prevail in simulating these results, the mask drives the activations of the letter nodes down so fast that the additional feedback to be gained from increased persistence of the activation of the relevant word node is of no benefit. As already noted, the model does not directly account for the greater dependence of the interior letters on order of context presentation. One way to account for this is to assume that subjects ordinarily follow an outside-in processing strategy—first establishing the end letters and then using the information derived from them to facilitate perception of the letters in the middle of the item via feedback. Finally, it turns out that the greater effect of adjacent letters on perception of the target falls out of the model without any further assumptions. The reason has to do with the statistical properties of the language. It turns out that adjacent letters in a given word tend to co-occur in the same word more frequently than nonadjacent letters. The phonological structure of the language puts more constraints on what letters can occur right next to each other than it places on what letters can occur at a greater distance from each other in words. Following an initial *P*, for example, only a vowel or a liquid consonant (*R* or *L*) may occur. But the letter separated from *P* by another letter might be almost any letter at all. This fact about the language is latent in our model, since all the words are stored in the set of nodes. Thus, when a word like *PLAY* is presented, increasing the duration of *P* is likely to activate more words containing *L* than words containing *A* or *Y*.

The model, then, fares rather well in accounting for these findings, as well as several others that we have not had space enough to mention. However, the model does have some difficulty accounting for the magnitude of the context enhancement effect obtained with pronounceable nonwords. The problem may be seen easily by considering an example, such as *BINT*, with a forced choice between *B* and *W*, say. What happens when the context is presented, in the model, is that the *_INT* tend to activate all those words containing these three letters, such as *DINT, HINT, LINT*. Any activation they may provide for words that begin with a *B* will have to be weaker, since because the item is a nonword, the remaining letter does not make a word with all three of the context letters. These words containing *B* may be weakly activated, but they have to contend with the inhibition generated by the activations of the "enemies" of the initial *B*. For other cases, the model shows a substantial pseudoword enhancement effect. Overall, however, the model underestimates the degree of the effect. We have considered a number of modifications to our present model that can account for this underestimation, including the possible involvement of nodes for letter clusters, phonological codes, and nodes for words of more or less than four letters. For details of these modifications, see Rumelhart and McClelland (1980).

SUMMARY AND CONCLUSION

Our model is basically very simple, and it is clear that a complete model of the role of context in the perception of letters would be considerably more complex. Nevertheless, the interactive nature of the processes involved give the model remarkable power and flexibility. Yet the processes carried out by the model are clearly not beyond the capability of simple neural circuits that we already know exist in the brain and nervous system. Through the use of computer simulation procedures we have been able to generate specific predictions from our model for nearly all the important phenomena of word perception. For the most part, these predictions have compared very favorably with observed results in a wide range of experimental studies. Obviously, however, there are many factors that go into reading and word perception that are not yet included in our model. Some of these factors are considered in some detail in McClelland and Rumelhart (1980) and in Rumelhart and McClelland (1980). Other factors have not yet been added to the model.

In addition to the substantive claims of the model we have developed, we are equally interested in the methodological implications of our work. We are becoming increasingly convinced that information-processing systems are properly viewed as consisting of numerous, relatively simple processing units (like our nodes) whose complexity results from the pattern of interactions that occur among the units and whose control structure is characterized by the modulation of levels of activation associated with the processing units. Such models, although simple in conception, gain their enormous processing power through the operation of populations of such units. We believe that computer simulations offer the clearest handle on the operations of such systems. Thus, we consider our efforts here as the beginning of an exploration into a kind of processing system seldom applied to phenomena as complex as reading. We are encouraged with our discoveries thus far.

ACKNOWLEDGMENTS

Preparation of this paper was supported by NSF Grant BNS-76-15024 to D. E. Rumelhart, by NSF Grant BNS-76-14830 to J. L. McClelland, and by the Office of Naval Research under Contract N00014-79-C-0323.

REFERENCES

Adams, M. J. Models of word recognition. *Cognitive Psychology*, 1979, *11*, 133–176.
Baron, J., & Thurston, I. An analysis of the word-superiority effect. *Cognitive Psychology*, 1973, *4*, 207–228.
Bouwhuis, D. G. *Visual recognition of words*. Eindhoven: Greve Offset B. V., 1979.
Broadbent, D. E. Word-frequency effect and response bias. *Psychological Review*, 1967, *74*, 1–15.
Broadbent, D. E., & Gregory, M. Visual perception of words differing in letter digram frequency. *Journal of Verbal Learning and Verbal Behavior*, 1968, *7*, 569–571.
Carr, T. H., Davidson, B. J., & Hawkins, H. L. Perceptual flexibility in word recognition: Strategies affect orthographic computation but not lexical access. *Journal of Experimental Psychology: Human Perception and Performance*, 1978, *4*, 674–690.
Cattell, J. M. The time taken up by cerebral operations. *Mind*, 1886, *11*, 220–242.

Grossberg, S. A theory of visual coding, memory, and development. In E. L. J. Leeuwenberg & H. F. Buffart (Eds.), *Formal theories of visual perception*. New York: Wiley, 1978.

Howes, D. H., & Solomon, R. L. Visual duration threshold as a function of word-probability. *Journal of Experimental Psychology*, 1951, *41*, 401–410.

Huey, E. B. *The psychology and pedagogy of reading*. New York: Macmillan, 1908.

Johnston, J. C. A test of the sophisticated guessing theory of word perception. *Cognitive Psychology*, 1978, *10*, 123–154.

Johnston, J. C., & McClelland, J. L. Visual factors in word perception. *Perception & Psychophysics*, 1973, *14*, 365–370.

Johnston, J. C., & McClelland, J. L. Experimental tests of a hierarchical model of word identification. *Journal of Verbal Learning and Verbal Behavior*, in press.

Juola, J. F., Leavitt, D. D., & Choe, C. S. Letter identification in word, nonword, and single letter displays. *Bulletin of the Psychonomic Society*, 1974, *4*, 278–280.

Kucera, H., & Francis, W. *Computational analysis of present-day American English*. Providence, R.I.: Brown University Press, 1967.

Luce, R. D. *Individual choice behavior*. New York: Wiley, 1959.

Manelis, L. The effect of meaningfulness in tachistoscopic word perception. *Perception & Psychophysics*, 1974, *16*, 182–192.

Massaro, D. W. (Ed.). *Understanding language: An information processing analysis of speech perception, reading, and psycholinguistics*. New York: Academic Press, 1975.

Massaro, D. W., & Klitzke, D. The role of lateral masking and orthographic structure in letter and word recognition. *Acta Psychologica*, 1979, *43*, 413–426.

Massaro, D. W., Venezky, R. L., & Taylor, G. A. Orthographic regularity, positional frequency, and visual processing of letter strings. *Journal of Experimental Psychology: General*, 1979, *108*, 107–124.

McClelland, J. Preliminary letter identification in the perception of words and nonwords. *Journal of Experimental Psychology: Human Perception and Performance*, 1976, *1*, 80–91.

McClelland, J., & Johnston, J. The role of familiar units in perception of words and nonwords. *Perception & Psychophysics*, 1977, *22*, 249–261.

McClelland, J. L., & Rumelhart, D. E. *An interactive activation model of the effect of context in perception, part I* (Chip Report 91). La Jolla, Calif.: Center for Human Information Processing, 1980.

Miller, G. A., Bruner, J. S., & Postman, L. Familiarity of letter sequences and tachistoscopic identification. *Journal of Genetic Psychology*, 1954, *50*, 129–139.

Rumelhart, D. E. Toward an interactive model of reading. In S. Dornic (Ed.), *Attention and performance VI*. Hillsdale, N.J.: Lawrence Erlbaum Associates, 1977.

Rumelhart, D. E., & McClelland, J. L. *An interactive activation model of the effect of context in perception, part II* (Chip Report 95). La Jolla, University of California, San Diego, Calif.: Center for Human Information Processing, 1980.

Rumelhart, D. E., & Siple, P. The process of recognizing tachistoscopically presented words. *Psychological Review*, 1974, *81*, 99–118.

Smith, F. Familiarity of configuration vs. discriminability of features in the visual identification of words. *Psychonomic Science*, 1969, *14*, 261–262.

Spoehr, K., & Smith, E. The role of orthographic and phonotactic rules in perceiving letter patterns. *Journal of Experimental Psychology: Human Perception and Performance*, 1975, *1*, 21–34.

3 PRINCIPLES FOR PRONOUNCING PRINT: THE PSYCHOLOGY OF PHONOGRAPHY

Robert J. Glushko
University of California, San Diego
Bell Laboratories, Whippany, N.J.

Jabberwocky

'Twas brillig, and the slithy toves
Did gyre and gimble in the wabe;
All mimsy were the borogoves,
And the mome raths outgrabe.

—Lewis Carroll

I begin this chapter on reading aloud with the nonsense poem ''Jabberwocky,'' not because what I write does not make any sense, but because dealing with nonsense is what reading and pronunciation are fundamentally all about. Every text is a mixture of familiar and unfamiliar words. For beginning readers, more of the words are novel or unfamiliar, but the ability to make sense of nonsense, to assign a pronunciation to a new pattern of squiggles, remains an important skill even for adult readers.

STANDARD THEORY: TWO MECHANISMS FOR READING ALOUD

Since reading material consists of both familiar and unfamiliar words, standard theory in psychology and reading education proposes that readers use two mechanisms (or strategies or procedures or processes) to deal with the two kinds of words (see Katz & Feldman, Chap. 4, this volume). A familiar word can be named by a *lexical* or *whole-word* or *graphemic* mechanism that retrieves a stored pronunciation from memory using letter or supraletter features as the access code. This word-specific (or perhaps morpheme-specific: Taft, 1979) procedure is complemented by a *phonological* or *phonic* mechanism that generates a pronunciation for an unfamiliar word using lexicon-independent spelling-to-sound rules. These rules are usually thought of as abstract relationships between single letters or letter units (graphemes) and single phonemes, or general principles such as the role of a terminal *e* to mark the tense or long pronunciation for a preceding vowel.

This two-mechanism framework for reading aloud seems strengthened by the existence of two kinds of words—*regular* words, which follow the rules of spelling-to-sound correspondence; and *exception* words, which break them. Regular words like *Hate* can be pronounced correctly by retrieving their stored pronunciations or by using spelling-to-sound rules, but exception words like *Have* can only be pronounced by retrieving the correct pronunciation from memory. This "two-mechanisms-are-better-than-one" logic is consistent with a reliable finding that regular words take less time to pronounce than exceptions (Baron & Strawson, 1976; Glushko, 1979b; Gough & Cosky, 1977; Stanovich & Bauer, 1978).

Despite its plausibility, however, this two-mechanism model of reading aloud is incorrect. The existing evidence for abstract spelling-to-sound rules is indeterminate. In three experiments, I explicitly seek evidence for abstract phonological rules yet consistently find only specific spelling-to-sound knowledge. I conclude that the two-mechanism structure of models for reading aloud is based more on ideology than on data. The elusive phonological mechanism has evolved out of a taxonomic distinction between regular and exception words that is not manifested in the mechanisms of pronunciation.

In the spirit of this conference, I propose a more interactive framework for reading aloud: As letters in a word are identified, an entire neighborhood of words that share orthographic features is activated in memory, and the pronunciation emerges through the coordination and synthesis of many partially activated phonological representations. Familiar and unfamiliar words, and regular words and exceptions, are pronounced through a unitary process of activation and synthesis rather than by separate lexical and phonological mechanisms. Whereas reading aloud requires lexical and phonological knowledge, phonological knowledge is primarily lexical. Even if the two knowledge bases were disjoint (and there is no clear evidence either way), they would not require different retrieval mechanisms. The varied uses of lexical and phonological knowledge in language processing make it more reasonable to assume a single, content-free retrieval process—"activation," as I define it here—rather than two separate and specialized lexical and spelling-to-sound processors.

This new view of reading aloud imposes a new definition of spelling-to-sound regularity and has implications for reading instruction. In addition, this new model of pronunciation fits into a broader psychological context for language understanding and speech production and is more consistent with nonpsychological procedures for producing speech from text.

IS THERE EVIDENCE FOR SPELLING-TO-SOUND RULES?

What knowledge about the spelling-to-sound structure of the language underlies a reader's ability to pronounce an unfamiliar word? Most readers of "Jabberwocky" agree with Lewis Carroll's pronunciations for *slithy* and *toves*: "The I in SLITHY is long, as is WRITHE; and TOVES is pronounced so as to rhyme with GROVES" (Carroll, 1960, p. 268 originally published 1933). Let's begin by trying to explain this second fact about the consensual pronunciation of *toves*.

Most people assume that the most efficient solution to the problem of dealing with novel letter strings is to have a small set of very general principles or rules for spelling-to-sound correspondence. One rule of this generality in English is that a final *e* after a single vowel and a simple consonant makes the vowel "tense" or "long." Readers knowing this rule could pronounce *toves* as /tovz/ and deal with any unfamiliar word ending in a vowel, consonant, and an *e*.

Unfortunately, it is not possible to capture the spelling-to-sound structure of the English language using only rules as broad as the *e*-marker principle. Some sequences of vowel–consonant–*e* allow more than one pronunciation. For example, the multiple pronunciations for the *ove* pattern might limit the generality of the rule that a reader might induce to a multiletter rule for that specific pattern. This specific rule—namely, that *ove* → /ov/—could then be used to pronounce *toves* correctly. Of course, a reader might be directly reminded of *cove* or *stove* when confronted by *toves* and pronounce it by analogy without going through a mediating rule.

The demonstration here is trivial but important. The pronunciation of a novel letter string like *toves* with a "correct" or "regular" pronunciation like /tovz/ does not reveal the level of generality of the knowledge of spelling-to-sound correspondences that made the pronunciation possible. Yet this ambiguity or indeterminacy is overlooked by psychologists and teachers of reading, who often assume that being able to pronounce unfamiliar words is evidence for abstract spelling-to-sound rules.

I hate to sound like a behaviorist, but I shall try to explain this compulsion most people have to interpret "regular" pronunciation as evidence for abstract spelling-to-sound rules. The "two-mechanism trap" so pervasive in the psychology of reading and reading education is analogous to the "psychological reality trap" of a decade ago. Just as the syntactic transformations of generative grammar have no necessary role in the perception of sentences, orthographic and phonological descriptions have no necessary role in the recognition and pronunciation of printed words. The spelling-to-sound trap took longer to fall into, however, and its explanation requires a digression into the history and theory of orthography.

Spelling-to-Sound Rules in Linguistics

The spelling-to-sound structure of English is invariably described as rules that relate letters or letter units (graphemes) to phonemes (e.g., $b \rightarrow /b/$; $ea \rightarrow /i/$) (Chomsky & Halle, 1968; Dewey, 1971; Haas, 1970; Venezky, 1970; Wijk, 1966). Since different descriptive systems share these common units of analysis, at first glance they seem more or less the same. Nevertheless, just as the alphabetic orthographies of Serbo-Croatian (Katz & Feldman, Chap. 4, this volume) or Spanish more closely preserve the pronunciation of words than that of English, different descriptive characterizations of English differ in the kinds of spelling-to-sound structure they represent.

Any particular linguistic description of relations between spellings and phonological representations ultimately rests on a theory of what an orthography does and how it is supposed to do it (see Glushko, 1979a; Klima, 1972). The oldest and most pervasive view is that the alphabetic orthography of English ought to represent as simply as possible the sounds of words and nothing else. Since the 12th century, when a monk named Orm sought to mandate spelling reform in Old English, many spelling reformers and dictionarians have approached the orthography with a letter-to-phoneme descriptive theory and goal in mind. Some current work maintains this 8-century-old tradition (Dewey, 1971; Wijk, 1966).

Contemporary linguistic theory rejects this simple phonemic view of orthography (Chomsky & Halle, 1968; Schane, 1973; Venezky, 1970). According to the theory of generative phonology (Chomsky & Halle, 1968; Schane, 1973), the letters in the alphabetic orthography of English primarily preserve morphological structure and only represent sound structure when it is not predictable by general phonological rules. This orthographic convention makes the *lack* of a direct correspondence between letters and phonemes optimal; for example, the traditional problem of the "silent" *b* in *bomb* is resolved since the second *b* preserves morphemic identity with *bombard* and *bombardier*.

The "Regular" and "Exception" Distinction.   Any system of rules relating spellings to pronunciations implies a binary classification of the words in the language—"regular" words, which follow the rules or form the basis for them; and "exception" words, which do not. A recurring question in psychology and education is: "How many words are exceptions?" According to some estimates, as many as 20% of all word types in English "break the rules" (Hanna & Hanna, 1959), including as many as 50% of the 1000 most frequently occurring ones (Hunnicutt, 1976). On the other hand, Venezky (1970) argues that exceptions to the rules of English spelling are rare, "mere oddities, begging for historical justification [p. 101].'' The reason for this disagreement is that the regular and exception categories are neither easily nor consistently defined (Venezky, 1976):

Regular spelling-to-sound relationships are assumed to be desirable features of an orthography and words with *regular spellings* are assumed to be healthy fodder for the child learning to read, yet what *regularity* means in these contexts has never been properly defined. The problem with the term *regular* is that it implies a frequent recurrence of some entity, yet does not indicate either what entity is to be observed or what measure is to be used [pp. 22–23].

The solution to this problem is that "the entity to be observed" in descriptions of spelling-to-sound structure depends on the underlying theory of what the orthography does. The Ormian notion of orthography as a simple cipher of sounds does not allow morphological information to be part of orthographic rules, so it leaves a larger class of exceptions than theories like Venezky's do. For example, spelling reformers such as Dewey (1971) bemoan the fact that *ph* in English fails to correspond invariantly to a single phoneme. In Venezky's morphophonemic analysis, however, the pronunciation of *ph* is perfectly predictable: Within a single mor*ph*eme, *ph* corresponds to a single phoneme /f/, and across morpheme boundaries as in to*ph*at, *ph* represents the two phonemes /p/ and /h/. If etymological and historical features supplement morphophonemics in orthographic descriptions, there are so few true exceptions that "in themselves they are of no interest" (Chomsky & Halle, 1968, p. ix).

In summary, there is no single set of spelling-to-sound rules and no single partition of words into "regular" and "exception" classes. The considerations that underlie a system of linguistic rules are complex and somewhat arbitrary. It makes little sense to ask how many words are exceptions except in the context of a particular spelling-to-sound description and its associated theory of orthography. Unfortunately, few teachers of reading and few psychologists seem to recognize the complexity of the problem.

Spelling-to-Sound Rules in Reading Instruction

Since the 16th century, proposals for spelling reform have generally been cloaked in pedagogical terms, so teachers of reading came to assume that these letter-to-phoneme representations of spelling-to-sound structure were appropriate rules to teach beginners (cf. Davies, 1974; Huey, 1908/1968). The most influential reform proposal is the Initial Teaching Alphabet devised by Pitman (Downing, 1967), which introduces extra letters into the conventional alphabet to produce an invariant letter-to-phoneme orthography. In principle, however, any theory of orthography could generate instructional rules for a reading curriculum (see C. Chomsky, 1970, for a curriculum based on generative phonology). The success of any theory and its associated curriculum cannot be determined on formal linguistic grounds, but only by how closely the rules and assumptions underlying them are consistent with the linguistic insights and cognitive abilities of beginning readers (Lesgold & Curtis, Chap. 13, this volume; Rozin & Gleitman, 1977; Savin, 1972).

When the simple phonemic view of orthography was transplanted from linguistics to education, it was escorted by its accompanying classification of words as "regular" and "exceptions." The large number of exceptions in a phonemic description of spelling in English profoundly affected the teaching of reading since the rules, by definition, were incapable of dealing with the exception words. This large residual class of exception words seemed to demand a different method of instruction. As a purely taxonomic classification became a pedagogically significant one, the seeds of the "Great Debate" in reading instruction (Chall, 1967) were sown by historical accident.

Although a linguistic description of spelling-to-sound structure may be a necessary feature of a reading curriculum, by no means can it be a sufficient one. The goal of reading is to understand print, and generating phonological representations from letters is a subgoal only to the extent that it facilitates comprehension. The instructional value of a set of spelling-to-sound rules can only be determined in the context of this search for meaning from print.

Spelling-to-sound Rules in Psychological Models

Perhaps because the spelling-to-sound structure of English is most often described as rules relating letters to phonemes, psychologists generally propose that adult readers use rules of this type in pronouncing unfamiliar words. But even though this is an assumption, it is treated as axiomatic. According to Frederiksen and Kroll (1976): "Since pseudowords have no representation in lexical memory, they can be pronounced only through an application of previously-acquired rules for grapheme–phoneme translation, as these exist for English spelling patterns [p. 362]." Similar claims are made by Coltheart (1978), Forster and Chambers (1973), Gough and Cosky (1977), Mason (1978), and Stanovich and Bauer (1978).

Psychologists fail to realize that any set of spelling-to-sound rules and its associated classes of regular and exception words are only relevant to their reading research if they accept its underlying theory of orthography. This fundamental criterion is rarely met. Psychologists usually assume a restricted view of orthography as little more than a phonemic representation of speech, which implies a simplistic view of spelling-to-sound rules as direct mappings from letters to phonemes. At the same time, the linguistic rule systems that psychologists invoke as examples of such rules (usually Venezky, 1970) use historical, etymological, and morphological information to "regularize" deviations from a simple letter-to-phoneme correspondence. Although such regularity is important in a complete linguistic description of English, it is not given by the orthography itself. It can hardly be of much use to a reader who encounters a word for the first time.

Once psychologists make the error of assuming without test that grapheme–phoneme rules are psychologically real, they are compelled to commit a second error: They inevitably assume that the distinction between regular and exception words implied in such linguistic descriptions must be represented in the psychological mechanisms for reading and pronunciation. The argument typically goes like this: Since words that break the rules cannot be pronounced using those rules, there must be another nonphonological mechanism by which all exceptions are pronounced. Mason (1978) wrote:

> The exception words necessitate a visual access of the lexicon for naming, because they cannot be phonologically recoded and pronounced by application of spelling-to-sound correspondence rules elaborated by Venezky (1970) [p. 568].

And Barron (1980) stated:

> Regular words (e.g., GLOBE, CHURCH, SWEET) conform to spelling rules and can be read and spelled by using either a phonological or a visual-orthographic strategy. Irregular words (e.g., SAID, BROAD, SWORD), on the other hand, are exceptions to spelling rules and cannot be read or spelled successfully by using a phonological strategy [p. 196].

These claims make sense only if knowledge of spelling-to-sound structure is represented as grapheme–phoneme rules of a particular type. But this premise is true only by assumption!

The psychological house of cards is now almost complete. An assumption that grapheme–phoneme rules are psychologically real leads to the assumption of a psychological distinction between regular and exception words. This second assumption is then marshaled as evidence for the psychological reality of grapheme–phoneme rules. Coltheart (1978) put it this way:

> Current work [a latency difference in naming] suggests that the classification of words as regular or exceptions actually has "psychological reality"; subjects behave differently with the two types of word. This is strong evidence in favor of the view that non-lexical phonological encoding uses a grapheme–phoneme correspondence procedure, since other methods for such encoding do not distinguish between regular words and exceptions, and hence cannot explain why this distinction is reflected in behavior [p. 159].

Coltheart is simply wrong here. If readers use spelling-to-sound knowledge in the form of probabilistic grapheme–phoneme rules or as specific rules for particular multiletter patterns, or if they pronounce words by analogy, then exception words might take longer to pronounce than regular words without any explicit representation of the regular/exception distinction.

Readers undoubtedly know a great deal about the spelling-to-sound structure of the language, and linguistic descriptions of this structure can suggest hypotheses about this knowledge. But there is no necessary relationship between linguistic descriptions of the spelling-to-sound regularity in the language and a reader's knowledge and use of such structure.

Neuropsychological Evidence from the "Acquired Dyslexias"

Another traditional source of support for the two-mechanism model of reading is the neuropsychological syndrome of acquired dyslexia (Marshall & Newcombe, 1973; Patterson & Marcel, 1977; Shallice & Warrington, 1975). Yet the evidence from this source for abstract lexicon-independent spelling-to-sound rules is as ambiguous as the "evidence" derived from logical analysis of the orthographic and phonological structure of the language.

At first glance, the two basic categories of patients who acquire reading disabilities after brain injuries seem to demonstrate the independent existence of visual and phonological mechanisms of reading. "Deep" or "phonemic" dyslexics pronounce and recognize familiar words but are unable to assign any reasonable pronunciation to novel letter strings. These patients apparently have an intact visual access mechanism with a loss of the phonological rules. "Surface" dyslexics, however, pronounce words and nonwords equally poorly. Visual recognition of words is no longer possible, but phonological recognition sometimes succeeds (or comes close) when the phonological translation of a printed letter string "sounds like a word." This syndrome is interpreted as a loss of direct visual access with partial damage to the phonological mechanism.

Nevertheless, the arguments against the "psychological reality" evidence for spelling-to-sound rules apply equally well to this clinical evidence. Deep dyslexic patients may have lost access to knowledge of spelling-to-sound structure, but there is no basis for concluding that this knowledge must have been represented as abstract spelling-to-sound rules.

In general, the clinical evidence is too weak to constrain neuropsychological models to the level of detail expected in cognitive models. The dyslexic syndromes are open to many alternative explanations involving: (1) damage to the memory representations of lexical or spelling-to-sound knowledge; (2) damage to the process(es) that make(s) use of these two types of knowledge; or (3) damage to both memory representations and processes.

A more provocative response to the clinical arguments for two mechanisms in reading is the recent claim by Marcel (1980) that the standard descriptions of the dyslexic categories are misleading. Marcel carefully reanalyzed the dyslexic patients' responses and criticized the usual "cursory and restricted" analyses of these primary data. Marcel's analysis suggests that there is considerable lexical influence in the responses of surface dyslexics, and that their responses are too idiosyncratic to be explained as the malfunctioning or restricted functioning of grapheme–phoneme rules. Marcel rejects the standard two-mechanism model of reading and proposes that the two dyslexic syndromes arise as impairments at different points in a unitary reading process. This new model of the dyslexias is roughly equivalent to the activation and synthesis model that I propose for normal adult readers. Marcel and I share the idea that phonological translation is not accomplished by grapheme–phoneme rules, but by lexical activation of more specific phonological knowledge.

EVIDENCE FOR SPECIFIC SPELLING-TO-SOUND KNOWLEDGE

Let's return to the *toves* examples from "Jabberwocky." The most common pronunciation of *toves* as /tovz/ is ambiguous. It does not identify the generality of a reader's knowledge of spelling-to-sound structure. However, some people pronounce *toves* as /tʌvz/ to rhyme with *loves*. This other pronunciation for *toves*, which we have so far ignored, is much more informative; some specific knowledge, such as the pronunciation of *loves*, is obviously involved. If abstract spelling-to-sound rules alone are used to pronounce unfamiliar words, how could readers come up with pronunciations that break the rules?

Experiment 1

In an initial experiment (Glushko, 1979b, Experiment 1), I conducted a more rigorous test of this "Jabberwocky" intuition that the pronunciation of novel words could be affected by words that resemble them. I constructed the stimuli for the experiment in sets of four. For each "exception" word like *pint*, I chose a "regular" word like *pink* that differed from it only in its terminal consonant. Then, using these regular and exception words, I made up "regular pseudowords" like *bink* and "exception pseudowords" like *bint* that differed by only their initial consonants from *pink* and *pint*. The two-mechanism view says that all novel words are pronounced by rules, so it predicts no differences in pronunciation or latency between the two types of pseudowords that differ only in the regularity of the words that they resemble. These two letter strings are so closely matched that the only thing that distinguishes them is whether or not they have an exception word that resembles them.

I used "exception" in the preceding paragraph because of historical precedent, but I do not accept its traditional definition. Instead, I used a definition of "exception" that does not assume any spelling-to-sound rules. I began by compiling a set of words that end with the same vowel and terminal consonant—here, *-int*—and I observed that most of them have the same pronunciation for this spelling pattern. *Pint* alone embodies a different spelling-to-sound correspondence, which makes it an exception. This is an intuitive definition, but it seems justified given the salience of rhyme for adults and the primacy with which this phonological judgment develops in children. Defining exceptions in terms of the consistency of their pronunciations with other words sidesteps the need to invoke a theory of rules or even to assume that there are rules at all.

I used 43 different exception words, which—given the constraints I imposed—comes close to exhausting the set in English. The 43 quadruples of matched letter strings like *pint–pink–bint–bink* here were presented in random order to each of 12 subjects, all college students and native speakers of English. The subjects were instructed to pronounce each letter string as quickly and accurately as possible. Note that for pseudowords, a correct pronunciation is the regular one.

Results.   The results clearly demonstrated the effects of specific knowledge in pronouncing both words and pseudowords. The mean correct pronunciation latencies for the four kinds of letter strings were collapsed over the 43 items of each type for each subject, and also collapsed over the 12 subjects for each item in each of the four item types. The effects were the same in both analyses. Correct pronunciations for exception pseudowords like *bint* (which resembles the exception *pint*) took 646 msec, 29 msec longer than those for regular pseudowords like *bink* that have no exception neighbors. This penalty imposed on exception pseudowords was about the same size as the familiar regularity effect that slows the pronunciation of exception words. Exception words took 618 msec, 20 msec longer than the matched regular words.

The regularity effect for words and the regularity effect for pseudowords are really one and the same, resulting from the interference in constructing a pronunciation when the activated knowledge of spelling-to-sound structure is inconsistent. The best evidence for the conflict between different kinds of spelling-to-sound structures came from the errors made in pronouncing the exception letter strings. On almost 18% of the trials with exception pseudowords, readers pronounced the pseudoword with an irregular pronunciation given to the vowel. Thus a pseudoword like *tave* was not pronounced regularly like /tev/ but irregularly as /taev/ with the exceptional vowel found in the exception *have*. Another example of "exceptionalization" of pseudowords is *heaf* pronounced as /hɛf/. A precisely analogous form of "exceptionalization" took place on a small proportion of the trials with exception words. These were errors in which the word was given an incorrect pronunciation from another exception word with similar spelling. For example, the exception word *tomb* was made to rhyme with the exception *comb*. Similar mispronunciations occurred with *move* pronounced to rhyme with *love* and *done* pronounced to rhyme with *gone*.

AN ACTIVATION AND SYNTHESIS VIEW OF READING ALOUD

These results from this first experiment pose severe problems for the consensual model of reading aloud in which words and pseudowords are pronounced by separate bodies of knowledge used by separate mechanisms. The only way that the standard model could account for a regularity effect for pseudowords is through conflict between existing exception words and abstract spelling-to-sound rules. The cost of this loophole, however, is too high, since allowing the stored pronunciations of existing words to contribute to the pronunciation of pseudowords eliminates the need for abstract spelling-to-sound rules. It appears that words and pseudowords are pronounced in essentially the same way. Novel words are not pronounced solely through the operation of an independent set of abstract spelling-to-sound rules. Instead, I suggest that readers use orthographic and phonological information simultaneously from many sources to construct a pronunciation for the letter string, much as readers use lexical, syntactic, and contextual knowledge to understand a sentence or larger units of text (Rumelhart, 1977). Grapheme–phoneme rules might play a part, but more specific knowledge, such as the stored pronunciations of existing words, appears to be more important.

A word as stored in memory consists in part of an orthographic entry associated with a phonological representation. Words in the lexicon are interconnected according to orthographic and phonological similarity. This multiple organization enables a phonological access of memory in recognizing speech and a visual or orthographic access in most reading tasks. As a letter string is identified, its constituent letters activate the stored orthographic and phonological representations of words that contain them.

To make a lexical decision, a reader must wait until the activation in a set of orthographic entries is integrated over time to reach a response threshold (to enable a "word" response) or until a deadline passes without any item reaching threshold (for a "nonword" response). To pronounce a letter string, a reader must wait for the coordination and synthesis of an articulatory program from the activated phonological information. In both tasks, the eventual response is determined through a constructive process that identifies the presented pattern by emphasizing the commonalities and attenuating the differences among the activated orthographic and phonological components. This characterization of the interactive processes in reading is intentionally vague and evasive, because my data offer few constraints at this end of the spelling-to-sound process. I accept the models of Hayes-Roth (1978; Hayes-Roth & McDermott, 1978) or Rumelhart (1977; Rumelhart & McClelland, Chap. 2, this volume) as reasonable "top-ends" for the time being.

"Activation" Versus "Analogy"

The first experiment provided clear evidence for a strong component of specific or "analogical" information in the process by which people read unfamiliar as well as familiar words. Nevertheless, I try to refrain from using the concept of analogy in my description of the workings of the mechanism. First, analogy implies a conscious aspect to the process of activation that is not reflected in what readers think they are doing and that could not occur in the half second or so required to pronounce words. This sense of analogy was recently invoked by Baron (1977, 1979) in studies of reading aloud, primarily using children as subjects.

A second reason for my use of activation instead of analogy is more basic. In my new view of reading aloud, activation is a *fundamental* process, not merely a *supplement* to abstract spelling-to-sound rules as in Baron's model. Once existing words are allowed to participate in the pronunciation of unfamiliar letter strings, there is no need for separate lexical and phonological mechanisms. Since there is no firm evidence that orthographic units of letter or letter-cluster size are themselves directly associated with phonological correspondences—that is, there is no certainty that explicit spelling-to-sound rules exist independent of the words that embody them—it is redundant to propose a separate rule mechanism. Analogical processing in Baron's sense, or neighborhood activation in my usage, is a generalized lexical retrieval mechanism, and the direct lexical retrieval of a particular stored pronunciation reduces to the activation of the "closest" analogy to a target letter string.

Analogy is an old notion in linguistics and psychology (see Esper, 1973, for a thorough historical treatment) and is repeatedly invoked in descriptions of linguistic productivity, language change, and concept formation. As an explanatory principle, however, analogy has rarely made a serious impact for the simple reason that it can be circular. The notion of analogy rests on the more basic idea of similarity—words that are similar to the novel word can presumably serve as analogies to it. But without a metric for similarity and without a specification of how similar is similar enough, the concept of analogy by similarity offers little insight.

This weakness is easy to see in Carroll's analogical explanation for the pronunciation of the nonsense words in "Jabberwocky." Why is *writhe* the most appropriate analogy for *slithy*? Why not *slither* or *lithium*? Why is *groves* the analogy for *toves,* instead of *loves* or *moves*? It has been too easy to invoke analogy by hindsight and too difficult to predict it, but only prediction suffices if analogy (or activation) is to be taken seriously.

A NEW DEFINITION OF SPELLING-TO-SOUND REGULARITY

Starting with a word like *have,* we ask, "What words are orthographically and phonologically similar enough to it to be activated during its pronunciation?" There are many possible partitions of the neighborhood around *have,* ranging from small sets of words that are very similar to *have* (such as those ending in *-ave* or beginning with *ha-*) to broad classes that have only abstract resemblances (such as all words with a final "silent" $=e$). It is obvious that a model has to specify which words are involved to make sense of a notion of analogical activation and interference. (Barron, Chap. 12, this volume, attempts to go much further and relates quantitative measures of neighborhood size to reading performance.)

Nevertheless, I already have made such a specification—at least implicitly in claiming that letter strings that differed only in their initial consonants were close enough to be in the same analogical domain. In the first experiment, I assumed that *pint* was a neighbor to *bint* but not to *pink*—at least not a near enough neighbor to get in *pink*'s way. Since exception pseudowords like *bint* were slowed in pronunciation, apparently by the presence of *pint,* this assumption to make up stimuli seemed validated.

If one accepts the idea that orthographic neighbors influence pronunciations, then one must reject the traditional distinction between regular and exception words. The classification of words as regular or exception depends on a theory of orthography and reading. Therefore, if a word like *have* is an exception because it embodies a different spelling-to-sound structure than regular words that resemble it, then these regular words like *wave* and *gave* are somewhat exceptional for the symmetric reason that they have a different pronunciation than *have*. In an activation framework, words are not regular or exceptional in themselves but only in the context of the other words that are activated while they are read.

In this revised classification, words like *have* are exceptions as before, but there is a profound change in the categorization of what standard theory calls regular words. Words like *hate* are still regular, since all words ending in -*ate* have the same vowel pronunciation, but words like *wave* and *gave* are regular and *inconsistent* since they are in the same orthographic neighborhood as the exception *have*. They are presumably close enough to the exception so that when they are pronounced, *have* might be activated and "get in the way."

Experiment 2

There is a straightforward experimental prediction that follows from this new theoretical partition of the lexicon. "Regular and inconsistent" words like *wave,* which might activate competing bodies of spelling-to-sound knowledge, should take longer to pronounce than closely matched "regular and consistent" words like *wade* that have no nearby exception neighbors. This would be a regularity effect that distinguishes between two supposedly regular words!

In this experiment (Glushko, 1979b, Experiment 3) I matched each of 41 exception words like *have* with a necessarily regular and inconsistent word like *wave* that differs from *have* only in the initial consonant. Regular and consistent controls for each of these words were constructed by changing the terminal consonant. In this example, *have* was paired with *haze,* and *wave* was paired with *wade*. The 164 words from these 4 sets were presented in random order to 16 adult readers.

Results. The results were clear and just as the new view of reading aloud had predicted. There was a reliable difference in pronunciation latency between the regular and consistent words like *wade* (529 msec) and their regular but inconsistent counterparts like *wave* (546 msec). The "standard" regularity effect was also obtained in this experiment. Exception words like *have* (550 msec) took longer to pronounce than matched regular and consistent words like *haze* (529 msec). All four of these differences were reliable over items as well as subjects.

These results confirm that a word need not be regular even if it has a unique pronunciation that follows the rules. *Wave* and *wade* are both regular according to the traditional definition and differ only in the collective spelling-to-sound consistency of the words they resemble. Regularity is a local concept, not a global one defined over the lexicon as a whole. The taxonomic distinction between regular and exception words is simply not relevant to psychological models of reading aloud.

A SEARCH FOR ABSTRACT SPELLING-TO-SOUND RULES

I began this chapter with an argument that there was no unambiguous evidence that abstract spelling-to-sound rules were used in reading aloud. I then reported two experiments in which specific spelling-to-sound knowledge played a large role. I built a new framework for reading aloud based on the activation of existing pronunciations, and assigned no role to the traditional cornerstone formed by abstract spelling-to-sound rules.

But perhaps there really are two fundamentally different kinds of spelling-to-sound knowledge—abstract rules as well as specific pronunciations—and abstract rules are simply hard to find. Since such rules are just the explicit representation of the regular structure embodied by words in the language, rules "in the pure form" are necessarily masked by the activation of regular words whose pronunciations they describe. It may be impossible to obtain unequivocal evidence for abstract rules in experiments like the ones I have so far reported that rely on the implicit activation of spelling-to-sound knowledge.

Experiment 3

Recently I set out to evaluate these elusive effects of abstract spelling-to-sound rules operating alone. The idea evolved from the design of my earlier experiments. I had always included filler words and pseudowords to break up any accidental repetitions of similar patterns that could introduce an artifactual bias in pronunciations. For example, I never allowed *pint* to come right before or right after *bint*. I was relying on the implicit activation of stored pronunciations to affect the pronunciation of a given letter string.

Finally it dawned on me. Rather than work to avoid the accidental repetition of potentially relevant knowledge, I could make systematic use of repetition with the priming technique used by Meyer, Schvaneveldt, and Ruddy (1974) and others. When letter strings are presented in pairs, the stimulus structure is no longer defined by the properties of each word in isolation, but by the relationship between the two items in the pair. In this way I could explicitly measure the relative effects of neighbors of various types on the pronunciation of a particular target letter string. In addition, by making the prime-target relationship abstract, I could assess the effects of abstract spelling-to-sound principles independent of the specific words that usually embody them.

I systematically varied the orthographic and phonological similarity of the items in six kinds of pairs. The prime or target could be a word or a pseudoword. The target items in each set of six pairs shared consonant–vowel structure and their initial phoneme, so any differences in their pronunciation latencies had to result from differences in facilitation that they received from the prime. Same pairs (e.g., *dice–dice*) and Control pairs (e.g., *trap–dine*) obviously represent end points. There were three kinds of pairs in which primes and targets shared specific (and hence abstract, as well) spelling-to-sound information: In Init pairs (e.g., *fire–dire*), the two words differed only by the initial consonant; in Vow pairs, the prime and target shared all letters except the medial vowel (e.g., *dome–dime*); in Term pairs (e.g., *(daze–date)*), the words differed only in the terminal consonant. Finally, in Rule pairs (e.g., *mole–duke*) the prime and target had no pronounced letters in common but followed the same general principle of spelling-to-sound correspondence. In this example, both *mole* and *duke* follow the final silent *-e* rule in which *-e* marks the long pronunciation for the preceding vowel.

In half the experimental blocks, each of the 12 subjects pronounced the prime, and in the other half, the subjects signaled a lexical decision about the prime by pressing one of two response keys. Each subject completed 176 trials in each priming task. To make these two priming tasks as different as possible, a large proportion of the nonword primes were pseudohomophones like *hoam* and *boal*. Since these nonwords sound like words, if subjects tried to locate lexical entries on a phonological basis, they would incorrectly label the pseudohomophones as words. This manipulation is analogous to the articulatory suppression techniques used by Baddeley and Lewis (Chap. 5, this volume) that attempt to dissociate phonological and nonphonological processing.

I wanted to compare the priming effects of these two tasks, because my new activation and synthesis framework for reading aloud makes a clear prediction that contrasts with that of the standard two-mechanism model. In my model, phonological activation is an inevitable or automatic consequence after lexical access occurs on an orthographic or visual basis. Even though the lexical decision task with pseudohomophones neither requires nor benefits from such phonological activation, the automatic phonological activation should lead to

TABLE 3.1
Results of Priming Experiment—Correct Target Pronunciation
Latencies (Msec)

Priming Task	Same	Init	Spelling-to-Sound Relation Betwen Prime and Target			Control	Mean
			Vow	Term	Rule		
Pronunciation	566	606	613	631	643	652	623
Lexical Decision	625	643	644	655	676	671	655
	596	625	629	643	661	662	

priming of the target pronunciation. According to standard theory, however, when the pseudohomophones slam the phonological door to lexical memory, the completely separate lexical route will be used, so there should be little or no facilitation on a subsequent pronunciation.

Results.   Table 3.1 shows the mean correct pronunciation latencies for target items for the six kinds of pairs in the two priming conditions. In both priming tasks, pronunciation and lexical decision, the spelling-to-sound relationship between the prime and the target makes a difference, and the effects on the target latency are roughly the same. When specific letters from the prime are repeated in the target (in Init, Vow, and Term pairs), the target is pronounced faster than when no information is repeated. This 30-millisecond facilitation by specific spelling-to-sound information may not seem large, but it is a substantial portion of the priming effect in Same pairs, which represents the largest obtainable effect given the particular stimuli and experimental conditions used. Targets differing only by the initial consonants (in Init pairs) are the largest beneficiaries of priming effects, confirming the rhymes-are-closest assumption that underlies the stimulus structure of the one-word-at-a-time pronunciation experiments that I reported earlier. Finally, repeating an abstract spelling-to-sound principle in Rule pairs yielded an insignificant 1-millisecond advantage over targets in Control pairs, which had neither specific nor abstract structures in common with their primes.

FOUR SUMMARY CLAIMS

Now that I have tried my best to find evidence for abstract spelling-to-sound rules and have come up empty once more, I can be more confident that they do not play some large but hidden role in the process of reading words aloud. I am not sure that such rules do not exist somewhere in the mind of the reader, but I suggest that it is more productive to consider a new view of reading aloud that is not distracted by their lifeless presence. To this end, I make four summary claims that review the evidence I have presented in this chapter and outline the theory in a more organized form.

1. Phonological Activation Is Automatic.   Phonological representations of a word and of those words in its orthographic neighborhood are automatically activated during its visual recognition. The word need not be explicitly pronounced for this activation to occur. Similar activation arises in making a lexical decision with pseudohomophone distractors, a task that neither requires nor benefits from phonological translation of the letter string. Further testimony to the inevitability of this phonological translation is that it occurs while reading Chinese, even though phonological access of memory is precluded by the Chinese symbol-to-morpheme orthography (Tzeng, Hung, & Wang, 1977).

2. Phonological Activation Is of a Single Type.   All letter strings are recognized and pronounced by the same knowledge activated in the same way, rather than by separate bodies of knowledge using different procedures. The characteristic latency differences between words and pseudowords, and between regular and exception words, naturally follow from an activation framework without the need to propose ad hoc mechanisms that explicitly incorporate these two distinctions. Regular and exception words are not fundamentally different; they just have different pronunciations. Both kinds of words are pronounced by the same mechanism.

Once activated, phonological knowledge remains available for some time to facilitate or impede a subsequent pronunciation; these priming effects are no different in kind from the activation effects associated with the recognition or pronunciation of a letter string without prior context.

If words were pronounced by a separate phonological mechanism independent of existing words, the mechanisms of reading aloud would be irrelevant to normal reading. Instead, there is no reason to suppose that the orthographic and phonological activation involved in the present experiments is any different in kind from the spreading activation invoked to explain how semantic and syntactic constraints in sentences facilitate the recognition of expected words and inhibit unexpected ones (e.g., Fischler & Bloom, 1979; Miller & Isard, 1963). This phonological activation may be the storage medium in the phonological working memory proposed as an essential resource in sentence comprehension (Kleiman, 1975; Levy, 1978).

3. Latency and Accuracy Penalties Result from Interference When the Activated Phonological Knowledge Is Inconsistent.   There are three distinct regularity effects that are unified by an activation explanation: (1) "Exception" words are more difficult to pronounce than "regular" words; (2) pseudowords that resemble exception words ("exception pseudowords") are more difficult to pronounce than "regular pseudowords"; (3) "regular and inconsistent" words, which resemble exception words, are more difficult to pronounce than "regular and consistent" words, which have no exception neighbors.

Regularity effects have a similar origin in inconsistent activation for both the lexical decision and pronunciation tasks. The size of the interference effects depends on the overlap between the entries activated in the visual network and those activated in the phonological network. For "regular and consistent" words, orthographic similarity and phonological similarity are equivalent. Lexical entries activated on an orthographic basis are appropriate candidates for phonological synthesis, and vice versa. This convergence focuses activation on a small set of contenders, so lexical decisions or pronunciations can be produced quickly because it is easy for the response to reach threshold or for phonological synthesis to stabilize. For exception words and letter strings that resemble them, however, phonological and orthographic similarity need not parallel one another. The inconsistency dissipates activation over a larger set of lexical entries, and the eventual outcome takes longer to emerge. As in a horse race, the more conflict, the more pushing and shoving in the stretch, the slower the eventual winning time.

Bauer and Stanovich (1980) recently reported two experiments that confirm this claim that regularity effects are postlexical. They obtained a regularity effect in the time required to make a lexical decision for "regular" and "exception" words (according to the classical definitions), and the size of the effect was not altered by degrading stimulus quality or by using mixed-cased (alternating lower- and uppercases) letter strings. They concluded that although lexical access may be slowed by disrupting the visual quality of a word, once lexical access occurs, phonological activation proceeds in the same way. In other words, once a word is activated, how it came to be activated is irrelevant.

Bauer and Stanovich reasoned as follows. Suppose there are two separate pathways to the lexicon—one visual and one phonological, the standard two-mechanism model. According to this traditional view, regularity effects arise when a stored pronunciation retrieved by visual access conflicts with a constructed pronunciation computed by lexicon-independent spelling-to-sound rules. If the visual route to the lexicon were disrupted, then the regularity effect should increase, since there would be greater reliance on the phonological route, and more time would pass before the conflict occurs. Alternatively, in the activation and synthesis model, regularity effects emerge from conflict among phonological representations that are activated only after visual lexical access. Under these conditions, disrupting the visual access route to the lexicon should not affect the size of the regularity effect.

4. *The Activated Phonological Knowledge Is Specific Rather than Abstract.*   A regularity effect for pseudowords and a regularity effect that differentiates two classes of regular words are clearly incompatible with the idea

that spelling-to-sound structure is represented and used as grapheme–phoneme rules. Abstract principles of spelling-to-sound structure do not provide any facilitation of a subsequent pronunciation.

ACTIVATION AND SYNTHESIS AS GENERAL PROCESSING CONCEPTS

In an activation and synthesis framework, complete pronunciations are not retrieved one at a time from the lexicon. Instead, as letters in the target item are identified, an entire neighborhood of words that share orthographic features are activated in memory, and the eventual response emerges through coordination and synthesis of many partially activated phonological representations. The sequence of partial specification, activation of a set of candidates, and response selection based on characteristics of the competing memory items may be a general procedure for memory retrieval (Norman & Bobrow, 1979) and is shared by several other models for language production and comprehension.

For example, MacKay (1972, 1973) suggests that the class of speech errors known as "blends" (e.g., *draft* + *breeze* → *dreeze*) are produced when a concept activates two synonyms that are fused during an articulatory synthesis stage. Most blends (like the preceding example) involve the initial consonants of one word combining with the vowel and terminal consonants of a synonymous word. The high frequency of this particular speech error is consistent with the salience of, and greater facilitation by, neighbors that share all but the initial consonants with target words in the present experiments.

Similarly, Kuczaj (1977) notes that a common error for children learning to use the past tense is to attach the past-tense marker to irregular forms that do not require it. When children say *swammed, camed,* or *wented,* it might reflect the activation and combination of competing past forms, and it suggests that verbs are not explicitly marked as "regular" or "irregular" in the lexicon.

Implications for Reading Instruction

To the extent that a model of reading aloud by adult readers is a description of the target skill for beginning readers, the activation and synthesis view of reading aloud has important implications for the teaching of reading. Abstract rules of spelling-to-sound correspondence are not as salient as specific examples when skilled readers encounter familiar letter strings. A pedagogy of reading predicated on a need to establish two separate kinds of reading mechanisms may be misguided. In adult readers, the functions supposedly performed using the "whole-word" method (the lexical mechanism) and the "phonics" or "analytic" method (the phonological mechanism) can be subsumed under a unitary process of lexical activation. "Exception" words, which "break the rules" of spelling-to-sound correspondence, are pronounced by the same mechanism as "regular" words, which "follow the rules."

However, I do not advocate that teachers abandon phonics. The college readers I studied in these three experiments are highly skilled, and their specialized and automated reading processes bear little resemblance to the rudimentary information-processing skills of the beginner. I have shown that grapheme–phoneme rules do not play a large role when adult readers pronounce unfamiliar words, but it seems undeniable that phonic or analytic instruction works for beginning readers. Spelling-to-sound rules may be useful for beginning readers as organizing principles or mnemonic devices until lexical activation becomes an automatic consequence of letter recognition. Lesgold and Curtis (Chap. 13, this volume) are conducting an extensive longitudinal study of beginning readers to study this process through which phonological processing becomes automatic, so I leave further speculation to them.

Nevertheless, the obvious justification for a phonics curriculum—that the alphabetic orthography of English makes it efficient to use grapheme–phoneme rules—ignores the effects of hundreds or thousands of exposures to the same words for skilled readers. A dozen years of practice makes it easy for readers to learn and quickly retrieve thousands of individual pronunciations. Teachers must see grapheme–phoneme rules as tools to help readers acquire knowledge of the orthographic and phonological structure of the language, not as ends in themselves. Perhaps teachers might temper their emphasis on phonics purely out of sympathy with their beginners, who can have great difficulty understanding the abstractness of the phonemes represented in an alphabetic orthography (Rozin & Gleitman, 1977; Savin, 1972).

Consensus with Nonpsychological Approaches to Reading Aloud

It is useful and rewarding to note that the activation and synthesis view of reading aloud converges with research by engineers and computer scientists on reading machines for the blind (Allen, 1973) and on computer voice-response systems as an alternative to visual output (e.g., Allen, 1976; Flanagan, 1976; McIlroy, 1973). These nonpsychological systems for producing phonological representations from print share three important features with my model.

First, the primary mechanism of pronunciation in all these approaches is the retrieval of a stored pronunciation from memory. The traditional Holy Grail of reading aloud, a separate set of grapheme–phoneme rules, is always the mechanism of last resort. For example, in Allen's (1976) model of text-to-speech synthesis, the only essential rules are those that decompose complex words into their constituent roots and affixes, and the most important component is a morpheme dictionary of 12,000 pronunciations.

Second, none of the models needs to represent the distinction between regular and exception words. Since exception words are generally of high frequency in the language (they must be if they are to resist the tendency to conform to the general principles of spelling-to-sound structure in the language), they occur often enough in normal texts to warrant their inclusion in the pronouncing dictionary. There is no need to mark exceptions explicitly or to block the application of spelling-to-sound rules for them, as proposed in current linguistic theory (Anderson, 1974; Chomsky & Halle, 1968; Halle, 1973), since the rules are relevant only if lexical retrieval fails.

Finally, if grapheme–phoneme rules are used at all, there must be a large number of them to augment the dictionary's effectiveness significantly. The tantalizing economy of grapheme–phoneme rules in an alphabetic orthography, which has tempted psychologists and educators for a long time, is shattered by the harsh criterion of making the system capable of pronouncing unrestricted text—rules alone simply won't work. In Allen's system there are over 400 complex, context-sensitive rules that must be ordered, and Allen emphasizes that these rules are adequate only in the context of the complete speech synthesis system because so much work is done by the dictionary and morpheme analyzer.

THE PSYCHOLOGY OF PHONOGRAPHY

A decade of psychological research on reading and word recognition converged on the idea that pronunciation required a separate set of abstract spelling-to-sound rules that had little to do with the mechanisms of normal reading. Unfortunately, the rules were off in a black box, and no one was quite sure about the size or abstractness of the spelling units on which the rules operated. This uncertainty was reflected in the names that psychologists gave to the spelling-to-sound device in their models of word recognition. Some researchers called it "phonological" (Coltheart, 1978; Stanovich & Bauer, 1978), while others characterized it as "phonemic" (Meyer, Schvaneveldt, & Ruddy, 1974; Rubenstein, Lewis, & Rubenstein, 1971) or "phonetic" (Shulman, Hornak, & Sanders, 1978), and still others called it "orthographic" (Baron & Stawson, 1976). The variety of names the same mechanism was going by should have told us something; what it told me was that we really couldn't tell what was going on as long as we focused on the "correct" or "regular" pronunciations of novel letter strings. An ideological fixation with the regular/exception distinction and, hence, with two-mechanism models obscured the similarity of reading research to that of other psychologists interested in language production, and also isolated psychology from research in other fields directed at the closely related problem of producing intelligible speech from text.

I hereby propose "phonography" as a neutral designation of the task of generating a pronunciation from a spelling, whether performed by reader or by reading machine. It may be difficult to rescue the adjective *phonographic* from its popular though less appropriate usage, but I think it will be worth the effort (Haas, 1970, has tried; and Barron, Chap. 12, this volume, is taking up the cause with me). I have tried to show that phonological translation is an automatic consequence of lexical access and that the means by which letter strings are pronounced are integrally related with normal reading and word recognition. There may be abstract spelling-to-sound rules, but no one has found them yet, and a view of reading aloud that overlooks their existence is more compatible with the perspective on the problem of reading aloud taken by engineers and computer scientists. Reseachers who are constrained to make phonography work have concluded that they don't need abstract spelling-to-sound rules, and psychology and reading instruction might benefit from this insight.

REFERENCES

Allen, J. Reading machines for the blind: The technical problems and the methods adopted for their solution. *IEEE Transactions on Audio and Electroacoustics*, 1973, *21*, 259–264.

Allen, J. Synthesis of speech from unrestricted text. *Proceedings of the IEEE*, 1976, *64*, 433–442.

Anderson, S. *The organization of phonology.* New York: Academic Press, 1974.

Baron, J. Mechanisms for pronouncing printed words: Use and acquisition. In D. LaBerge & S. Samuels (Eds.), *Basic processes in reading: Perception and comprehension.* Hillsdale, N.J.: Lawrence Erlbaum Associates, 1977.

Baron, J. Orthographic and word-specific mechanisms in children's reading of words. *Child Development*, 1979, *50*, 60–72.

Baron, J., & Strawson, C. Use of orthographic and word-specific knowledge in reading words aloud. *Journal of Experimental Psychology: Human Perception and Performance*, 1976, *2*, 386–393.

Barron, R. Visual-orthographic and phonological strategies in reading and spelling. In U. Frith (Ed.), *Cognitive processes in spelling.* London: Academic Press, 1980.

Bauer, D., & Stanovich, K. Lexical access and the spelling-to-sound regularity effect. *Memory and Cognition*, 1980, *8*, 424–432.

Carroll, L. *The humorous verse of Lewis Carroll.* New York: Dover, 1933.

Chall, J. *Learning to read: The great debate.* New York: McGraw-Hill, 1967.

Chomsky, C. Reading, writing, and phonology. *Harvard Educational Review*, 1970, *40*, 287–309.

Chomsky, N., & Halle, M. *The sound pattern of English.* New York: Harper & Row, 1968.

Coltheart, M. Lexical access in simple reading tasks. In G. Underwood (Ed.), *Strategies of information processing.* London: Academic Press, 1978.

Davies, W. *Teaching reading in early England.* New York: Harper & Row, 1974.

Dewey, G. *English spelling: Roadblock to reading.* New York: Teachers College Press, 1971.

Downing, J. *Evaluating the initial teaching alphabet.* London: Cassell, 1967.

Esper, E. *Analogy and association in linguistics and psychology.* Athens, Ga.: University of Georgia Press, 1973.

Fischler, I., & Bloom, P. Automatic and attentional processes in the effects of sentence context on word recognition. *Journal of Verbal Learning and Verbal Behavior*, 1979, *18*, 1–20.

Flanagan, J. Computers that talk and listen: Man–machine communication by voice. *Proceedings of the IEEE*, 1976, *64*, 405–415.

Forster, K., & Chambers, S. Lexical access and naming time. *Journal of Verbal Learning and Verbal Behavior*, 1973, *12*, 627–635.

Frederiksen, J., & Kroll, J. Spelling and sound: Approaches to the internal lexicon. *Journal of Experimental Psychology: Human Perception and Performance,* 1976, *2,* 361–379.

Glushko, R. Cognitive and pedagogical implications of orthography. *Quarterly Newsletter of the Laboratory of Comparative Human Cognition,* 1979, *1,* 22–26. (a)

Glushko, R. The organization and activation of orthographic knowledge in reading aloud. *Journal of Experimental Psychology: Human Perception and Performance,* 1979, *5,* 674–691. (b)

Gough, P., & Cosky, M. One second of reading again. In N. Castellan, D. Pisoni, & G. Potts (Eds.), *Cognitive theory* (Vol. 2). Hillsdale, N.J.: Lawrence Erlbaum Associates, 1977.

Haas, W. *Phono-graphic translation.* Manchester, England: Manchester University Press, 1970.

Halle, M. Prolegomena to a theory of word formation. *Linguistic Inquiry,* 1973, *4,* 3–16.

Hanna, J., & Hanna, P. Spelling as a school subject: A brief history. *National Elementary Principal,* 1959, *38,* 8–23.

Hayes-Roth, F. Learning by example. In A. Lesgold, J. Pellegrino, S. Fokkema, & R. Glaser (Eds.), *Cognitive psychology and instruction.* New York: Plenum, 1978.

Hayes-Roth, F., & McDermott, J. An interference matching technique for inducing abstractions. *Communications of the ACM,* 1978, *21,* 401–411.

Huey, E. *The psychology and pedagogy of reading.* Cambridge, Mass.: MIT Press, 1968. (Reprint of original Macmillan edition, 1908.)

Hunnicutt, S. Phonological rules for a text-to-speech system. *American Journal of Computational Linguistics Microfiche,* 1976, *57,* 1–72.

Kleiman, G. Speech recoding in reading. *Journal of Verbal Learning and Verbal Behavior,* 1975, *14,* 323–339.

Klima, E. How alphabets might reflect language. In J. Kavanaugh & I. Mattingly (Eds.), *Language by ear and by eye.* Cambridge, Mass.: MIT Press, 1972.

Kucjaz, S. The acquisition of regular and irregular past tense forms. *Journal of Verbal Learning and Verbal Behavior,* 1977, *16,* 589–600.

Levy, B. Speech recoding during sentence processing: Reading and listening. *Visible Language,* 1978, *12,* 81–102.

MacKay, D. The structure of words and syllables: Evidence from errors in speech. *Cognitive Psychology,* 1972, *3,* 210–227.

MacKay, D. Complexity in output systems: Evidence from behavioral hybrids. *American Journal of Psychology,* 1973, *86,* 785–806.

Marcel, A. Surface dyslexia and beginning reading: A revised hypothesis of the pronunciation of print and its impairments. In M. Coltheart, K. Patterson, & J. Marshall (Eds.), *Deep dyslexia.* London: Routledge & Kegan Paul, 1980.

Marshall, J., & Newcombe, F. Patterns of paralexia: A psycholinguistic approach. *Journal of Psycholinguistic Research,* 1973, *2,* 175–199.

Mason, M. From print to sound in mature readers as a function of reader ability and two forms of orthographic regularity. *Memory & Cognition,* 1978, *6,* 568–581.

McIlroy, M. *Synthetic English speech by rule* (Bell Telephone Laboratories Technical Memorandum #73-1271-7. Murray Hill, N.J. Bell Laboratories, 1973.

Meyer, D., Schvaneveldt, R., & Ruddy, M. Functions of graphemic and phonemic codes in visual word-recognition. *Memory & Cognition,* 1974, *2,* 309–321.

Miller, G., & Isard, S. Some perceptual consequences of linguistic rules. *Journal of Verbal Learning and Verbal Behavior,* 1963, *2,* 217–228.

Norman, D., & Bobrow, D. Descriptions: An intermediate stage in memory retrieval. *Cognitive Psychology,* 1979, *11,* 107–123.

Patterson, K., & Marcel, A. Aphasia, dyslexia, and the phonological coding of written words. *Quarterly Journal of Experimental Psychology,* 1977, *29,* 307–318.

Rozin, P., & Gleitman, L. The structure and acquisition of reading II: The reading process and the acquisition of the alphabetic principle. In A. Reber & D. Scarborough (Eds.), *Toward a psychology of reading.* Hillsdale, N.J.: Lawrence Erlbaum Associates, 1977.

Rubenstein, H., Lewis, S., & Rubenstein, M. Evidence for phonemic recoding in visual word recognition. *Journal of Verbal Learning and Verbal Behavior,* 1971, *10,* 635–647.

Rumelhart, D. Toward an interactive model of reading. In S. Dornic (Ed.), *Attention and performance VI.* Hillsdale, N.J.: Lawrence Erlbaum Associates, 1977.

Savin, H. What a child knows about speech when he starts to learn to read. In J. Kavanaugh & I. Mattingly (Eds.), *Language by ear and by eye.* Cambridge, Mass.: MIT Press, 1972.

Schane, S. *Generative phonology.* Englewood Cliffs, N.J.: Prentice-Hall, 1973.

Shallice, T., & Warrington, E. Word recognition in a phonemic dyslexic patient. *Quarterly Journal of Experimental Psychology,* 1975, *27,* 187–199.

Shulman, H., Hornak, R., & Sanders, E. The effects of graphemic, phonetic, and semantic relationships on access to lexical structures. *Memory & Cognition,* 1978, *6,* 115–123.

Stanovich, K., & Bauer, D. Experiments on the spelling-to-sound regularity effect in word recognition. *Memory & Cognition,* 1978, *6,* 410–415.

Taft, M. Lexical access via an orthographic code: The basic orthographic syllable structure (BOSS). *Journal of Verbal Learning and Verbal Behavior,* 1979, *18,* 21–40.

Tzeng, O., Hung, D., & Wang, W. Speech recoding in reading Chinese characters. *Journal of Experimental Psychology: Human Learning and Memory,* 1977, *3,* 621–630.

Venezky, R. *The structure of English orthography.* The Hague: Mouton, 1970.

Venezky, R. *Theoretical and experimental base for teaching reading.* The Hague: Mouton, 1976.

Wijk, A. *Rules of pronunciation for the English language.* London: Oxford University Press, 1966.

4

Linguistic Coding in Word Recognition: Comparisons Between a Deep and a Shallow Orthography

Leonard Katz and Laurie B. Feldman
University of Connecticut
and
Haskins Laboratories

The point of departure for this chapter is the following set of questions: What kinds of information are provided to readers by their orthography; how much of this potential information is actually used; and how does this selection vary with reading experience? In particular, we are concerned with the phonological infor- mation provided by alphabetic orthographies. We ask how the use of such infor- mation for word recognition changes with a reader's skill and with the nature of the correspondence between that individual's orthography and his or her spoken language. We are interested in the relation of speech to the reading process because it seems to us reasonable that the information-processing structures that readers evolve when learning to become skilled readers grow out of the structures they have developed for processing their spoken language. One of the points we pursue in this chapter is that although perceiving language by eye is not the same as by ear, there are important correspondences between the information in the spoken word and the information a reader actually codes from print. An alterna- tive view of word recognition emphasizes the use of visual codes that have no general linguistic properties.

We begin with a discussion of the characteristics of phonological and non- phonological codes and their potential uses in word recognition in reading. Then we suggest that the kind of code that is used for lexical access depends on the kind of alphabetic orthography facing the reader. Specifically, it depends on how directly the orthography reflects the phonetic surface. Languages in which the spelling-to-sound correspondences are simple and invariant (as in Serbo- Croatian) will readily support information-processing structures for reading that utilize the language's surface phonological features. On the other hand, in an orthography that bears a complex relation to speech (a deep orthography such as

English), phonologically structured mechanisms for processing words will be less well developed. These conjectures are given some support by studies we present that compare adult speakers of English and Serbo-Croatian on a lexical decision task. A second factor that interacts with the use of phonological information for recognizing words is the maturity of the reader. Our evidence suggests that younger readers tend to rely more on phonological information and less on nonphonological (e.g., word-specific) mechanisms than do older readers.

PHONOLOGICAL AND NONPHONOLOGICAL CODES

The prevailing view of word recognition is that it is a process that is supported by two broad classes of codes—phonological and visual. We would like to suggest a framework for discussing these codes more precisely. In particular, it will be useful to define the terms *phonological* and *visual* so as not to imply opposites. Rather, a given code may be described as phonological or nonphonological *and* as visual or nonvisual.

Any information-processing mechanism may be described at an abstract level as a transfer function or transform applied to a specified input and producing a specified output. For example, transforms can be described that map partitions of a printed word (input) onto units (output) that match information stored in the reader's memory. The initial stages of processing print can be described by transforms whose output consists of letter features or supraletter features. The information-processing mechanisms that instantiate these processes may be interactively organized (in the sense of Rumelhart, 1977) or hierarchically organized (in the sense of Estes, 1976); our use of a language of transforms is neutral with respect to mechanism but descriptive with respect to code. The final stages of processing result in the selection of a unique word. The word will be, of course, more or less semantically ambiguous; sentential constraints must be introduced to resolve the intended meaning. For the present discussion, however, we are concerned only with the search for the lexical entry and with the character of the codes that address it.

The character of a code is described by the range of a transform (its output dimension). For example, the range of a syllable code is the set of syllables in the reader's tacit knowledge of speech; the range of a word-specific code is the set of visual patterns stored in memory, each of which defines a unique morpheme or a word. Not all codes (not all stages) need consist of one-to-one or many-to-one mappings. For example, the transforms that take word shape and word length information as their inputs must be one-to-many mappings; additional information must be specified in order to select a unique lexical entry. Similarly, if there is a phonological code whose domain (i.e., input) consists of single letters, it must have one-to-many mapping somewhere in the process of its assignment of letters to speech units (e.g., as an abstract phoneme) prior to the introduction of phonotactic constraints. In addition, the transform must also convey positional information along with its content.

Phonological codes are those codes whose transforms carry their input into categories defined by linguistic units such as single phonemes, morphophonemes, syllables, and certain morphemes. All of these are codes whose units generalize across words. A reader may use the information coded in these linguistic units (for example, two or three specific syllables) as memory addresses that access whole words in the mental lexicon or that are prelexical addresses (inputs) to other codes that, in turn, access whole words. Simultaneous use may be made of more than one kind of code.

Visual codes are spatially defined. It seems likely that some important visual codes would be those whose ranges are the number of character spaces (i.e., word length), letter features, and features of letter sequences and groupings (i.e., macrofeatures). Some visual codes may be *nonphonological* in the sense that their ranges cannot be made isomorphic to the range of any phonological code. A word-specific code is not phonological. Its range consists of particular lexical entries, not of speech units that generalize across words. And clearly, those codes whose ranges are the input to a word-specific code are not phonological; the domain of a word-specific code must consist of spatially defined arrays of whole words; these are the letter features or supraletter macrofeatures of whole words together with relations among them. The set of letter features is not isomorphic to any set of phonological units. However, other visual codes may be described as *phonological* in the sense that their ranges are identical to some phonological code. For example, a code based on visual patterns, each of which corresponds to a syllable in speech, is a phonological code. The input to the code's transform consists of a collection of units such as letter features or supraletter features. These features are sufficient to point to, or define, a unique output—a particular syllable. This syllable information may or may not be represented as a phonetic code (or an articulatory code, etc.); it may be represented as a visual code. Nevertheless, it is a syllable code in the sense that it can be shown to be isomorphic to the effective set of syllables in speech.

If we are concerned with the relation between speech and reading, and particularly with the role played by knowledge of the spoken language in the learning and performance of reading, it may make more sense to distinguish between phonological and nonphonological effects as we have defined them rather than limiting our examination of phonological effects to the phonetic effects of inner speech alone, considering all other effects to be merely "visual."

The ultimate output of both phonological and nonphonological codes must be the word. If we think of the word as a node in memory in an associative semantic net, then appropriate word-specific information or phonological information constitutes an address to that node. Thus, we conceptualize both kinds of codes as accessing the same semantics. There is no logical necessity for a higher-order nonphonological visual code to access the semantic node *through* a phonological code; access can be directly to the semantic node that represents the word. But of course, this is a question that is the source of much controversy. Whether readers typically use a connection between higher-level nonphonological and phonological codes or not, it is clear that there must be at least one connection between such codes at a lower level. That this must be so is undeniable because visually coded letter information must be the input to a device whose output consists of phonemes; readers can sound out novel words. Even if a reader uses an analogy strategy for pronouncing novel words (see Glushko, Chap. 3, this volume), at least part of the process involves grapheme-to-phoneme transforms.

A point that needs to be emphasized is that it is the word, the lexical entry itself, that must be contacted first in memory prior to accessing the semantics associated with the word. The reader cannot "go directly to meaning" if the term *direct* is used to mean that some collection of semantic information can be directly addressed (with what unique code?), bypassing the node representing the word that defines—ties together—its associated semantics. A word bears a more or less arbitrary relation to its semantics. There is little, if any, semantic information (though some syntactic information) to be culled from applying general rules to orthography. An arbitrary signal, the word, links the writer's intention to the reader's understanding. It may appear to be a minor point, but it seems to us that missing this point has been a source of confusion in discussions about the recovery of meaning from print.

In this chapter, we are concerned with a particular kind of phonological code—namely, the syllable. We present evidence suggesting that syllable codes can be formed in at least two different ways: (1) by a transform that takes as its input phonologically coded information, or (2) by a transform whose input is visually coded nonphonological information. For the former, Spoehr and Smith (1973) and Hansen and Rodgers (1965) present schemes based on phonologically defined input for parsing printed words into syllables. Their schemes, based on earlier descriptions of rules for articulating phonemes and phonemic clusters by Liberman, Ingemann, Lisker, Delattre, and Cooper (1959), involve transforms whose domain consists of elements that are derived from the letters in a word conditionalized by phonotactic rules. The output consists of syllables or syllablelike units called vocalic center groups, which are minimal pronunciational units in which the important articulatory constraints are specified. A vocalic center group contains one vowel or diphthong plus from zero to three consonants or semiconsonantal elements, all constrained by the phonological rules of English. Most one-syllable words contain one vocalic center group; most two-syllable words contain two.

The input to the vocalic-center-group process consists of letters and letter clusters—elements of a visual graphemic code—each of which is defined by the process as a consonatal or vocalic element. Then rules derived from speech specify which of the units are to be concatenated into a common higher-order unit—the syllable—and which are to be divided between syllables. The syllables that are the output of the process are specified in only a symbolic manner; their actual mode of representation may be phonetic or spatial-visual or something else. The important characteristic of the process is that its operation is according to rules derived from speech. The transform may be said to operate on phonological principles, because it recodes its input—graphemically coded letters—into phonologic elements—phonemes identified as consonants or vowels—and then uses phonotactic rules of speech to determine the final groupings of these phonologic elements. Finally, the output of the process consists of syllable information and is therefore isomorphic to a speech code.

A second way of forming a syllable code is with a transform that operates as a simple visual pattern-matching device with either sequences of letter features or supraletter macrofeatures of the spatial array as its input. This second device may evolve in the following way: While learning to read, the beginning reader may adopt, by and large, a grapheme-to-phoneme method of coding syllables. In order to perform the task of letter-to-sound conversion correctly and to achieve appropriate coarticulation of the syllable complex, the reader may very likely produce a complete temporary visual image of the syllable. Such a visually coded percept may be the result of the reader utilizing a visual scratch-pad buffer or a visual working buffer as he or she attempts correctly to partition the word syllabically. After producing the correct syllables (verified by finding the correct word), the correctly partitioned visual units are available to become associated either to the correct phonologically coded units (the syllables) or directly *to the output* of the syllables, thereby effectively replacing the original pathway. Our description of the creation of phonological codes from units of print larger than the letter is close to that given by LaBerge and Samuels (1974). Note that we are suggesting that a code whose input is defined visually but whose output is isomorphic to a phonological code (e.g., the syllable) should also be termed a phonological code. This sidesteps the issue of the nature of the representation of the coded units—that is, is the output represented phonetically or spatially?—but we believe that the problem of the representation, even if soluble (see Anderson, 1978), is less important for theory and application than is an understanding of the logical form of the information being processed.

THE IMPORTANCE OF PHONOLOGICAL CODING

The reader who uses a well-structured phonological processing system for word recognition would appear to have some advantages over a reader who relies on nonphonological visual processing instead. There is some agreement that comprehension in reading depends substantially on the manipulation of phonetic codes in a limited-capacity short-term memory (cf. Baddeley, 1978; Levy, 1977; Perfetti & Lesgold, 1977). It seems plausible that lower-order phonologically coded information (e.g., phonetic representations, phonemes, syllables) would be the most efficient and the least error prone in accessing the phonologically coded whole word that is needed for working memory. Visual codes have an arbitrary link with whole-word names and, therefore, would generally have less redundancy to guide their search for the correct word name.

There is also indirect evidence that having a well-structured phonological processing system is important to reading. Children who are skilled readers rely more on phonological coding and prefer it to nonphonological coding. This has been demonstrated in many ways—by some of the participants of this conference and by others. There is the well-known pioneering work of Conrad (1972), who related the poor reading ability of deaf children to their impoverished or attenuated verbal short-term memory. Vellutino (1977) and his associates found that the poorer reader's memory deficit is confined to verbally codable material. Hogaboam and Perfetti (1978) studied children's vocalization latency and same–different judgments as a function of type of experience with words (aural exposure or printed exposure). Although large differences were found between skilled and less skilled readers (defined by a comprehension test), there were no major qualitative differences between the two groups; experience with letter strings simply facilitated decoding less for the less skilled readers. Subword processes were implicated as the source of the less skilled readers' generally slower responding; the authors suggested that the slower assignment of phonetic codes to letters or letter groups (syllables) was the critical mechanism. I. Y. Liberman and D. Shankweiler and their associates (e.g., Liberman, Liberman, Mattingly, & Shankweiler, 1980; Shankweiler, Liberman, Mark, Fowler, & Fischer, 1980) have demonstrated that cognitive processing differences between good and poor young readers occur in situations in which phonetic working memory is stressed. They find that good readers are more skillful in utilizing verbally coded information and prefer its use over nonverbal codings even when the choice of verbal code results in inferior performance. For example, Mann, Liberman, and Shankweiler (1980) recently found that good readers performed better than poor readers when recalling ordinary sentences but fell to the level of the poor readers when required to recall sentences that contained several words with a common rhyme. Here, the phonetic confusability of the rhyming words was damaging to the good readers, presumably because they coded the words phonetically for verbal short-term memory. A similar manipulation involving meaningful and meaningless sentences failed to affect the good and poor readers differentially. Also, they find that young good readers develop a tacit awareness of the existence of two major phonological variables, syllables and phonemes, at an earlier age than poorer readers.

ORTHOGRAPHY AND PHONOLOGICAL CODING

Alphabetic orthographies may be characterized by the depth—that is, the extent—to which they are phonetic representations of speech. One of the factors that determines orthographic depth is the morphophonological depth of the language. For example, in English, the plural of a noun is signaled in speech by one of three phonemically distinct sounds; for example, the plurals of *kit, kid, kiss* are *kIts, kIdz, kIssaz*. The correct plural ending phoneme is specified by a morphophnological rule: That we tacitly know such a rule is easily demonstrated; we can all agree on the plurals of the following three pseudowords: *bluk, blug,* and *blus.* The second factor that determines orthographic depth is the degree to which the orthography represents this morphophonological level instead of the surface phonetics. The morphemic invariance for all three plural phonemes is recognized and captured by the orthography that assigns to the /s/ and /z/ phonemes the same grapheme, the letter *s*. Another example of morphophonological depth is the vowel shift rule given by Chomsky and Halle (1968), which specifies vowel changes such as *grateful-gratitude, serene-serenity, divine-divinity*. The members of each pair have a common root morpheme despite the phonemic difference. The orthography captures this invariance of meaning by creating a "graphic morpheme" representing both sets of phones with the same grapheme. English orthography allows the reader to use this knowledge of English phonology in order to decode the printed word into speech. As Chomsky and Halle point out, it is unnecessary for the orthography to indicate predictable phonetic variants as long as the reader is knowledgeable about the spoken language; they go even further, conjecturing that the orthography is optimally efficient in transcribing English in the sense that it maps onto a morphophonemic representation that is the same as that for the spoken language.

The character of the morphophonemic code can, of course, be described as phonological. Morphophonemic units are used as units of information that eventually address an item in a speech lexicon that is structured for morphophonemic and phonetic codes. However, the fact that graphemic invariance is used to represent morphophonemes gives weight to the argument that readers will use this graphemic invariance for a visual code to access the item in a visually based lexicon instead of a speech lexicon. This presumes that there is a good deal of linguistic structure to such a visual lexicon; morphemes that are parts of words must be represented as well as whole words. Rules (linguistic rules) must exist to conjoin and manipulate morphemes and other visually described units. It seems plausible that even a process of recognizing words by means of the visual patterns within words will involve phonological codes for part of its operation.

The end result of a visually based process must be the same as that for any process: A unique word must be identified in memory. As we stated earlier, it is the word itself, with its syntactic and semantic identity, that must be found. Finding a fuzzy approximation to the word—for example, a constellation of syntactic and semantic characteristics shared by the several words that contain within them a given morpheme—will not generally produce an unambiguous meaning. A process of comprehension based on fuzzy information will require even more input from the comprehender's world knowledge, situational knowledge, etc., than is usual. If the ambiguity of word meaning and syntactic category becomes too severe, either the burden on verbal working memory will become great as the reader tries harder to infer what the intended message was, or the reader will fail to understand the message at any acceptable level.

Although the complexity of English orthography may be an asset for the skilled reader, the task of word recognition for the beginning reader is more difficult than would be the case with a shallow orthography—that is, one in which there is an invariant grapheme–phoneme relationship. Serbo-Croatian is represented by such a shallow orthography. A century ago, the Yugoslav *Vuk Karadžić* organized the alphabet and spelling according to the principle, "Write it as it sounds, and say it as it is written." In addition, Serbo-Croatian has a less complex morphophonology than English. Thus, Serbo-Croatian imposes less of a burden on the beginning reader than does English. On the other hand, Serbo-Croatian words that are related morphemically but pronounced differently (e.g., words similar to *heal* and *health* in English) will be spelled differently, so their graphemic patterns may give no hint of the underlying semantic similarity. Therefore, the difference between Serbo-Croatian and English orthographies may be described as follows: Serbo-Croatian orthography generally represents the phonemic level of the spoken language, whereas English orthography generally represents the morphophonemic level.

Given this difference between English and Serbo-Croatian, it might be expected that the kinds of codes that are used in word recognition will differ where the two orthographies differ. For example, phoneme and syllable codes may be used more often in Serbo-Croatian because their derivation is more directly related to the spelling and, presumably, is therefore more efficient than in English. Morphophonemic information should be favored less in Serbo-Croatian than in English, where it is represented in print as an invariant spelling pattern. (Morphemic information is, of course, available as invariant spellings in both orthographies.) Moreover, the superficial inconsistency of phonologically coded information in English may lead English readers to depend less on all kinds of phonological codes even when they are applicable; we are suggesting the possibility of linguistic differences in coding preference.

Presumably, there are both costs and gains associated with the coding style differences we are hypothesizing. For English readers, comprehension may be slowed by a more circuitous route to the recovery of a phonetically coded representation for use in verbal working memory. However, word recognition itself may be speeded by direct access mechanisms that produce visual codes of invariant spelling patterns. The latter mechanisms, however, require the existence of a visually coded lexicon; this may involve the use of processing capacity to construct and strengthen new visual codes during the process of word recognition. Our comparison of American and Yugoslavian readers does not speak to these questions of costs and gains. Rather, we are concerned first with the more fundamental question of whether or not Yugoslavian and American readers differ in style of coding for word recognition.

THE AMERICAN EXPERIMENTS: WORD RECOGNITION
FROM A DEEP ORTHOGRAPHY

The experiments reported here looked for evidence of effects on word recognition in English due to a major phonological variable, the syllable. Two questions were asked: (1) Is the syllable a component of word recognition in reading? (2) If it is, are there differences among readers of different abilities in their use of syllabic information in recognizing words? The major experimental manipulation concerns the integrity of the syllable units in each stimulus item; two-syllable stimuli were divided either at the syllable boundary or off the boundary. Three levels of reading experience (or ability) were studied: skilled and average fifth-grade students and college adults. For the children, two aspects of word recognition were studied. First, encoding skill was studied in a naming experiment in which articulation of the printed stimulus was required. Second, because articulation does not require lexical access, a lexical decision experiment was also run. For the adults, only the lexical decision task was used.

EXPERIMENT 1

Naming: Fifth Graders

Fifth-grade children pronounced printed two-syllable words and pseudowords that had been altered by the addition of an oblique slash either between the two letters at the syllable boundary or between two other letters, off the syllable boundary. Regular syllabification was performed according to the rules suggested by Spoehr and Smith (1973). Irregular divisions, off the syllable boundary, were also made. Forty-five high-frequency words were selected from the 1000 most frequent third-grade words in the Carroll, Davies, and Richman (1971) norms. Each word was used to produce a similar pseudoword, examples of which are the following pairs: *letter–lutter, region–rogion, among–omang, coming–cimong, perhaps–parheps*. Each item of a pair was divided with a slash—once regularly (i.e., appropriately syllabified) and once irregularly. The serial position of the slash was counterbalanced across items. Subjects were presented either with all words or all pseudowords, but in either case, they saw the regular and irregular forms of each item in different halves of the session. The 90 items were viewed one at a time in a Gebrands T-scope after being preceded by five practice and two dummy trials. Vocal reaction time to each item was measured.

For a group of 51 fifth-grade children, 25 skilled readers and 26 average readers were chosen. The mean reading-class levels on a scale of 0 to 9 and mean Comprehensive Test of Basic Skills (CTBS) reading-grade equivalences were 6.6 and 8.7 for the skilled readers and 3.2 and 5.1 for the average readers. A child's reading-class level was determined by the reading supervisor together with the teacher, based mainly on the child's classroom performance. A between-subjects design was used, with 11 skilled readers and 13 average readers in the real-word condition and 14 skilled and 13 average readers in the pseudoword condition.

Errors were classified into one of two types: *incomplete utterances* (e.g., partial vocalizations) and *mispronunciations*. Incomplete utterances were scored as such only when followed immediately by a correct pronunciation. Long hesitations between the two syllables were also scored as incomplete. With regard to scoring mispronunciations, the experimenter's criterion for a correct pronunciation was generous for both real words and pseudowords. The effect of reading ability was significant, with skilled readers making only 1.04 errors whereas the average readers averaged 3.21 errors, $F(1,47) = 6.06$, $MS_e = 6.67$, $p = .018$. No other effects involving reading ability were significant. Fewer errors were made on real words than on pseudowords, $F(1,47) = 13.17$, $MS_e = 6.67$, $p < .001$; and fewer errors were made on regularly syllabicated stimuli than on irregular stimuli, $F(1,47) = 6.05$, $MS_e = 4.29$, $p = .017$. The interaction of these two variables was also significant, $F(1,47) = 4.05$, $MS_e = 4.29$, $p < .05$, and is given in Table 4.1. Clearly, the disruptive effect of irregular syllabification was stronger for pseudowords than for high-frequency real words, although a syllable effect existed for both.

The results were slightly different for mispronunciations. There was no significant difference between skilled and average readers on these errors; skilled readers made an average of 1.43 errors, whereas average readers made 1.96 errors. As before (see Table 4.1), there were significant effects for the word-pseudoword comparison, $F(1,47) = 14.47$, $MS_e = 75.03$, $p < .001$, and the regular–irregular syllabification comparison, $F(1,47) = 8.65$, $MS_e = 20.17$, $p = .006$; but their interaction was not significant, unlike the result for incomplete utterances. For the latter measure, the significant interaction suggests that syllabification is more important for naming novel stimuli than for naming frequent words. Although the interaction leading to this suggestion is only marginally significant, the same interpretation is supported more strongly by the response latency data.

TABLE 4.1
Errors (Mean Number of Incomplete Utterances and Mispronunciations)
and Naming Latencies (in Msecs) for Correct Pronunciations

Stimulus Division	*Real Words*		*Pseudowords*	
	Regular	*Irregular*	*Regular*	*Irregular*
Incomplete utterances	.65	.87	1.69	3.53
Mispronunciations	.61	1.07	1.90	3.22
Latencies	655	656	1007	1055

The mean latencies, in milliseconds, were 771 for skilled readers and 915 for average readers, $F(1,41) = 13.23$, $MS_e = 39784$, $p < .001$. No other effects involving reading ability were significant. Table 4.1 presents the mean latencies for regularly and irregularly syllabified words and pseudowords, averaged over both reading ability groups. Not surprisingly, real words were pronounced faster than pseudowords, $F(1,47) = 89.53$, $MS_e = 39784$, $p < .001$; and the effect of regularity is also significant, $F(1,47) = 13.28$, $MS_e = 1148$, $p < .001$. However, the interaction of the two variables clearly accounts for the main effect of regularity; irregular syllabification is detrimental only when pronouncing pseudowords, $F(1,47) = 12.32$, $MS_e = 1148$, $p < .001$. The finding of a syllable effect on the naming of pseudowords is striking in the light of negative evidence for syllable involvement in naming either words or pseudowords from Henderson, Coltheart, and Woodhouse (1973); Forster and Chambers (1973); and Fredriksen and Kroll (1976). The data are clear with respect to the effect of syllable regularity on pseudoword naming; both errors and latencies indicate that regularly syllabified stimuli are easier to process than irregular stimuli. The results for real words are contradictory; syllable effects are suggested by both types of error responses but not by latencies.

With regard to reader ability differences in the processing of syllable information, the experiment found no interactions between reader ability and syllable regularity. Therefore, it cannot be said that the substantial reader ability differences that were found appear to be related to the processing of syllable information in the present experiment. However, evidence from inspection of the means for skilled and average readers, together with the relatively low power of the test of the interaction between reading ability and syllable regularity, prevents us from endorsing the null hypotheses in this case.

EXPERIMENT 2

Lexical Decision: Fifth Graders

The second experiment was designed to assess whether children use a syllable code in accessing lexical memory. In addition, Experiment 2 extended the study of real words to include low-frequency as well as high-frequency real words. The finding of syllable effects on latencies for pseudowords but not for high-frequency words in Experiment 1 suggested that if a similar result obtained in Experiment 2, the lexical access of low-frequency words would be found to be more like that of pseudowords in requiring syllable-coded information. Both skilled and average reader groups were studied.

Eighteen skilled and 18 average fifth-grade readers were selected. The mean reading-class levels and CTBS reading-grade equivalences were 8.56 and 10.4 for the skilled readers and 2.67 and 6.3 for the average readers. The children were studied in May and June and were given the CTBS in June. Therefore, as expected, their CTBS scores are somewhat higher than those of the children in the first experiment (run earlier in the school year), whose CTBS scores dated from the end of the previous school year.

Six 2-syllable high-frequency and six 2-syllable low-frequency words were selected from the Carroll, Davies, and Richman (1971) fifth-grade norms. The high-frequency words had a range of from 145 to 959 occurrences in a sample of 634,283 tokens, with a mean frequency of 411. The low-frequency words ranged from a frequency of 1 to 10 occurrences, with a mean of 3.5. Each low-frequency word was required to be similar in length to a specific high-frequency word and to preserve morphemes such as -er and -ing in the high-frequency word. For each high- and low-frequency word, a control pseudoword was constructed by changing one or more consonants or vowels in the word. Some of the words were composed of suffixes attached to stems that were themselves words (e.g., *poster*, *wanted*). For the set of low-frequency words, the frequency of the stem was always lower than that of the entire word; for the set of high-frequency words, the stem was always more frequent than the entire word.

Pilot testing established a pool of words and pseudowords that were reliably judged correctly. In pilot tests, stimuli were printed on a sheet of paper, and fifth-grade poor readers were asked to circle those stimuli that were real words. The final set of stimuli is presented in Table 4.2. Thus the 24 stimuli may be viewed as being divided into 6 sets of 4 conditions each, with each set consisting of a high-frequency word, a low-frequency word, and two pseudowords. Within each set, the 4 stimuli are structurally similar with regard to orthography and syllabification; the similarity is greater between a pseudoword and its real-word counterpart. Each stimulus was syllabified once regularly and once irregularly, as in the previous experiment, to produce 48 stimuli.

Two lists, each containing all 24 original stimuli, were constructed. For List A, 3 of the 6 stimuli in each of the 4 conditions (high- and low-frequency words, pseudoword controls for high- and low-frequency words) were syllabified regularly, and 3 items were divided irregularly. Each list contained a quasi-random sequence of conditions. List B was identical to List A except that a stimulus that was divided regularly in List A was divided irregularly in List B, and vice versa (see Table 4.2). Stimuli were placed on 10 × 15-cm tachistoscope cards as in Experiment 1.

Nine skilled and 9 average readers received List A followed by List B, and the remaining 9 children in each reader ability group received the lists in reverse order. Randomized within each list were the factorial combinations of the 4 conditions (high- and low-frequency words, two pseudoword controls) by two levels of syllable regularity.

Subjects were told to decide whether each stimulus displayed was a real word or not, based on their knowledge of meaning. If they did not know the meaning of a stimulus, they were told to judge it as not a word. The experimenter showed

TABLE 4.2

Latencies in Msec and Number of Correct Responses for Skilled and Less Skilled Readers When Subject Was Correct on Both the Rgular and Irregular Forms of a Stimulus[a]

		Skilled		Less Skilled			Skilled		Less Skilled
wa/ter	(17)	674	(18)	808	wu/ter	(18)	954	(17)	952
w/ater		700		847	w/uter		814		864
pos/ter	(18)	738	(18)	883	wos/ler	(18)	827	(17)	965
p/oster		734		782	w/osler		878		938
wan/ted	(18)	769	(15)	892	lun/ted	(18)	888	(18)	1025
wa/nted		821		1007	lu/nted		851		1087
dus/ted	(18)	750	(15)	1097	sto/ded	(18)	1037	(17)	1370
du/sted		786		1117	st/oded		987		1068
sto/ry	(18)	757	(18)	945	spo/ry	(16)	1130	(13)	1399
st/ory		764		797	sp/ory		1043		1309
hol/ly	(14)	1050	(15)	1004	hob/ly	(16)	1116	(10)	1269
ho/lly		869		929	ho/bly		1109		1251
look/ing	(16)	764	(18)	771	woak/ing	(16)	971	(11)	1238
lo/oking		901		1120	wo/aking		1110		1176
soak/ing	(13)	832	(13)	1093	boak/ing	(17)	956	(11)	1286
so/aking		850		965	bo/aking		975		1203
morn/ing	(17)	788	(16)	954	mern/ing	(18)	952	(18)	1061
morni/ng		892		942	merni/ng		959		1134
jok/ing	(14)	723	(15)	872	jul/ing	(17)	941	(17)	1075
joki/ng		949		1176	juli/ng		942		1161
lit/tle	(18)	794	(16)	944	lut/tle	(18)	951	(17)	1110
l/ittle		793		934	l/uttle		990		1107
nib/ble	(16)	916	(14)	1001	wim/ble	(13)	999	(12)	1047
n/ibble		951		1010	w/imble		991		1009

[a] Within each block of four words, the order is high frequency to low frequency and regular to irregular. For pseudowords, the order is high-frequency control to low-frequency control and regular to irregular.

the child four cards representing real and pseudowords, two divided regularly and two divided irregularly. The slash in each stimulus was explained away as the experimenter's way of making the task more challenging. Then four practice trials were given. The child pressed a telegraph key with his or her dominant hand to make a "word" response; the other hand was used for a "not-word" response. The first list was then presented, beginning with a dummy trial. The cards were changed after the first list, and then the second list, beginning with a dummy trial, was presented.

Skilled readers made fewer errors out of 48 trials (1.8 or 3.7%) than did average readers (4.0 or 8.3%), $F(1,34) = 15.5$, $MS_e = .179$, $p < .001$. The mean errors for the four types of stimuli were: high-frequency words, 1.44; low-frequency words, 3.89; pseudoword high-frequency controls, 2.22; pseudoword low-frequency controls, 4.0; $F(3,102) = 6.12$, $MS_e = .146$, p

< .001. No effects involving syllabification were significant. The higher error rate for low-frequency words than for high-frequency words is not unexpected, but the higher error rate for pseudoword low-frequency controls than for high-frequency controls may seem puzzling. Possibly, the greater error rate for pseudoword low-frequency controls results from subjects' greater difficulty in letter and letter-cluster identification. The low-frequency pseudowords are less orthographically regular, and it is this irregularity that could have slowed the early stages of processing print (Katz, 1977a). Together with a normal speed–accuracy trade-off in operation, the slowing down of the early stages of processing would lead to increased errors as subjects attempted to maintain a criterion response latency in spite of impoverished information.

An analysis of variance was performed for reaction times on correct responses. As in the error analyses, the main effects of reader ability and item type were significant, whereas the main effect of syllable regularity was not. Importantly, however, one interaction was significant—syllable regularity by item type. No other terms approached significance. The reader ability mean latencies were 900 msec for skilled readers and 1036 msec for average readers, $F(1,34) = 6.21$, $MS_e = 426,433$, $p = .01$. Table 4.3 presents the mean latencies for the combinations of syllable regularity and item types. For the item type effect, $F(3,102) = 47.47$, $MS_e = 23, 321$, $p < .001$. For the interaction, $F(3,102) = 6.26$, $MS_e = 10,394$, $p < .001$.

Table 4.3 shows that latencies within high frequency and within low frequency are ordered from fastest to slowest as follows: regular words, irregular words, irregular pseudoword controls, and regular pseudoword controls. For the word conditions, latencies to regularly syllabified words were faster than to irregularly divided words, whereas for the pseudoword conditions, the reverse was the case. The reason for the absence of a main effect of syllable regularity and the significance of its interaction with conditions are clear. A word is more easily identified if it has a phonologically correct syllable division, whereas a pseudoword is less easily identified as such if it has a phonologically correct syllable division. Thus, it appears that processing based on the syllable is part of

TABLE 4.3
Mean Reaction Times in Milliseconds for Regularly and Irregularly
Syllabified Words and Pseudowords in Each Condition

Word Frequency	High		Low	
Syllabification	Regular	Irregular	Regular	Irregular
Pseudowords	1055	1024	1074	1057
Words	804	891	919	953

the lexical decision process; both words and pseudowords appear more wordlike when they are regularly syllabified. Moreover, inspection of Table 4.3 indicates that the magnitude of the syllable regularity effect is at least as large for high-frequency words as for low-frequency words.

An additional analysis of the latency data was performed that included, for each child, only those responses for which both the regularly and irregularly syllabified forms were correct; if only one of the pair was correct, both responses were eliminated from the analysis. Table 4.2 contains these mean latencies for each item in each item type for skilled and average readers. The number of data points for each is included in parentheses. An ANOVA on these more conservative data presented results similar to the previous ANOVA. In particular, the interaction of syllable regularity × item type was again significant, $F(3,102)$ = 6.31, MS_e = 9114, p < .001. Inspection of individual stimuli in Table 4.2 suggests that the syllable effect tends to be stronger when the syllable boundary coincides with a morpheme boundary (e.g., *look/ing* vs. *lo/oking*) but not always (e.g., *morn/ing* vs. *morni/ng*), and the syllable effect also occurs when no morpheme is involved (e.g., *wa/ter* vs. *w/ater*). Thus, inspection of the individual stimuli supports the overall analyses already reported; children recognize words, in part, by means of syllables within the words.

EXPERIMENT 3

Lexical Decision: Adults

The stimuli and procedures of Experiment 3 were identical to those in Experiment 2. The subjects were 21 college students. Their response errors were few and unsystematic. Mean latencies were computed for each subject in each of the eight combinations of syllabic division (regular, irregular) and item type (high- and low-frequency words and their respective pseudoword controls).

The effect of condition was significant, $F(3,60)$ = 59.5, MS_e = 4501, p < .001, but neither syllabic regularity nor its interaction with conditions approached significance. The means, in milliseconds, for the four conditions were as follows: high-frequency words = 545; low-frequency words = 593; high-frequency control pseudowords = 679; low-frequency control pseudowords = 721. All means were significantly different from one another by post hoc t tests (Cohen & Cohen, 1975) at p < .05. These data clearly show a word frequency effect but no sign of any effect involving syllabification. Inspection of the means for the eight combinations of regularity and conditioning supported the ANOVA; only small, unsystematic differences existed between cells as a function of syllable regularity. Contrary to the results found on lexical decision with children, college students did not appear to use syllabic information in recognizing words. The difference between high- and low-frequency control pseudowords can be accounted for on the basis of the greater orthographic redundancy of the high-frequency controls whose spelling patterns are more English-like (cf. Katz, (1977b); this redundancy may be an aid to letter identification.

In summary, the first three experiments give us part of the story we expected—syllable-coding effects for children but not for adults, suggesting a shift away from surface phonological codes with increasing maturity in reading. For adults, at least, the lack of a syllable regularity effect is consistent with the results of Frederiksen and Kroll (1976), Forster and Chambers (1973), and others who varied the number of syllables in a word rather than the integrity of the syllabic unit, as in the present study. The adult results are also consistent with the findings of Kleiman (1975), among others, for the predominance of direct visual codes in adult word recognition (see Levy, 1978, for a review).

Although we found no evidence relating reading ability differences to the use of syllable coding, we are not inclined to argue for the validity of that finding. Two factors temper our judgment; one is the fact that we did not study a wide range of reading ability, and the second is the large size of the error mean squares that were used to test reading ability effects.

THE YUGOSLAVIAN EXPERIMENT: WORD RECOGNITION FROM A SHALLOW ORTHOGRAPHY

Lexical Decision

We wished to assess the notion that the degree of depth in a reader's orthography will influence the kind of coding he or she characteristically uses for word recognition. An excellent contrast to English, with its complex, deep orthographic relation to the surface phonetics of speech, is Serbo-Croatian, whose shallow orthography closely mirrors the surface phonetics. Because we found some evidence of syllabic coding with American children but none with American adults, an opportunity for a strong test of our hypothesis was given by observing Yugoslavian adults.

There were 55 subjects, 1st- and 2nd-year psychology students at the University of Belgrade, who participated as a requirement of the introductory psychology course. They had participated in previous lexical decision and naming studies. As in our American study, we presented stimulus items, words and pseudowords, that were either regularly syllabified or irregularly divided. Here, however, syllable regularity was made a between-groups factor. In addition, the regular and irregular divisions were signaled in one of two different ways. The first way was to use the same technique we had used with the American studies—that is, a slash between two letters, the slash taking up one character space. The two groups were called slash regular (for regular syllabification, at a syllable boundary) and slash irregular (for irregular division of the item, off a syllable boundary). As with the American studies, we expected that disruption of the integrity of a syllable should slow lexical devision; if syllable coding is used, then the slash-irregular group should be slower than slash regular.

The second technique to manipulate syllabification took advantage of a unique characteristic of Serbo-Croatian—namely, that it has two rather distinct alphabets. Our subjects, like most Yugoslavs, had learned both kinds of script. They were facile in both and would switch from one to the other frequently during a normal academic day. With this second technique, syllabification was signaled by spelling part of the item in one alphabet and part in the other alphabet. There were two such groups; in one, the integrity of the syllable was maintained by keeping the letters within a given syllable homogeneous but varying the script between syllables. This group was called the alphabet-transition-regular group, because the transition from one script to the other was regular; that is, it occurred at a syllable boundary. In the other group, the integrity of one of the syllables in each item was broken by switching from one script to the other, off a syllable boundary at a point corresponding to the irregular slash for that word in the slash-irregular condition (alphabet-transition-irregular group).

Our motivation for including an alphabet-change manipulation was to remove or reduce the possibility of word-specific coding. A roughly analogous technique in English would be to switch from uppercase to lowercase letters (or vice versa). By making nonphonological visual coding more difficult, we intended to increase the likelihood of phoneme or syllable coding. If syllable coding was enhanced, we would expect to find an effect of syllable disruption that was stronger than that for the two slash groups. On the other hand, if phoneme coding was increased but not syllable coding, we would find an effect of syllable disruption equal to or smaller than that for the slash groups. Along with these four experimental groups, a fifth group was run in which the items contained no slash or alphabet transition; these words and pseudowords were printed normally, and the group was labeled "pure."

The two scripts of Serbo-Croatian are a Roman alphabet, rather similar to the English alphabet and a Cyrillic alphabet. Both scripts are ciphers on each other; that is, they address the same phonemes in Serbo-Croatian. The two scripts have some alphabetic characters in common. Of these, the so-called common letters represent the same phoneme in both scripts (e.g., *k, t, a, e, o,* and others). There are also the so-called ambiguous letters, which represent different phonemes in the two scripts (e.g., the letter *c,* which has the sound of *ts* in Roman and *s* in Cyrillic). These placed restrictions on stimulus construction. Clearly, common and ambiguous letters could not be used to signal alphabet transitions; only unique letters could be used at a boundary. In addition, items whose syllables were morphemes were avoided.

Each group contained the same 32 items, half words and half pseudowords. The 16 words were all common nouns. Eight of them contained two syllables, and 8 contained three syllables. Each of the 16 pseudowords was constructed by changing one vowel and one consonant from the middle portion of a word. For the pure, slash-regular, and slash-irregular groups, half of each set of 16 stimuli were printed in Roman and the other half in Cyrillic. For the two alphabet-transition groups, half the items began with Cyrillic and switched to Roman, whereas for the other half, the reverse was true. For the two irregular groups (slash irregular and alphabet transition irregular), half the irregular divisions occurred one letter to the left of the correct (regular) syllable division, and half occurred one letter to the right of the correct division. Thus, half the time a left-to-right scan produced an entire syllable plus one letter before a division, and half the time this scan produced only part of a syllable.

To summarize the design: There were four groups of 11 subjects each that constituted the factorial combination of Syllable Regularity (regular/irregular) and Form of Syllabification (slash/alphabet transition). Within each group, there were 16 words and 16 pseudowords each consisting of 8 two-syllable and 8 three-syllable items. In addition, there was a group of 11 subjects who received the same stimuli as the slash group, but without any divisions within each item (the pure group).

Stimuli were presented on a Scientific Prototype three-channel tachistoscope. Subjects responded by tapping, with both hands, one of two telegraph keys; the farther key signaled yes and the nearer one, no. Ten practice items were run with questions on the procedure permitted after each. Then two dummy trials were run, 1 word and 1 pseudoword, which were designed to give data on a subject's general response speed; these data were used later as control data for an analysis of covariance. The run of 32 experimental items followed the dummy trials without a break.

Because it was possible to run only small numbers of subjects and trials, the major analysis was an analysis of covariance that attempted to compensate for the low power by removing variability due to differences among subjects in general response speed. Before presenting the analysis of covariance, however, we first present the unadjusted means for the five conditions (Table 4.4). In particular,

TABLE 4.4
Unadjusted Latencies: Means and Percentage Error (in Parentheses) in Each Item Type Condition for Words, Pseudowords, and Response Speed Control

Form of Syllabification	Slash		Alphabet Transition		
	Regular	Irregular	Regular	Irregular	Pure
Example	kon/zul	konz/ul	konзy∧	konzy∧	konzul
Control	591 (0)	599 (1)	644 (1)	657 (2)	607 (0)
Pseudowords	709 (3)	789 (6)	773 (4)	777 (5)	736 (6)
Words	625 (6)	691 (2)	624 (6)	623 (5)	612 (0)

the data of interest are the response speed control latencies, each of which is the mean of the two dummy trials. Inspection of Table 4.4 indicates that control latencies were nearly equal for the regular and irregular groups within each Form of Syllabification, suggesting that an analysis of covariance on this factor would be easily interpretable. Furthermore, although the response control latencies for the two alphabet-transition groups appear to be slower than those for the two slash groups by about 50 msec, an F test run on the response speed control latencies failed to produce a significant difference, and in fact, its mean square was small. Therefore, it seemed reasonable to proceed with an analysis of covariance.

Table 4.5 presents the adjusted mean latencies for the four groups of the factorial design. Inspection of Table 4.5 suggests that the slash-irregular group was slower than the other three, which were approximately equal to one another. In addition, there are large differences between words and pseudowords, with the larger differences occurring for the two alphabet-transition groups. An analysis of covariance confirmed these suggestions; Syllable Regularity $\times$ Form of Syllabification was significant, $F(1,39) = 4.58$, $MS_e = 25613$, $p = .039$. In addition, Word/Pseudoword $\times$ Form of Syllabification was significant, $F(1,40) = 12.72$, $MS_e = 6854$, $p < .001$. There is a larger word/pseudoword difference for the alphabet-transition groups than for the slash groups. Not shown in Table 4.5 is a significant effect of the number of syllables. Two-syllable words and nonwords had a mean latency of 684 msec, and three-syllable items had a mean latency of 721 msec, $F(1,40) = 23.61$, $MS_e = 4988$, $p < .001$. The significant effect of two versus three syllables cannot be interpreted as unequivocal evidence in favor of phonological processing, however, because number of syllables was confounded with number of letters (5.9 and 6.9 letters). Finally, t tests comparing the pure group against the other four showed no differences with the two alphabet-transition groups and with the slash-regular group on either unadjusted or adjusted latencies. Comparisons between the pure group and the slash-irregular group gave marginally nonsignificant results for unadjusted latencies, $t(20) = 1.85$, $p = .08$, and for adjusted latencies, $t(20) = 1.99$, $p = .06$.

TABLE 4.5
Mean Adjusted Reaction Times in Milliseconds for Regularly and
Irregularly Syllabified Words and Pseudowords in Each Condition

Form of Syllabification	Slash		Alphabet Transition	
	Regular	Irregular	Regular	Irregular
Example	kon/zul	konz/ul	konɜy∧	konzy∧
Pseudowords	730	805	756	751
Words	646	708	608	597

The results for the two slash groups indicated that the disruption of the natural syllabification of an item slows lexical search for both words and nonwords. Thus, there is the suggestion that a syllable code is used by adult readers of Serbo-Croatian as one of the codes for word recognition. However, the lack of such an effect for the two alphabet-transition groups appears, at first glance, to run counter to the syllable code hypotheses. An explanation of the difference between the two forms of signaling syllabification may lie in a discussion of the character of the input to a hypothetical syllable-coding device.

We suggested earlier that phonological syllable codes found in reading can be formed in at least two distinct ways—by a transform that takes as its input phonologically coded information (e.g., phonemes and associated phototactic rules) or by a transform whose input is visually coded nonphonological information (e.g., a spatially defined pattern of supraletter macrofeatures). Our results suggest that the latter process was operative for our subjects. Of the several explanations of the results that we can think of, all have in common the conjecture that syllabic information is normally derived from print by a device that is tuned to visually coded patterns corresponding to syllables. When the pattern of print in a word is visually heterogeneous (as in the alphabet-transition groups in the present study or in the mixed-case conditions often used in English studies), visual coding is apparently disturbed, and, therefore, so is syllable coding.

For the alphabetic-transition groups, subjects apparently did not attempt to use visual codes beyond the transform that carries letters into phonemes. Note that this is still an efficient code for Serbo-Croatian. Indeed, it seems to have degraded the recognition of real words very little, although pseudoword latencies were slowed (cf. the significant Word/Pseudoword × Form of Syllabification term). The absence of degradation for words suggests further that phoneme and syllable codes operate in parallel and that when the syllable code is not used, there is enough spare capacity in the phoneme processor to take on additional activity.

The notion that phonological coding is characteristic of lexical access in Serbo-Croatian receives support from a series of experiments reported by G. Lukatela and his associates (Lukatela, Savić, Gligorijević, Ognjenović, & Turvey, 1978; Lukatela & Turvey, 1980). Subjects in a lexical decision task were presented with stimuli that were ostensibly printed only in the Roman alphabet. However, an occasional stimulus was presented that was printed only in common and ambiguous letters; these had a pronunciation if read in the Cyrillic alphabet as well as a pronunciation in the Roman alphabet. It was found that lexical decision latency to such a phonologically bivalent stimulus was slower than to a uniquely Roman stimulus—but only if it was a real word in at least one of the two alphabets. Phonologically bivalent stimuli that were pseudowords in both alphabets were rejected as quickly as pseudowords made of uniquely Roman letters. From these and other data, the authors concluded that phonological coding is characteristic of the reading of Serbo-Croatian words and that it is an automatic and extremely rapid process. In our experiment, the alphabet-transition groups were not significantly slower than the slash-regular and pure groups. There was little if any cost for processing the visually unfamiliar mixed-alphabet stimuli. This also supports the notion that phonological processing of both alphabets occurs automatically in our experiment.

SUMMARY

The major question that we asked was how a particular phonological code, syllable information, is used in printed word recognition. It was found that subjects used syllable information more when reading printed Serbo-Croatian, which represents speech by a shallow alphabetic orthography, than when reading English, whose orthography represents a deeper, morphophonological level of speech. The greater accessibility and efficiency in obtaining phonological information from printed Serbo-Croatian appears to make syllable coding a more viable process for Yugoslav readers. American fifth graders, in contrast to American adults, also used syllable coding for printed word recognition. This suggests that as reading ability matures, phonological coding is supplanted by nonphonological codes that are more efficient for English in terms of speed of accessing the mental lexicon.

ACKNOWLEDGMENTS

The authors are indebted to many people whose ideas and criticisms have been incorporated; in particular, there are our colleagues C. Fowler, M. Gurjanov, A. Liberman, I. Liberman, G. Lukatela, V. Mann, I. Mattingly, M. Savić, D. Shankweiler, and M. Turvey. We are grateful for special cooperation and assistance from J. Gawrys, V. Harding, and E. Yatroussis of the Tolland Public Schools and P. Ognjenović and D. Popodić of the University of Belgrade. Special thanks to B. Gligorijević and B. Lorenc. This research was supported in part by NIH Grants HD-08495 to the University of Belgrade and HD-01994 to Haskins Laboratories.

REFERENCES

Anderson, J. R. Arguments concerning representations for mental imagery. *Psychological Review,* 1978, *85,* 249–277.

Baddeley, A. Working memory and reading. In P. A. Kolers, M. E. Wrolstad and H. Bouma (Eds.). *The proceedings of the conference in the processing of Visual Language,* Eindhoven.

Carrol, J. B., Davies, P., & Richman, B. *Word frequency book.* New York: American Heritage, 1971.

Chomsky, N., & Halle, M. *The sound pattern of English.* New York: Harper & Row, 1968.

Cohen, J., & Cohen, P. *Applied multiple regression/correlation analysis for the behavioral sciences.* Hillsdale, N.J.: Lawrence Erlbaum Associates, 1975.

Conrad, R. Speech and reading. In J. F. Kavanaugh & I. G. Mattingly (Eds.), *Language by ear and by eye: The relationships between speech and reading.* Cambridge, Mass: M.I.T. Press, 1972.

Estes, W. K. (Eds.) *Handbook of Learning and Cognitive Processes: IV. Attention and Memory.* Hillsdale, N.J.: Lawrence Erlbaum, 1976.

Forster, K. I., & Chambers, S. M. Lexical access and naming time. *Journal of Verbal Learning and Verbal Behavior,* 1973, *12,* 627–635.

Frederiksen, J. R., & Kroll, J. F. Spelling and sound: Approaches to the internal lexicon. *Journal of Experimental Psychology: Human Perception and Performance,* 1976, *2,* 361–379.

Hansen, D., & Rodgers, T. S. An exploration of psycholinguistic units in initial reading. In *Proceedings of the Symposium on the Psycholinguistic Nature of the Reading Process.* Detroit: Wayne State University, 1965.

Henderson, L., Coltheart, M., & Woodhouse, D. Failure to find a syllable effect in number naming. *Memory & Cognition.* 1973, *1,* 304–306.

Hogaboam, T. W., & Perfetti, C. A. Reading skill and the role of verbal experience in decoding. *Journal of Educational Psychology,* 1978, *70,* 717–729.

Katz, L. Reading ability and single-letter orthographic redundancy. *Journal of Educational Psychology,* 1977, *69,* 653–659. (a)

Katz, L. *The word frequency effect and orthographic regularity.* Paper presented at the Psychonomic Society meetings, St. Louis, Mo. 1977. (b)

Kavanagh, J. F., & Venezky, R. L. (Eds.) *Orthography, Reading and Dyslexia,* Baltimore: University Park Press, 1980.

Kleiman, G. Speech recoding in reading. *Journal of Verbal Learning and Verbal Behavior,* 1975, *14,* 323–339.

LaBerge, D., & Samuels, S. J. Toward a theory of automatic information processing in reading. *Cognitive Psychology,* 1974, *6,* 293–323.

Levy, B. A. Reading: Speech and meaning processes. *Journal of Verbal Learning and Verbal Behavior,* 1977, *16,* 623–638.

Levy, B. A. Speech analysis during sentence processing: Reading and listening. *Visible Language,* 1978, *12,* 81–101.

Liberman, A. M., Ingemann, F., Lisker, L., Delattre, P., & Cooper, F. S. Minimal rules for synthesizing speech. *Journal of the Acoustical Society of America* , 1959, *31,* 1490–1499.

Liberman, I. Y., Liberman, A. M., Mattingly, I. G., & Shankweiler, D. *Orthography and the beginning reader.* J. F. Kavanagh, and R. L. Venezky (Eds.), *Orthography, Reading and Dyslexia,* Baltimore: University Park Press, 1980.

Lukatela, G., Savić, M., Gligorijević, B., Ognjenović, P., & Turvey, M. T. Bi-alphabetical lexical devision. *Language and Speech,* 1978, *21,* 142–165.

Lukatela, G., & Turvey, M. T. *Some experiments on the Roman and Cyrillic Alphabets.* J. B. Kavanagh & R. L. Venezky (Eds.), *Orthography Reading and Dyslexia.* Baltimore: University Park Press. 1980.

Mann, V., Liberman. I. Y., & Shankweiler, D. A. *Children's memory for sentences and word strings in relation to reading ability.* Memory and Cognition, 1980, *8,* 329–335.

Perfetti, C. A., & Lesgold, A. M. Discourse comprehension and sources of individual differences. In M. A. Just & P. A. Carpenter (Eds.), *Cognitive processes in comprehension.* Hillsdale, N.J.: Lawrence Erlbaum Associates, 1977.

Rumelhart, D. Toward an interactive model of reading. In S. Dornic (Ed.), *Attention and performance VI.* Hillsdale, N.J.: Lawrence Erlbaum Associates, 1977.

Shankweiler, D., Liberman, I. Y., Mark, L. S., Fowler, C. A., & Fischer, F. W. The speech code and learning to read. *Journal of Experimental Psychology: Human Learning and Memory,* 1980, *6,* 531–545.

Spoehr, K. T., & Smith, E. B. The role of syllables in perceptual processing. *Cognitive Psychology,* 1973, *5,* 71–89.

Vellutino, F. R. Alternative conceptualizations of dyslexia: Evidence in support of a verbal-deficit hypothesis. *Harvard Educational Review,* 1977, *47,* 334–354.

5 Inner Active Processes in Reading: The Inner Voice, the Inner Ear, and the Inner Eye

Alan Baddeley and Vivien Lewis
MRC Applied Psychology Unit
Cambridge, England

Our interest in reading has stemmed from an interest in memory, more particularly from an interest in working memory and in the types of memory code involved in the complex skill of reading. That being so, our approach to the central theme of this volume is likely to differ somewhat from that adopted in most of our colleagues' chapters.

Given two factors, both under the control of the experimenter, such as semantic context and stimulus clarity, it is relatively straightforward to ask the simple question of whether the two interact or have additive effects on performance. Provided one avoids floor and ceiling effects, a statistical interaction has interesting implications for any model of the reading process, although as Betty Ann Levy points out, such interpretations may be less straightforward than at one time seemed likely. If such an interaction is found, then it is clearly necessary to begin to postulate models that attempt to account as precisely as possible for the interacting processes. Unfortunately, although the concept of working memory implies interaction between a range of subcomponents of the system, we do not yet know enough about these to look at the interactive processes involved. We therefore examine the evidence for a range of types of memory encoding that may be involved in reading, but we are not in a position to speculate particularly fruitfully about the details of their interaction.

Our approach to the role of coding in reading has been based on the techniques and procedures that have been applied to the study of coding in short-term memory over the past decade. The initial focus of our interest was on the role of phonemic coding in reading. This seemed likely to prove an interesting bridging topic between the study of memory and the study of reading for two reasons; first, the role of phonemic coding in short-term and working memory has been studied intensively and with some degree of success. Second, the role of phonemic coding in fluent reading has been an important but puzzling problem in the reading literature for virtually the whole of this century. The present chapter describes a series of experiments attempting to confront the reading problem with the concepts and techniques derived from the memory laboratory in the hope of throwing light on both reading and memory. It is necessary, however, to begin with a brief outline of the role of phonemic coding in working memory.

In studying the immediate serial recall of strings of consonants, Conrad (1964) observed that intrusion errors tended to be phonemically similar to the correct item; hence, the letter *B* was more likely to be misrecalled as *P* than as *F*, whereas the letter *S* was more likely to be misrecalled as *F* than as the phonemically dissimilar better *B* This was not due to mishearing, since the effect occurred with visual presentation. Conrad and Hull (1964) went on to show that sequences of letters with similar-sounding names such as *B G T P C* were less likely to be correctly recalled than a string of dissimilar letters such as *K Q L R Y*. Wickelgren (1965) showed that this effect was largely due to the subject's difficulty in recalling the order of the items correctly. Using sequences of words, it was shown (Baddeley, 1966b) that the effect was crucially dependent on phonemic similarity; strings of words that were similar in sound (*man, map, can, mad, cap*) were hard to remember, whereas sequences that were similar in meaning (*great, huge, large, big, long*) did not present any very great problems for immediate recall. Sequences of words that looked similar but were different in sound (*rough, dough, bough, cough, through*) were also easy to recall. The situation changed dramatically when the paradigm was switched from one of immediate recall of strings of 5 words to the delayed recall and long-term learning of sequences of 10 words. Under these conditions, phonemic similarity ceased to be important, and similarity of meaning became crucial (Baddeley, 1966a).

The evidence cited so far is all based on similarity, either similarity between intrusions and the items they supplant, or similarity as a factor that impairs recall of the order of the presented items. The second class of evidence for the role of some form of speech coding in memory came from suppression techniques in which a secondary task is used to inhibit speech coding. In the case of phonemic coding, the standard means of disruption is the technique of articulatory suppression. This requires the subject to articulate some item or items rapidly and repeatedly, normally at a level quiet enough to avoid any substantial auditory masking but clear enough to allow the experimenter to monitor the subject's behavior. To minimize any memory load effects, subjects are usually required to recite either a single item, such as the word *the,* or else to repeat some highly overlearned sequence, such as *one two three four five six.* Suppression has been shown to impair digit span and, more importantly, to interact with the phonemic similarity effect (Levy, 1971; Murray, 1968; Peterson & Johnson, 1971). More specifically, provided material is presented visually, subjects undergoing articulatory suppression fail to show a phonemic similarity effect.

Baddeley and Hitch (1974) suggested that the phonemic similarity and suppression effects both reflected the operation of a subcomponent of working memory that they termed the *articulatory loop*. They suggested that this was not synonymous with short-term memory, but comprised a subcomponent or slave system of working memory that can maintain phonemically encodable material through subvocal rehearsal. They supported their claim by reference to the word length effect, a tendency for memory span to decrease as the length of the words to be remembered increases (Baddeley, Thomson, & Buchanan, 1975). The word length effect has been shown to depend on the physical spoken duration of the constituent words, not on the number of phonemes; hence a sequence of disyllabic words that can be spoken relatively quickly (e.g., *bishop, cricket*) is better recalled than a sequence of words that take longer to articulate (e.g., *Friday, cyclone*), suggesting that the articulatory loop is a time-based system. The system appears to be capable of holding approximately 2 seconds' worth of speech. Subsequently, Nicholson (in press) has shown that the developmental change in digit span can be predicted from the change in the rate at which children can rehearse, while Ellis and Hennelly (1980) have shown that the lower digit span found in Welsh-speaking schoolchildren can be attributed to the greater spoken duration of Welsh digits. As is the case for phonemic similarity, the word length effect can be abolished if the material is presented visually and the subject prevented from articulating (Baddeley, Thomson, & Buchanan, 1975). The concept of an articulatory loop therefore appears to give a very coherent account of the role of phonemic coding in short-term memory.

Both historically and developmentally, speech precedes reading. In both cases, the early stages of reading were and are associated with speaking, with reading aloud preceding silent reading. A classic question in reading research has been the issue of whether some form of phonemic coding continues to be important in fluent adult reading. We do not review the evidence for and against this view here since there are several recent reviews (Baddeley, 1979; Baron, 1976; Levy, 1978a, 1978b). In general, the evidence remains equivocal; phonemic coding does appear to be important in certain tasks of which reading is a component (e.g., Levy, 1975), but it does not appear to be essential for all aspects of reading (Baddeley, 1979). The remainder of the present chapter is concerned with taking the techniques and concepts developed to study the role of phonemic coding in working memory and applying them to a study of reading tasks. The first section is concerned with the role of phonemic similarity in reading; the second, with articulatory suppression; a third section studies the effect of combining these two operations.

RUDE JUDE PURSUED: PHONEMIC SIMILARITY AND READING

Baddeley and Hitch (1974) attempted to study the role of phonemic similarity in reading by presenting their subjects with sentences largely comprising phonemically similar words, then comparing the speed and accuracy with which subjects processed such sentences with their performance on dissimilar control sentences. It was argued that if comprehension depended on some form of phonemically encoded representation of the sentence, then the similarity among the words should impair performance, just as it did in the case of immediate memory span. The subject's task was to read sentences such as *Rude Jude chewed his crude stewed food,* or semantically equivalent but phonemically dissimilar control sentences such as *Rough curt Jude ate his plain boiled meal.* Subjects were required to decide whether each sentence was or was not correct. Incorrect sentences were produced by transposing the order of two adjacent words. Subjects were consistently slower at processing the similar sentences, although this effect was unfortunately not consistent across all the sentences sampled. In view of this, we decided that we should replicate the effect before drawing any conclusions.

Rude Jude Replication 1

This was based on the original study by Baddeley and Hitch (1974), but used a larger and more carefully constructed set of sentences, of which examples are shown in Table 5.1. The study included two types of anomalous sentence. The first simply involved permuting the order of two words, whereas the second type of anomalous sentence was obtained by substituting for the target word a semantically anomalous word. Since we have previously suggested that the articulatory loop is particularly concerned with processing order information, it seemed possible that phonemic similarity might impair detection of anomalies of word *order* while leaving the subject able to detect semantic anomalies.

A total of 17 members of the Applies Psychology Unit (A.P.U.) subject panel classified 80 sentences. These comprised 40 semantically appropriate sentences, 20 sentences with anomalous word order, and 20 with anomalous word substitution. The items were presented in a different random order for each subject by means of the "mousetrap." This is a device in which each stimulus is typed on

TABLE 5.1
Illustration of the Material Used in the First Rude Jude Replication Study

	Similar	*Dissimilar*
Appropriate	Crude rude Jude chewed his stewed food.	Rough curt Jude ate his boiled meal.
Word Order Anomaly	Crude rude chewed Jude his stewed food.	Rough curt ate Jude his boiled meal.
Word Substitution Anomaly	Crude rude Jude queued his stewed food.	Rough curt Jude lined his boiled meal.

Examples of Other Appropriate Similar Sentences

The sad mad lad had a bad dad.
I poked the bloke who woke, spoke, and joked.
Vain Jane strains with pain in the rain.
We dine at nine with fine wine from the vine that is mine.
Slow Joe's nose glows like a red rose.

TABLE 5.2
Results of the First Rude Jude Replication Study:
Effect of Similarity on Speed of Verification

| | Speed of Verification (Secs) | | |
| | Possible | Impossible | |
		Substitution	Transposition
Similar	2.79	2.86	2.35
Dissimilar	2.62	2.68	2.23
Similarity Effect	.17	.18	.12

an index card that is stacked behind a shutter. When the subject indicates that he is ready, the shutter is raised, starting a timer. The subject then presses one of two buttons—left if she thinks the sentence is semantically permissible, and the right if not. This drops the shutter and stops the timer. The experimenter then records the time and removes the card, thereby setting up the next card.

The mean classification time for the three conditions is shown in Table 5.2. Analysis of variance showed a significant effect of similarity whether the data are analyzed by subject, $F (1, 16) = 30.4$, $p < .001$, or by sentence, $F (1, 19) = 12.0$, $p < .01$. Subjects were reliably faster at detecting transposition errors than they were at detecting impossible substitutions or classifying sentences as semantically acceptable. There was a mean overall error rate of 14.5%, but this was not significantly affected by similarity. There was a small tendency for subjects to make more errors on the false items than on the true items when performance was analyzed by subjects, although this did not reach significance when analyzed across sentences.

Although we were gratified to have replicated our main result and to have obtained an effect that held across sentences as well as subjects, we were slightly surprised to observe no interaction between the type of sentence and similarity. More specifically, we had expected to find the largest effect for transpositions and little or no effect in the case of substitution. It seemed possible, however, that the presence of some sentences in which word order was crucial may have forced subjects to adopt a strategy emphasizing order information for all sentences. We therefore decided to carry out a further experiment in which the anomalous sentences were all based on the substitution of inappropriate words, excluding the class of sentence where order information provides the only clue to anomaly.

Rude Jude Replication 2

In this study 10 additional subjects classified a total of 20 semantically permissible and 20 anomalous sentences. Again the order of presentation of sentences

TABLE 5.3
Results of the
Second Rude Jude
Replication Study

	Verification Time (Secs)	
	Possible	Impossible Substitution
Similar	2.54	2.81
Dissimilar	2.50	2.61
Similarity Effect	.04	.20

was random; and half the sentences again contained a large number of phonemically similar words, whereas half were semantically equivalent but phonemically dissimilar sentences. The results are shown in Table 5.3. Although there was an overall tendency for similarity to slow down performance when analyzed across subjects, F (1, 9) = 16.6, $p < .01$, on this occasion we observed a significant interaction between similarity and sentence type, F (1, 9) = 7.5, $p < .05$, which, as Table 5.3 shows, reflects the absence of the similarity effect in the case of semantically permissible sentences. When analyzed across sentences, however, neither the interaction ($F < 1$) nor the main similarity effect, F (1, 9 = 3.9, .05 < p < .10), was significant.

Similarity again had no effect on errors, whether analyzed across subjects or sentences ($F < 1$ in each case). There was, however, a significant tendency for subjects to make more errors on the semantically anomalous sentences than on the permissible ones—by subjects, F (1, 9) = 13.3, $p < .01$; by sentences, F (1, 19) = 10.1, $p < .05$.

In conclusion, it appears that our similarity effect is not dependent on requiring the subject to detect order errors. There were, however, some worrying features to our results; once again the effect is significant for subjects but not for sentences. Furthermore, we found no trace of an effect of similarity on errors. This is puzzling since the phonological similarity effect in short-term memory shows up primarily in errors that stem from difficulty in maintaining order information (Wickelgren, 1965). We return to this point after exploring further the effect of articulatory suppression on reading.

ARTICULATORY SUPPRESSION AND READING

There is an extensive literature on the effect of interfering with articulation on various reading tasks. The resulting evidence is far from clear. There is no doubt that articulatory suppression will impair performance if the reading task also requires the subject to remember the literal wording of the material read (Levy,

1975). However, since there is clear evidence that recall itself can be impaired by suppression, it is highly questionable that these results can be interpreted as reflecting the process of reading per se. For that reason, we ourselves have opted to study the effect of suppression on reading using only tasks that have no overt memory demand over and above that necessary to comprehend the material. This seems to be a necessary condition if one wishes to make claims about the role of articulation in reading rather than memory.

Previous evidence in this area is somewhat equivocal. We ourselves found that our subjects could decide on the truth of simple sentences such as *Canaries have wings* and *Canaries have gills* while suppressing, showing no increase in processing time or errors (Baddeley, 1979). However, Kleiman (1975) found that a concurrent digit-shadowing task did impair the performance of his subjects on a task involving evaluating rather more complex sentences and a task involving rhyme judgments. Furthermore, in a study using electromyography and attempting to train subjects to read without articulation, Hardyk and Petrinovitch (1970) found that their subjects could read simple prose without laryngeal electromyographic activity but that with difficult material, evidence of subvocalization always occurred. We therefore decided to extent our study of articulatory suppression to rather more complex material than the evaluation of the simple statements we had previously used.

Articulatory Suppression and the Detection of Anomaly

Subjects were presented with a total of 96 sentences of which 64 were semantically meaningful whereas 32 contained an anomalous word. The semantically anomalous word was, in fact, related to the word it supplanted in one of several ways, being either visually similar, phonemically similar, both visually and phonemically similar, or dissimilar on both counts. Unfortunately, it proved very difficult to generate sets that balanced the various types of similarity in an entirely satisfactory way, particularly since visual and phonemic similarity tend to be closely associated; and for that reason we do not discuss the effects of similarity further.

The sentences were considerably more complex than those used in the previous study. Examples are: *She doesn't mind going to the dentist to have fillings, but doesn't like the pain [rent] when he gives her the injection at the beginning* and *After the football match, the goalkeeper had some pain [rain] in his left leg which he got from being hit hard by the center forward.* The words in brackets are examples of the semantically anomalous word substituted for the preceding word in order to make the sentence in question anomalous. A test sequence comprised 32 anomalous sentences; 32 control sentences, which were created using the same criteria and served as the basis for anomalous sentences for other subjects; and 32 filler sentences. The filler sentences were included to reduce the overall probability of anomaly, thereby making the task, it was hoped, somewhat more like normal reading. All subjects verified half the sentences under control conditions and half under articulatory suppression; this involved the subject in repeatedly counting from 1 to 6, with the sentence being exposed halfway through each subject's first counting sequence. Subjects were monitored and encouraged to keep their rate of counting at about four digits per second. A total of 32 members of the A.P.U. subject panel were tested, half beginning with the suppression and half with the control condition.

Figures 5.1 and 5.2 show the effect of articulatory suppression on the speed and accuracy of sentence verification. We found a clear effect of articulatory suppression whether analyzed across subjects, F (1, 31) = 17.43, p < .001, or across sentences, F (1, 31) = 27.87, p < .001. As Table 5.4 shows, there is also a significant effect of whether the sentence was semantically permissible or not (for subjects, F (1, 31) = 31.54; for sentences, F (1, 31) = 16.26; p < .001 in each case). In addition, however, there is a highly significant interaction between suppression and semantic anomaly (for subjects, F (1, 31) = 17.74; for sentences, F (1, 31) = 19.09; p < .001 in each case). A Newman Keuls test suggested that the interaction was largely due to a very high error rate when

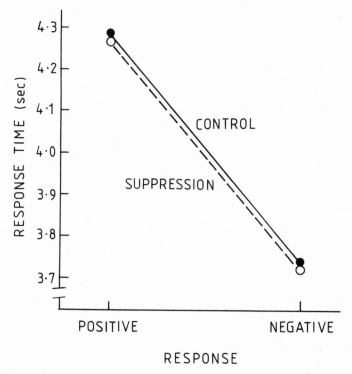

FIG. 5.1. The influence of articulatory suppression on the speed of classifying sentences as meaningful (positive) or meaningless (negative).

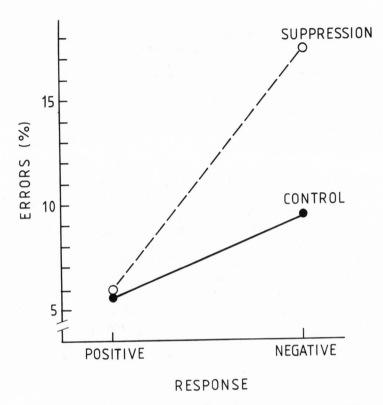

FIG. 5.2.   The influence of articulatory suppression on the accuracy of classifying sentences as meaningful (positive) or meaningless (negative).

subjects are required to read semantically anomalous sentences while suppressing, this condition leading to significantly higher error rates than the other three, which do not differ among themselves.

SUPPRESSION AND PHONEMIC SIMILARITY COMBINED

The experiments we have described so far could be accounted for by making the simple and plausible assumption that phonemic coding is necessary for verifying complex but not simple sentences. There remained, however, a number of worrying secondary features to our results. Why, for example, does the phonemic similarity effect produce an impairment in speed while having no effect on errors, in contrast to articulatory suppression, which appears to leave speed unaffected while causing a clear decrease in accuracy? We were also worried by the failure of the phonemic similarity effect to be consistently significant when

TABLE 5.4
Effect of Articulatory Suppression on the
Accuracy of Sentence Verification
(Percentage Errors)

	Sentence Type	
	Permissible	Anomalous
Control	5.47	8.20
Suppression	5.86	17.48

tested across sentences, although it came through clearly enough when tested on a subject basis. We decided therefore to explore the situation further by testing the stronger prediction from the short-term memory analogy—namely, that the phonemic similarity effect should disappear when combined with articulatory suppression.

Our next experiment was therefore based on our first Rude Jude replication study, with the exception that the additional variable of articulatory suppression was introduced. The same 20 sentences were used in both the similar and dissimilar form, and both transposition and substitution errors were inserted. Of the 16 A.P.U. panel members tested, 8 began with the control condition and then performed the task under articulatory suppression, which once again involved counting repeatedly from 1 to 6; the remaining 8 subjects performed in the opposite order.

The effects of similarity on verification time for the various types of sentence are shown in Table 5.5. When analyzed across subjects, there proved to be a significant effect of similarity, F (1, 15) + 8.87, $p < .01$, although the effect interacted with type of sentence, F (2, 30) = 4.75, $p < .05$. Somewhat paradoxically, the effect appears to be greater for the semantically acceptable sentences than for either of the anomalous sentences, exactly the opposite pattern to that obtained in a previous experiment. When analyzed across sentences, however, the similarity effect failed to reach significance, F (1, 19) = 3.37, $p < .05$. There was no effect of articulatory suppression on processing speed; indeed, there was a nonsignificant tendency for subjects to process faster while suppressing.

The distribution of errors for the various conditions is shown in Table 5.6. There is no effect of similarity on error rate ($F < 1$) for both subjects and sentences. There is a clear tendency for suppression to increase error rate whether measured across subjects, F (1, 15) = 21.5, $p < .001$, or across sentences, F (1, 19) = 25.0, $p < .001$. In addition, there is a highly significant effect of sentence type (across subjects, F (2, 30) = 21.1, $p < .01$; across sentences, F (2, 38) = 17.7, $p < .001$), and this in turn interacts with suppression (across subjects, F (2, 30) = 5.04, $p < .05$; across sentences, F (2, 38) = 6.94, $p < .01$). As is clear from Table 5.6, the effect occurs because the transpositions are harder to detect than substitutions or true sentences and, furthermore, are much more

TABLE 5.5
The Effect of Phonemic Similarity and Articulatory Suppression
on Speed of Sentence Verification (Secs per Sentence)

| | Similarity | | |
| | Possible | Impossible | |
		Substitution	Transposition
Similar	2.78	2.69	2.57
Dissimilar	2.63	2.68	2.46
Similarity Effect	.15	.01	.11

| | Suppression | | |
| | Possible | Impossible | |
		Substitution	Transposition
Control	2.75	2.77	2.52
Suppression	2.66	2.59	2.51
Suppression Effect	.09	.18	.01

subject to disruption by articulatory suppression. Indeed, a number of subjects were virtually at chance level when attempting to detect transpositions under suppression.

The pattern of errors obtained under conditions of suppression are very much what one might expect on the assumption that the articulatory loop is involved in verifying these more complex sentences. Order information is particularly vul-

TABLE 5.6
The Effect of Phonemic Similarity and Articulatory Suppression
on Mean Percentage of Errors in Sentence Verification

| | Similarity | | |
| | Possible | Impossible | |
		Substitution	Transposition
Similar	9.4	14.1	23.8
Dissimilar	5.3	10.9	27.8
Similarity Effect	4.1	3.2	−4.0

| | Suppression | | |
| | Possible | Impossible | |
		Substitution	Transposition
Control	5.0	9.4	15.9
Suppression	9.7	15.9	35.6
Suppression Effect	4.7	6.5	19.7

nerable, just as one might expect from the short-term memory literature. In short, we are producing clear evidence for an effect of articulatory suppression on performance. Note first, however, that the effect is on errors only; preventing subjects from using the articulatory loop may make them less accurate, but it certainly does not slow them down. The second feature of interest is that the effects of articulatory suppression are completely at variance with those of similarity. The similarity effect has no effect on errors and shows no evidence at all of the predicted interaction with suppression. In view of the consistency and magnitude of this interaction in the short-term memory literature (Levy, 1971; Murray, 1968; Peterson & Johnson, 1971), the absence of such an interaction is striking. It clearly suggests that the similarity effect in comprehension cannot be attributed to the articulatory loop. How then should it be explained?

There is one variable that we have consistently confounded with phonemic similarity—namely, visual similarity. Words that sound alike are typically spelled in a similar way. This did not worry us during the earlier experiments, since we were extending the data observed in short-term memory, where it has been shown (Baddeley, 1966b) that in contrast to the massive effects of phonemic similarity, visual similarity has little effect on performance. However, given that the STM analogy is clearly not appropriate, visual similarity returns as a potentially important factor, particularly in a task that is as visually dependent as reading. We therefore decided to check this, measuring the visual similarity of the words in a sentence by counting the number of shared letter pairs. Hence a phonologically similar sentence like *The lone crone was shown the phone thrown on the stone* would have a relatively high score of 28 repeated digrams, whereas a sentence like *I sigh and cry as the sly guy dies* would have a relatively low score. In order to obtain as reliable a measure as possible of the mean verification time for each sentence, we took the average of the scores obtained over the three replications and correlated this with mean digram score for both similar and dissimilar sentences. The resulting distribution is shown in Fig. 5.3, from which it is clear that there is a substantial correlation between mean verification time and the digram measure of visual similarity ($r = .60$, $p < .001$).

Although one might expect an artifactual correlation due to the confounding of phonemic and visual similarity, closer examination of Fig. 5.3 suggests that this is not the reason for the relationship. Consider the middle values of similarity, for which there is a reasonable amount of overlap with both phonologically similar and dissimilar sentences represented. Within this band, if phonemic similarity is the important factor, then one should notice that for any given level of visual similarity, those items that are more phonologically similar should be processed consistently more slowly. If anything, however, the tendency is in the opposite direction. On the evidence presently available, then, we were clearly premature in ruling out visual similarity as an important variable. It may well be the failure to take this factor into account that has led to our recurrent difficulty in obtaining similarity effects that are consistent across sentences; although all the

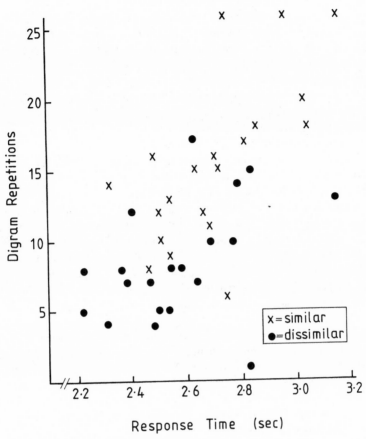

FIG. 5.3.   The mean time to verify phonemically similar and dissimilar sentences as a function of visual similarity. Visual similarity is measured in terms of the number of repeated letter digrams.

phonemically similar sentences are clearly distinct from the control sentences in degree of phonemic similarity, differences in visual similarity are far less consistent.

Suppose we did accept the suggestion that visual similarity is an important factor in reading; would this imply the operation of an internal visual code? It seems likely that some form of internal visual representation does mediate between the printed word and comprehension in reading. Rayner (1975) and McConkie (1979) have postulated an *integrative visual buffer* that takes visual information from successive fixations and integrates them during reading. McConkie (1979) describes one study in which the subject reads text printed in alternating upper- and lowercase letters (e.g., *It ApPeArS tHaT pItCh NaMiNg AbIlIt Y cAn Be*). The subject's eye movements were monitored, and on each saccade the display was changed so that each upper case letter became lowercase (e.g., *iT aPpEaRs ThAt PiTcH nAmInG aBiLiTy CaN bE*). Not only were the subjects quite able to read under these conditions; they did not even notice the change. This seems to suggest that the information was being stored at some level that was more abstract than that of the simple visual representation of the letter, since this would surely be disrupted by the continual change. McConkie argues against a semantic representation on the basis of Rayner's (1975) demonstration of comparable integration effect across fixations that appeared to occur when semantic information had not yet been obtained.

Evidence for some form of visual input store for words has also been produced by Morton (1979), who postulates separate visual input, auditory input, and output logogen systems. The basis for this assumption is a series of experiments following the demonstration by Winnick and Daniel (1970) that the reading of a word may be facilitated by previously presenting that word in written form, whereas no such facilitation occurs when a picture or definition of the word is given, despite the fact that in both cases the subjects themselves produce the word. As in the McConkie demonstration, the effect appears to occur at an abstract visual level, since the reading of a typewritten word was facilitated just as much by a previous presentation of that word in cursive script as it was by the presentation of a visually identical typewritten version.

It is tempting to attribute the similarity effects observed in the Rude Jude experiments to the operation of an integrative visual buffer, but on available evidence, this would be premature. It is, for example, entirely possible that the Rude Jude effect may be visual but entirely due to the subject losing his or her place in the sequence. At present, then, we have evidence that the Rude Jude effect is not based on inner speech, but we are unable to rule out an interpretation in terms of auditory imagery.

The Inner Ear or the Inner Eye?

Although visual similarity offers one potential explanation of the Rude Jude effect, it is not the only one. In discussing the role of phonemic coding in reading, it has previously been suggested (Baddeley, 1979) that subvocalization may not be the only form of phonemic coding to accompany reading. From an introspective viewpoint, the internal monologue that often appears to accompany reading does not seem to depend on direct subvocalization and does appear to go on even during suppression. This putative phenomenon, which we shall term the "inner ear," does not seem to depend on articulation and may represent some form of auditory imagery. It seems obvious that some form of auditory imagery does exist, since we can imagine the sound of a creaking door or a symphony orchestra or the call of a sea gull—all sounds that we are not capable of articulating at all accurately. However, introspective evidence is notoriously unreliable, and we therefore decided to attempt to collect independent evidence that some form of phonemic coding can proceed during articulatory suppression.

Does the Inner Ear Depend on the Inner Voice?

The primary evidence supporting the introspectively plausible view that inner speech was possible without overt articulation came from two studies. The first of these was an experiment by Kleiman (1975) in which subjects were required to perform a number of tasks that involved reading material while shadowing an auditory sequence of digits. Kleiman observed that speed of making rhyme judgments was particularly hard hit by shadowing but that subjects were still performing quite accurately. However, since a demanding shadowing task was used, it is not always easy to separate the general information-processing demands of the task from the specifically articulatory component. An unpublished study by Folkard (1978), suggests that this is unlikely, since he observed that subjects were able to judge very accurately whether two words rhymed or not while suppressing with relatively little impairment in speed. We decided to explore this task further, first asking whether such phonological coding was dependent on lexical access. It seems possible, for example, that a subject will have an auditory image for a familiar word, but may well not be able to evoke such an image of an unfamiliar but pronounceable nonword.

Rhyme Judgment Experiments

In our first rhyme judgment experiment, subjects were given lists of 50 items—half of which sounded like real words when pronounced (e.g., *cayoss, yorn*), and half of which were not phonologically similar to real words (e.g., *bambil, trid*). The subject's task was to categorize each item as similar in sound to a real word or dissimilar, working as quickly and accurately as possible and making a tick mark by the similar items but putting a cross by those that were dissimilar to words. Sixteen female members of the A.P.U. subject panel attempted to process two such lists—one under control conditions, and the other while counting continually from 1 to 6. Half began with the control and half with the suppression condition. The mean reading time and error frequencies are shown in Table 5.7. It is clear from this that not only were subjects able to perform this task while suppressing, but they did so almost as quickly and accurately as under control conditions, the difference failing to reach significance for either speed or errors.

The first experiment required subjects to decide whether or not nonsense sequences were wordlike. Such a task clearly depends upon a phonological lexicon or at least on some form of long-term phonological representation. The next experiment explores the possibility that subjects can make rhyme judgments about pairs of nonwords that are unfamiliar and presumably are therefore not represented in a lexicon. Subjects were therefore required to decide whether pairs of nonwords would be phonologically identical if spoken. Once again, subjects were timed as they processed a list of 50 items—half of which were phonologically equivalent (*frelame—phrelaim, kerm—curm*), whereas half were phonologically different (*galinp—gallemp, dake—dagh*). The same 16 subjects

TABLE 5.7
Articulatory Suppression and the Phonemic
Categorization of Nonwords

Do the Following Sound Like Real Words?

CAYOSS
BOMBIL
TRID
YORN

	Control	*Suppression*
Mean time per item (sec)	1.88	2.02
Mean % errors	14.40	18.50

$C < S$ for 10 of the 16 subjects on each score.

performed the task, ticking the items they thought were identical in sound and putting a cross by the others. Half began with the suppression condition, and half began in the control condition. The results shown in Table 5.8 are essentially similar to those of the last study. There is no doubt that subjects can perform this task very efficiently while suppressing; the time taken to process items in the two conditions was virtually identical, although there is a marginally significant increase in errors under suppression, an effect shown by 11 of the 16 subjects ($.05 < p < .1$).

It is clear that subjects could not have been performing the previous experiment on the basis of lexical information, since only nonwords were involved. It is conceivable, however, that subjects may have been matching sequences on the basis of simple grapheme–phoneme rules. Although such a procedure seems a little unlikely, it is at least logically possible and would not necessarily involve any form of auditory or articulatory coding.

TABLE 5.8
Articulatory Suppression and Nonword Rhyme Judgments

Do the Following Nonwords
Rhyme?

FRELAME	PHRELAIM
GALINP	GALLEMP
KERM	CURM
DAKE	DAGH

	Control	*Suppression*
Mean time per item (sec)	2.34	2.34
Mean % errors	8.37	13.25

Of 16 subjects, 7 are faster on control and 11 more accurate (N.S.).

TABLE 5.9
Articulatory Suppression and Word–Nonword Rhyme Judgements

	Do the Following Pairs Rhyme?	
	DOZEN	DUSSEN
	OCEAN	OSHUN
	TROUBLE	TRAPPEL
	ACCENT	AKSEN

	Control	*Suppression*
Mean time per item (sec)	1.88	1.92
Mean % errors	6.37	6.62

Of the 16 subjects, 11 are faster on control and 8 more accurate.

In our third experiment we attempted to eliminate the possibility that subjects were simply matching sequences on the basis of highly overlearned rules by requiring judgments of phonological similarity between words that were largely irregular in grapheme–phoneme structure and nonwords that, although regular, would have no lexical representation. The same subjects were tested as previously, and this time they judged lists of 50 pairs of items—half of which consisted of phonologically similar word–nonword pairs (e.g., *dozen—dussen, ocean—oshun*), whereas half were phonologically distinct (*trouble—trappel, accent—aksen*). Table 5.9 shows the mean speed and accuracy of processing under control and suppression conditions. Once again, there is a very slight tendency for subjects to be slower and less accurate under suppression, but the effect does not approach significance.

We initiated the three experiments just described in order to reassure ourselves that it is possible to make rhyme judgments while suppressing and in order to attempt to gain some clue as to how the task is performed. In view of Kleiman's results, however, we expected to observe clear and consistent impairment in performance. Although our results do show a consistent trend in the direction of poor performance under suppression, the difference never reached an acceptable level of significance and suggests that the effect of preventing articulation is, at best, minimal. Furthermore, the constraints we expected to find while performing this task under suppression simply did not appear; subjects seem to be able to perform under suppression all the phonological tasks that they can perform under control conditions and, what is more, to perform them as quickly and almost as accurately. Introspection suggests that the task is performed by auditory imagery, the inner voice of subvocalization. If you are not convinced at this point, we suggest you try the following demonstration: Begin counting repeatedly from 1 to 6; while continuing to count, try to read the sentence in uppercase letters that follows; each of the words in the sentence has been replaced by a nonword that is phonologically roughly equivalent to the word replaced (e.g., *taybul* for *table*).

KANN YOO REDE ANDD KONPRIHENNED THISS CENTANS WYLE SERPRESING VOAKULYSAYSHUN?

Our experiments using articulatory suppression suggest that preventing subjects from subvocalizing may make them less likely to detect substitution or transposition errors in a text, even though they are alerted to the probability of such errors occurring. This implies that some form of articulatory coding may occur but does not, of course, imply that it normally does. Indeed, the ability of subjects to process material rapidly, and in the case of brief sentences such as *Canaries have wings,* accurately suggest that subvocalization may be unnecessary under less demanding conditions. While we were thinking about this particular problem, a new line of evidence presented itself.

It has in recent years become popular among some car owners to attach an adhesive, transparent sun visor to the top of their windshields. It is possible to have various names and slogans printed, and quite commonly, one will see two names—typically, a male name such as *Fred* over the driver's side, and a female name such as *Jean* over the passenger's seat. Presumably, this is a slightly less painful and permanent alternative to the more ancient custom of tatooing the name of one's beloved somewhere on one's anatomy. One of us was somewhat puzzled a little while ago to see a car with the single, rather un-British name of *Ersnmyne* in the center of the visor. It took some time to realize that the car did not belong to an egocentric alien, but was simply keeping its options open with a phonetic rendering of *Hers and Mine.* In order for such a representation to work, it is necessary to assume that reading an item is accompanied by a phonological representation that can then access the meaning. In this case it certainly did not, or at least not without several minutes of pondering. It did, however, suggest that one way of tackling the question of whether phonetic coding occurs during normal reading might be through a study of puns.

A pun is essentially a play on words whereby a single sentence or phrase can have two separate meanings. For the pun to work, of course, the listener must be able to perceive both meanings of the crucial word. The convention of punning demands that the two words be phonologically identical, or at least very similar, but not necessarily spelled in the same way. If, when a word is read, meaning is accessed via its auditory or articulatory image, then both written and spoken puns should be relatively insensitive to whether the two lexical items are spelled the same way. On the other hand, if an auditory or phonological code typically does not occur during reading, puns that rely on two lexical items that are pronounced the same but spelled differently should be much less likely to work when written than when spoken. An example is the old chestnut: "I just bought this budgie since it was going cheap"; reply: "But don't all budgies go cheep?" The difference is likely to be even greater when the pun extends over several words and requires a restructuring of the original lexical units. Consider this example from the BBC radio program "The Goon Show":

Enter Colonel Bloodknock who has just flown down from the Scottish Islands: "I'm from the Isle of Yew." Seagoon replies "I love you too—shall we dance?"

A similar case is the rather bad pun contained in the title of the present chapter; is it likely to be detected spontaneously in written form? Sometimes, perhaps, and since the pun on the title of this volume works better in an American than an English accent, will it be perceived more by American speakers than by English speakers? Or perhaps it will depend on the reader's acoustic image of how the writer would say it. Clearly, that particular experiment is hardly likely to be done in time to include the result in the present chapter, but it did seem worthwhile to ask the simple question of whether people who make written puns professionally are more likely to opt for visually identical puns than those who are professional makers of spoken puns or, for that matter, than amateur punsters. If some type of phonemic code inevitably accompanies reading, there is no reason to expect any difference in distribution between written and spoken puns. A clear indication that professional writers of puns avoid nonidentical puns, however, would suggest that readers cannot be relied on to generate and recognize a phonemic recoding of a written word.

For some reason best known to themselves, newspaper headline writers, at least in Britain, appear to be addicted to puns. We therefore combed the headlines of two national British newspapers—the *Daily Express,* a right-wing tabloid; and the *Guardian,* a rather more "intellectual" daily with views slightly left of center. We classified each pun as identical, which meant that the two separate lexical items indicated by one word were both spelled the same way; or nonidentical. Examples of the first type are *Light relief* (an *Express* article on lamps) and *Bakers who didn't use their loaf* (a *Guardian* article about a bakers' union bungle). Nonidentical examples included *No weigh to treat a lady* (an *Express* story about a lady skier who had been excluded from a team for being overweight) and *Snake in the bras trapped* (a *Guardian* item on a boa constrictor caught in a ladies' underwear factory).

An equivalent sample of spoken puns was collected by listening to radio and TV programs—in particular, comedy shows and panel games. In most cases, it was possible to record the actual pun; but occasionally there was a rapid burst of puns, and in these cases only the occurrence of the pun and whether it was visually identical or not were recorded.

Both these sources could be regarded as rather atypical of normal punning. It is, unfortunately, much more difficult to get a baseline for puns under less artificial conditions. A request to colleagues at the A.P.U. to note any puns they came across over a period of a week evoked a number of examples, many of which were rather hard to classify, and when these were excluded, one was left with about a dozen moderately clear examples, approximately equally distributed between identical and nonidentical. A much larger sample, however, was provided by the U.S. horror magazine *Famous Monsters,* which was organizing a

TABLE 5.10
Distribution of Identical and
Nonidentical Puns in
Different Media[a,b]

	Identical	Nonidentical
Newspapers	68	18
Radio & TV	25	37
Monster Panel	14	48

[a]$\chi^2 = 50.0$, $d.f. = 2$, $p < .001$.
[b]Excluding Monster Jokes: $\chi^2 = 23.3$, $d.f. = 1$, $p < .001$.

horror jokes competition and gathered a panel of five (D. R. Acular and four colleagues) to generate a large number of such "jokes." These largely consisted of puns and probably represent what will be produced if one consciously attempts to produce as many puns on a given topic as possible within a limited period of time. Table 5.10 shows the distribution of identical and nonidentical puns for newspaper headlines, radio and TV shows, and the horror joke set. Analysis of Table 5.10 using a chi-square test indicated significant differences between the three sources ($\chi^2 = 50.0$, $d.f. = 2$, $p < .001$). This is clearly due at least in part to the very skewed distribution of horror jokes, but when these are excluded, there is still a highly significant effect ($\chi^2 = 23.3$, $d.f. = 1$, $p < .001$). As predicted, newspaper headline writers tend to opt for puns in which the two lexical items both have the same spelling, whereas for the spoken puns, the trend is in the opposite direction. The much more extreme bias shown by the horror jokes indicates that provided one's criterion is sufficiently lax, there may be a larger range of possible nonidentical puns than there are identical ones. It seems likely, then, that our results reflect a self-imposed constraint by the headline writers, rather than a preference for nonidentical puns on TV and radio.

Observational evidence of this indirect nature can obviously not be regarded as conclusive. It does, however, present a new phenomenon that can readily be explained on the assumption that reading does not *necessarily* involve mediation by an auditory or articulatory representation.

DISCUSSION

The series of experiments described does not represent a completed piece of work, and we are not in a position to draw any unequivocal conclusions. However, it is perhaps worth commenting on the possible interpretations and remaining problems. Our concern has been primarily with the types of memory code that may be involved in reading. The question at issue can be divided into a number of subquestions. The first of these is whether a particular type of coding *can* be used in reading. If it can, then the question arises of whether it is essential and, if not essential, under what conditions it will be used and what the consequence of its not being used will be. Given that reading itself does not appear to be a simple unitary function, it seems very unlikely that the answer to these questions will be straightforward. We suspect that there is evidence for at least three types of short-term or buffer storage in the reading process—namely, articulatory coding (the inner voice), acoustic coding (the inner ear), and visual coding (the inner eye). We discuss these in turn.

It is clear that subjects can subvocalize when reading. There is, however, evidence that this is not necessary for accessing the meaning of individual words, short phrases and sentences (e.g., Baddeley, 1979), or, it would seem, newspaper headlines. There is clear evidence that when a substantial memory load is involved, however, subvocalization may be necessary for accurate performance (Levy, 1975). What is less clear is whether the comprehension of prose is likely to be impaired if articulation is not allowed. We ourselves begin with the assumption that articulation was probably not necessary, on the basis of our previous work on short sentences. We subsequently discovered that although subvocalization does not allow the subject to work any more rapidly, it does apparently allow him or her to process complex material more accurately. We do, however, still need to run a further control study to ensure that the observed decrement is due to preventing articulation and not simply a general secondary task effect. In our earlier studies where we were observing no effect of suppression, such a control was obviously not necessary; it has subsequently become necessary, and although we would be surprised if the equivalent effect occurred when a subject was required to perform a nonarticulatory secondary task such as tapping while reading, the results reported by Betty Ann Levy in Chapter 1 indicate that this is a precaution we must take before drawing firm conclusions.[1]

Our rhyme judgment experiments reinforce our suspicion that some form of nonarticulatory phonemic coding may be available during reading. Before drawing any firm conclusions, however, we need to answer two questions. The first of these concerns the discrepancy between our results and those of Kleiman (1975), who observed a clear decrement in the speed of making rhyme judgments when subjects were shadowing. One possible clue to the reason for the discrepancy comes from an unpublished study by Besner (1980), who examined the effect of articulatory suppression on the speed and accuracy of rhyme judgments made concerning either pairs of words or pairs of nonwords. He found no effect of suppression on the ability to judge whether two nonwords rhymed but did find an effect when words were involved.[2] This somewhat unexpected result would

---

[1] We have now ruled out this interpretation; errors increase under suppression while concurrent tapping has no effect.

[2] We have been unable to replicate this result.

indicate that rhyme judgments may be based on two separate processes, only one of which is available for words. This in turn would imply that some form of nonarticulatory image may be available but would suggest that it might not be involved in normal reading. Suppose, however, that nonword rhymes are judged using some system that does not depend on articulation; does this necessarily imply an auditory image? Clearly not, since it is entirely possible that the judgment is made using some deeper component of the articulatory process that is not interfered with by concurrent articulatory suppression. At present, then, although it is introspectively obvious that auditory imagery occurs, we are sadly lacking in techniques for exploring it; a nonarticulatory technique for disrupting auditory imagery would clearly be a very useful experimental tool, but unfortunately, it is a tool that has not yet been developed.

Our third hypothetical short-term code is visual, the inner eye. Our own results merely indicate that a phenomenon previously attributed to phonemic coding, the Rude Jude effect, could be due to visual similarity. The case is still not proven, and even if visual similarity does prove to be the crucial factor, it remains to be demonstrated that the effect is not due to some more peripheral process, such as difficulty in keeping one's place within the letter sequence. However, the previously cited evidence from McConkie (1979), Rayner (1975), and Morton (1979) all suggest that some form of visual buffer storage does occur. Any adequate interpretation of the role of working memory in reading will need to take this into account.

We initially ventured into the study of reading because there appeared to be a very straightforward mapping of a simple component of working memory onto the process of reading. As a result of attempting to pursue this apparently simple relationship, we have become increasingly convinced that not one but several forms of temporary information storage are involved in the reading process, a process that itself is far from unitary. Reading is not a skill but a range of skills that the fluent reader may deploy in different ways to tackle different tasks. Reading is, however, an extremely important and well practiced skill, and as such it provides a valuable if demanding test bed for the concepts and techniques of cognitive psychology. Whether the concept of working memory is helping us to understand reading, we are not sure; we are convinced; however, that the process of reading is helping us to understand working memory.

REFERENCES

Baddeley, A. D. The influence of acoustic and semantic similarity on long-term memory for word sequences. *Quarterly Journal of Experimental Psychology,* 1966, *18,* 302–309. (a)

Baddeley, A. D. Short-term memory for word sequences as a function of acoustic, semantic and formal similarity. *Quarterly Journal of Experimental Psychology,* 1966, *18,* 362–365. (b)

Baddeley, A. D. Working memory and reading. In P. A. Kolers, M. E. Wrolstad, & H. Bouma (Eds.), *The processing of visible language.* New York: Plenum Press, 1979.

Baddeley, A. D., & Hitch, G. J. Working memory. In G. A. Bower (Ed.), *The psychology of learning and motivation* (Vol. 8). New York: Academic Press, 1974.

Baddeley, A. D., Thomson, N., & Buchanan, M. Word length and the structure of short-term memory. *Journal of Verbal Learning and Verbal Behavior*, 1975, *14*, 575–589.

Baron, J. Mechanisms for pronouncing printed words: Use and acquisition. In D. LaBerge & S. J. Samuels (Eds.), *Basic processes in reading*. Hillsdale, N.J.: Lawrence Erlbaum Associates, 1976.

Besner, D. Personal communication, 1980.

Conrad, R. Acoustic confusion in immediate memory. *British Journal of Psychology*, 1964, *55*, 75–84.

Conrad, R., & Hull, A. J. Information, acoustic confusion and memory span. *British Journal of Psychology*, 1964, *55*, 429–432.

Ellis, N. C., & Hennelly, R. A. A bilingual word-length effect: Implications for intelligence testing and the relative ease of mental calculation in Welsh and English. *British Journal of Psychology*, 1980, *71*, 43–51.

Folkard, S. Personal communication, 1978.

Hardyk, C. D., & Petrinovitch. L. R. Subvocal speech and comprehension level as a function of the difficulty level of reading material. *Journal of Verbal Learning and Verbal Behavior*, 1970, *9*, 647–652.

Kleiman, G. M. Speech recoding in reading. *Journal of Verbal Learning and Verbal Behavior*, 1975, *24*, 323–339.

Levy, B. A. The role of articulation in auditory and visual short-term memory. *Journal of Verbal Learning and Verbal Behavior*, 1971, *10*, 123–132.

Levy, B. A. Vocalization and suppression effects in sentence memory. *Journal of Verbal Learning and Verbal Behavior*, 1975, *14*, 304–316.

Levy, B. A. Speech analysis during sentence processing: Reading versus listening. *Visible Language*, 1978, *12*, 81–101. (a)

Levy, B. A. Speech processing during reading. In A. M. Lesgold, J. W. Pellegrino, J. W. Fokkema, & R. Glaser (Eds.), *Cognitive psychology and instruction*. New York: Plenum Press, 1978. (b)

McConkie, G. W. On the role and control of eye movements in reading. In P. A. Kolers, M. E. Wrolstad, & H. Bouma (Eds.), *Processing of visible language I*. New York: Plenum Press, 1979.

Morton, J. Facilitation in word recognition: Experiments causing change in the logogen model. In P. A. Kolers, M. E. Wrolstad, & H. Bouma (Eds.), *Processing of visible language I*. New York: Plenum Press, 1979.

Murray, D. J. Articulation and acoustic confusability in short-term memory. *Journal of Experimental Psychology*, 1968, *78*, 679–684.

Nicholson, R. The relationship between memory span and processing speed. In M. Friedman, J. P. Das and N. O'Connor (Eds.) *Intelligence and learning*. New York: Plenum Press (In Press).

Peterson, L. R., & Johnson, S. T. Some effects of minimizing articulation on short-term retention. *Journal of Verbal Learning and Verbal Behavior*, 1971, *10*, 346–354.

Rayner, K. The perceptual span and peripheral cues in reading. *Cognitive Psychology*, 1975, *7*, 65–81.

Wickelgren, W. A. Short-term memory for phonemically similar lists. *American Journal of Psychology*, 1965, *78*, 567–574.

Winnick, W. A., & Daniel, S. A. Two kinds of response priming in tachistoscopic recognition. *Journal of Experimental Psychology*, 1970, *84*, 74–81.

6
An Interactive Analysis of Oral Reading

Joseph H. Danks and Gregory O. Hill
Kent State University

Models of reading and language comprehension have come to be dominated by the distinction between bottom-up and top-down sources of information and processing control (Danks & Glucksberg, 1980). Until recently, most information-processing models of reading have emphasized bottom-up processing (e.g., Gough, 1972; LaBerge & Samuels, 1974; Massaro, 1975). Such models attempt to formalize the intuitive observation that reading comprehension begins with the perception of print and ends with the construction of an abstract meaning representation. However, strictly bottom-up processing models have difficulty explaining some demonstrable aspects of reading performance. The crux of the difficulty is that readers and listeners frequently can anticipate parts of a linguistic message before bottom-up processing is completed. They habitually employ that ability to facilitate both perception and comprehension.

Evidence of anticipatory processing is found in two general classes of phenomena. One class results from the vagaries, ambiguities, and imperfections of typical human communication. The ease with which readers compensate for typographical errors, often without even noticing them, is an example of how the ability to anticipate an input provides a degree of insensitivity to minor linguistic violations (cf. Marslen-Wilson & Welsh [1978] for a similar effect in speech shadowing).

The other class of phenomena that poses difficulties for strictly bottom-up processing models is the facilitating effects of contextual information. Numerous demonstrations have shown that speed and accuracy of processing at one level are dependent on information from a more abstract level of representation (Rumelhart, 1977; Wildman & Kling, 1978–1979). Letter recognition is facilitated by lexical information; lexical access (word recognition) is faster when syntactic, semantic, and factual information from sentences and paragraphs is available; semantic interpretation is aided by contextual information about the topic or theme; and paragraph comprehension is aided by general world knowledge. One or two of these contextual effects might be handled plausibly by modifications in a basically bottom-up model—for example, by the addition of feedback loops or by reordering processing stages. But the pervasiveness of top-down effects throughout all levels of representation indicates that bottom-up processing is only part of a more complicated picture.

There have been few purely top-down models proposed as alternatives to bottom-up models, and with good reason. Bottom-up effects can be readily demonstrated. Readers do not create the meaning of what they are reading wholly from prior knowledge. As a general principle, there is a greater reliance on less abstract information and bottom-up processing with difficult or unfamiliar material. However, if the text is not too difficult or unfamiliar, top-down information can facilitate processing greatly. The key to the benefits of top-down processing lies in the tremendous redundancy at all levels of analysis. Although redundancy tends to bog down any attempt at comprehensive bottom-up processing of all the information in the signal, it opens the door to a more efficient use of lower-level information.

The most realistic alternatives to bottom-up models are interactive models that envision both bottom-up and top-down directions of information flow (Danks, 1978). However, because of the traditional dominance of bottom-up models, interactive models have concentrated on describing the influence of contextual information. In order to demonstrate clearly the interaction between bottom-up and top-down processing, such models have focused on intermediate levels of processing where both types of processing have an opportunity to function. The most commonly chosen level is lexical access or word recognition. Visual-perceptual information and syntactic, semantic, and prior-knowledge information converge in lexical access. So it is a convenient point at which to demonstrate both bottom-up and top-down effects.

Selection of lexical access as the focus of study may not be the most felicitous choice, however, in that the interactions found there may not generalize to processing at other levels. There seems to be a fundamental change in the nature of comprehension at levels more abstract than lexical access. Words and letters can be thought of as self-contained units possessing a relatively enduring identity. It is meaningful to talk about word and letter "re-cognition" processes because we encounter those same units repeatedly. Beyond the level of words, however, a somewhat different picture emerges. Sentences and paragraphs do not have the relatively constant representations that we attribute to letters and words. Since almost every sentence that readers encounter is unique in their experiences, it does not make sense to talk about a sentence "re-cognition" process. The correspondence between the physical input and the mental representation is much less evident above the level of individual words.

STUDIES OF ORAL READING

Oral reading is a task used frequently in schools for teaching and evaluating reading skills (Durkin, 1978–1979), but we understand very little of the processing requirements of oral reading or how it relates to silent reading. The predominant requirement of oral reading is that each word be recognized and verbalized in serial order. In most oral reading, processing probably is carried beyond simple word identification, but higher-level comprehension is not generally the central focus. In contrast, silent reading does not require the serial recognition of every word and typically focuses on overall comprehension.

When oral reading is followed by a comprehension test—for example, recall, recognition, summarization, or question answering—there are two major tasks confronting the reader (Danks & Fears, 1979). One is to verbalize each word in succession. To accomplish this task, the reader must explicitly recognize each word. By this we presume that he or she locates the word in the mental lexicon and then uses the articulation information represented there to pronounce it. It is possible that a reader might use only lower-level information, such as grapheme–phoneme correspondences, spelling patterns, or syllabic structure, to pronounce each word without accessing it in the mental lexicon. However, since readers do not "read" pronounceable nonwords without hesitation, complete dependence on lower-level information is unlikely.

The oral reader's secondary task is to understand phrases, sentences, paragraphs, and themes of the text so as to be able to satisfy the demands of the comprehension test. The reader usually attempts to satisfy both the verbal performance and the comprehension tasks at the same time, although the press of the performance demand is greater. Analysis of oral performance provides an excellent opportunity to study the interaction of lexical access and text comprehension processes in a relatively natural reading situation.

Oral reading has the advantage of yielding a continuous on-line response that is roughly cotemporaneous with the visual input. It is the reading counterpart to shadowing speech (cf. Lindig, 1976; Marslen-Wilson, 1975). In shadowing, the listener is presented with continuous speech and must produce the corresponding verbalization immediately while continuing to receive new input. In oral reading, the reader produces an oral rendition of the printed text shortly after the intake of the visual information. The main difference is that in oral reading the reader controls the intake of information, but in shadowing the listener does not. This difference corresponds to the general difference between listening and reading.

Rationale

In the experiments described in this chapter, we assessed how different types of textual information were used in oral reading by selectively violating or removing information from the text. If a particular type of information was used in meeting either the oral production or the comprehension demand, there was a disruption in the oral performance at the moment when the altered information was needed. The basic procedure was to alter several critical words in a long story, violating one or more types of textual information at each location. We then analyzed readers' oral productions for disruptions at or around each critical word.

Across several experiments, using readers at different levels of reading skill (defined by grade), we manipulated lexical, syntactic, semantic, and factual information as illustrated in a segment of text presented in Fig. 6.1. The story is about a high school girl who is severely injured when a train hits her school bus. In the example, her mother has just heard about the accident and is worried about the daughter.

1. *Lexical.* The critical word (*injured* in the example) was replaced with a pronounceable nonword (*brugen*). The nonword followed the rules of English orthographic structure and was readily pronounceable. If the reader were relying solely on grapheme–phoneme correspondences to pronounce the word, there would be no disruption of oral performance. But if the reader were using lexical information, word recognition would be impossible, because the nonword could not be found in the reader's mental lexicon. The lexical violation would disrupt

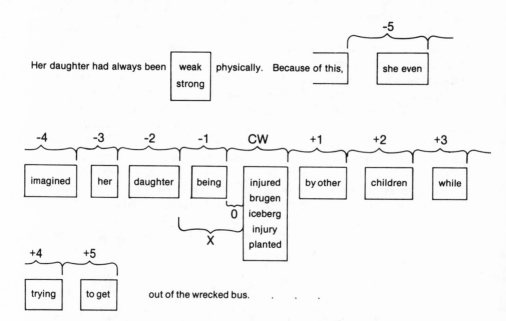

FIG. 6.1.   A portion of a story illustrating the different types of textual violations.

comprehension as well, because there was no syntactic or semantic information associated with the nonword.

2. *Syntactic + Semantic.*   Both syntactic and semantic information was distorted by replacing the critical word with a word that was the incorrect part of speech and that was semantically anomalous as well (*iceberg* in Fig. 6.1). Here the word could be accessed in the mental lexicon, but it was inappropriate for the syntactic and semantic context of the sentence.

3. *Syntactic.*   Syntactic information alone was distorted by retaining the root morpheme of the critical word but changing the inflection such that it indicated a part of speech that could not occur at that point in the sentence. In the example in Fig. 6.1, *injured,* a verb, was changed to *injury,* a noun. Although some semantic information is carried in the syntactic categories, most of the semantic information remains in the root. In this case, the reader could determine the meaning of the text relatively easily.

4. *Semantic.*   To violate semantic information but not disturb lexical or syntactic information, the critical word was replaced with a word that was the correct part of speech but that was semantically anomalous; for example, *planted* replaced *injured.* Although the readers could determine grammatical structure, they had to concoct an implausible meaning. The best they could do was to imagine a very unusual circumstance in which the anomalous word could be interpreted metaphorically.

5. *Factual.*   Factual information is what the reader accumulates from the proceeding text while reading a story. While reading, he or she constructs a representation of what the writer is conveying. New information is added to that representation. We violated factual information by introducing an inconsistency between the critical word and the preceding sentence. Unlike the other manipulations, neither the critical word nor the sentence containing it was altered. The sentence immediately before the sentence with the critical word was altered such that the critical word was factually inconsistent with the sense of the altered sentence. In the example in Fig. 6.1, the word *weak* in the preceding sentence was replaced with *strong.* The fact that her daughter was strong was inconsistent with the mother worrying about her being injured. There was nothing syntactically or semantically wrong with either sentence. They simply communicated inconsistent information.

All modifications were selected to assure that the readers would be unlikely to conceive of a continuation after the critical word that would eliminate the violation. For the factual manipulation, there did exist a plausible substitution for the critical word. Otherwise, the reader might sense something was amiss prior to reading the critical word. For example, if the daughter were strong, the mother might imagine her being safe, unharmed, helpful, or a heroine.

For purposes of analysis, five word units before and five word units after a critical word were identified (see Fig. 6.1). These were one or two words (rarely three words) that readers tended to pronounce together. Word units did not correspond to any specific syntactic or semantic structures. The major dependent variable was the frequency (later converted to a probability) of a major disruption occurring during the oral production of each word unit. Major disruptions were defined as pauses of at least 1 sec duration, substitutions, omissions, reversals, stammerings, mispronunciations, repetitions, and regressions. Only one disruption was scored per word unit. A baseline probability of a major disruption was established in a control condition in which the original critical word was left unaltered. This baseline probability was subtracted from each of the violation conditions. The interaction of violation conditions by word-unit position was the critical test and was evaluated using both readers and critical word segments as random factors.

The basic rationale was to look for disruptions in oral reading performance surrounding each of the violation types. If there were disruptions in oral performance, the readers presumably were attempting to use the violated information to recognize the critical word and/or to construct a meaning for the text. Furthermore, the relative position of the disruptions resulting from the different violations would indicate the order in which the information typically was used.

According to a bottom-up model, only lexical information was strictly necessary for oral production, although the reader would need to determine the grammatical structure to read with appropriate prosody. If the reader were using solely grapheme–phoneme correspondences to pronounce the words and did not access the word in the lexicon prior to uttering it, then the disruption from the lexical violation would occur after the critical word had been said. Syntactic and semantic information would be used primarily to determine the meaning of the clause, so those disruptions would occur after the critical word at the clause boundary. Violations of factual information would be important only after the meaning of the clause had been determined. The reader would attempt to integrate the meaning of the clause with the representation of the preceding text and then would encounter the inconsistency.

How syntactic, semantic, and factual information would exert top-down influence on lexical access would depend on the particular interactive model adopted. If syntactic, semantic, and/or factual information were used in lexical access, disruptions from violating that information would occur at the same time as those resulting from lexical violations. Whether the disruptions occurred at the same position and had about the same extent would indicate the functional relation among the information sources. Violating two information sources, as in the syntactic + semantic manipulation, would lead to different patterns of disruption depending on the interactions among the information sources.

Skilled Reading

The first experiment with skilled readers used 12 paragraphs averaging about 125 words each from a contemporary novel. One critical word was selected in each paragraph. In four versions of the story, lexical, syntactic + semantic, and semantic violations were introduced at three critical words each. The remaining three critical words in each version were controls and were left unchanged. Across the four versions, manipulations were counterbalanced across critical words. Ten college students, who were unscreened for reading skills, read each version aloud. In order to ensure that they paid some attention to comprehension, they were required to give a brief summary of each paragraph immediately after reading it.

As shown in Fig. 6.2, the principal point of disruption resulting from lexical violations occurred at the critical word (word unit 0). Most of these disruptions were pauses as the readers hesitated before uttering the pronounceable nonword. Unable to locate that lexical item in their mental lexicons, they balked and sometimes had difficulty in pronouncing the nonwords just on the basis of phoneme–grapheme correspondences. The disruptions from the syntactic + semantic violation followed the disruption from the lexical almost perfectly. They both differed significantly from the control at the critical word and at word unit +1. Syntactic or semantic information or both were being used to locate the lexical item, so that removal of that information disrupted the readers. Since the patterns of disruption resulting from the lexical and syntactic + semantic violations were essentially the same, these information sources must have been

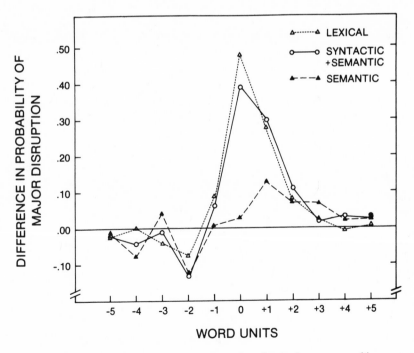

FIG. 6.2. Disruptions in skilled readers' oral reading performances resulting from lexical, syntactic + semantic, and semantic violations.

active at the same time, although they may have operated independently (Lazerson, 1974–1975).

The disruption from the semantic violation did not occur until word unit +1, however, and was relatively much smaller. In reading this story, semantic information was not being used for lexical access. The violation was discovered later, perhaps when clause integration occurred. When we considered the story more carefully, we realized why the semantic information may not have been used as readily. The story was excerpted from a novel that was written in an abstract, metaphorical style. The semantic violations were anomalies that easily could have been mistaken for intentional but incomprehensible metaphors. The readers adopted the quite reasonable strategy of not giving high priority to semantic information because it was frequently figurative or anomalous.

The next experiment used a concrete, emotionally involving story (2171 words long) about a high school girl who was severely injured when a train hit her school bus (see sample of text in Fig. 6.1). We dropped the lexical violations and added factual ones. The syntactic + semantic and the semantic violations were retained. However, given the general context of a concrete, literal story, the semantic information would be more useful in lexical access and the anomalies more pronounced. The other procedures and analyses remained unchanged except that the story was divided into four sections with four critical words (one of each condition) in each section. Readers gave a summary after reading each quarter of the story.

Both the syntactic + semantic and the semantic violations produced a disruption at the word unit before the critical word (word unit −1; see Fig. 6.3). The peak disruption from the syntactic + semantic violation was significantly larger than that resulting from the semantic violation alone, but the semantic violation had a longer lasting effect, remaining significantly different from the control at word units +3 and +5. Since both syntactic + semantic and semantic violations yielded disruptions before the critical word was produced, both syntactic and semantic information was being used during lexical access. Both violations were also disruptive after the critical word was produced, indicating failures during the comprehension-integration task as well. The factual inconsistency was disruptive only after the critical word had been uttered (word unit +1). So factual information was not involved in lexical access, but only in sentence meaning integration.

The syntactic + semantic violation had a larger disruptive effect earlier than did the semantic violation. A violation in both of two independent information sources would be noticed before a condition in which only one source was violated. So the syntactic + semantic violation may have been a violation of two independent knowledge sources (Siler, 1973–1974). The next experiment separated the syntactic and semantic violations and attempted to enhance the factual violations.

The third experiment used the same story as the second, but several of the factual violations were rewritten to make them even more inconsistent, and the

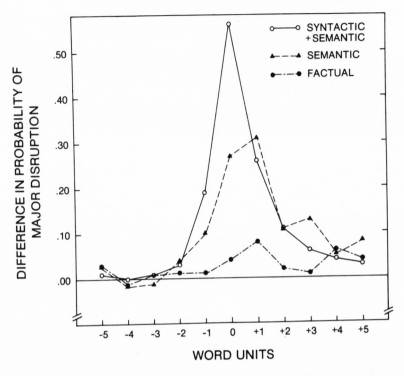

FIG. 6.3. Disruptions in skilled readers' oral reading performances resulting from syntactic + semantic, semantic, and factual violations.

syntactic + semantic violations were replaced with syntactic-only violations. The rest of the procedure and analyses remained the same except that the subjects answered 10 multiple-choice questions after each quarter of the text instead of giving summaries. Scores on the multiple-choice test were nearly perfect.

As shown in Fig. 6.4, the syntactic and the semantic violations produced very similar disruption curves. Both were significantly different from the control at word unit -1 and peaked at the critical word. The semantic violation produced a slightly longer disruptive effect (to word unit $+3$) than the syntactic (only to word unit $+2$). The biggest difference was in the magnitude of the disruption at the critical word. Most of the disruptions in the syntactic violation (54% of all disruptions) were restorations of the correct part of speech. Excluding restorations of the original critical word from the syntactic and semantic conditions, the proportions of disruptions at the critical word were virtually identical—.33 for syntactic and .34 for semantic. The restoration of the original critical word in the syntactic violation condition was a top-down effect resulting from syntactic constraints on the part of speech. Syntactic + semantic violations were never restored in the previous experiments. So the difference between syntactic +

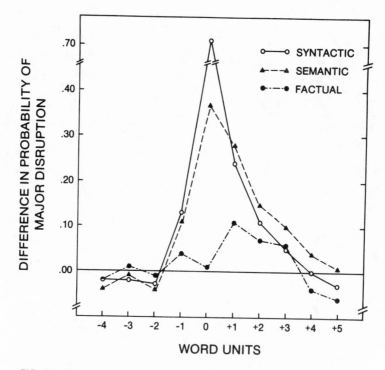

FIG. 6.4   Disruptions in skilled readers' oral reading performances resulting from syntactic, semantic, and factual violations.

semantic and semantic-only disruptions observed in the second experiment evidently resulted from the combined effect of violations of two independent knowledge sources.

The factual violation produced a larger effect than in the preceding experiment, but it still was first effective at word unit +1 and not at or before the critical word. In contrast to syntactic and semantic information, factual consistency did not have any apparent influence on lexical access of the critical word but was involved in sentence meaning integration. Lindig (1976) obtained similar results of factual violations on speech-shadowing performance.

Violations of lexical, syntactic, and semantic information disrupted oral production at about the same point before the critical word was uttered. From the perspective of lexical access, lexical information is bottom-up, and syntactic and semantic information is top-down. Yet the pattern of their disruptive effects was quite similar. All three information sources were contributing to lexical access. When any one information source was violated, the normally automatic process was disturbed, forcing a reliance on careful bottom-up processing to be sure what word was actually printed.

The occurrence of disruptions for several word units after the critical word represents more than a simple perseveration of the initial disruption, however. After the critical word had been uttered, the reader attempted to make sense of the inserted word. How could the clause be interpreted so that the word would not be inconsistent with the representation the reader was constructing for the sentence, paragraph, and story? This comprehension difficulty was evident with all violations, including the factual. Even though the disruption from the factual violation was much smaller, it occurred consistently for several words after the critical word.

Were the post-critical-word disruptions synchronized with the end of the clause? In preparing the stories, we did not attempt to control the location of the clause boundaries after the critical word. However, a post hoc analysis of the data in the last two experiments suggested that there may have been a peak of disruption at the clause boundary. Sometimes a peak at the clause boundary was the only disruption; sometimes it was in addition to one at the critical word; and sometimes it was missing entirely. However, the data were too few to draw strong conclusions about whether there were disruptions at the clause boundary.

Learning to Read

What is the interaction of information sources as a child is learning to read? A reasonable first hypothesis is that the child is paying most attention to bottom-up information, because that is where most instruction is focused and that is where the child is having the most difficulty. As bottom-up processing becomes more automatic (LaBerge & Samuels, 1974), children are gradually able to use more abstract information for lexical access and meaning integration. Alternatively, children initially might be overly dependent on context and prior knowledge simply because they lack proficiency in processing bottom-up information. As they gain skill in decoding, bottom-up information would become relatively more useful to them, and the balance between bottom-up and top-down processing would shift.

To investigate this question, the basic experimental paradigm used with skilled readers was adapted for children learning to read—second, fourth, and sixth graders. Stories were selected from primers one grade below the children's actual grade. The readabilities (Fry, 1968) of the stories were 1.6, 3.5, and 5.6, and the stories were 881, 1354, and 1617 words long. The stories were divided into four sections, and five critical words were selected in each quarter. Lexical, syntactic, semantic, and factual violations were developed for each critical word following the same criteria as for the skilled readers. Five versions of each story were constructed so that violations were counterbalanced across critical words and subjects. There were 50 children tested at each grade level, 10 on each version of the story. In order to ensure that the children paid some attention to

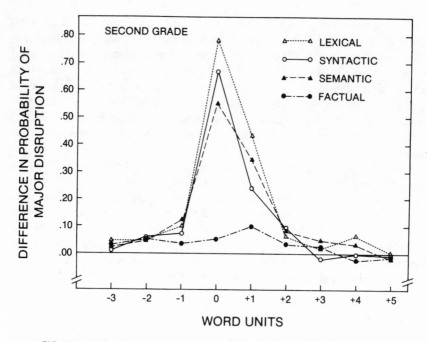

FIG. 6.5 Disruptions in second graders' oral reading performances.

comprehension, the children were asked three to four simple questions after reading each quarter of the text. The scoring of major disruptions was the same as described for skilled readers.

The disruption curves for the second, fourth, and sixth graders are shown in Figs. 6.5, 6.6, and 6.7, respectively. Although there were some differences across the three grades, the results were very similar. Lexical, syntactic, and semantic violations all produced their largest disruptions at the critical word and, to a lesser extent, at word unit +1. A few of the conditions were significantly different from the control as early as word units −2 or −1—namely, lexical in sixth at −2, lexical in second and fourth at −1, syntactic in fourth and sixth at −1, and semantic in second and fourth at −1. Likewise, there were a few significant effects at word units +2 and +3—namely, syntactic in second at +2 and semantic in fourth at +2 and +3. But the dominant effect was at and immediately after the critical word.

The factual violation produced small but significant disruptions in all three grades—at word unit +1 in the second and fourth grades and at the critical word in the sixth grade. Factual information may have been filling some useful role in lexical access for the sixth graders, but not for the second and fourth graders. The small size and the location of the children's factual disruptions indicated that

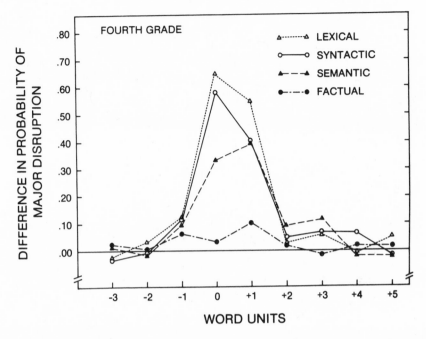

FIG. 6.6. Disruptions in fourth graders' oral reading performances.

resolving a factual inconsistency was more critical at meaning integration than at lexical access.

The major conclusion was that syntactic and semantic information influenced lexical access of the critical word as much as lexical information itself (cf. Isakson & Miller, 1976; Miller, 1975). The magnitudes of the disruptions were ordered from lexical violations producing the largest disruption, followed closely by syntactic and semantic violations. Perhaps these children were well along the way to being skilled readers, so that bottom-up processing was relatively automatic, thus permitting top-down processes to operate (Isakson & Miller, 1976). Their reading rates indicated that this was not the case, however. Estimating reading rates from the control condition, the second graders read at 123 syllables/minute, fourth graders at 161 syllables/minute, sixth graders at 181 syllables/minute, and college students at 270 syllables/minute. The children's reading on the whole was not as fluent as that of skilled readers; they read more slowly and haltingly.

In a comparison of the children's results with those of skilled readers, there were no major differences as a function of skill level. These particular children may have been more highly skilled than one would expect from their grade levels (standardized reading-test scores were not available), but still they were not

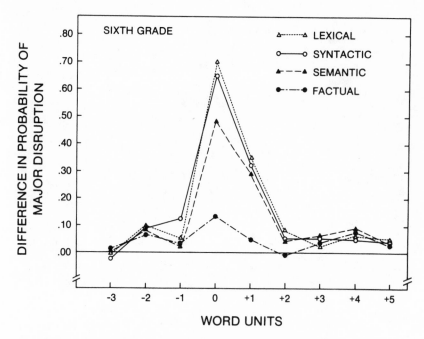

FIG. 6.7. Disruptions in sixth graders' oral reading performances.

reading at adult levels. The use of relatively easy, grade-appropriate stories may have allowed the children to use more skilled reading strategies. Also, some of the children's inefficiencies may have been masked by their slow reading rates. Whatever the reasons, there were no significant differences in the pattern of results across grades.

AN INTERACTIVE ANALYSIS OF ORAL READING

We now consider an interactive analysis of oral reading and how such an analysis applies to our results. There are two interactive models that are related to the one proposed here—Rumelhart's (1977) parallel-interactive model of reading and Marslen-Wilson and Welsh's (1978) direct lexical access model of speech perception. Although there are convergences among the models, neither Rumelhart's nor Marslen-Wilson and Welsh's has been developed in the direction of oral reading.

An Oral Reading Model

The primary task in oral reading is to verbalize each word of the text in succession. It is a constant demand on the reader, one that cannot be ignored. There are many points in a reading comprehension process at which the oral production might originate (Danks & Fears, 1979). Extraction of grapheme–phoneme correspondences might supply sufficient information for articulation. At the other extreme, a meaning representation of an entire sentence might be constructed first; a sentence production process might be initiated in the same way that sentences are produced in conversations. Neither of these extremes seems likely. The former would have readers articulate orthographically regular nonwords in context without any hesitation. However, readers do not do this (cf. disruptions from the nonword violation). The latter position would require that eye–voice spans encompass entire clauses, but eye–voice spans are not that large (Levin, 1979; Vázquez, Glucksberg, & Danks, 1977–1978).

A more plausible assumption is that oral production is initiated following lexical access, at least for familiar words. Once readers locate a word in their lexicon, they then have available the articulatory information necessary to pronounce it. There is no claim that lexical access is direct without any phonological mediation, only that initiation of an oral response does not occur until after the word has been accessed. The oral response does not originate in any phonological mediation that might be used in lexical access. When encountering an unfamiliar word, readers—especially children being taught with a phonics-based program—sometimes "sound out" the word slowly by breaking it into phoneme and/or syllable units. Then they repeat it, blending the parts together. In these cases, the first pronunciation is directed by letter–sound correspondences and the repetition, by the articulatory code accessed in the mental lexicon.

Lexical Access.   Our model of lexical access is closely related to Marslen-Wilson and Welsh's (1978) direct access model. They proposed that a cohort of words is activated in the mental lexicon strictly on the basis of incoming perceptual information, which in their studies of speech shadowing was a phonemic analysis of the initial syllable of each word. Candidate words in the cohort then are evaluated against the continuing perceptual analysis and against syntactic and semantic constraints. Any word that is inconsistent with any constraint, whether it be perceptual or contextual, is deactivated. The elimination process continues until only one candidate remains in the cohort. That survivor is recognized as the target word.

Applying this model to reading, cohorts of words are activated by an initial visual analysis. However, we think that semantic and syntactic information, especially semantic, also can activate words for the cohort. In conversations, listeners frequently anticipate what speakers are going to say—as when a speaker pauses, apparently searching for a word, and the listener obligingly supplies it. Sometimes the listener anticipates correctly, sometimes not; but in either case the anticipation is present. We are not proposing a hypothesis-testing procedure in which contextually based predictions are produced and evaluated serially by comparison to perceptual information. Rather, we are proposing that many alternatives are activated simultaneously, each of which is consistent with some current information, either perceptual or contextual. These alternatives then are evaluated in parallel.

The evaluation procedure differs from Marslen-Wilson and Welsh's as well. Their procedure is a process of elimination. Members of the cohort are tested for consistency with semantic and syntactic information, as well as with the results of the continuing perceptual analysis. Inconsistent items are eliminated from the cohort until one is left. We propose a two-stage process. Initially, an elimination process tests members of the cohort for consistency with all available information, especially syntactic and semantic. This evaluation is fast and can be based on incomplete perceptual information. If only one item remains in the cohort, it is accepted. However, if more than one item remains or if no item remains, then a relatively slow, careful perceptual analysis is conducted to obtain relatively complete letter, syllable, and word information. Most of the time the elimination process is sufficient, but sometimes the reader must rely primarily on perceptual information.

Once a word has been located in the mental dictionary, information about how to pronounce that word is sent to a buffer where speech articulation is organized. This articulation process is assumed to be nearly the same as spontaneous speech production. The only difference is that in oral reading, subsequent syntactic and semantic information might be needed to specify some pronunciation or intonation patterns. For example, whether the printed word *record* is pronounced with first- or second-syllable stress may be determined by syntactic or semantic information later in the sentence. The use of subsequent syntactic and semantic information is not needed in natural speech production because the speaker already knows whether *record* is a noun or a verb, just as he or she knows what intonation pattern is appropriate for the message. In contrast, the relevant information may not be available to the oral reader until the end of a clause or sentence. The reader can scan quickly ahead in an attempt to locate the information or can select an interpretation using whatever information is available at that point.

Clause (and Sentence) Comprehension.   At the same time as the reader is articulating the words, he or she is also selecting an appropriate meaning for each word (Swinney, 1979) and integrating those meanings in order to understand what is being read. This step is necessary to satisfy the secondary task demand of producing a recall or summary after the reading is finished. In some cases, the reader may be forced to wait until reaching a clause boundary to execute the meaning integration (Carroll & Bever, 1976; Carroll, Tanenhaus, & Bever, 1978). But in general, the reader attempts to integrate meanings word by word, as quickly as possible (Marslen-Wilson, Tyler, & Seidenberg, 1978; Tyler & Marslen-Wilson, 1977).

As with lexical access, there are two processing options. Initially, the reader attempts a fast integration of each word's meaning with the representation that has been constructed up to that point. This process is efficient but requires the use of considerable top-down, contextual information about the meaning of what is written. With relatively easy or familiar material, the reader can succeed in performing this integration with minimal attentional and processing effort. Upon reaching the end of a clause, which is a conceptual as well as syntactic demarcation, the reader has in mind a coherent representation of the entire text up to that point.

Sometimes, however, word-by-word integration does not succeed. For example, in our semantic violation, the readers were unable to integrate the critical word. In more typical texts, there are ambiguities and vagaries to confound a reader's word-by-word integration. When such failures occur, a reader can postpone integration for a short time in hope that new information will resolve the difficulty. The individual meanings are stored in a temporary memory buffer. At the end of the clause or sentence, the reader is forced to integrate as best as possible because he or she cannot store and retain the meanings of individual words for very long. Since most clauses and sentences are conceptually integrated, the reader can reasonably expect a resolution at that point. At the end of a clause or sentence, the reader attempts to clarify the meaning of the clause by carefully analyzing its syntactic structure. In this respect, a careful syntactic analysis is a bottom-up process that provides definitive structural information specifying how to integrate the word meanings. If there is no resolution, the reader can suspend forward processing and regress in an attempt to find additional information or can plunge ahead, leaving a lacuna in the composite representation.

In summary, first the reader attempts a word-by-word integration of the meanings, based on prior knowledge and semantic expectancies about what is being communicated. If that process fails, the reader relies on a careful analysis of the syntactic structure ending at the clause boundary. The former process is fast and efficient, but risky. The latter is slow, but more likely to succeed.

In an oral reading task, how would these two processing strategies be evidenced? If word-by-word integration goes awry, oral performance would be disrupted at that point. For example, disruptions occurred both before and after a semantically anomalous word, one that could not be integrated, had been uttered. The disruption after the critical word could not have resulted from problems of lexical access because the word had to be accessed to be uttered. So a disruption after the critical word reflected difficulty with meaning integration. Attention appeared to be diverted from oral production to meaning integration. However, it is not clear that either oral production or meaning integration requires much attention in the normal case. Skilled readers can easily read aloud without attention, as any parent who reads stories to children can testify. Meaning integration also appears relatively effortless. Yet somehow, difficulty with word-by-word integration distracted the reader's attention from oral production and resulted in a disruption. If word-by-word integration has failed and a careful syntactic analysis is required, then the reader may have to pause at the clause boundary to allow time (and attention) for the slower analysis to occur. In the experiments reported here, the location of the clause boundary was uncontrolled, so that disruptions at the clause boundary were not observed in the primary analysis. However, a post hoc analysis at the first clause boundary following each critical word indicated that there was a disruption at that point.

How is a coherent representation of the entire text constructed? In word-by-word integration, each word is integrated with a composite representation of the entire text up to that point, not just with the representation for that clause or sentence. If a clause requires additional processing at the clause boundary in order to be understood, then the reader has to adjust the meaning of the clause to fit the composite representation. Such an adjustment is especially necessary if the meaning of the clause is inconsistent with another proposition already integrated in the representation. The factual inconsistency in our experiments blocked the formation of a coherent representation. Elementary school children sometimes allow inconsistent propositions to remain in their mental representations (Markman, 1979), but skilled, adult readers usually do not. If the inconsistency involves sufficiently critical information for the understanding of a text, a reader may stop, regress, and attempt to solve it. Alternatively, he or she may alter either the interpretation of the prior existing portion of the inconsistency (Loftus, 1975; Loftus, Miller, & Burns, 1978) or the perception of the new information. If the information is not crucial for understanding the whole text, the reader may postpone an attempt at resolution indefinitely. At recall, when that understanding must be made public, he or she may attempt a resolution, omit the inconsistent information, or repeat the inconsistency unaware. In any case, resolution of the difficulty is not a pressing demand and can be postponed in hope of finding clarification later.

Oral Reading Task Demands

Based on this analysis of oral reading, we can identify three implicit tasks for oral readers. The first is lexical access, which provides the information necessary to produce the oral rendition. It also is the primary source of semantic information to be used in forming a representation of the meaning of the text, but it is the immediate demand for oral production that drives lexical access. It cannot be postponed—as it might be in silent reading when an unknown word is encountered—without producing a major disruption in oral production. Because of the immediacy of the demand, disruptions in lexical access appear as disruptions in oral production before the critical word has been uttered.

The second implicit task is clause understanding and integration. Normally, this task proceeds word by word, but when that integration fails—as it would with our semantic violations—then more careful structural analysis must occur. There would be a disruption in oral production at the point within the clause where word-by-word integration failed. Attention would be diverted from oral production to meaning integration. The demand for meaning integration can be delayed to the end of the clause but no longer because of memory limitations. One result of a more careful analysis at the clause boundary is a disruption in oral production there.

The third implicit task is ensuring that the representation is coherent. Successful word-by-word integration satisfies this demand perforce. However, if an inconsistency remains at the end of a clause—as there would following a factual violation—the demand for coherency can be postponed to the end of the text or until an overt comprehension response, such as recall or summarization, is required.

What effect does the demand for an oral production have on these three implicit tasks? Some effects have been mentioned already. The competition for cognitive resources can result in less attention being allocated to integrating a meaning representation and to ensuring its coherence. For skilled readers, comprehension and oral production processes are sufficiently automatic that both can be carried out in parallel. Division of attention would be most evident when the comprehension process encounters difficulty. However, the sharing of cognitive resources may be facilitated by the fact that the mechanics of articulation slow down the intake of new information. The silent reading rates of skilled adult readers are approximately halved in oral reading. Many skilled readers read difficult texts aloud in order to assist understanding. If the rate becomes too slow, however, as in a child who is having difficulty with basic decoding skills, comprehension may be affected adversely. Individual word meanings would have to be retained too long in a temporary memory buffer and would be forgotten.

Having to read every word in sequence may alter the comprehension processes. In silent reading, skilled readers may not look at and access every word, especially highly predictable words (but for evidence to the contrary, see Zola, 1979; described by McConkie & Zola, Chap. 7, this volume). Skilled readers may not access the words in the order in which they appear on the page, either. Instead, they may jump ahead or regress in an attempt to optimize information intake. This strategy is analogous to that employed by many English-speaking students with an intermediate-level knowledge of German: Jump to the verb at the end of the clause before reading the rest of the clause.

Finally, auditory feedback from hearing oneself read aloud may change processing. Readers who spontaneously restored the correct part of speech to the syntactic violations may have paused after words because they realized that what they had uttered was not what was printed. Auditory feedback provides an external feedback loop by which automatic oral production can be monitored.

Interpretation of Oral Reading Results

How does this analysis of oral reading explain the results of the experiments? Each basic finding is considered in terms of the analysis.

1. Lexical, syntactic, and semantic violations disrupted oral production before the critical word was uttered (i.e., at word units −1 and 0). All three types of information were used in lexical access. By definition, lexical violations disrupted lexical access. Since the nonword was not in the lexicon, it could not be accessed. Syntactic and semantic violations disrupted oral production before the critical word was uttered to the same extent as did insertion of a nonword. So syntactic information and semantic information were critical for lexical access as well.

2. Lexical, syntactic, and semantic violations disrupted oral production after the critical word was uttered (i.e., at word units +1 and +2). Disruptions in these locations indicated that lexical, syntactic, and semantic information was being used to construct a meaning of the sentence or clause. Semantic disruptions after the critical word tended to be somewhat larger than syntactic ones (cf. Fig. 6.4), suggesting continuing attempts at meaning integration.

3. When both syntactic and semantic properties were violated, disruptions began before the critical word was uttered and were more pronounced than when semantic information alone was violated. Syntactic and semantic information came from functionally independent knowledge sources, both of which were active in lexical access. In terms of the model, violation of both information sources resulted in the more rapid elimination of all members of the initial cohort during lexical access. Since the slower perceptually dependent process was required at an earlier point, the disruptions also occurred earlier.

4. Readers frequently restored syntactic violations to the original and contextually appropriate part of speech. The part of speech was altered by changing the inflection on the root morpheme. There is a left-to-right scanning bias in reading (McConkie & Rayner, 1976), as well as in speech perception (Marslen-Wilson & Welsh, 1978). Initial analysis of the first letters or syllable would be consistent with the orthographic, syntactic, and semantic constraints of a single lexical entry—namely, the original critical word. It would be the only word remaining in the cohort at an early point in the elimination process. With the relatively early elimination of all but one lexical item from the cohort, perceptual processing of the latter portion of the printed word could be discontinued, and the original word would be uttered, restoring the altered inflection.

5. Semantic violations in conceptually difficult text disrupted oral performance only after the critical word was uttered—that is, at word units +1, +2,

and +3 in Fig. 6.2. When the material was conceptually difficult, readers were unable to generate semantic expectations about upcoming words. They had few expectations with which to select items for the initial cohort, nor was there semantic information that could eliminate items from the cohort. After a lexical item was identified, primarily through perceptual and syntactic information, the reader could not integrate the meaning of the semantically anomalous word, resulting in a disruption after the critical word was uttered.

6. Factual inconsistencies between successive sentences disrupted oral performance only after the critical word had been uttered (word unit +1) and not before. Factual violations did not disrupt lexical access. There is nothing in the model that precludes factual expectancies from activating or eliminating items from the cohort. Perhaps the factual violations were not strong enough to produce inconsistent expectancies. Or perhaps factual information simply is not involved in lexical access. Factual inconsistencies did interfere with word-by-word meaning integration, however, although the disruption was relatively small.

7. In a post hoc analysis, some disruptions in oral performance occurred at the clause boundary immediately following the critical word. This pattern was most evident following factual violations. Assuming that this tentative finding is confirmed in future experiments, disruptions at the clause boundary indicated that readers were making another attempt to understand the clause with the violation. They may have reread the sentence silently; they may have regressed to the preceding sentence; or they may have engaged some covert problem-solving strategy. Language is flexible enough that most apparently inconsistent statements can be resolved eventually. This fact became obvious to us when constructing materials for the experiments. It was difficult to exclude the possibility of plausible alternative interpretations.

8. In the experiment with children, the same basic pattern of results was obtained at all grade levels. General processing strategies apparently were the same across differences in reading skill. There are several qualifications on that conclusion. First, reading skill differences were defined by grade, not by test scores. Good and poor readers at the same grade level might yield different patterns of results. Second, the stories were easy, somewhat below estimated reading-grade level. With difficult texts, differences in processing strategies might emerge as children acquire reading skill. Third, the youngest children were second graders in the second semester. Substantial changes in processing strategies may occur during the first 1½ years of learning to read (Miller & Isakson, 1978; but contrast with Lovett, 1979). In spite of these qualifications, the similarity of oral disruption patterns in Figs. 6.2 through 6.7 was striking. Processing differences may have existed, but the dominant impression was one of constancy.

These results are consistent with an interactive model of oral reading. Although we have not detailed all of the arguments and rationale, it does not seem possible for any plausible bottom-up model to explain these results. Perhaps one could be developed (e.g., McClelland's [1979] cascade model), but we are disposed to look toward interactive models as a more promising avenue. Other interactive models, such as Rumelhart's (1977) and Marslen-Wilson's (Marslen-Wilson et al., 1978; Marslen-Wilson & Welsh, 1978), are consistent with our results which do not discriminate among these models in any significant way. There are many experimental demonstrations that require interactive models, of which ours is one, but these demonstrations do not tell us very much about how the interaction works. The nature of the interaction among information sources needs to be specified more precisely through experimentation.

ACKNOWLEDGMENTS

The experiments discussed here were conducted in collaboration with Lisa Bohn, Ramona Fears, Jeff Hall, and Ruth Miller. Their contributions to the research program are gratefully acknowledged. Preparation of this paper and the reported experiments were supported by Grant No. NIE-G-78-0223 from the National Institute of Education.

REFERENCES

Carroll, J. M., & Bever, T. G. Sentence comprehension: A case study in the relation of knowledge to perception. In E. C. Carterette & M. P. Friedman (Eds.), *Handbook of perception: Language and speech* (Vol. VII). New York: Academic Press, 1976.

Carroll, J. M., Tanenhaus, M. K., & Bever, T. G. The perception of relations: The interaction of structural, functional, and contextual factors in the segmentation of sentences. In W. J. M. Levelt & G. B. Flores d'Arcais (Eds.), *Studies in the perception of language:* Chichester, England: Wiley, 1978.

Danks, J. H. Models of language comprehension. *Polish Psychological Bulletin*, 1978, *9*, 183–192.

Danks, J. H., & Fears, R. Oral reading: Does it reflect decoding or comprehension? In L. B. Resnick & P. A. Weaver (Eds.), *Theory and practice of early reading* (Vol. 3). Hillsdale, N.J.: Lawrence Erlbaum Associates, 1979.

Danks, J. H., & Glucksberg, S. Experimental psycholinguistics. *Annual Review of Psychology*, 1980, *31*, 391–417.

Durkin, D. What classroom observations reveal about reading comprehension instruction. *Reading Research Quarterly*, 1978–1979, *14*, 481–533.

Fry, E. B. A readability formula that saves time. *Journal of Reading*, 1968, *11*, 513–516; 575–578.

Gough, P. B. One second of reading. In J. F. Kavanagh & I. G. Mattingly (Eds.), *Language by ear and by eye.* Cambridge, Mass.: MIT Press, 1972.

Isakson, R. L., & Miller, J. W. Sensitivity to syntactic and semantic cues in good and poor comprehenders. *Journal of Educational Psychology*, 1976, *68*, 787–792.

LaBerge, D., & Samuels, S. J. Toward a theory of automatic information processing in reading. *Cognitive Psychology*, 1974, *6*, 293–323.

Lazerson, B. H. The influence of highly variable spelling upon the reading performance of skilled readers of Modern English. *Reading Research Quarterly*, 1974–1975, *10*, 583–615.

Levin, H. *The eye-voice span.* Cambridge, Mass.: MIT Press, 1979.

Lindig, K. D. *Contextual factors in shadowing connected discourse.* Unpublished doctoral dissertation, University of Chicago, 1976.

Loftus, E. F. Leading questions and the eyewitness report. *Cognitive Psychology,* 1975, *7,* 560–572.

Loftus, E. F., Miller, D. G., & Burns, H. J. Semantic integration of verbal information into a visual memory. *Journal of Experimental Psychology: Human Learning and Memory,* 1978, *4,* 19–31.

Lovett, M. W. The selective encoding of sentential information in normal reading development. *Child Development,* 1979, *50,* 897–900.

Markman, E. M. Realizing that you don't understand: Elementary school children's awareness of inconsistencies. *Child Development,* 1979, *50,* 643–655.

Marslen-Wilson, W. D. Sentence perception as an interactive parallel process. *Science,* 1975, *189,* 226–228.

Marslen-Wilson, W., Tyler, L. K., & Seidenberg, M. Sentence processing and the clause boundary. In W. J. M. Levelt & G. B. Flores d'Arcais (Eds.), *Studies in the perception of language.* Chichester, England: Wiley, 1978.

Marslen-Wilson, W. D., & Welsh, A. Processing interactions and lexical access during word recognition in continuous speech. *Cognitive Psychology,* 1978, *10,* 29–63.

Massaro, D. W. Primary and secondary recognition in reading. In D. W. Massaro (Ed.), *Understanding language.* New York: Academic Press, 1975.

McClelland, J. L. On the time relations of mental processes: An examination of systems of processes in cascade. *Psychological Review,* 1979, *86,* 287–330.

McConkie, G. W., & Rayner, K. Asymmetry of the perceptual span in reading. *Bulletin of the Psychonomic Society,* 1976, *8,* 365–368.

Miller, J. W. Disruptive effect: A phenomenon in oral reading. *Reading Horizons,* 1975, *15,* 198–207.

Miller, J. W., & Isakson, R. L. Contextual sensitivity in beginning readers. *Elementary School Journal,* 1978, *78,* 325–331.

Rumelhart, D. E. Toward an interactive model of reading. In S. Dornic (Ed.), *Attention and performance VI.* Hillsdale, N.J.: Lawrence Erlbaum Associates, 1977.

Siler, E. R. The effects of syntactic and semantic constraints on the oral reading performance of second and fourth graders. *Reading Research Quarterly,* 1973–1974, *9,* 583–602.

Swinney, D. A. Lexical access during sentence comprehension: (Re)consideration of context effects. *Journal of Verbal Learning and Verbal Behavior,* 1979, *18,* 645–659.

Tyler, L. K., & Marslen-Wilson, W. D. The on-line effects of semantic context on syntactic processing. *Journal of Verbal Learning and Verbal Behavior,* 1977, *16,* 683–692.

Vázquez, C. A., Glucksberg, S., & Danks, J. H. Integration of clauses in oral reading: The effects of syntactic and semantic constraints on the eye–voice span. *Reading Research Quarterly,* 1977–1978, *13,* 174–187.

Wildman, D. M., & Kling, M. Semantic, syntactic, and spatial anticipation in reading. *Reading Research Quarterly,* 1978–1979, *14,* 128–164.

Zola, D. *The perception of words in reading.* Paper presented at Psychonomic Society meetings, Phoenix, 1979.

7

Language Constraints and the Functional Stimulus in Reading

George W. McConkie and David Zola
Center for the Study of Reading, University of Illinois

In the struggle to understand how perception takes place in a particular task such as reading, two primary questions can be asked: First, what is serving as the functional stimulus for the perception; and second, what is the nature of the perceptual activities by which the use of this stimulus information yields its effects? The first of these questions is the most directly empirical in nature. If empirical data can specify the functional stimulus for perception under certain conditions, then the task of understanding the mental activities of perception under those conditions can be addressed more profitably. Without good evidence about what is actually serving as the stimulus, further theorizing about perceptual activities is on somewhat shaky ground, being based on unsupported assumptions concerning what aspects of the visual information are actually being used.

The purpose of the present chapter is to consider the nature of the functional stimulus in reading—that is, what aspects of the text stimulus are being attended to or used for reading. The discussion of this topic requires that a distinction be made between visual information and contextual information. This is a common distinction in the literature, but the boundary between the two categories varies depending on the author's purposes and theoretical inclination. For the present chapter, we adopt a more extreme position than is usually taken. We use the term *visual information* to refer only to the visual characteristics of the text that are available during a particular fixation during reading. *Contextual information* refers to all other information the reader has up to that point that places constraints on what the presently available visual information might be. This contextual information might have been gained from earlier portions of the text or simply be available from prior knowledge of the language, the nature of passages, the author's writing style, the topic being discussed, and so forth.

The particular question we wish to address is whether contextual information produces changes in what visual information is acquired and used for reading during a fixation—that is, whether contextual information influences the functional stimulus. This is treated as an empirical question. We consider to some degree the evidence from tasks that do not involve normal reading, as well as studies of reading itself. We evaluate the evidence for the frequently made claim that contextual information influences what visual information is attended to and used during reading.

The assumption that such influences exist has been prominent in the reading field for decades. The primary concern has been with the way contextual information influences visual processing. Different theorists have provided different possible explanations (e.g., see Goodman, 1967; Hochberg, 1970; Neisser, 1967; Rumelhart, 1977). This assumed use of contextual information to control what serves as the functional stimulus in reading is often spoken of, in the language of this volume, as an example of higher-level processes influencing lower-level processes.

STUDIES INVOLVING TASKS OTHER THAN SKILLED, SILENT READING

There have been many studies that have demonstrated contextual facilitation of perception in tasks using language-based stimuli (e.g., letters, words, and sentences). Two types of such research deal with perception of language in noise and perception of printed language presented tachistoscopically.

Perceiving Language in Noise

Most of this research has been done with auditory presentation of language. Miller, Heise, and Lichten (1951), for instance, asked subjects to identify words presented in noise and found that the amount of information necessary for word identification was a function of the number of alternative possible words that could occupy that location in the language. As the range of alternatives decreased, more noise could be tolerated; that is, less information from the word itself was needed for correct identification to occur. For example, the word *trees* was readily identified in the sentence *Apples grow on trees,* even when the noise level presented with that word was very high. The authors interpreted this result as indicating that the contextual environment in which a word is presented allows the listener to limit the range of alternatives, thus facilitating the perception of the word, possibly by allowing its identification with less stimulus information. Miller and Isard (1963) further extended these results by demonstrating that both semantic and syntactic information can produce such a context effect. Thus, the context provides multiple sources of information that can limit potential word alternatives. This work made it clear that under impoverished stimulus conditions, listeners can and do use contextual information from their conceptual and linguistic knowledge to interpret what they hear. A related finding using visual noise in reading was reported by Sawyer (1971). She showed that grammatical constraints influenced subjects' ability to read blurred parts of sentences.

Perceiving Briefly Presented Words

Another line of research demonstrating contextual facilitation of word identification has involved subjects in identifying words presented very briefly, using either a tachistoscope or computer display to control the length of the stimulus presentation. O'Neil (1953) and Rouse and Verinis (1962) showed that preceding a to-be-identified target word with a context word, which is associatively related to it, made it possible to identify the target word with shorter presentations. Samuels (1969) made this same demonstration and also showed the influence of word familiarity using semantically related adjective–noun pairs. Tulving and Gold (1963) extended this finding to more normal language materials. They found that preceding the presentation of the target word with a sentence, which the target word would then complete, reduced the presentation time necessary for accurate identification of that word. Tulving, Mandler, and Baumal (1964) suggested that in this task, sources of stimulus information from the word are interchangeable with sources of contextual information. Morton (1964) took this logic one step further, claiming that a reader utilizes some available contextual information to predict the target word, thus allowing the reader to use fewer visual cues to perceive the word. Jacobson (1973) demonstrated the same facilitation in oral reading and visual masking tasks, and even demonstrated an effect using cross-model presentation (context presented aurally; target word, visually).

In a manner similar to the research on the perception of language in noise, these and many other studies have shown that under impoverished stimulus conditions, a person uses contextual information to aid word identification and that with greater contextual constraint, a target word can be identified with less stimulus information.

Generalizing to Reading

It is but a small step from this body of research to suggest that in normal reading, people may be able to "trade off" these sources of information in their perception of text. When the reader is about to encounter a given word, the contextual information is already in mind, so it seems quite reasonable to believe that efficiency might result from making full use of this information in the identification of the next word, thus reducing the amount of visual information that is required from the word itself. There are two reasons why this might be seen as contributing to efficiency in reading. First, a reduction in the amount of visual analysis of the word may be a means of reducing the number of mental operations needed in its identification, thus providing a time savings. This assumes, of course, that putting available contextual information to use for word identification purposes is cognitively easier or faster than acquiring and using additional visual information. Second, using the mind–computer analogy, which is so common in cognitive psychology today, we might suppose that the slowest aspect of mental computing is the I/O (input/output) activity. Thus, operating on information that is already in the mind may be substantially faster than taking in new information. If this were the case (as it typically is with computers), then efficiency could be gained by utilizing existing information (contextual information) as fully as possible and depending minimally on the acquisition of information from visual stimuli.

Several mechanisms have been proposed in the literature by which this sort of efficiency in reading might be achieved, each attempting to explain how the reader succeeds in depending more heavily on contextual information in order to reduce the amount of visual information that must be extracted from the text itself. Neisser (1967) and Levin and Kaplan (1970) suggested an analysis-by-synthesis approach (also see a description by Wanat, 1971) patterned after work on the understanding of oral language by Halle and Stevens (1967). Goodman (1967) proposed a more extreme version in which readers were described as making specific guesses about the words yet to be visually encountered, with minimal visual information then being used simply to confirm or disconfirm these guesses. McConkie and Rayner (1976b) suggested that such guesses may not be necessary and that the reader simply may take in information from a word over time as needed. Such visual information was thought to be used as it was acquired in combination with contextual information, in something like a discrimination net, seeking a unique reading of the word. Once a decision was made, the acquisition of new visual information could be terminated. Brown (1970) suggested that the acquisition of visual information from a word may occur in a fixed sequence, which he called a "noticing order." More gross visual aspects are acquired first—for example, word length, general overall word shape, and perhaps initial and terminal letters. Finer details indicating internal letters would only be acquired later. Again the process of acquiring visual information could be discontinued once the word was identified, thus producing the desired efficiency in visual processing.

Such proposals depict the reader as not wasting processing time on the analysis of visual detail that is not needed for discriminating between alternative possible words permitted by the context. This is very much a "top-down" approach to thinking about perception during reading. Perception is conceived of as involving the judicious positioning of the eyes based on one's knowledge of what is likely to be present next in the text, with perhaps some gross visual cues from the visual periphery to help in this decision (Hochberg, 1970); and as involving an extreme attentional selectivity during fixations—that is, choosing to attend to those aspects of a word that are likely to be useful in making the decisions involved in efficient identification or confirmation. Under high-language-constraint conditions, one would expect that much of the visual detail of the text would never be cognitively encountered by the reader since that detail is not needed under such conditions. Either the eyes would skip over it completely (that is, fixations would be far enough apart that this particular visual pattern would never occupy a retinal location that permits detailed resolution), or it would be given only cursory visual analysis (that is, although it may occupy a retinal region where the detail could be resolved, in fact the reader effectively ignores it).

It is important to note that the research basis for this position largely involved perception under impoverished stimulus conditions. When people are attempting to identify words from insufficient visual information, they are able to use information from the context to help. In such a task it seems likely that subjects are forced to adopt a strategy that maximizes the use of nonvisual information if they are to perform adequately. Subjects could use contextual information to narrow the range of possibilities or use it to aid in determining which aspects of the stimulus to attend to. The sophistication of the visual system in accomplishing this task is attested to by the conscious experience one has in a tachistoscopic task. With no contextual information, a 40-msec presentation followed by a mask can leave one with the feeling of having simply seen a smudge or perhaps a letter or two. An appropriate context produces a drastic improvement of clarity. There is a feeling of having clearly seen the word, and there is a remarkable improvement in the accuracy of the report.

In the normal reading situation, however, people are seldom faced with inadequate stimuli. The text is typically clear and is constantly present for observation. Thus it is quite possible that the types of strategies that are so useful in the impoverished stimulus situation are unnecessary and not employed during normal reading. Is there any evidence that certain aspects of the available visual information are ignored during the reading of clear, persistent text?

There are two lines of research that suggest that certain stimulus information is not utilized in making word identification decisions: errors in oral reading, and proofreaders' errors.

Oral Reading Errors

As people read orally, they occasionally make errors, sometimes inserting words that are not in the original text, sometimes leaving out words, and sometimes replacing text words with other words. These replacements have been of particular interest and have been dubbed "miscues" by Goodman (1969). Miscues are taken as an indication of which aspects of the text were actually used in the word identification process and, hence, as a rather direct indication of the detailed aspects of the reader's perceptual and linguistic processing. Many of these types of errors are contextually appropriate; that is, given the language up to that point, the miscue tends to be an appropriate continuation of the sentence (though it may not combine properly with text not yet encountered, of course). This observation is taken as evidence that contextual information was used in identifying the words. Such errors often preserve aspects of the original text word, such as initial letters, length, and so forth. This fact is taken as evidence that such aspects of the original text were also used in word identification. Those aspects of the printed word that do not jibe with the spoken word are assumed to indicate aspects of the original stimulus that were not used in the identification process. The very existence of such errors is taken as evidence that certain words or parts of words are not perceived by readers.

It should be noted that most of this miscue analysis has been done with children who are learning to read. It seems quite possible that developing readers have difficulty using all the available information at any given moment in order both to achieve an understanding of the message of the text and to produce a spoken version of it that will be acceptable to the listener. In the task of reading aloud, it is a requirement that one say something. Thus, even when the person may be having difficulty, it is still necessary to produce the most appropriate spoken language possible, and the reader does this. To some degree, the miscues indicate the basis on which the language was generated. Interestingly, readers, and particularly older readers, occasionally produce a synonym for a word that is actually in the text. This would suggest that the meaning of the text was perceived and that a word then was chosen for production based strictly on the meaning. It seems likely that the visual characteristics of the word were used in obtaining the meaning (unless, of course, it was strictly guessed from the context) and then not used in selecting a word for production. This points up the problem, in the task of reading aloud, of trying to distinguish between what information was used in understanding language and what information seems to have been used in selecting the words to say (see Allport, 1979, for a further discussion of the distinction between the use of information for understanding vs. production). It is not known how accurately the miscue data indicate what visual information the reader actually attended to, or even what information might have been used by the same person for identifying the word had it not been for the requirement of producing an oral response. Thus, although the existence of miscues in oral reading can be explained by a reader's failure to attend to some visual information, such an explanation is not required by it.

Proofreaders' Errors

Another source of evidence that parts of the text stimulus are ignored during reading comes from proofreaders' errors. It is often difficult to find certain spelling and typographic errors in text. However, once they are seen, the errors are quite obvious. At the same time, it must be noted that other errors are not only readily perceptible but seem to "jump out" at the reader under normal reading conditions. A related observation comes from studies (e.g., Frith, 1979; Smith & Groat, 1979) where subjects are asked to mark all instances of a certain letter in a passage. Certain letters are more likely to be missed in some locations in the text than in others. One reasonable explanation for these phenomena is that during reading, much visual information is not needed and, hence, is not attended to and that these reading habits carry over into other tasks involving textual materials. Thus, errors and letters are missed because they lie at locations that are not visually analyzed during reading. In fact, with this assumption, such tasks can be used to identify which parts of the text tend to be skipped over during reading.

Again it must be recognized that such an explanation is not forced by these phenomena. It seems quite possible, for instance, that reading habits may interfere with these tasks but not in the manner proposed. The likelihood of finding an error or locating a letter in a specific location may well reflect the ease one has in decomposing that portion of text into letter elements for consideration rather than reflecting whether or not visual information from such letters is normally attended to and used in reading.

In this brief review, we have attempted to show that although there are phenomena that are compatible with the notion that certain aspects of textual stimuli are being selectively ignored during reading, the evidence for this position is far from conclusive. In order to study the question more directly, methods are needed for indicating what aspects of the stimulus are being encountered as people are in the act of reading. This is extremely difficult to achieve, but one possible approach is described later.

STUDIES OF PERCEPTION DURING READING

A number of studies have been conducted that deal more directly with perception during reading. In this section, the results of these studies are examined to see whether they provide evidence that readers use different visual information under different contextual conditions—that is, evidence for top-down control over the functional stimulus in reading. First, however, it is necessary to consider some aspects of perception that might be influenced by contextual information.

It is obvious from the outset that the perception of meaning from text at any moment is influenced by the meaning of the earlier portions of the passage. We do not suppose that this generalization is in question. Rather, here we deal with only one aspect of perception: the question of the functional stimulus. Does contextual information influence what aspects of the textual stimulus are encountered and used during reading?

There are at least three ways in which such an influence might occur. First, contextual information may influence where the eyes are sent for fixations.

Where the eyes are centered determines what visual information is potentially available for use in reading. The greatest visual detail is only available from that small region of text that happens to lie directly on and around the fovea. Visual acuity drops off rapidly in the more peripheral visual areas. Second, contextual information may influence the general size and location of the textual region attended to during a fixation. Although there are physiological limits on the level of detail available from different retinal areas, recent research has also demonstrated that attentional factors determine whether potentially available information is actually perceived. With the eyes centered at the same location, a subject is quite capable of attending to different visual regions, thus influencing the likelihood that visual patterns will be detected or used from these different regions (e.g., see Engel, 1976; Rayner, McConkie, & Ehrlich, 1978; Sperling & Melchner, 1978). Third, research by Neisser and Becklen (1975) indicates that narrowing the region within which visual information is used is probably not the only effect of attention. Their results suggest that subjects can give attention to the same general area but respond to different aspects of the stimulus pattern presented there. Thus, it may be that people can attentionally select certain aspects of the stimulus within the general attended region and ignore other aspects.

Our purpose here is to review studies in which relatively skilled readers are involved in the act of reading in order to determine whether contextual information is influencing the three different aspects of perception in reading just described. Essentially, this review consists of an attempt to find evidence for top-down controls on perception in reading. The region being attended to during a fixation is considered first, then the basis for eye movement guidance, and finally the specific visual detail from the text that is used in reading. Definitive answers are not yet available for any of these questions, but some evidence is available on each issue.

The Text Region Attended

Eye movement records indicate, with some accuracy, the locations in the text where the eyes were centered during reading. However, this alone does not indicate what region of text was being perceived during each of these fixations or even whether the text was being seen at all. Visual researchers have studied at the level of visual detail that can be perceived at different retinal locations and how this visual detail interacts with other factors such as the presence of other stimuli at specific locations in the visual field (e.g., see Bouma, 1973). This research can indicate what visual information is potentially available from a passage when the eyes are centered at a specific location, but it does not indicate what region within this area is actually attended to during a fixation in reading or whether the attended region varies from fixation to fixation. This requires research with subjects who are actually engaged in reading a passage. Such investigation is still in its infancy, but research techniques are now available that make it possible (e.g., see McConkie, Zola, Wolverton, & Burns, 1978; Reder, 1973).

In general, research conducted thus far seems to indicate that the region attended to during a fixation is influenced by the reading task itself. However, there is not yet clear evidence that the size or location of this region is varying from fixation to fixation on the basis of contextual factors.

During reading, one does not have the impression of getting meaning from the text on the lines above and below the line being read, although words on these lines are frequently within visual regions where they could be identified if desired. In several studies (e.g., Willows, 1974) extraneous textual materials have been placed between the lines of text, and evidence has been produced that such materials are perceived and influence what is retained from the text. This research has not yet been done using eye-movement-monitoring techniques to determine whether such extraneous materials are sometimes directly fixated. Also, the materials have frequently been printed in ways that might be expected to attract attention; for example, they have been printed in a different color and with different spacing patterns from the rest of the text. Thus, it is still not clear whether, in normal reading, information is acquired from lines other than the one being read.

McConkie and Rayner (1976a) demonstrated that skilled readers use little, if any, visual information more than four letter positions to the left of the fixation point (the letter on which the eyes are centered in the text) during a fixation in reading. Present research is being conducted in our laboratory to determine whether information is even picked up that far to the left of the fixation point. Bouma (1973) has shown that words can be identified when presented farther to the left than this. Thus, we seem to have a clear example of attentional selectivity occurring during reading. Apparently the visual region attended to during fixations in reading lies primarily on and to the right of the center of vision. Whether this differs for Hebrew readers, who read from right to left, or whether it changes when the reader makes regressive (leftward) movements during reading are interesting questions needing study.

There is also some evidence that a region of text tends not to be given attention on two successive fixations. This is in contrast to Smith's (1971) suggestion that the perceptual span is wide enough to permit the same word to be seen on several fixations, thus contributing to accuracy of its identification. In one study (McConkie, 1978) pairs of words were identified that differed in a single letter (for instance, *leaks* and *leans*). Sentences were written in which either word was appropriate (e.g., John did not store his tools in the garage because it _____ too much). College students then read these sentences from a computer-controlled cathode-ray tube (CRT) as their eye movements were recorded. During each forward eye movement, the critical letter differentiating the two words was switched; that is, the word *leaks* was present during one fixation, the word *leans* during the next, *leaks* during the next, etc. Thus, the word was different on successive fixations. If the word in the critical location was identified on two fixations, some difficulty should have been encountered. The results indicated that the subjects were entirely unaware that any change was taking place in the display, and their eye movement records showed no evidence of disruption from the display changes; that is, there were no differences between change and no-change conditions in mean fixation durations, saccade lengths, or number of regressive eye movements. Subjects could generally report what word they saw in the sentence. We tend to believe their reports because in the sentences where the critical word was not changing (one of the words was continuously present), the subjects were very accurate at selecting the word that was present. Thus, it seems likely that once a region of text has been perceived, or read, that region is not reconsidered during the next fixation even though it may lie well within the visual area in which identification would be possible.

If the text regions attended on successive fixations are discrete from one another, this would suggest that the variability typically present in the lengths of saccades during reading may be reflecting a similar variability in the size of the text regions being attended to during different fixations. Thus, the distance the eyes are sent for a saccade in reading may reflect how far to the right of the fixation point "reading" was successful (McConkie, 1979b; McConkie, Hogaboam, Wolverton, Zola, & Lucas, 1979). This speculation appears to be receiving some support from a series of studies presently being conducted by a member of our research group (Hogaboam, 1979). In these studies, subjects read a passage from a CRT as their eye movements are being monitored. During occasional saccades, the text is replaced with a line of Xs. Thus, the text is gone when the eyes stop for the next fixation. When this happens, the subjects' task is to report the last few words they remember reading, to indicate anything they can say about the next word (e.g., its first letter or approximate length), and to guess what the next word might be. The results indicate that subjects can sometimes report the word to which their eyes are being sent (about 30% of the time), but they very seldom report the word to the right of it. Thus, it appears that sometimes readers have enough information about the word to which their eyes are being sent for the next fixation to be able to identify it if needed, but most of the time this is not the case.

This then leads to the question that is of most interest in this volume, and that cannot be answered at this time. Is the variability in the size of the region apparently attended to and interpreted during a fixation related to contextual variables? Investigating this question is one of the planned "next steps" in our research program, but no conclusive answer can be given at this time.

Where the Eyes Are Sent

Speculations about the basis on which the mind decides where to send the eye during reading have ranged over a wide area, from those suggesting little or no specific guidance (Bouma & deVoogd, 1974; Shebilske, 1975) to those suggesting that the eyes are sent precisely to locations based on where the most informative regions of text will be (Hochberg, 1970; Smith, 1971). Data presently being analyzed from a study we have conducted provide evidence that the eyes are being sent to rather specific locations, but the data provide no evidence concerning the basis for that guidance. As college students were reading from a CRT, the text was shifted on the screen two letter positions to the left or right during certain saccades. This caused the eyes to stop for the next fixation at a location two letter positions away from that point in the text where they normally would have stopped. The subjects reported that they had not been aware that the text had moved, but this manipulation had a substantial effect on their eye movement patterns. When the text was shifted to the left, causing the eyes to stop two letter positions farther along the line than they normally would have, a large number of short, regressive movements of about two to three letter positions in length were produced. A similar shift to the right reduced the normal number of regressive movements by one-half and produced an increase in short forward saccades. Thus, the eyes seem to be sent to a rather specific location in the text during a saccade in reading; experimentally displacing that location by just two letter positions clearly affects the person's reading behavior.

There is also considerable evidence indicating that the eyes tend to be sent to some regions in text rather than others during reading (Levy-Schoen & O'Regan, 1979; Rayner, 1978). Rayner (1975) and Abrams and Zuber (1972) found a tendency for the eyes to avoid being centered in empty spaces, including the spaces between sentences. Rayner and McConkie (1976) reported a relation between the length of a word and the probability of fixating a letter in the word. O'Regan (1979) has demonstrated a tendency to send the eyes farther when the next word is a longer word and a tendency to skip the word *the* in one syntactic frame (but not in another). He also reported a greater tendency to fixate a particular region if it contained a three-letter verb than if it contained the word *the*. All these results point to the existence of some sort of control of eye movements in reading (though reading is still possible in the absence of this control, as demonstrated by Bouma & deVoogd, 1974). However, this line of research leaves much to be discovered about the rules on which this control is based, and even about the degree to which it is based on contextual versus visual information.

One reasonable possibility, stated most clearly by Hochberg (1970), is that in some way, the mind avoids sending the eyes to regions where the language is highly predictable because such regions are relatively uninformative. Instead the eyes are sent to more informative regions. Thus the reader's knowledge of the language and of the topic being discussed may be brought into play to aid perception by guiding the eyes in a manner that contributes to efficiency. O'Regan's *the*-skipping effect could be seen as an example of this.

Zola (1979) has attempted to test this possibility in a recent study. He identified seven- or eight-letter nouns that could be highly constrained in passage contexts by single preceding seven- or eight-letter adjectives. For instance, in a paragraph concerning a movie theater, the word *buttered* can make it highly probable that the next word will be *popcorn*. Zola wrote 250 paragraphs, each containing one such target word, preceded immediately by its constraining word. These paragraphs, up to the target word, were given to 150 college students who indicated what the next few words would probably be. The target word was given by at least 85% of the subjects and for many paragraphs, by 100% of them. A second version of each passage was also prepared in which the constraining adjective was replaced by another adjective of equal length; for instance, *buttered popcorn* was replaced by *adequate popcorn, optical illusion* by *curious illusion*, etc. When given these paragraphs up to the target word, students guessed the next word less than 15% of the time. Thus, by the choice of an adjective in these paragraphs, the target noun could be highly constrained or left with considerably less constraint. In the high-constraint condition, the target noun had practically no information value.

Subjects then read 100 of these paragraphs while their eye movements were being recorded, and the data were analyzed to determine the frequency with which the target noun was directly fixated under high- and low-constraint conditions. Zola found that subjects made fixations on the target noun over 96% of the time regardless of the level of constraint. Thus, there was no observable tendency to skip the target noun when it was almost completely specified by the context. Fixation durations on the target noun averaged about 14 msec shorter in the high-constraint condition, indicating that the language constraint was facilitating processing in some manner. In this study, there seemed to be no tendency for skilled readers to skip over a highly predictable word as they were reading. These results do not support the hypothesis of high-level control of eye movements based on language constraints.

Regressive eye movements have typically been believed to result from some confusion on the part of the reader in which some part of the text read earlier was not correctly identified (Huey, 1908/1968). Thus, it has often been suggested that high-level processes detect the incompatibility resulting from earlier misreading, and that the eyes are then sent back to perform a reanalysis of the earlier text to correct the misreading. This would be an example of high-level processes controlling an aspect of perception. Carpenter and Just (1977, Chap. 8, this volume) provide one example of indeterminacy in the text stimulating regressive movements. When the referent to a pronoun was ambiguous, the reader's eyes tended to regress to one of the possible referents, mentioned earlier, and the interpretation of the passage was then generally harmonious with that being taken as the referent of the pronoun. These researchers report that the eyes tended to go rather directly to one potential referent or the other, suggesting that the reader remembered rather precisely the physical location of the words, rather than a tendency for the eyes to scan the text in search of an appropriate referent. Thus it is not clear that the regression was stimulated by a need to search for an appropriate referent; perhaps it simply reflected the referent chosen together with the fact that the choice was not entirely clear. The regression may have been the result of the referent choice rather than being involved in its cause. Clearly, this interesting phenomenon needs further investigation.

In studies mentioned earlier, Hogaboam has also collected some data in which the text was masked and removed from the screen while the reader was making a particular regressive eye movement (say, the second regression on the eighth line of text). The subject then reported the last word read. Relatively few of these instances have been recorded thus far, but the data show a consistent pattern. The word that the subjects give is the last word fixated prior to the regression. Thus, the subjects have identified this word. The regression is not being stimulated by the eyes outrunning the mind and having to go back to some point where word identification faltered. In addition, in this study subjects often report the last several words read, although they are only required to report one. It is of interest that no instances have been observed where these reports show any of the kinds of confusions or misreadings that are typically suggested to be the stimulus for regressive eye movements. Research is continuing in the attempt to learn what the stimulus for regressive movements in reading is.

To date, our research—which admittedly is far from providing final answers on these questions—has not manifested data patterns that require the complex, high-level eye movement control based on language constraints that has been commonly suggested in reading theories.

Attended Aspects of the Visual Stimulus During Reading

Given that the eyes are centered at a certain location for a fixation and that attention is given to a particular region of the text, the final question concerns whether language constraints influence what aspects of the text are used in reading. This is, of course, a very difficult question to study, particularly with subjects actually engaged in reading a passage, and it requires extensive research effort. However, a few initial observations can be made at this time.

One possibility that has been suggested, particularly by Goodman (1967), is that the reader anticipates the text about to be encountered and then only uses a minimal amount of visual detail to test these anticipations. This suggests that the text is in some sense known before the eyes are sent to it. If this were the case, we might expect that if the text were suddenly to go blank during an eye movement and the readers were asked what words were likely to come next, they would respond readily and with a fair degree of accuracy. In Hogaboam's (1979) study, which used this procedure, subjects reported with great accuracy a word no farther to the right than that to which they were sending their eyes on that eye movement, and usually not that far. Frequent prompting and encouragement were required to get them to try to guess the next word, which was often the word to which the eyes were being sent. They felt very unsure, and in fact the accuracy of their guesses was quite poor. Thus, the data indicated an important distinction between the words that had been read, which the subjects reported with confidence and high accuracy, and those that lay farther to the right, about which the subjects were reluctant to guess. The readers did not seem to have active, conscious hypotheses concerning the text that lay beyond the words that had been read, even when they had been or were about to be fixated. Although this is not a critical test of hypothesis and verification models of reading, the results place rather severe constraints on any such theory.

Another relevant observation comes from studies in which we have had subjects read sentences containing one of two words that differ by a single letter at a given word position (the *leaks–leans* example has been cited earlier). In these sentences, the discrimination between two alternative readings of the sentence depends on the accurate identificaton of a single letter. In many of the sentences, the discriminating letters are visually quite similar in shape (e.g., *beans* and *bears*). Yet subjects are very accurate in reporting what the sentences actually say. If subjects were basing their reading on only parts of the visual information from the words, it would seem likely that more misidentifications would be observed in the reading of this material. On the other hand, it may be that the perceptual system operates in a way that causes it to focus on the acquisition of exactly those letters that are so critical to making the discriminations between such possible alternative words. This possibility needs further study.

A final set of observations comes from a study by Zola (1979), previously mentioned, in which the degree of constraint of target nouns in short paragraphs was varied by manipulating the immediately preceding adjective. There were other conditions in this study in which the target words were altered in various ways in order to determine whether such errors would be disruptive to reading. Four experimental conditions had spelling errors of differing severity. A control condition had no spelling errors. In the minimal-error condition, the fourth letter of the target noun (always a seven- or eight-letter word) was replaced by its most visually similar letter, as determined by visual similarity data collected earlier. Thus, the smallest possible change permitted by the English alphabet was made in the most redundant part of the word; certainly this is information not needed for identification of the word, especially under high-redundancy conditions (Pillsbury, 1897). Other error conditions were more severe. In the third condition, the fourth letter was replaced by its most visually dissimilar letter from the same category, where letters were categorized as either ascenders, descenders, or others. In the fourth condition, the fourth letter was replaced by its most similar letter, and the fifth letter was replaced by a letter from a different category. This error condition caused a small change in the external shape of the target word. And in the fifth condition, the initial, fourth, and final letters were replaced.

The study was done under the assumption that if a reader only attended to that part of the visual stimulus that was necessary to select among contextually allowable alternatives, then more visual information would be needed from the target word in the low-constraint condition than in the high-constraint condition.

Under high-constraint conditions, relatively little visual information would be needed for word identification—perhaps only word length and initial and final letters. If this assumption were correct, then subjects would not attend to other aspects of the visual stimulus; unneeded visual information would not be processed; and errors that did not violate the needed information would have no effect on reading. Thus, under lower visual constraint, more visual detail should be used in word identification, and less severe errors should cause difficulty in reading.

The view of perception in reading just described would suggest that only the most severe errors would affect reading under high-constraint conditions where the target word could usually be identified on the basis of the prior context alone; less severe errors would cause difficulty in the low-constraint condition; and the minimal-error condition would have no effect in either condition, since the level of visual detail being changed was probably not needed for word identification under either condition.

The task given to the subjects was simply to read the passages and prepare to answer comprehension questions about them. The subjects were told that errors had been put in the text, but that their task was to ignore the errors and simply read for understanding. Subjects were given practice trials in which they read several paragraphs that contained errors. Throughout the study, a comprehension test was administered after each block of six paragraphs. The questions never involved information stated in sentences containing the errors. Subjects were not asked to comment about the errors during the experiment. Thus an active effort was made to orient the subjects toward reading for retention and away from attending to the errors. In fact, in each block of 72 lines, there were only eight errors, two of these being minimal errors. Thus, errors were infrequent in the text.

The study involved 20 college students, each reading 100 paragraphs, with each paragraph containing one target noun. Thus each subject read 10 paragraphs under each of the 10 conditions (2 levels of constraint by 5 levels of error). The eye movement data were examined in detail to determine whether the errors had an effect on fixation durations, saccade lengths, and frequency of regressive movements in the area of the error, as compared to the no-error control conditions.

The results do not appear to support the description of perception in reading given earlier. As already indicated, there was no tendency for subjects to fixate the target nouns less frequently in high- than in low-constraint conditions or to differ in where they fixated the word. It was not the case that small errors affected reading only in the low-constraint condition. Even the minimal errors seemed to have an effect on subjects' reading behavior, under both the high- and low-constraint conditions. There is no condition in which the high-constraint paragraphs showed no effect of errors but the low-constraint condition did. Thus, it appears that under both extremely high and low-constraint conditions, visual detail was being encountered and used in reading that an information-theoretic-related position would claim was not needed. More extreme errors caused greater disruption in the reading patterns, as might be expected, and subjects in the high-constraint conditions had an easier time dealing with severe errors than subjects in the low-constraint conditions. But it appears that under even the highest constraint, the subjects were attending to a great deal of the visual detail of the target noun, at least frequently enough to produce mean differences in eye movement measures as compared to the no-error condition.

The results from Zola's study appear to be yielding data patterns that stand as a rather direct challenge to some common notions of top-down influences on the selection of visual information during reading. This study was specifically designed to provide the opportunity for contextual influences on the functional stimulus to be manifested in the data patterns. However, no evidence has been found that readers encounter more of the visual stimulus of a word when there is less contextual constraint on the word; that they use only a small amount of the visual information to verify their hypotheses concerning the word; or that they employ some sort of noticing order from gross to fine detail in the word that terminates when sufficient information has been garnered to permit word identification given the present context. Rather, it appears that readers are responding to most of the visual detail of the stimulus even under high-language-constraint conditions. Whether they are conscious of the presence of small errors that are affecting their reading is, of course, another question requiring further research.

WHERE IS CONTEXTUAL FACILITATION?

The conclusion that seems to be emerging from the research already discussed is that whereas it may be possible for people to use contextual information to help identify a word when the stimulus alone is insufficient, under adequate stimulus conditions the stimulus is rather fully used. Efficiency is apparently not gained by circumventing visual analysis. In fact, relying heavily on visual information may be more efficient in normal reading than having to depend too much on contextual information for word identification. Recently, there have been suggestions that as children become better readers, they depend more heavily on the visual information from the text, rather than contextual information (e.g., Perfetti & Roth, Chap. 11, this volume; Stanovich, Chap. 10, this volume).

Although the studies reviewed here call into question a common explanation for the effects of contextual constraint on reading, at the same time they further document the existence of such effects. The question still remains. How should we explain the facilitation that results from contextual constraint during reading? O'Regan (1979) has shown that under some conditions, the eyes are sent farther when the next word is an article (undoubtedly more predictable) than when it is a verb. Wanat (1971) has found that subjects spend less time looking at more constrained regions of sentences. Zola (1979) has shown a shorter fixation on a word when it is more highly constrained by its context. How can we account for such instances of facilitation if they do not result from reduced perceptual analysis?

One alternative that appears tempting is provided by recent research on priming, which comes from studies dealing with semantic memory. This research indicates that preceding the presentation of a word with the presentation of a semantically related word reduces the time necessary to make lexical decisions about it (Meyer & Schvaneveldt, 1971). In some way, the activation produced by one word selectively facilitates the processing of a second related word. Of particular interest is the report that the first word can have this effect even when it has been presented for such a short time that the subject cannot indicate what the word was and sometimes is not even aware that a word was presented; that is, the priming word was below perceptual threshold (Marcel & Patterson, 1978). Without the priming word even being identified in any normal sense, its meaning seems to have been perceived, and the arousal of that meaning seems to have had an influence on decisions about a semantically related word presented later. This research, if replicated, suggests that the perception of words, including gaining meaning from them, can be a very direct sort of activity and is not something that might benefit from becoming entangled in decisions about what visual information to respond to (and in what order) on the basis of contextual information.

This body of research on priming raises an alternative way of conceptualizing perception in reading that will likely attract some attention in the future. Is it possible that at the beginning of a fixation, all the words that lie in a retinal region within which sufficient visual clarity is available for their identification rapidly arouse their meanings in the brain? If this were the case, then attentional processes would need to be thought of as selecting from among spatially tagged semantic information, rather than from visual patterns. The primary task of attentional processes would not then be the analyses of visual information in order to identify what word or words were on the page, but rather would be selecting from those potential meanings, which are rather directly provided, the particular ones that will next contribute to the construction of an understanding of the message of the text. From this view, contextual facilitation may aid in the arousal of those meanings through priming (Fischler & Bloom, 1979), and attentional selectivity would then be occurring with higher-level representations, rather than at the level of visual information. Exploring this possibility requires experimental techniques that will indicate whether readers are in some way responding to the meanings of words that lie outside the region being directly attended to during fixations.

We have one further observation to make that may place some constraints on this way of conceptualizing perception during reading. We have constructed sentences and short paragraphs in which either of two words could occupy particular word positions. These two words differed by only a single letter. As subjects read the materials, one of the words was present for the first 80 or 100 msec of each fixation. The text was then disrupted briefly by presenting a 20-msec mask (a line of Xs) or by shifting the entire line one letter position to the right and then returning it to its original position. When the original text returned, a letter had been changed in the target word, which of course resulted in a different word occupying that location for the rest of the fixation. After reading these texts, the subjects were asked questions designed to reveal which word they read in the sentence and were then asked whether they saw more than one word. In this pilot work, sometimes a subject reported only the first word presented, sometimes only the second word, and sometimes reported having seen both words. Thus, in some instances, the subjects seemed to have employed the meaning from that word early during the fixation and sometimes, only later during the fixation. It does not seem to be true that the meanings of all words are settled upon during the initial few milliseconds of a fixation, nor that a change in meaning at some point in the visual field will be detected.

The preliminary results from this pilot study seem to support the position that information from different regions of the visual field is used in reading at different times during the fixation. Thus, if meanings are aroused rapidly at the beginning of a fixation, as the priming literature might suggest, it still seems that the employing of these meanings for the purpose of understanding the text is an activity that takes place over the time of the fixation in some sort of systematic fashion. In addition, these results suggest that given this way of thinking about perception in reading, one would have to conclude that meanings can be masked and changed during a fixation without conscious awareness that such a change has occurred.

Whether or not a priming-based theory of this sort can account for contextual facilitation during normal reading is a question that will require considerable thought and research ingenuity. Perhaps most important at the present time is the need for more careful studies that document and describe the effects of contextual constraints during reading. Only by having a number of well-established observations about these effects will we be in a position to select among alternative possible explanations.

CONCLUSION

In this chapter we have attempted to review the evidence available to support the notion that the visual information used in reading is a function of the contextual information available. Results from studies of language identification in noise and of word identification from tachistoscopic presentation clearly indicate that contextual information can be used to facilitate word identification under inadequate stimulus conditions. However, these results do not provide strong evidence that such an interaction is occurring during normal reading. Other forms of evidence using tasks more similar to reading (proofreading errors and errors in reading aloud), though compatible with this position, also do not require it.

Three aspects of perception were identified that might be affected by contextual information: where the eyes are sent, the visual region attended to, and the visual information within that region that is used for reading. The studies conducted to date that investigate perception during reading are not definitive on these issues. However, there currently appears to be no clear evidence that the contextual information environment exerts control over what visual information is used in reading—that is, over the functional stimulus. In fact, subjects appear to be responding to considerable visual detail of words that are almost completely constrained by their prior context. From present evidence, it seems quite possible that contextual facilitation is not achieved by reducing the amount of visual information a reader acquires from individual words.

ACKNOWLEDGMENTS

The research described in this chapter was supported by grants MH32884 and MH24241 from the National Institute of Mental Health to the first author, and by contract no. US-NIE-C-400-76-0116 from the National Institute of Education to the Center for the Study of Reading, University of Illinois at Urbana–Champaign. The authors express their thanks to Thomas W. Hogaboam for his contributions in the preparation of this chapter.

REFERENCES

Abrams, S. G., & Zuber, B. L. Some temporal characteristics of information processing during reading. *Reading Research Quarterly*, 1972, *7*, 40–51.

Allport, A. Word recognition in reading. In P. A. Kolers, M. E. Wrolstad, & H. Bouma (Eds.), *Processing visible language* (Vol. 1). New York: Plenum Press, 1979.

Bouma, H. Visual interference in the parafoveal recognition of initial and final letters of words. *Vision Research*, 1973, *13*, 767–782.

Bouma, H., & deVoogd, A. H. On the control of eye saccades in reading. *Vision Research*, 1974, *14*, 273–284.

Brown, R. Psychology and reading. In H. Levin and J. P. Williams (Eds.), *Basic studies on reading*. New York: Basic Books, 1970.

Carpenter, P. A., & Just, M. A. Reading comprehension as eyes see it. In M. A. Just & P. A. Carpenter (Eds.), *Cognitive processes in comprehension*. Hillsdale, N.J.: Lawrence Erlbaum Associates, 1977.

Engel, F. L. *Visual conspicuity as an external determinant of eye movements and selective attention*. Published thesis, Eindhoven, 1976.

Fischler, I., & Bloom, P. A. Automatic and attentional processes in the effects of sentence contexts on word recognition. *Journal of Verbal Learning and Verbal Behavior*, 1979, *18*, 1–20.

Frith, U. Reading by eye and writing by ear. In P. A. Kolers, M. E. Wrolstad, & H. Bouma (Eds.), *Processing visible language* (Vol. 1). New York: Plenum Press, 1979.

Goodman, K. S. Reading: A psycholinguistic guessing game. *Journal of the Reading Specialist*, 1967, *6*, 126–135.

Goodman, K. S. Analysis of oral reading miscues: Applied psycholinguistics. *Reading Research Quarterly*, 1969, *5*, 9–30.

Halle, M., & Stevens, K. N. Remarks on analysis by synthesis and distinctive features. In W. Wathen-Dunn & L. E. Woods (Eds.), *Models for the perception of speech and visual form*. Cambridge, Mass.: M.I.T. Press, 1967.

Hochberg, J. Components of literacy: Speculations and exploratory research. In H. Levin & J. P. Williams (Eds.), *Basic studies on reading*. New York: Basic Books, 1970.

Hogaboam, T. W. *The relationship of word identification and eye movements during normal reading*. Paper presented at the annual meeting of the Psychonomic Society, Phoenix, Arizona, November 1979.

Huey, E. B. *The psychology and pedagogy of reading*. New York: Macmillan, 1908. (Republished by M.I.T. Press, Cambridge, Mass., 1968.)

Jacobson, J. Z. Effects of association upon masking and reading latency. *Canadian Journal of Psychology*, 1973, *27*, 58–69.

Levin H., & Kaplan, E. L. Grammatical structure and reading. In H. Levin & J. P. Williams (Eds.), *Basic studies on reading*. New York: Basic Books, 1970.

Levy-Schoen, A., & O'Regan, K. The control of eye movements in reading. In P. A. Kolers, M. E. Wrolstad, & H. Bouma (Eds.), *Processing visible language* (Vol. 1). New York: Plenum Press, 1979.

Marcel, A. J., & Patterson, K. E. Word recognition and production: Reciprocity in clinical and normal studies. In J. Pequin (Ed.), *Attention and performance VII*. Hillsdale, N.J.: Lawrence Erlbaum Associates, 1978.

McConkie, G. W. *Where do we read?* Paper presented at the annual meeting of the Psychonomic Society, San Antonio, Texas, November, 1978.

McConkie, G. W. *Eye movement data in the study of silent reading*. Paper presented at the annual meeting of the American Education Research Association in San Francisco, California, 1979. (a)

McConkie, G. W. On the role and control of eye movements in reading. In P. A. Kolers, M. E. Wrolstad, & H. Bouma (Eds.), *Processing visible language* (Vol. 1). New York: Plenum Press, 1979. (b)

McConkie, G. W., Hogaboam, T. W., Wolverton, G. S., Zola, D., & Lucas, P. A. Toward the use of eye movements in the study of language processing. *Discourse Processes*, 1979, *2*, 157–177.

McConkie, G. W., & Rayner, K. Asymmetry of the perceptual span in reading. *Bulletin of the Psychonomic Society*, 1976, *8*, 365–368. (a)

McConkie, G. W., & Rayner, K. Identifying the span of the effective stimulus in reading: Literature review and theories of reading. In H. Singer & R. B. Ruddell (Eds.), *Theoretical models and processes of reading*. Newark, Del.: International Reading Association, 1976. (b)

McConkie, G. W., Zola, D., Wolverton, G. S., & Burns, D. D. Eye movement contingent display control in studying reading. *Behavior Research Methods & Instrumentation*, 1978, *10*, 154–166.

Meyer, D. E., & Schvaneveldt, R. W. Facilitation in recognizing pairs of words: Evidence of a dependence between retrieval operations. *Journal of Experimental Psychology*, 1971, *90*, 227–234.

Miller, G. A., Heise, G. A., & Lichten, W. The intelligibility of speech as a function of the context of the test materials. *Journal of Experimental Psychology*, 1951, *41*, 329–335.

Miller, G. A., & Isard, S. Some perceptual consequences of linguistic rules. *Journal of Verbal Learning and Verbal Behavior*, 1963, *2*, 217–228.

Morton, J. The effects of context on the visual duration threshold for words. *British Journal of Psychology*, 1964, *55*, 165–180.

Neisser, U. *Cognitive psychology*. New York: Appleton-Century-Crofts, 1967.

Neisser, U., & Becklen, R. Selective looking: Attending to visually-specified events. *Cognitive Psychology*, 1975, *7*, 138–150.

O'Neil, W. M. The effect of verbal association on tachistoscopic recognition. *Australian Journal of Psychology*, 1953, *5*, 42–45.

O'Regan, J. K. Moment to moment control of eye saccades as a function of textual parameters in reading. In P. A. Kolers, M. E. Wrolstad, & H. Bouma (Eds.), *Processing visible language* (Vol. 1). New York: Plenum Press, 1979.

Pillsbury, W. B. A study in apperception. *American Journal of Psychology*, 1897, *8*, 315–393.

Rayner, K. Parafoveal identification during a fixation in reading. *Acta Psychologica*, 1975, *39*, 271–282.

Rayner, K. Eye movements in reading and information processing. *Psychological Bulletin*, 1978, *85*, 618–660.

Rayner, K., & McConkie, G. W. What guides a reader's eye movements? *Vision Research*, 1976, *16*, 829–837.

Rayner, K., McConkie, G. W., & Ehrlich, S. Eye movements and integrating information across fixations. *Journal of Experimental Psychology: Human Perception and Performance*, 1978, *4*, 529–544.

Reder, S. M. On-line monitoring of eye position signals in contingent and noncontingent paradigms. *Behavior Research Methods & Instrumentation*, 1973, *5*, 218–228.

Rouse, R. O., & Verinis, J. S. The effect of associative connections on the recognition of flashed words. *Journal of Verbal Learning and Verbal Behavior*, 1962, *1*, 300–303.

Rumelhart, D. E. Toward an interactive model of reading. In S. Dornic (Ed.), *Attention and performance VI*. Hillsdale, N.J.: Lawrence Erlbaum Associates, 1977.

Samuels, S. J. Effects of word associations on the recognition of flashed words. *Journal of Educational Psychology*, 1969, *60*, 97–102.

Sawyer, D. J. *Intra-sentence grammatical constraints in readers' sampling of the visual display.* Unpublished doctoral dissertation. Department of Education, Cornell University, 1971.

Shebilske, W. Reading eye movements from an information-processing point of view. In D. Massaro (Ed.), *Understanding language*. New York: Academic Press, 1975.

Smith, F. *Understanding reading*. New York: Holt, Rinehart & Winston, 1971.

Smith, P. T., & Groat, A. Spelling patterns, letter cancellation and the processing of text. In P. A. Kolers, M. E. Wrolstad, & H. Bouma (Eds.), *Processing visible language* (Vol. 1). New York: Plenum Press, 1979.

Sperling, G., & Melchner, M. J. The attention operating characteristic: Examples from visual search. *Science*, 1978, *202*, 315–318.

Tulving, E., & Gold, C. Stimulus information and contextual information as determinants of tachistoscopic recognition of words. *Journal of Experimental Psychology*, 1963, *66*, 319–327.

Tulving, E., Madler, G., & Baumal, R. Interaction of two sources of information in tachistoscopic word recognition. *Canadian Journal of Psychology*, 1964, *18*, 62–71.

Wanat, S. F. Linguistic structure in reading: Models from the research of Project Literacy. In F. B. Davis (Ed.), *The literature of research in reading with emphasis on models* (The final report for Project No. 2: The Literature Search. Contract No. OEC-0-70-4790 [508]). New Brunswick, N.J.: Graduate School of Education, Rutgers—The State University, 1971.

Willows, D. M. Reading between the lines: Selective attention in good and poor readers. *Child Development*, 1974, *45*, 408–415.

Zola, D. *The perception of words in reading*. Paper presented at the annual meeting of the Psychonomic Society, Phoenix, Arizona, November, 1979.

8 Cognitive Processes in Reading: Models Based on Readers' Eye Fixations

Patricia A. Carpenter and Marcel Adam Just
Department of Psychology
Carnegie-Mellon University
Pittsburgh, Pa. 15213

OVERVIEW

This chapter develops a process model of reading comprehension, as well as a more general theoretical framework to explain why and how reading changes with the task, the text, and the reader. The model focuses on the processes of word encoding, case role assignment, and text integration and tries to account for how long readers spend on various parts of a text. Readers make longer pauses at points of increased processing that correspond to encoding infrequent words, integrating information from more important clauses, and making inferences at the ends of sentences. The model predicts the gaze duration of college students on each clauselike unit of scientific text as a function of the involvement of each of these processes. The durations of some of the processes change when the reader's goals change—for example, when the same text is read under different instructions. The flexibility of reading is ascribed to processing goals that control the extent to which the stages of encoding, case role assignment, and integration are executed.

Since eye fixations may be an unfamiliar form of data, Table 8.1 presents an excerpt that may dispel some misconceptions and illustrate some characteristics of eye fixations that motivate the reading model. This table presents a protocol of a college student reading a technical passage about the properties of nonradioactive isotopes. The reader's task was to read a paragraph and then perform a simple true–false comprehension test. The sequence of fixations within each sentence is indicated by the successively numbered fixations above the word being fixated. The duration of each fixation (in msec) is shown below the fixation number.

TABLE 8.1
The Eye Fixations of a College Student Reading a Technical Passage
in Order Later to Verify True–False Statements.

The sequence of fixations within each sentence is indicated by the successively numbered fixations above the word being fixated. The duration of each fixation (in msec) is shown immediately below the fixation number.

4	11
286	466

1	2	3	5	6	7	8	9
166	200	167	299	217	268	317	399

Radioisotopes have long been valuable tools in scientific and medical

5
183

10	1	2	3	4	6	8	7	9
463	317	250	367	416	333	183	450	650

research. Now, however, four nonradioactive isotopes are being produced.

4	8
366	183

1	2	3	5	6	7	9	10	11
250	200	367	400	216	233	317	283	100

They are called "icons"—four isotopes of carbon, oxygen, nitrogen, and

12	13
683	150

sulfur.

One possible misconception is that readers are selective about which words they fixate in the previously unread portions of the text. The data here (and most of our other data) indicate that under virtually all nonskimming conditions, most content words (over 80%) and many function words are fixated. Another possible misconception is that the time spent on all words is approximately equal once word length is taken into account. The data in Table 8.1 show this not to be the case. For example, the words *radioisotopes* and *icons* were fixated for a long time. This chapter shows that the longer fixations are due to longer processing caused by the words infrequency and their thematic importance (so that the reader integrates them with previous long-term knowledge). Also, the fixations at the end of each sentence tend to be long. For example, this reader had fixations of 399 msec and 483 msec on *medical research* at the end of the first sentence, and 450 msec and 650 msec on *being produced* at the end of the second sentence. These long fixations are later shown to reflect a processing episode that is evoked at the end of a sentence.

The link between eye fixation data and the theory rests on two assumptions. The first, called the immediacy assumption, is that a reader tries to understand each content word of a text as he or she encounters it, even at the expense of making guesses that sometimes turn out to be wrong. "Understanding" refers to processing at several levels, such as encoding the word, choosing one meaning of it, assigning it to its referent, and determining its status in the sentence and in the discourse. The immediacy assumption posits that the interpretations at all levels of processing are not deferred; they occur as soon as possible, a qualification that is clarified later.

The second assumption, the eye–mind assumption, is that the eye remains fixated on a word as long as the word is being processed. So the time it takes to process a newly fixated word is directly indicated by the gaze duration. Of course, comprehending that word often involves the use of information from preceding parts of the text, without any backward fixations. So the concepts corresponding to two different words may be compared to each other, for example, while only the more recently encountered word is fixated. The eye–mind assumption can be contrasted with an alternative view that data acquired from several successive eye fixations are internally buffered before being semantically processed (Bouma & deVoogd, 1974). This alternative view was proposed to explain an unusual reading task in which the phrases of a text were successively presented in the same location. However, the situation was unusual in two ways. First, there were no eye movements involved, so the normal reading processes may not have been used. Second, and more telling, readers could not perform a simple comprehension test after seeing the text this way. By contrast, several studies of more natural situations support the eye–mind assumption that readers pause on words that require more processing (Carpenter & Daneman, 1981; Just & Carpenter, 1978). The eye–mind assumption posits that there is no appreciable lag between what is being fixated and what is being processed. In the research that is described, the durations of the individual fixations on a particular word or phrase of the text are cumulated into a single gaze duration. Then the immediacy and eye–mind assumptions are used to interpret the gaze duration data in the development of a model of reading comprehension.

The chapter has four major sections. The first briefly describes a theoretical framework for considering the processes and structures in reading. The second section describes the eye fixation experiment in reading. The third describes the model itself, with subsections describing each component process of the model, and applies the model to a quantitative analysis of the eye fixation results. The fourth section describes mechanisms that allow for changes in reading processes in different situations and provides results from a second experiment that pin-point some of the changes.

THEORETICAL FRAMEWORK

Reading can be construed as the coordinated execution of a number of processing stages, such as word encoding, lexical access, assigning semantic roles, and relating the information in a given sentence to previous sentences and previous knowledge. Some of the major stages of the proposed model are depicted schematically in Fig. 8.1. The diagram depicts both processes and structures. The stages of reading in the left-hand column are shown in their usual sequence of execution. The long-term memory on the right-hand side is the storehouse of knowledge, including the procedural knowledge used in executing the stages on the left. The working memory in the middle mediates the long-term memory and the comprehension processes. Although it is easy to agree informally on the general involvement of these processes in reading, it is more difficult to specify

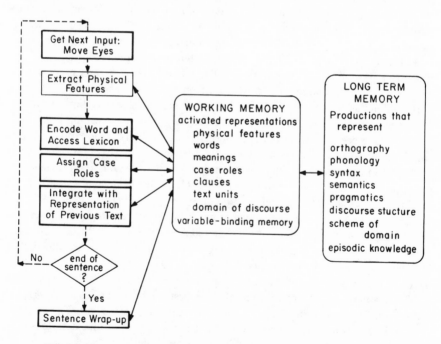

FIG. 8.1.   A schematic diagram of the major processes and structures in reading comprehension. Solid lines denote data-flow paths, and dashed lines indicate canonical flow of control.

the characteristics of the processes, their interrelations, and their effects on reading performance.

The nature of comprehension processes depends on a larger issue—namely, the architecture of the processing system in which they are embedded. Although the human architecture is very far from being known, production systems have been suggested as a possible framework because they have several properties that might plausibly be shared by the human system. (Detailed discussions of production systems as models of the human architecture are presented elsewhere; Anderson, 1976; Newell, 1973, 1980.) There are three major properties of particular relevance here.

1. Structural and procedural knowledge is stored in the form of condition-action rules, such that a given stimulus condition produces a given action. The productions "fire" one after the other (serially), and it is this serial processing that consumes time in comprehension and other forms of thought. In addition to the serial productions, there are also fast, automatic productions that produce spreading activation among associated concepts (Anderson, 1976; Collins & Loftus, 1975). These automatic productions operate in parallel to the serial productions and in parallel to each other (Newell, 1980). These productions are fast and automatic because they operate only on constants; that is, they directly associate an action with a particular condition (such as activating the concept "dog" on detecting "cat"). By contrast, serial productions are slow because they operate on variables as well as constants; they associate an action with a class of conditions. A serial production can fire only after the particular condition instance is bound to the variable specified in the production. It may be the binding of variables that consumes time and capacity (Newell, 1980). This architectural feature of two kinds of productions permits serial comprehension processes to operate in the foreground while in the background, automatic productions activate relevant semantic and episodic knowledge.

2. Productions operate on the symbols in a limited-capacity working memory. The symbols are the activated concepts that are the inputs and outputs of productions. Items are inserted into working memory as a result of being encoded from the text or being inserted by a production. Retrieval from long-term memory occurs when a production fires and activates a concept, causing it to be inserted into working memory. Long-term memory is a collection of productions that are the repositories of both procedural and declarative knowledge. In the case of reading, this knowledge includes orthography, phonology, syntax, and semantics of the language, as well as schemas for particular topics and discourse types (cf. Schank & Abelson, 1977). A new knowledge structure is acquired in long-term memory if a new production is created to encode that structure (Newell, 1980). This occurs if the structure participates in a large number of processing episodes.

One important property of working memory is that its capacity is limited, so that information is sometimes lost. One way that capacity can be exceeded (causing forgetting) is that the level of activation of an item may decay to some subthreshold level through disuse over time (Collins & Loftus, 1975; Hitch, 1978; Reitman, 1974). A second forgetting mechanism allows for processes and structures to displace each other, within some limits (Case, 1978). Heavy processing requirements in a given task may decrease the amount of information that can be maintained, perhaps by generating too many competing structures or by actively inhibiting the maintenance of preceding information. There is recent evidence to suggest that working memory capacity (as opposed to passive memory span) is strongly correlated with individual differences in reading comprehension performance, presumably because readers with greater capacity can integrate more elements of the text at a given time (Daneman & Carpenter, 1980).

3. Production systems have a mechanism for adaptive sequencing of processes. The items in the working memory at a given time enable a given production to fire and insert new items, which in turn enable another production, and so on. In this way, the intermediate results of the comprehension process that are placed in working memory can influence or sequence subsequent processing. There is no need for a superordinate controlling program to sequence the mental actions.

The self-sequencing nature of productions is compatible with the model depicted in Fig. 8.1. The composition of each stage is simply a collection of productions that share a common higher-level goal. The productions within a stage have similar enabling conditions and produce actions that serve as conditions for other productions in the same stage. The productions within a stage need not be bound to each other in any other way. Thus the ordering of stages with a production system is accomplished not by direct control-transfer mechanisms, but an indirect self-sequencing accomplished by one production helping to create the conditions that enable the "next" production to fire.

This architecture permits stages to be executed not only in a canonical order but also in noncanonical orders. There are occasions when some stages of reading appear to be partially or entirely skipped; some stages seem to be executed out of sequence; and some "later" stages sometimes seem to be able to influence "earlier" stages (Levy, Chap. 1, this volume). Stages can be executed earlier than normal if their enabling conditions exist earlier than normal. For example, if a context strongly primes a case role, then the case assignment could precede the lexical access of a word. Having read *John pounded the nail with a* _____, a reader can assign the last word to the instrumental case on the basis of cues provided by the words *pound* and *nail,* before encoding *hammer.* This organization can permit "context effects" in comprehension, where a strong preceding context shortens reading time on a given word or clause. This might occur if a processing stage that is normally intermediate between two others is partially or entirely eliminated. It could be eliminated if the preceding stage plus the context provided sufficient enabling conditions for the later stage. Analogously, a misleading context could lengthen comprehension time by providing elements that enable conflicting processes.

The production system organization can also explain how "later" stages can influence "earlier" stages, so that higher-level schemas can, for example, affect word encoding. If the productions of the normally later stage are enabled earlier than usual, then their outputs can serve as inputs to the normally earlier stage. The ordering of stages does not have to be entirely reversed to obtain this top-down influence. It may be sufficient for just a portion of the productions of the "later" stage to fire in order to influence the "earlier" stage.

In this view of processing stages, several stages can be executed contemporaneously, in the sense that firings of productions of two or more stages may be interleaved. Consequently, data and control can be transferred back and forth among different stages, somewhat similarly to computer programs organized into co-routines. Co-routines are two or more subprograms that have equal status (i.e., there is no master–slave relationship); when one co-routine obtains control, it executes until it detects a condition indicating that it should relinquish control, and then another co-routine executes, and so on. One interesting difference between co-routines and the production system model is that co-routines generally transfer information between each other only along specified paths, used especially for this purpose. By contrast, productions "transfer" information by placing it in the working memory, so that all processes have access to it. In this sense, the working memory serves as a message center, and communication among stages is by means of the items in working memory. This is distinct from one stage feeding its output directly to another stage.

RESEARCH

The Texts

This section describes the texts that were used in the reading research because their properties, both local and global, have a large influence on the processing. The global organization of a narrative text has been shown to influence how a reader recalls the text (Kintsch & van Dijk, 1978; Mandler & Johnson, 1977; Meyer, 1975; Rumelhart, 1977; Thorndyke, 1977). The experiment reported next shows that the organization has at least part of its effect when the text is being read. Scientific texts were selected from *Newsweek* and *Time* because their content and style is typical of what students read to learn about technical topics. The passages discussed a variety of topics that were generally unfamiliar to the readers in the study. (When readers were asked to rate their familiarity with the topic of each passage, the modal rating was at the "entirely unfamiliar" end of the scale.) There were 15 passages, averaging 140 words each. One of the passages is shown in Table 8.2. The texts are moderately well written, and they

TABLE 8.2
A Scientific Paragraph Used in the Experiment

Radioisotopes have long been valuable tools in scientific and medical research. Now, however, four nonradioactive isotopes are being produced. They are called "icons"—four isotopes of carbon, oxygen, nitrogen, and sulfur. Each icon has one more neutron in its nucleus than the number usually found in carbon (12), oxygen (16), nitrogen (14), and sulfur (32). The odd neutron gives the isotopes a distinctive magnetic characteristic. These isotopes have some of the same characteristics that made radioisotopes useful for tracing chemical reactions and even powering some of the scientific instruments left on the moon by Apollo astronauts. But the icons do not have the damaging radiation of radioisotopes. Consequently, icons offer good prospects for pharmacological research, for pollution monitoring, and for clinical medicine.

are on the border line between "fairly difficult" and "difficult" on Flesch's readability scale (1951), with 17 words per sentence and 1.6 syllables per word.

A simplified grammar was developed to categorize the components of the texts. The grammar (shown schematically in Fig. 8.2) classifies the text units, often clauses but sometimes whole sentences or single words, into a structure that is quasi-hierarchical. This abbreviated grammar captures most of the regularities in our short passages (see Vesonder, 1979, for a more complete grammar for longer scientific passages). The initial sentences generally introduced a topic—a scientific development or event. The beginnings of the passage sometimes gave details of the time, place, and people involved with the discovery. Familiar concepts were simply named, and unusual concepts were accompanied by an

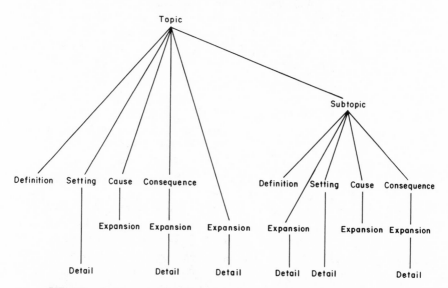

FIG. 8.2. A schematic diagram of the major text-grammatical categories of information in the scientific paragraphs.

TABLE 8.3
A Classification of the Icon Passage into Text-Grammatical Categories

Topic:	Radioisotopes have long been valuable tools in scientific and medical research.
Topic:	Now, however, four nonradioactive isotopes are being produced.
Definition:	They are called "icons"
Definition:	the four isotopes of carbon, oxygen, nitrogen, and sulfur.
Expansion (of topic):	Each has one more neutron in its nucleus than the number usually found in
Details:	carbon (12), oxygen (16), nitrogen (14), and sulfur (32).
Expansion:	The odd neutron gives the isotopes a distinctive magnetic characteristic.
Subtopic:	These isotopes have some of the same characteristics that made radioisotopes useful for
Detail:	tracing chemical reactions and even powering some of the scientific instruments left on the moon by Apollo astronauts.
Subtopic:	But the icons do not have the damaging radiation of radioisotopes.
Consequence:	Consequently, icons offer good prospects
Details:	for pharmacological research, for pollution monitoring, and for clinical medicine.

explicit definition. The main topic itself could be developed through specific examples or through subtopics that were then expanded with further descriptions, explanations, and concrete examples. Consequences, usually toward the end of the passage, gave the importance of the event for other applications. Table 8.3 shows how each text unit or sector in the *Icon* passage was classified according to these categories (consecutive sectors belonging to the same category have been merged in this table). All 15 passages were segmented into a total of 275 sectors. Each sector was then assigned to one of the five levels by one of the authors. The levels of the grammar were further confirmed by a pretest involving 16 subjects who rated the importance of each sector in its passage on a 7-point scale. The mean importance ratings differed reliably among the five levels, $F(4,270) = 40.04$, $p < .01$. Specifically, the means decreased monotonically down through the five postulated levels. So the grammar potentially has some psychological reality, and its relevance to reading will be demonstrated with the eye fixation data.

Method and Data Analysis

Before the model and data procedures are described in detail, this section presents the data collection and analysis procedures. The readers were Carnegie-Mellon undergraduates who read 2 practice texts followed by the 15 scientific texts in random order. One group of readers was asked to recall each paragraph immediately after reading it, whereas another group was given about 10 sentences to verify as true or false, also immediately after reading the paragraph. The subjects were asked to read naturally, without rereading or trying to memorize the paragraph, but with a goal of performing well in the recall or verification task. The readers' eye fixations were monitored and recorded as they read the texts.

The paragraphs were presented on a television monitor using upper- and lowercase and a conventional paragraph layout. The sentences were presented one at a time and cumulated on the screen to form the paragraph. The subject pressed a button when he or she came to the end of each sentence, at which point the screen was blanked except for a fixation point indicating where the next sentence began. The reader fixated the point and pressed the button. Then the next sentence was presented along with all of the previous sentences so that the entire paragraph appeared on the screen by the time the subject was reading the last sentence.

The reader's pupil and corneal reflections were monitored relatively unobtrusively by a television camera that was 2.5 feet away. The monitoring system, developed by Applied Science Laboratories, computed the point of regard (rather than eye movement or head movement) every 16.7 msec. If the subject's point of regard was within 1 degree of the fixation point, then the data for that sentence were scorable. This procedure was used to test whether accuracy of 1 degree was maintained throughout the paragraph. If 1-degree accuracy was not maintained, the data for the entire paragraph were discarded. Due to machine problems, eye fixation data were not obtained from 3 of the subjects in the recall condition and 1 in the verifiration condition. There were 13 remaining readers in the recall condition and 9 in the verification condition, who on average produced 10 entirely scorable paragraphs and 5 entire paragraphs for which the data were discarded.

The objective of the data reduction procedure was to convert the 60 observations per second to some dependent measure that could be meaningfully related to reading time. First, there was some reduction as the data were being acquired in real time. A new "fixation" was scored as having occurred if the point of regard changed by more than 1 degree (the size of a three-letter syllable). Furthermore, durations of blinks that were preceded and followed by fixations on the same location were attributed to the reading time on that location. Notice that this treatment of the data ignores traditional fixations and deals only with the time on a given part of the text, regardless of how many "real" fixations went into that time. The reason for this procedure is that such gaze durations are the most direct behavioral measures to relate to cognitive processes (Just & Carpenter, 1976).

Another program computed the duration of gaze of each subject on each of the 275 sectors. The pooling of all fixation durations on the several words of a sector helps to average over some measurement noise. Since the accuracy of the tracker was about 1 degree, the measure could be in error by about three letters. By pooling all the fixation durations in a sector, the inaccuracy becomes less important. The mean duration of gaze on each sector (i.e., the average over all the subjects in each experimental condition who produced scorable data for a given paragraph) was computed. The data were fit to the model with a multiple linear regression, in which the independent variables were the factors postulated to affect reading time and the dependent variable was the mean gaze duration of each of the 275 sectors.

THE READING MODEL

The next subsections describe the five major stages shown in Fig. 8.1: Get next input, encoding and lexical access, case role assignment, interclause integration, and sentence wrap-up. Each subsection describes the processes in that stage together with the factors that should affect the duration of those processes and hence the gaze durations.

Get Next Input

This is the first stage of a cycle that finds information, encodes it, and processes it. When the perceptual and semantic stages have done all the requisite processing on a particular word, the eye is directed to land in a new place, where it continues to rest until the requisite processing is done, and so forth. The specification of what constitutes "all of the requisite processing" is contained in a list of conditions that must be satisfied before the reader terminates the gaze on the current word and fixates the next one. These conditions include a specification of the goals of normal reading. For instance, one condition may be that a meaning of the word be accessed, and another condition may be that a case role be assigned. These conditions can also reflect more specific reading goals. A reader who is trying to memorize a text may have as a condition that the word or phrase be transferred to long-term memory. By setting the conditions appropriately, the reader can adjust the relevant processes to the situation at hand. When the goal conditions for processing a word are satisfied, the resulting action is to "get next input."

The command to get next input usually results in a saccade to the next part of the text—one or two words forward. The process that selects the placement of the next forward fixation does not have to be very complex or intelligent. The choice of where to place the next forward fixation appears to depend primarily on the length of the next word or two to the right of the current fixation (McConkie & Rayner, 1975). The length information, which is encoded parafoveally, is then used to program a rightward saccade. But if only the right margin is visible in the parafovea, then the eye is directed to the first word of the next line, producing a return sweep. In this case the information in peripheral vision is not adequate for accurate targeting. The return sweep is typically too short; the eye often lands on the second word of the new line for a very brief amount of time (50 or 75 msec) and then makes a corrective saccade leftward to the first word of the line (Bayle,

1942). On occasion, a comprehension stage may require a review of previously read text to reencode it or process it to deeper levels. In those cases, the get-next-input stage results in a regressive saccade to the relevant portion of the text.

The duration of the get-next-input stage is short, consisting of the time needed for a neural signal to be transmitted to the eye muscles. In monkeys, this takes about 30 msec (Robinson, 1972). This duration must not be confused with the typical 150–200-msec latency of a saccade to a visual stimulus that has spatial or temporal uncertainty (Westheimer, 1954). These latencies include stimulus detection, interpretation, and selection of the next fixation target. In normal reading, there is very little uncertainty about direction of the next saccade (it is almost always rightward for forward fixations, except for the return sweeps). Nor is there much uncertainty about distance. On average, the saccade distance may be simply the mean center-to-center distance between words, a distance that does not vary much relative to the physically possible variation in eye movements. Thus it is reasonable to suppose that the preprogramming time is very short here, consisting usually of a "go" signal and the time it takes that signal to be translated into a motor movement, about 30 msec (Robinson, 1972). The actual movements, the saccades, constitute about 5% to 10% of the total reading time. Recent analyses suggest that the saccade itself may destroy the visual persistence of the information from the preceding fixation so that it does not mask the input from the new fixation (Breitmeyer, 1980). Consequently, stimulus encoding may commence soon after the eye arrives at a new location.

Word Encoding and Lexical Access

The reading process involves encoding a word into an internal semantic format. It is assumed that prior to this encoding, the transduction from the printed word to the visual features has already taken place and that the features have been deposited into the working memory. Perceptual encoding productions use the visual features as conditions; their action is to activate the representation of the word. Once the representation of the word has been sufficiently activated, its corresponding concept is accessed and inserted into working memory. The concept serves as a pointer to a more complete representation of the meaning, which consists of a small semantic network realized as a set of productions. The major nodes of the network are the possible meanings of the word, the semantic and syntactic properties of the meanings, and information about the contexts in which they usually occur (see Rieger, 1979, for a related proposal). The word meanings are represented as abstract predicates, defined by their relations to other predicates.

The productions that encode a word generally trigger on orthographically based subword units, like syllables (Mewhort & Beal, 1977; Spoehr & Smith, 1973; Taft, 1979). However, there are times when alternative codes, including orthographic, phonological, and whole-word codes are used (Baron, 1977;

Kleiman, 1975; LaBerge & Samuels, 1974). Since the syllablelike encoding unit is believed to be the dominant one, the data should be analyzed in terms of the number of syllables in each word.

The mechanism underlying lexical access is the activation of a word's meaning representation by various sources. There are three ways that a concept's level of activation can be temporarily increased above its base level. One activation mechanism is perceptual encoding; the encoded representation of a word can activate its meaning. A second source is the parallel productions that produce spreading activation through the semantic and episodic knowledge base of the reader. The third source is activation by the serial productions that do the major computations in all the stages of processing. When a concept has been activated above some threshold by one or more of these sources, a pointer to its meaning is inserted into working memory. The activation level gradually decays to a subthreshold level unless some process reactivates it. If the word soon reoccurs in the text while the concept is still activated, lexical access will be facilitated because the activation level will still be close to threshold. When the activation level does decrease, it decreases to an asymptote slightly higher than the old base level. In this way, the system can learn from both local and long-term word repetitions. Frequently used words will have a high base level of activation and consequently will require relatively less additional activation to retrieve them. Thus, frequent words should take less time to access than infrequent words (Morton, 1969). Similarly, the various possible interpretations of each word will have different base activation levels, such that the more common interpretations have higher base activation levels. For example, whereas the word *does* has at least two very different meanings, the "third-person singular verb" interpretation would have a higher base activation because it is more common than the "female deer" interpretation (Carpenter & Daneman, 1981). The more common interpretation would then be accessed faster, since less additional activation would be required to bring the activation level to threshold. This model of lexical access can account for word frequency effects, priming effects, and repetition effects in reading.

Lexical access is complicated by the fact that some words have more than one meaning, so the appropriate interpretation must be selected or at least guessed at. When a polysemous word is accessed, the word representation that is retrieved is a pointer to a semantic network that includes the multiple representations. The interpretation that is selected is the one with the highest activation level, and several factors can affect the activation. First, some interpretations start off with a higher activation level; for instance, the "third-person singular" interpretation of *does* has a higher base activation level than the "deer" interpretation. Second, the automatic productions that produce spreading activation can contribute selectively to the activation level of one particular interpretation. The spreading activation can emanate from the preceding semantic and syntactic context, from the reader's knowledge of the domain, and from knowledge of the discourse style.

Third, the output of other stages operating on the same word may activate a particular interpretation. For example, although *hammer* can be interpreted as a noun or a verb, a sentence context that suggests an instrument to the case role assignment stage (e.g., *John hit the nail with a* _____) may help activate the noun interpretation. Fourth, when a word with many highly related meanings occurs in an impoverished context, there may be no single interpretation with higher activation than others, and the superordinate concept may be the selected interpretation of the word. This probably occurs for words that have many closely related interpretations, such as *get* and *take*.

The selection of only one interpretation of each word, posited by the immediacy assumption, provides a measure of cognitive economy. Selecting just one interpretation allows the system to dampen the activation of the unselected interpretations to keep them from activating their associates. Thus, the contextual effects would remain focused in the appropriate semantic domain. This permits a limited-capacity working memory to cope with the information flow in a spreading activation environment that may activate many interpretations and associations for any lexical item. This method of processing also avoids the combinatorial explosion that results from entertaining more than one interpretation for several successive words.

This aspect of the model is consistent with some recent results on lexical access that indicate that although multiple meanings of a word are initially activated, only one meaning remains activated after a few hundred milliseconds. In one experiment, the subjects simultaneously listened to a sentence and pronounced a visually presented word. When an ambiguous word (*rose*) was presented auditorily in a syntactic context (e.g., *They all rose*), the speed of pronouncing a simultaneous visual probe related to either meaning (*stood* or *flower*) was faster than in a control condition (Tanenhaus, Leiman, & Seidenberg, 1979). In another experiment, the subjects listened to a sentence and performed a lexical decision task on visually presented stimuli. When an ambiguous word (*bug*) was presented in a semantic context (*John saw several spiders, roaches, and bugs*), the speed of a simultaneous lexical decision related to either meaning (*insect* or *spy*) was faster than a control (Swinney, 1979). In both studies, the facilitation of the inappropriate meaning was obtained only within a few hundred milliseconds of the occurrence of the ambiguous word. If the probe was delayed longer, the inappropriate interpretation was no faster than the control. These results suggest that both meanings are available when an ambiguous word is being accessed, but the inappropriate meaning is lost from working memory after a short time.

As the interpretation of the text is constructed, a corresponding representation of the extensive meaning—the things being talked about—is also being built. If readers cannot determine the referents of the words in a passage, they will find the text difficult to understand. One example of this problem is highlighted in a passage from Bransford and Johnson (1973) that discussed a procedure that involved arranging ". . . things into different groups. Of course, one pile may be sufficient depending on how much there is. . . . [p. 400]." Subjects who weren't given the title "Washing Clothes" thought the story was incomprehensible. The referential representation helps the reader to disambiguate referents, infer relations, and integrate the text.

The immediacy assumption posits that there is an attempt to relate each content word to its referent as soon as possible. Sometimes this can be done when the word is first fixated, but sometimes more information is required. For example, whereas the semantic interpretation of a relative adjective like *large* can be computed immediately, the extensive meaning depends upon the word it modifies (for instance, *large insect* versus *large building*). The referent of the entire noun phrase can be computed only after both words are processed. The immediacy assumption doesn't state that the relating is done immediately on each content word but, rather, that it occurs as soon as possible. This is an important distinction that is made again in the discussion on integrative processes.

Assigning Case Roles

Comprehension involves determining the relations among words, the relations among clauses, and the relations among whole units of text. This section describes the first of these processes, that of determining the relations among the words in a clause (or, in Schank's [1972] terms, determining the dependencies among the concepts). These relations can be categorized into semantic cases, such as agent, recipient, location, time, manner, instrument, action, or state (Chafe, 1970; Fillmore, 1968). The case role assignment process usually takes as input a representation of the fixated word, including information about its possible case roles and syntactic properties. For example, hammers tend to be instruments rather than locations or recipients, and information about a word's usual case role can be an important contributor to the assignment process. But this normative information generally is not sufficient to assign its case role in a particular clause. Consequently, the assignment process relies on heuristics that use the word's meaning together with information about the prior semantic and syntactic context, as well as language-based inferences. The output of the process is a representation of the word's semantic role with respect to the other constituents in its clause.

Just as certain meanings suggest particular case roles, so too can the context prime a particular case role. Consider the sentence *John was interrogated by the* _____. The semantic and syntactic cues suggest that the missing word will be an agent, such as *detective*. The strength of the context becomes evident if the primed case does not occur; for example, *John was interrogated by the window*. The prior semantic context can precede the affected case assignment by more than a few words. In the sentences: *The lawyer wanted to know where in the room John had been interrogated; Mary told him that John was interrogated by the window;* the thematic focus of the first sentence on a location alters the interpretation of *by* and facilitates a locative case role assignment for *window*.

The specific heuristics that are used in case role assignment have received some attention (see Clark & Clark, 1977, for some examples). Many proposals have the suggestion that readers use the verb as a pivotal source of information to establish the necessary and possible case roles and then fit the noun phrases into those slots (Schank, 1972). But the immediacy assumption posits that the case role assignment for an item preceding the verb is not postponed in anticipation of the verb. Like the lexical access stage, the case assignment stage makes a best guess about a word's case when the word is fixated, rather than making the decision contingent on subsequent words. So the model would not accord any special status to verbs. Another suggested heuristic (that children appear to use) is to assign a sequence consisting of animate noun–verb–noun to the case roles of agent–action–object (Bever, 1970). Like all heuristics, this one sometimes fails, so young children sometimes misinterpret passive sentences (Fraser, Bellugi, & Brown, 1963). This heuristic may be employed by adults but in a modified version that conforms to the immediacy assumption. Rather than waiting for the three major constituents before assigning case roles, readers should assign an animate noun to the agent role as soon as they encounter it, in the absence of contrary prior context.

The immediate assignment of a case role implies that readers will sometimes make errors and have to revise previous decisions. For example, an adult who assigns the role of agent to an animate noun and then encounters a passive verb will have to revise the agent assignment. (Presumably, young children don't make this revision.) The immediacy of the case assignment process is evident in the reading of such sentences as *Mary loves Jonathan*. The immediacy assumption suggests that a reader would assign *Jonathan* the role of recipient; this would turn out to be an incorrect assignment if the sentence continued, *Mary loves Jonathan apples*.

Because case roles are assigned within clauses, the assignment process must include a segmentation procedure to determine clause boundaries within sentences. Sentences can sometimes be segmented into clauses on the basis of explicit markers, such as a subordinating conjunction (e.g., *because, when*). More often, the reader cannot tell with certainty where one clause ends and another starts until he or she has read beyond the clause boundary (or potential boundary). A general strategy for dealing with such cases has been suggested— namely, to assign a word to the clause being processed if possible (Frazier & Fodor, 1978). For example, the word *soil* in the sentence *When farmers are plowing the soil* can continue the initial clause (*When farmers are plowing the soil it is most fertile*) or start a new one (*When farmers are plowing the soil is most fertile*). The suggested strategy is to continue the initial clause until contrary information is encountered. Interestingly, the strategy discussed by Frazier and

Fodor presupposes the immediacy assumption; the segmentation decision arises because case roles are assigned as soon as the words are encountered.

There is no direct mapping between particular case roles and the duration of the assignment process. For example, there is no a priori reason to expect that assignment of instruments takes more or less time than locations. The time for a particular assignment might depend more on the context and properties of the word than on the particular case role being assigned. Detailed specification of the process is not within the scope of this chapter; it probably requires a large-scale simulation model to examine the complex interactions of different levels of processing.

Interclause Integration

The reader must relate clauses and sentences to each other in order to capture the coherence in the text. As each new clause or sentence is encountered, it must be integrated with the previous information acquired from the text or with the knowledge retrieved from the reader's long-term memory. Integrating the new sentence with the old information consists of representing the relations between the new and the old structures.

Several search strategies may be used to locate old information that is related to the new information. One strategy is to check whether the new information is related to the other information that is already in working memory either because it has been repeatedly referred to or because it is recent (Carpenter & Just, 1977a; Kintsch & van Dijk, 1978). Using this strategy implies that adjacency between clauses and sentences will cause a search for a possible relation. For instance, the adjacent sentences *Mary hurt herself, John laughed* seem related (John must be a cad), even though there is no explicit mention of the relation. This strategy also entails trying to relate new information to a topic that is active in working memory. This is a good strategy, since information in a passage should be related to the topic.

A second strategy is to search for specific connections based on cues in the new sentence itself. Sentences often contain old information as well as new. Sometimes the old information is explicitly marked (as in cleft constructions and relative clauses), but often it is simply some argument repeated from the prior text. Readers can use this old information to search their long-term text representation and referential representation for potential points of attachment between the new information and the old (Haviland & Clark, 1974). This second strategy may take more time than the first. In fact, it takes longer to read a sentence that refers to information introduced several sentences earlier than one that refers to recently introduced information (Carpenter & Just, 1977a).

There are two main points at which integration can occur. First, as each ensuing word of the text is encountered, there is an attempt to relate it to previous information (Just & Carpenter, 1978). Second, a running representation of the clause is maintained, with an updating as each word of the clause is read. This running clause representation consists of the configuration of clause elements arranged according to their case relations. This second type of integration involves an attempt to relate the running clause representation to previous information at each update. Integration occurs whenever a linking relation can be computed. Consider the sentence: *Although he spoke softly, yesterday's speaker could hear the little boy's question.* The point of this example is not so much that the initial integration of *he* and *speaker* is incorrect but that the integration is attempted at the earliest opportunity. This model implies that integration time may be distributed over fixations on different parts of a clause. Moreover, the duration of the process may depend on the number of concepts in the clause; as these increase, the number of potential points of contact between the new clause and previous information will increase. There is also evidence for integration triggered by the end-of-sentence; this process is discussed in more detail later.

Integration results in the creation of a new structure. The symbol representing that structure is a pointer to the integrated concepts, and this superordinate symbol is then available for further processing. In this way, integration can chunk the incoming text and allows a limited working memory to deal with large segments of prose. The macrorules proposed by Kintsch and van Dijk (1978) can be construed as productions that integrate.

Integration can also lead to forgetting in working memory. As each new chunk is formed, there is a possibility that it will displace some previous information from working memory. Particularly vulnerable are items that are only marginally activated, usually because they were processed much earlier and haven't recently participated in a production. For instance, the representation of a clause will decay if it was processed early in a text and was not related to subsequent information. This mechanism can also clear working memory of "lower-level" representations that are no longer necessary. For example, the verbatim representation of a previously read sentence may be displaced by the processes that integrated the sentence with other information (Jarvella, 1971). By contrast, the semantic elements that participate in an integration production obtain an increased activation level. This increases the probability that they will become a permanent part of long-term memory.

The main types of interclause relations in the scientific passages correspond to the text-grammatical categories described previously, such as definitions, causes, consequences, examples, and so forth. Text roles that are usually more important to the text and to the reader's goals, such as topics or definitions, are integrated differently than less important units, such as details. The more central units will initiate more retrievals of relevant previous knowledge of the domain (schematic knowledge) and retrievals of information acquired from the text but no longer resident in the working memory. In addition, more relations will be computed between the semantically central propositions and previous information, because centrality inherently entails relations with many other units. By contrast, details are often less important to the reader's goals and to the text. Moreover, when a detail is to be integrated, the process is simpler because details are often concrete instantiations of an immediately preceding statement (at least in these scientific texts), so they can quickly be appended to information still present in the working memory. Thus, higher-level units will take more time to integrate, because their integration is usually essential to the reader's goals and because integration of higher units involves more relations to be computed and more retrievals to be made.

The nature of the link relating two stuctures may be explicitly denoted in the text (with connectives like *because, therefore,* and *for instance*), or it may have to be inferred on the basis of schematic knowledge of the domain. For example, the causal relation between the sentences *Cynthia fell off the rocking horse. She cried bitter tears* is inferred from the reader's knowledge about the temporal and causal relation between falling and hurting oneself (Charniak, 1972).

One cost of immediate interpretation, case role assignment, and integration is that some decisions will prove to be incorrect. There must be mechanisms to detect and recover from such errors. The detection of a misinterpretation often occurs when new information to be integrated is inconsistent with previous information. So misinterpretation detection may be construed as inconsistency detection. For example, the sentence *There were tears in her brown dress* causes errors initially because the most frequent interpretation of *tears* is not the appropriate one here, and the initial interpretation is incompatible with *dress*. The eye fixations of subjects reading such garden-path sentences clearly indicate that readers do detect inconsistencies, typically at the point at which the inconsistency is first evident (Carpenter & Daneman, 1981). At that point, they use a number of error-recovery heuristics that enable them to reinterpret the text. They do not start reinterpreting the sentence from its beginning. The heuristics point them to the locus of the probable error. Readers start the backtracking with the word that first reveals the inconsistency—in this case, *dress*. If that word cannot be reinterpreted, they make regressions to the site of other words that were initially difficult to interpret, such as ambiguous words on which a best guess about meaning had to be made. The ability to return directly to the locus of the misinterpretation and to recover from an error makes the immediacy strategy feasible.

Sentence Wrap-Up

A special computational episode occurs when a reader reaches the end of a sentence. This episode, called sentence wrap-up, is not a stage of processing defined by its function but rather by virtue of being executed when the reader reaches the end of a sentence. The processes that occur during sentence wrap-up involve a search for referents that haven't been assigned, the construction of interclause relations (with the aid of inferences, if necessary), and an attempt to handle any inconsistencies that could not be resolved within the sentence.

The ends of sentences have two important properties that make them especially good places for integration. First, within-sentence ambiguities are usually clarified by the end of the sentence. For example, if a sentence introduces a new object or person whose identity can't be inferred from the preceding context, some cue to that identity is generally given by the end of the sentence. For that reason, if readers can't immediately determine the referent of a particular word, they can expect to be told the referent or given enough information to infer it by the end of the sentence. Indeed, readers do use the ends of sentences to process inconsistencies that they can't resolve within the sentence (Carpenter & Daneman, 1981). The second property is that the end of a sentence unambiguously signals the end of one thought and the beginning of a new one. It can be contrasted with weaker cues that signal within-sentence clause boundaries, such as commas, relative pronouns, and conjunctions, that can signal other things besides the end of a clause. Since ends-of-sentences are unambiguous, they have the same role across sentences, and they may be processed more uniformly than within-sentence clause boundaries.

There is ample empirical support for integrative processing at the ends of sentences. Previous eye fixation studies show that when a lexically based inference must be made to relate a new sentence to some previous portion of the text, there is a strong tendency to pause at the lexical item in question and at the end-of-sentence that contains it (Just & Carpenter, 1978). Readers were given paragraphs containing pairs of related sentences; the first noun in the second sentence was the agent or instrument of the verb in the first sentence:

1a. It was dark and stormy the night the millionaire was murdered.
1b. The killer left no clues for the police to trace.

In another condition, the integrating inference was less direct:

2a. It was dark and stormy the night the millionaire died.
2b. The killer left no clues for the police to trace.

It took about 500 msec longer to process sentence 2b than 1b, presumably because of the more difficult inference linking *killer* to *die*. There were two main places where the readers paused for those 500 msec, indicating the points at which the inference was being computed. One point was on the word *killer,* and the other was on the end of the sentence containing *killer.* Another eye fixation study showed that integration linking a pronoun to its antecedent can occur either when the pronoun is first encountered or at the end of the sentence containing the pronoun (Carpenter & Just, 1977b).

Reading-time studies also have shown that there is extra processing at the end of a sentence. When subjects self-pace the word-by-word or phrase-by-phrase presentation of a text, they tend to pause longer at the word or phrase that terminates a sentence (Aaronson & Scarborough, 1976; Mitchell & Green, 1978). The pause has been attributed to contextual integration processes, similar to the proposed interclause integration process here. Yet another source of evidence for sentence wrap-up processes is that verbatim memory for very recently comprehended text declines after a sentence boundary (Jarvella, 1971; Perfetti & Lesgold, 1977). The model attributes the decline to the interference between sentence wrap-up processes and the maintenance of verbatim information in working memory.

It is possible that wrap-up episodes could occur at the ends of text units smaller or larger than a sentence. For example, the data of Aaronson and Scarborough (1976) suggest that there are sometimes wrap-up processes at the ends of clauses. The decision of when and if to do wrap-up may be controlled by the desired depth of processing. For example, skimming may require wrap-up only at paragraph terminations, whereas understanding a legal contract may require wrap-up at clause boundaries. In fact, the clause boundary effects obtained by Aaronson and Scarborough are sensitive to the subjects' reading goals.

RESULTS

Data Analysis

The purpose of the analysis was to partition reading time into the various processes outlined in the model. Each of the 15 paragraphs was divided into sectors, as in the example in Table 8.3, producing a total of 275 sectors. The sectors were classified into the categories described by the grammar. A multiple regression analysis computed how the gaze duration on each sector was affected by the variables presumed to influence different stages of the processing. The regression analysis had eight independent variables that coded: the size of a sector, the number of infrequent words it contained, whether it was the last sector in a sentence, and five more variables that coded the text-grammatical level of the sector. More precise descriptions of these measures are presented with the results.

Verification Condition Results.   The analysis indicates how reading time was distributed across the various processing stages when readers anticipated a true–false comprehension test. The eight independent variables were associated with various processing stages, as indicated by the tripartite division of Table 8.4.

1. *Lexical encoding/access and case role assignment.*   Even though lexical encoding, lexical access, and case role assignment are believed to be separable

processes, their durations cannot be measured separately in this experiment. The combined duration of these processes should depend on two factors. The duration should increase with the size of the sector because larger sectors will have more words to encode and more case roles to be assigned. Sector length was measured in number of character spaces since this can easily be done by a computer program. In retrospect, it would have been preferable to measure the length of a sector in syllables, since the syllable might plausibly be a unit of lexical encoding (Spoehr & Smith, 1973). However, the number of syllables is typically highly correlated with the number of letters, with r above .75 in some similar texts we have examined. The second factor affecting the duration of these processes is the number of infrequent words in a sector, because the time taken to access the meaning of infrequent words is longer. "Infrequent" was operationally defined as occurring less than 25 times per million in the Kucera and Francis norms (1967). A word was counted as infrequent only on its first occurrence in the paragraph. These parameters for encoding, access, and case role assignment are shown in the top part of the table. The 22 msec per character indicates the time to encode words, retrieve their meanings, and assign case roles. As Table 8.4 indicates, the first occurrence of an infrequent word added 51 msec to the gaze, suggesting that one or more of the three—encoding, access, and case role assignment—takes longer for unusual words. Frequency effects are often attributed to the lexical access process (Glanzer & Ehrenreich, 1979). The additional intercept of 98 msec is a wastebasket parameter. It suggests that there is a minimal duration on a sector corresponding to the minimum encoding, access, and assignment duration.

TABLE 8.4
Application of the Model to the
Verification Condition

	Regression Weight (msec)
Encoding, lexical access, & case role assignment	
Time per character	22*
Time per infrequent word	51*
Intercept	98
Integration (time per content word)	
Topics	96*
Definitions/consequences	99*
Subtopics	57*
Expansions	49*
Details	9
Sentence wrap-up	309*

*t has $p < .01$.

2. *Clause integration.* The model posits that integration time should depend on the text-grammatical level of a clause and on the number of concepts it contains. The corresponding independent variable was the interaction of the indicator variables that represented the five text-grammatical levels and the variable that represented the number of content words in the sector, with content words defined as in Hockett (1958).

The text-grammatical role of the sector influenced the duration of the integration processes as shown in the middle portion of Table 8.4. Important sectors, such as topics and definitions, had much longer gaze durations than did unimportant sectors, particularly details, when sector length was controlled in an analysis of covariance, $t(269) = 7.67$ and 7.39 respectively, $p < .01$. For example, the additional time spent integrating topics was 96 msec per content word. Consequently, the introductory topic sentence for the icon passage, with 7 content words, required an additional 672 msec for integration. By contrast, the integration time for details was only 9 msec per content word, the only parameter that was not significantly different from zero. The results suggest that details did not receive processing much beyond what was required for encoding and case role assignment. Integration time increases with the number of content words in a sector because more relations are computed. As the number of content words increases, there are more potential relations to other information in the text and to the reader's prior knowledge.

Different text-grammatical roles are integrated to different extents. For example, readers may not relate details to as many different parts of their representations because details are perceived as less important than other kinds of information. In addition, the integration parameter reflects the probability of having to retrieve information from long-term memory. Because details are generally preceded by a relevant superstructure, they can be integrated faster than if they were to be related to information that has to be retrieved from long-term memory.

3. *The sentence wrap-up* stage should be reflected by an increase in the fixation duration on sectors that were at the ends of sentences. This was coded by another indicator variable. Sentence wrap-up contributes an additional 309 msec to sentence-terminal sectors, as shown in Table 8.4. This parameter reflects the inference making, consistency checking, and integration that occurs at the end of a sentence. The size of the parameter must be interpreted with caution because the procedure required readers to push a button at the end of each sentence, and the response preparation and execution may have contributed to this parameter. Recently, the end-of-sentence effect has been obtained in studies that presented the entire paragraph at one time, with subjects responding only at the end of the paragraph. The obtained parameter was smaller (71 msec) but still reliable.

The parameters can be used to estimate the reading time for individual sectors. The estimated reading times are compared to the observed reading times for the icon passage in Table 8.5. The observed and estimated times for this paragraph

TABLE 8.5
The Observed and Estimated Reading Times
for the Sectors of the Icon Paragraph

	Observed	Estimated
Radioisotopes have long been valuable tools in scientific and medical research.	3073	2857
Now, however, four nonradioactive isotopes are being produced.	2813	2322
They are called "icons"	1116	961
four isotopes of	646	582
carbon	193	260
oxygen	213	260
nitrogen	276	355
sulfur	343	621
Each icon has one more neutron in its nucleus than the number usually found in	2630	2370
carbon	519	379
oxygen (16)	506	379
nitrogen (14)	287	474
sulfur (32)	536	791
The odd neutron gives the isotopes a distinctive magnetic characteristic.	2526	2099
These isotopes have some of the same characteristics that made radioisotopes useful for	2226	2417
tracing chemical reactions	526	767
even powering some of the scientific instruments left on the moon	1666	1606
by Apollo astronauts	873	988
But the icons do not have the damaging radiation of radioisotopes.	2750	2448
Consequently, icons offer good prospects	943	1083
for pharmacological research	959	802
for pollution monitoring	639	765
and for clinical medicine	910	995

correlate quite highly, $r(21) = .98$, $p < .01$. Over all the paragraphs, the correlation is similarly high, $r(273) = .96$, $p < .01$.

This analysis can be used to estimate how reading time was distributed over the major processing stages. The proportions will vary with the text, but the icon passage gives an example of the distribution. For the icon passage, the model accounted for about 26.6 sec of the observed reading time of 27.2 sec. About 17.5 sec, or 66%, was consumed by the encoding and case role assignment processes. About 3.3 sec, or 12%, was consumed by the integration stage. About 2.5 sec, or 9%, was accounted for by the sentence wrap-up processes. Finally, another 2.2 sec, or about 8%, was consumed by the base time, which is an intercept parameter covering processes common to all sectors. The time for saccades was not included in the measured gaze durations, but it adds 5% to 10% overhead beyond the 27.2 sec.

The parameters in Table 8.4 are all significantly different from zero except for the integration time for details. In addition, the accuracy of the model can be compared to the variability in reading times among sectors. The standard deviation of reading times among the 275 sectors was 917 msec, reflecting the considerable variation in their length, text-grammatical role, and so forth. Compared to this variation, the model fits the data quite well; the standard error of estimate is 265 msec. The model accounts for 92% of the total variance among the 275 means. However, much of the variation among the means is due to differences in the sizes of the sectors. A model that contains only a variable representing the sector size accounts for 84% of the variance, leaving 16% that is unrelated to sector size. Thus the reading model, which accounts for 92% of the total variance, captures 50% of the variance unrelated to sector size.

The model characterizes some of the reading behavior of individual subjects and not just the average of their distributions of reading time. The median proportion of variance accounted for in the analysis of each subject's data was 77% in the verification task. Moreover, the parameter values for individual subjects stayed within a reasonable range of the parameter value of the subject means. For example, the encoding and case role assignment time was 22 msec for the data averaged over subjects, whereas the individual subjects' parameters ranged from 19 to 27 msec in the verification task. Infrequent words took longer for all but one subject in the verification task. All readers took longer to integrate the more important sectors in the text grammar. They also spent additional time at the ends of sentences, ranging from 157 to 525 msec. Thus the model applied to the group data is a reasonable index of individual reading performance as well.

VARIATION IN READING

It is obvious that people read very differently in different situations, but that there is still something that can be identified as "reading" across diverse tasks. A theory of reading should explain the commonalities and differences. The commonality across reading tasks may reflect the fact that all types of reading involve the basic processes of word encoding and lexical access, case role assignment, integration, and inference making. What differs between situations is the extent to which each process is evoked. For example, a reader who is checking for logical consistency may devote relatively more processing effort to integration. At the other extreme, some processes may be reduced to a bare minimum. For example, a skimmer may do very little syntactic processing. Since skimmers fixate relatively few words in a sentence, it might be difficult or impossible to establish complete syntactic coherence. These are examples of how the amount of processing devoted to a particular stage can vary across tasks. The model proposes that the amount of processing done of each type of stage is determined by the goals for that situation. The goals determine the conditions that must be satisfied—the kind and amount of information that the system needs before proceeding to the next word or clause. These goals, in turn, reflect the reader's objective in reading, the nature of the text, and the reader's knowledge of the content domain.

Perhaps the most important influence on reading is the reader's objective in reading. This often determines both what is read and how it is read. A reader will consult a technical journal for research information but pick up a novel for entertainment. However, the text's effects can be separated from the reader's objective, and both can have a large effect in their own right. The same scientific texts used in the experiment reported earlier are read differently when the antici-pated comprehension test is somewhat different, as the study reported next shows. The change can be localized to a specific process, with the help of the reading model. Eventually, a major part of a theory of reading will be a taxonomy of reading objectives and their effects on each of the processing stages. Presumably, the taxonomic approach would start with some of the more common functions of reading, such as reading to learn, to follow instructions, and to be entertained (cf. Sticht, 1977).

The second major influence, the text structure, interacts with the reading process at several levels. Variables such as word frequency and concreteness influence encoding time and readability (Coleman, 1971). Literary devices such as anaphoric reference and intersentential connectives trigger inference and in-fluence the speed of understanding (Carpenter & Just, 1977b). The current re-search shows that different parts of a text such as topic, subtopics, and details are read differently. In particular, semantically central units receive more integra-tion, in a way consistent with the model described earlier.

Another major influence on the reading process, aside from the task demands themselves, is the reader's knowledge of the content domain. Many of the comprehension processes depend on the reader's previous knowledge. Encoding and lexical access depend on previous knowledge of vocabulary; case role as-signment depends on the semantic knowledge associated with various concepts; integration and inference making may vary in both extent and direction, depend-ing on the reader's prior knowledge. Reading that is strongly driven by the reader's previous knowledge is called top-down because the higher-level concep-tual processes may operate sooner and therefore influence what are normally earlier, bottom-up processes. Thus, two people reading the same text with the same objective may read it differently if their previous knowledge of the content area differs.

THE RECALL CONDITION

The second experimental condition, in which subjects were asked to recall the passage instead of answering true–false questions about it, provides a test of this view of adjustment of reading goals to meet task demands. A priori, one might guess that readers who are expecting to recall would attend more to the higher-order structure of the text (such as theme statements) in order to help them organize their storage of to-be-recalled material. Also, since the passages contain technical details, readers might spend more time trying to integrate them if they intend to recall the details. By contrast, in the verification condition, the exact details did not have to be integrated completely, since the verification task presented sentences from the text, so the details were provided at the time of test.

Recall Condition Results

In the encoding and case role assignment stages, the results for the recall task (Table 8.6) are very similar to the results for the verification task. Readers spent about the same time for encoding and case role assignment (23 msec per character). Infrequent words had the same effect—adding an average of 51 msec on their first occurrence. The intercept was 93 msec per sector. These results suggest that readers were executing the encoding and case role assignments similarly in the two tasks.

The integration stage was sensitive to the differences between the tasks. Readers in the recall condition spent more time on details, 47 msec per word, as

TABLE 8.6
Application of the Model to the Recall Condition

	Regression Weight (msec)
Encoding, lexical access, &	
case role assignment	
Time per character	23*
Time per infrequent word	51*
Intercept	93
Integration (time per content word)	
Topics	65*
Definitions/consequences	106*
Subtopics	81*
Expansions	76*
Details	47*
Sentence wrap-up	192*

*t has $p < .01$.

opposed to 9 msec in the verification task, $t(20) = 1.93$, $p < .07$. The time spent on details in the recall condition was significantly greater than zero. Finally, the sentence wrap-up parameter (192 msec) was still fairly substantial.

The model's fit was as good as for the verification task. All of the models' parameters were significantly different from zero. The standard error of estimate was 263 msec, which is reasonable compared to the standard deviation of 947 msec among the reading times for the sectors. The regression accounted for 92% of the results for the recall means. In general, the fit was comparable in the two conditions.

In summary, the two tasks show striking similarities in the encoding and case role assignment stages. Both tasks resulted in careful reading of about the same rate, 315 words per minute (wpm) for the verification task and 295 wpm for the recall task. In both tasks, integration time decreased as the role varied from an important one (such as a topic or definition) to a less important one (such as a detail). However, there were some differences in the integration stage. Readers in the free-recall condition spent more time integrating details with the superordinate structure than did readers in the verification condition. The recall subjects were probably spending more time on integration because they knew they would later have to produce some of them, rather than merely recognize them. Thus, their criterion for integration was adjusted to meet their objectives.

Skimming

In an attempt to manipulate strongly the reader's task, five additional readers were asked to skim each paragraph and recall it immediately afterward. Four of the readers were unable to skim under these conditions, as indicated by their slow reading rate. However, there was one reader who did skim at 925 wpm. Her protocol, shown in Table 8.7, displays a very different behavior from the careful reading performance in the other conditions. Her fixations are shorter and more selective. She did not fixate every word or even every clause; in particular, she skipped details—like the numbers in line 5 and the list of applications for radioisotopes in line 8. She spent more time on important sectors, such as the first line and line 10, which mentions that icons lack radiation.

Her recall also indicates that she did not process details; it contains only the more important text-grammatical units. A typical example is her recall of the icon passage:

This paragraph was talking about a kind of substitute for radioactive isotopes called icons and how they have something in them that gives them a magnetic, kind of magnetic charge and how they're being used in different things. And they're not as dangerous as a radioactive isotope is.

TABLE 8.7
The Eye Fixations of a College Student Skimming the Passage

The sequence of fixations within each sentence is indicated by the successively numbered fixations above the word being fixated. The duration of each fixation (in msec) is shown immediately below the fixation number.

1	2		3	4	5	6		7
(183)	(133)		(217)	(100)	(267)	(67)		(116)

Radioisotopes have long been valuable tools in scientific and medical

8		1		2	3	4
(117)		(83)		(167)	(184)	(150)

research. Now, however, four nonradioactive isotopes are being produced.

1	2		3	4	5
(183)	(183)		(200)	(133)	(217)

They are called "icons"—four isotopes of carbon, oxygen, nitrogen, and

6	1	2	3	4	5
(67)	(183)	(67)	(83)	(150)	(200)

sulfur. Each icon has one more neutron in its nucleus than the number usually

8	7	6
(133)	(150)	(216)

found in carbon (12), oxygen (16), nitrogen (14), and sulfur (32). The odd

1	2		3	4		1
(200)	(116)		(217)	(183)		(201)

neutron gives the isotopes a distinctive magnetic characteristic. These isotopes

2	3	4	5
(67)	(67)	(150)	(200)

have some of the same characteristics that made radioisotopes useful for tracing

6	7	8	11	10	12
(217)	(216)	(217)	(133)	(183)	(83)

chemical reactions and even powering some of the scientific instruments left

(continued)

205

TABLE 8.7 (*Continued*)

9	13		1	2	4	3
(183)	(200)		(200)	(117)	(167)	(133)

on the moon by Apollo astronauts. But the icons do not have the damaging

8
(233)

5	6	7	1	2	3	4	5
(217)	(67)	(200)	(183)	(284)	(133)	(233)	(67)

radiation of radioisotopes. Consequently, icons offer good prospects for phar-

6	7	9	8	10
(200)	(133)	(200)	(216)	(284)

macological research, for pollution monitoring, and for clinical medicine.

Although the skimming data are only preliminary, they suggest that skimming may also rely on the ability to discriminate between various text-grammatical roles and to process selectively the units that are relevant to the reader's objective.

Memory

Memory performance should reflect, in part, how well each part of the text was integrated during comprehension. Clauses that are integrated to a greater degree are more likely to become part of long-term memory and should be recalled better. There are two factors that determine the extent to which a unit of text is integrated. First, those parts of the text structure that receive more integration time (e.g., topics and definitions) should be recalled better. Second, if a clause is referred to several times in the passage, either explicitly or implicitly, then it may be involved in an integration episode after each mention. Hence, recall of a given unit should be partially explained by integration time and by the number of times a unit is referred to in the text. This account resembles the one proposed by Kintsch and van Dijk (1978) except that the current account uses integration parameters estimated from the reading fixations.

The proportion of the 16 subjects who recalled each of the 275 sectors was analyzed as a function of two predictor variables: the integration parameter for that type of text unit (derived from the gaze duration analysis) and a count of the number of times a sector was referred to in the passage after its initial occurrence.

Both variables produced reliable effects, $t(272) = 5.60$, $p < .01$ for the integration time parameter and $t(272) = 5.79$, $p < .01$ for the number of repetitions. Thus certain aspects of comprehension are at least partial determinants of recall.

Text units that were at higher levels in the grammar (see Fig. 8.2) tended to be recalled better (see Fig. 8.3), replicating the text-role effects found with other types of texts (Meyer, 1975; Thorndyke, 1977). The model partially explains this result in terms of the processes that occur during comprehension. In addition, retrieval processes also may play a role in this effect. For example, there may be many paths from less important concepts that lead to topics, but not vice versa. There may also be response-output effects. Furthermore, a complete model of recall will have to consider how the particular facts and concepts in the text map onto the reader's previous knowledge. Although the passages used were generally unfamiliar, particular facts surely differed in their familiarity, and this could affect recall (Spilich, Vesonder, Chiesi, & Voss, 1979).

The verification results were not amenable to this kind of analysis. Each passage had been followed by four to six true and four to six false probes, with each true probe containing information from several text units. The true probes

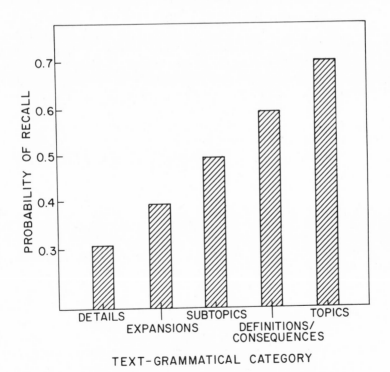

FIG. 8.3.   The probability of recall of each text-grammatical category.

were verified fairly accurately, with a mean accuracy of 75% correct and an average response time of 4040 msec.

In summary, the model shows that an account of the comprehension process can be used to account partially for recall performance. To explain recall totally will require a precise account of the role of prior long-term knowledge and the role of retrieval and reconstruction processes in recall.

DISCUSSION

The results support several aspects of the reading model and the general theoretical framework. At the encoding and case assignment stages, clauses with infrequent words took more time to process. At the integration stage, units that were higher in the text grammar received longer gaze durations. This greater duration reflects a more extensive integration process, both in terms of the number of times information would be retrieved from long-term memory and in the number of relations that would be computed. Details, because they are relatively unimportant to the discourse structure, took less time to be integrated than did other categories of information. Verification readers may have had a lower criterion for integration of details since they only had to recognize them. However, readers in the recall condition paid more attention to details. Finally, the end of a sentence can trigger additional processing, including inference making and integration. The differences in criteria for the two tasks were apparent only at the integration stage; however, the theory suggests that encoding, case role assignment, integration, and sentence wrap-up may all vary if the reader's goals change sufficiently. The model and the analytic techniques make it possible to identify where tasks have their effects. Thus, it is possible to go beyond global statements of task effects and to quantify where and how reading objectives influence reading.

Eye Fixations, Reading, and Listening

The reported research demonstrates that readers do not distribute their gazes uniformly during reading; they look longer at text units where they are doing more processing. This selective allocation of processing resources during reading can be compared to analogous mechanisms in listening. Although a listener cannot control the rate of input or relisten to the spoken discourse, there are mechanisms that functionally resemble the pacing and rereading role of eye fixations. For example, the echoic memory allows a listener to store some part of the auditory message temporarily, at least partially compensating for the large external memory available to the reader. The listener may also use the speaker's pauses to do extra processing at points of high computational demand. Moreover, the listener is aided in identifying important text roles and relations by the speaker's repetition, stress, and gesture. To the extent that these devices allow a listener some selectivity in processing, auditory comprehension may resemble its reading counterpart.

Although reading and listening comprehension have some analogous mechanisms, they may not produce equivalent comprehension. The theoretical framework accounts for this with its notion of variable goals for each stage. The goals for the comprehension stages for reading may differ from those in listening because the processes may not be able to perform to the same specifications in the two modalities. For example, a listener might not be able to integrate to the same extent as a careful reader. If the auditory material were presented too quickly, the listener might allow inconsistencies to go unchecked or else risk missing the incoming information. With sufficiently sensitive methodologies, it should be possible to find systematic differences between the results of reading and listening to the same text.

The Immediacy Assumption

The model's ability to account for gaze durations in terms of the comprehension processes provides some validation for the immediacy and eye–mind assumptions. Readers interpret a word while they are fixating it, and they continue to fixate it until they have processed it as far as they can. This kind of processing eliminates the memory load and computational explosion that would result if a reader kept track of several possible meanings, case roles, and referents for each word and computed the final interpretation at the end of a clause or sentence. This architectural feature also allows a limited-capacity processor to operate on a large semantic network without being bombarded by irrelevant associations. After a single interpretation has been selected, the activation of the unselected meanings can be dampened to their base levels so that they will not activate their semantic associates any further. This minimizes the chances that the reader will be conceptually driven in many directions at the same time.

The cost of this kind of processing is fairly low because the early decisions usually are correct. This is accomplished by taking a large amount of information into account in reaching a decision. The processes have specific heuristics to combine semantic, syntactic, and discourse information. Equally important, the processes operate on a data base that is strongly biased in favor of the common uses of words and phrases, but one that also reflects the effects of local context. The cost is also low because the reader can recover from errors. It would be devastating if there were no way to modify an incorrect interpretation at some later point. However, there are error-recovery heuristics that seem fairly efficient, although the precise mechanisms are only now being explored (Carpenter & Daneman, 1981).

The fact that a reader's heuristics for interpreting the text are good explains why the "garden-path" phenomenon isn't the predominant experience in comprehension; it only happens occasionally. Perhaps the most common, everyday "garden-path" experiences occur when reading newspaper headlines—for example, *Carter views discussed*. The incorrect initial interpretation occurs because headlines are stripped of the syntactic and contextual cues that guide the processing of normal text. Similarly, many jokes and puns explicitly rely on the contrast between two interpretations of an ambiguous word or phrase (Shultz & Horibe, 1974). Even garden-path sentences sometimes seem funny. The humor in all these cases resides in the incongruity between the initial interpretation and the ultimate one. Garden-path sentences are also infrequent because writers usually try to avoid ambiguities that might encourage or allow incorrect interpretations. These kinds of sentences are useful tools for studying comprehension because they indicate where the usual comprehension strategies fail. But the fact that they are not frequent indicates that a reader's heuristics usually are sufficient.

The current research demonstrates that specific fixation patterns can be related to specific comprehension processes (cf. also Carpenter & Just, 1977a; Just & Carpenter, 1976, 1978). This approach has its roots in reading research earlier in the century, when many researchers considered eye fixations to be excellent indicators of comprehension (Buswell, 1920, 1937; Dearborn, 1906; Huey, 1908/1968; Judd & Buswell, 1922). Eye fixations were correctly interpreted as the result, not the cause, of reading processes. Readers who had difficulty comprehending a passage would show an unusual pattern of eye fixations because of their cognitive problems. The primary measures used in those studies were mean fixation duration and mean number of fixations, averaged over an entire passage. It was found that both measures increased for texts that were intuitively classified as difficult. The analyses were global, and there was little systematic effort to relate pauses to particular parts of a text. Nevertheless, the general implications of this early research and the more process-oriented analyses of the current results demonstrate that eye fixations are extremely useful indicators of ongoing comprehension processes. The study of eye fixations in reading offers a means of attaining a goal that Huey (1908) set for psychology:

> To completely analyze what we do when we read would be almost the acme of a psychologist's achievements, for it would be to describe very many of the most intricate workings of the human mind, as well as to unravel the tangled story of the most remarkable specific performance that civilization has learned in all its history [p. 6].

ACKNOWLEDGMENTS

The order of authors was decided by the toss of a coin. The research was supported in part by grant NIE-G-77-0007 from the National Institute of Education and grant MH-29617 from NIMH. We thank J. Anderson, L. Noordman, V. Noordman-Vonk, L. Reder, and H. Simon for their comments on earlier drafts of the manuscript.

REFERENCES

Aaronson, D., & Scarborough, H. S. Performance theories for sentence coding: Some quantitative evidence. *Journal of Experimental Psychology: Human Perception and Performance*, 1976, *2*, 56–70.

Anderson, J. R. *Language, memory, and thought*. Hillsdale, N.J.: Lawrence Erlbaum Associates, 1976.

Baron, J. Mechanisms for pronouncing printed words: Use and acquisition. In D. LaBerge & S. J. Samuels (Eds.), *Basic processes in reading: Perception and comprehension*. Hillsdale, N.J.: Lawrence Erlbaum Associates, 1977.

Bayle, E. The nature and causes of regressive movements in reading. *Journal of Experimental Education*, 1942, *11*, 16–36.

Bever, T. G. The cognitive basis for linguistic structures. In J. R. Hayes (Ed.), *Cognition and the development of language*. New York: Wiley, 1970.

Bouma, H., & deVoogd, A. H. On the control of eye saccades in reading. *Vision Research*, 1974, *14*, 273–284.

Bransford, J. D., & Johnson, M. K. Considerations of some problems of comprehension. In W. G. Chase (Ed.), *Visual information processing*. New York: Academic Press, 1973.

Breitmeyer, B. G. Unmasking visual masking: A look at the "why" behind the veil of "how." *Psychological Review*, 1980, *87*, 52–69.

Buswell, G. T. An experimental study of the eye–voice span in reading. *Supplementary Educational Monographs*, *17*. Chicago: University of Chicago, 1920.

Buswell, G. T. How adults read. *Supplementary Educational Monographs, 45*. Chicago: University of Chicago, 1937.

Carpenter, P. A., & Daneman, M. Lexical access and error recovery in reading: A model based on eye fixations. *Journal of Verbal Learning and Verbal Behavior*, 1981, *20*, 137–160.

Carpenter, P. A., & Just, M. A. Integrative processes in comprehension. In D. LaBerge & S. J. Samuels (Eds.), *Basic processes in reading: Perception and comprehension*. Hillsdale, N.J.: Lawrence Erlbaum Associates, 1977. (a)

Carpenter, P. A., & Just, M. A. Reading comprehension as eyes see it. In M. A. Just & P. A. Carpenter (Eds.), *Cognitive processes in comprehension*. Hillsdale, N.J.: Lawrence Erlbaum Associates, 1977. (b)

Case, R. Intellectual development from birth to adulthood: A neo-Piagetian interpretation. In R. Siegler (Ed.), *Children's thinking: What develops?* Hillsdale, N.J.: Lawrence Erlbaum Associates, 1978.

Chafe, W. L. *Meaning and the structure of language*. Chicago: University of Chicago Press, 1970.

Charniak, E. *Toward a model of children's story comprehension* (Tech. Rep. No. 266). Cambridge, Mass.: MIT Artificial Intelligence Laboratory, 1972.

Clark, H. H., & Clark, E. V. *Psychology and language*. New York: Harcourt Brace Jovanovich, 1977.

Coleman, E. B. Developing a technology of written instruction: Some determiners of the complexity of prose. In E. Z. Rothkopf & P. Johnson (Eds.), *Verbal learning research and the technology of written instruction*. New York: Teachers College Press, Columbia University, 1971.

Collins, A. M., & Loftus, E. F. A spreading activation theory of semantic processing. *Psychological Review*, 1975, *82*, 407–428.

Daneman, M., & Carpenter, P. A. Individual differences in working memory and reading. *Journal of Verbal Learning and Verbal Behavior*, 1980, *19*, 450–466.

Dearborn, W. *The psychology of reading* (Columbia University Contributions to Philosophy and Psychology). New York: The Science Press, 1906.

Fillmore, C. J. The case for case. In E. Bach & R. T. Harms (Eds.), *Universals in linguistic theory*. New York: Holt, Rinehart & Winston, 1968.

Flesch, R. F. *How to test readability*. New York: Harper, 1951.

Fraser, C., Bellugi, U., & Brown, R. Control of grammar in imitation, comprehension, and production. *Journal of Verbal Learning and Verbal Behavior,* 1963, *2,* 121–135.

Frazier, L., & Fodor, J. The sausage machine: A new two-stage parsing model. *Cognition,* 1978, *6,* 291–325.

Glanzer, M., & Ehrenreich, S. L. Structure and search for the internal lexicon. *Journal of Verbal Learning and Verbal Behavior,* 1979, *18,* 381–398.

Haviland, S. E., & Clark, H. H. What's new? Acquiring new information as a process in comprehension. *Journal of Verbal Learning and Verbal Behavior,* 1974, *13,* 512–521.

Hitch, G. J. The role of short-term working memory in mental arithmetic. *Cognitive Psychology,* 1978, *10,* 302–323.

Hockett, C. F. *A course in modern linguistics.* New York: Macmillan, 1958.

Huey, E. B. *The psychology and pedagogy of reading.* New York: Macmillan, 1908. (printed in Cambridge, Mass., by the MIT Press in 1968.)

Jarvella, R. J. Syntactic processing of connected speech. *Journal of Verbal Learning and Verbal Behavior,* 1971, *10,* 409–416.

Judd, C. H., & Buswell, G. T. Silent reading: A study of the various types. *Supplementary Educational Monographs, 23.* Chicago: University of Chicago, 1922.

Just, M. A., & Carpenter, P. A. Eye fixations and cognitive processes. *Cognitive Psychology,* 1976, *8,* 441–480.

Just, M. A., & Carpenter, P. A. Inference processes during reading: Reflections from eye fixations. In J. W. Senders, D. F. Fisher, & R. A. Monty (Eds.), *Eye movements and the higher psychological functions.* Hillsdale, N.J.: Lawrence Erlbaum Associates, 1978.

Kintsch, W., & van Dijk, T. A. Toward a model of text comprehension and production. *Psychological Review,* 1978, *85,* 363–394.

Kleiman, G. M. Speech recoding in reading. *Journal of Verbal Learning and Verbal Behavior,* 1975, *14,* 323–339.

Kucera, H., & Francis, W. N. *Computational analysis of present-day American English.* Providence, R.I.: Brown University Press, 1967.

LaBerge, D., & Samuels, S. J. Toward a theory of automatic information processing in reading. *Cognitive Psychology,* 1974, *6,* 293–323.

Mandler, J. M., & Johnson, N. S. Remembrance of things parsed: Story structure and recall. *Cognitive Psychology,* 1977, *9,* 111–151.

McConkie, G. W., & Rayner, K. The span of the effective stimulus during a fixation in reading. *Perception & Psychophysics,* 1975, *17,* 578–586.

Mewhort, D., & Beal, A. L. Mechanisms of word identification. *Journal of Experimental Psychology: Human Perception and Performance,* 1977, *3,* 629–640.

Meyer, B. *The organization of prose and its effect on recall.* Amsterdam: North-Holland, 1975.

Mitchell, D. C., & Green, D. W. The effects of context and content on immediate processing in reading. *Quarterly Journal of Experimental Psychology,* 1978, *30,* 609–636.

Morton, J. Interaction of information in word recognition. *Psychological Review,* 1969, *76,* 165–178.

Newell, A. Production systems: Models of control structures. In W. G. Chase (Ed.), *Visual information processing.* New York: Academic Press, 1973.

Newell, A. Harpy, production systems and human cognition. In R. Cole (Ed.), *Perception and production of fluent speech.* Hillsdale, N.J.: Lawrence Erlbaum Associates, 1980.

Perfetti, C. A., & Lesgold, A. M. Discourse comprehension and sources of individual differences. In M. A. Just & P. A. Carpenter (Eds.), *Cognitive processes in comprehension.* Hillsdale, N.J.: Lawrence Erlbaum Associates, 1977.

Reitman, J. S. Without surreptitious rehearsal, information in short-term memory decays. *Journal of Verbal Learning and Verbal Behavior,* 1974, *13,* 365–377.

Rieger, C. J. Five aspects of a full-scale story comprehension model. In N. V. Findler (Ed.), *Associative networks.* New York: Academic Press, 1979.

Robinson, D. A. Eye movements evoked by collicular stimulation in the alert monkey. *Vision Research*, 1972, *12*, 1795-1808.

Rumelhart, D. E. Understanding and summarizing brief stories. In D. LaBerge & S. J. Samuels (Eds.), *Basic processes in reading: Perception and comprehension.* Hillsdale, N.J.: Lawrence Erlbaum Associates, 1977.

Schank, R. C. Conceptual dependency: A theory of natural language understanding. *Cognitive Psychology*, 1972, *3*, 552-631.

Schank, R. C., & Abelson, R. P. *Scripts, plans, goals and understanding: An inquiry into human knowledge structures.* Hillsdale, N.J.: Lawrence Erlbaum Associates, 1977.

Shultz, T., & Horibe, F. Development of the appreciation of verbal jokes. *Developmental Psychology*, 1974, *10*, 13-20.

Spilich, G. J., Vesonder, G. T., Chiesi, H. L., & Voss, J. F. Text processing of domain-related information for individuals with high and low domain knowledge. *Journal of Verbal Learning and Verbal Behavior*, 1979, *18*, 275-290.

Spoehr, K. T., & Smith, E. The role of syllables in perceptual processing. *Cognitive Psychology*, 1973, *5*, 71-89.

Sticht, T. G. Comprehending reading at work. In M. A. Just & P. A. Carpenter (Eds.), *Cognitive processes in comprehension.* Hillsdale, N.J.: Lawrence Erlbaum Associates, 1977.

Swinney, D. A. Lexical access during sentence comprehension: (Re)consideration of context effects. *Journal of Verbal Learning and Verbal Behavior*, 1979, *18*, 645-659.

Taft, M. Recognition of affixed words and the word frequency effect. *Memory & Cognition*, 1979, *7*, 263-272.

Tanenhaus, M. K., Leiman, J. M., & Seidenberg, M. S. Evidence for multiple stages in the processing of ambiguous words in syntactic contexts. *Journal of Verbal Learning and Verbal Behavior*, 1979, *18*, 427-440.

Thorndyke, P. W. Cognitive structures in comprehension and memory of narrative discourse. *Cognitive Psychology*, 1977, *9*, 77-110.

Vesonder, G. T. *The role of knowledge in the processing of experimental reports.* Unpublished doctoral dissertation, University of Pittsburgh, 1979.

Westheimer, G. H. Eye movement responses to a horizontally moving visual stimulus. *Archives of Ophthalmology*, 1954, *52*, 932-943.

9

Sources of Knowledge in Reading Comprehension: Cognitive Development and Expertise in a Content Domain

Gay L. Bisanz[1] and James F. Voss

A theory of reading comprehension should specify how a reader's knowledge interacts with the reader's goal and with features of a given text (Carpenter & Just, Chap. 8, this volume; Kintsch & van Dijk, 1978; Miller & Kintsch, 1979). However, attempts to study how individuals use their knowledge to comprehend and interpret text are relatively new. In this chapter we are concerned with the question of how various types of knowledge and levels of expertise influence the comprehension process. By the term *knowledge* we mean the organized semantic information a child acquires during the course of development, as well as information that pertains to a particular subject-matter domain. In addition, *knowledge* may refer to procedures and strategies that individuals employ when they use their semantic information to understand and interpret text.

The question of how knowledge influences comprehension can be examined in the context of both cognitive development and individual differences in knowledge of a content domain. In the next section, the relation between children's knowledge and story comprehension is discussed. Results are presented supporting the thesis that comprehension should be investigated in relation to the types of knowledge that children have at different levels of cognitive development. Methods for exploring this thesis are emphasized. It is also suggested that even though younger children may have the semantic knowledge necessary to understand a given text, they may not have developed strategies that enable them to extract appropriate meaning. In the subsequent section, comprehension is examined in relation to levels of knowledge within a particular content

[1]Now at the Centre for the Study of Mental Retardation and the Department of Psychology, University of Alberta, Edmonton, Alberta, Canada.

domain—namely, the game of baseball; and the importance of developing strategies to utilize domain-related information in text comprehension is discussed. In the final section, some general comments are made regarding the role of knowledge in comprehension.

CHILDREN'S KNOWLEDGE AND STORY COMPREHENSION

One of the primary tasks for psychologists interested in children's story comprehension is to characterize what it means to "understand" at different levels of intellectual development. To do this, it is necessary to identify and study developmental changes in the knowledge and skills important to comprehension. Previous research on simple stories has been focused primarily on knowledge of story structure. However, current research on more complex stories has indicated the importance of (1) identifying when different types of knowledge have been acquired, and (2) studying how these types of knowledge interact in the process of text comprehension.

Research on Simple Problem-Solving Stories

At least two broad classes of knowledge have been considered in relation to text comprehension by children: (1) knowledge of relevant content domains, and (2) knowledge of classes of text. Simple stories that involve goal-directed problem-solving sequences on the part of a character have been a primary vehicle for studying the role of these two types of knowledge. This is not surprising since many of the stories that children generate, hear, or read involve these problem-solving sequences (Botvin & Sutton-Smith, 1977; Goldman, 1978; Stein & Glenn, 1979). There is general agreement that knowledge of human social interactions is one of the most important content domains involved in the understanding of problem-solving stories (see Bower, 1978). However, with some exceptions (e.g., Goldman, 1978; Stein & Goldman, in press), the role that this knowledge plays in children's comprehension has received relatively little attention.[2] Instead, research has been focused primarily upon knowledge of the class of text itself, and specifically upon the individual's knowledge of the structure of such stories.

Attempts to characterize the structure of simple stories (e.g., fables, folktales, myths, children's stories that focus on the problem-solving behavior of a single protagonist) have often taken the form of story grammars (e.g., Mandler &

---

[2]This discussion does not deal with research on the development of children's social cognition where very short stories have been used to assess skills like moral reasoning; rather, the focus here is on research intended to examine children's understanding of text.

Johnson, 1977; Rumelhart, 1975; Stein & Glenn, 1979; Thorndyke, 1977). It has been assumed that these grammars represent knowledge in the form of expectations that an individual has about setting information and the nature and sequence of events associated with the problem-solving behavior of the story protagonist. If we ignore certain variations in terminology and detail, the categories of story information related to problem-solving behavior typically identified in these grammars include: (1) the *initiating event,* defined as a problem or change of state that provokes a reaction by the character; (2) the character's *internal reaction,* the critical feature of which is the activation of a goal; (3) the character's *attempt*—that is, actions by the character intended to achieve the goal; and (4) the *outcome,* which refers to the character's success or failure at the endeavor.

A large portion of the research on children's story understanding has investigated how story schemata (defined in terms of the categories of story information identified by grammars) may play a role in the retrieval of information from memory. Using story grammars to analyze the relation between text structure and children's recall, this research has called into question claims by Piaget (1926/1960) and Fraisse (1963) that the recall of younger children fails to reflect temporal order and conventional cause-and-effect relations. Indeed, when stories are "well-formed"—that is, conform to a grammar—adults and children older than age 6 have little trouble recalling these relations (Mandler & Johnson, 1977; Stein & Glenn, 1979). In addition, Mandler (1978) has provided evidence that the recall of children 7 or 8 years of age may actually be more dependent upon familiar schemata than recall by adults. Furthermore, Mandler and Johnson (1977) have suggested that the greater emphasis that young children place on the recall of setting, initiating event, and outcome information relative to older children and adults may reflect the changing nature of story schemata at various points in development.

In addition to the two broad classes of knowledge already considered, there is a third class, called "strategic knowledge for understanding" by Brown, Collins, and Harris (1978). This refers to strategies the individual is able to apply that facilitate comprehension. Though not much is known about such strategies, we should note that they may be relatively simple, such as taking advantage of the known "syntax" of particular types of stories by making sure that every "slot" of the story schema is filled. Alternatively, these strategies may be more complex and subtle, such as recognition by the reader of constraints placed upon a story outcome by relationships developing among subplots.

Although interactions among these three broad classes of knowledge have been acknowledged, as indicated earlier, the major focus of research has been on knowledge of story structure. Little work has been conducted on the other two types of knowledge and their interaction. At this point children's comprehension should be studied in terms of the interaction of developing social knowledge, knowledge of text structure, and strategic knowledge. This broadening of focus could clarify our understanding of the comprehension process and tie the study of children's story understanding to research on the text processing of novices and experts within a content domain. We briefly describe a study that illustrates the importance of examining the acquisition and interactions among these various types of knowledge.

Current Work on Multiple-Character Stories

A Scaling Analysis of Multiple-Character Stories.   Our concern for the need to identify the sources of knowledge that are important to children's story understanding is the result of a study conducted to examine children's ability to construct themes that relate the goals and actions of several story characters (Bisanz, 1977; Bisanz & Voss, 1978). The method developed to study such themes involved having an author write a story that related the actions of characters along *two* thematic dimensions (Bisanz, LaPorte, Vesonder, & Voss, 1978). After hearing such a story, subjects made similarity judgments about the characters based on the relationships of the characters within the story. Multidimensional scaling techniques were employed to analyze the data. A major assumption was that dimensions derived from applying scaling techniques to these similarity judgments represented a way to describe the themes that interrelate the story characters.

The story employed was a fairy tale in which the problem-solving behaviors of nine characters share a common setting and ending, and the goals of the characters are interdependent. The focus of the plot is on a goal conflict between a lion, king of the beasts, who gets stuck in a trap and wants to get out (the "story protagonist"), and a tiger, who wants to keep the lion in the trap so *he* can become king (the "story antagonist"). In the scaling analysis, actions and characteristics of both major and minor characters located each animal along thematic dimensions labeled: (1) helpfulness (helpful vs. not helpful to the lion), and (2) leadership (leader vs. follower in resolving the story conflict).

Seven-, 10-, and 18-year-olds participated in this study. The major finding was that subjects in all age groups constructed the author's helpfulness theme; however, the likelihood of constructing the second theme increased with age and was only strongly evident in the 18-year-olds' scaling solution. We attributed this consistent improvement in the ability to construct thematic relations over age to several factors, including: (1) knowledge as it relates to text structure, (2) knowledge of a relevant content domain, (3) strategic knowledge, and (4) text characteristics. A discussion of the 7-year-olds' performance serves to illustrate hypothesized effects of the first three factors.

The 7-year-olds failed to construct the second story theme. If the construction of thematic relations is conceptualized as a type of strategic knowledge that involves *a search for large patterns of story information,* the 7-year-olds' difficulties may be attributable to any or all of the general classes of knowledge previously considered. As is discussed later, we have begun to conceptualize the construction of themes more precisely as: (1) a search for "prototypic" sequences of story events revolving about the goal of a major character, or (2) the relating of particular story events to a common idea—for example, the wise and evil uses of power. Construction of the former type of theme is dependent upon the individual having sufficient experience with the particular class of text to recognize prototypic sequences, and construction of *both* classes of themes is heavily reliant upon the individual's knowledge of social interactions. The degree to which 7-year-olds have had experiences with stories such as we employed is unclear; however, their knowledge of social relations is known to be developing rapidly (Shantz, 1975). Thus it may be that 7-year-olds lacked knowledge of the class of text, knowledge of the relevant content domain, the strategic knowledge of searching for and relating large patterns of story information, or possibly some combination of these types of knowledge.

Based on this study, we speculated that improvement in the ability to construct themes over development was due, in part, to the acquisition and application of different sources of knowledge at each age level. Thus, the scaling methodology proved useful for deriving initial hypotheses about developmental changes in the ability to construct thematic relations, and these hypotheses pointed to the need for consideration of the interaction among knowledge sources during comprehension. However, a problem with the scaling technique was that without more precise analyses of the types of story events that subjects used in making their similarity judgments, it was difficult to assess the effects that various sources of knowledge may have had on performance at different points in development. We briefly describe two lines of research that used the story previously described in attempts to provide the more precise frameworks necessary for developing hypotheses about levels of knowledge acquisition that may influence children's comprehension performance.

Specifying Components of Macrostructure.   Kintsch and van Dijk (1978) and others (e.g., Carpenter & Just, Chap. 8, this volume; Spilich, Vesonder, Chiesi, & Voss, 1979) have developed models of text comprehension and production based on the assumption that the semantic structure of discourse has two general levels. The first level, the microstructure, involves individual propositions and their relations. The second, the macrostructure, specifies a more global level of meaning that is largely derivable from the first and consisting of propositions that characterize the text as a whole. Macrostructure propositions (1) are assumed to have a higher probability of recall than microstructure propositions, and (2) are derived in relation to the reader's goals and knowledge represented in the form of a "controlling" schema. As we illustrate, a hypothesis about the macrostructure of a story can provide a precise framework for examining changes in knowledge that can affect comprehension.

One hypothesis that we had regarding the scaling results previously described was that subjects at all ages were making their similarity judgments based upon propositions reflecting the story's macrostructure. We developed a hypothesis about the macrostructure of the story consistent with the information that older subjects might have used in making their similarity judgments. We then posited how that macrostructure may change over the course of development in a manner consistent with the pattern of results obtained in the scaling study.

Our hypothesis about the macrostructure of this text has four components, with a primary and secondary component of macrostructure associated with each of the themes identified in the scaling analysis. The actions of major characters were related to primary components, whereas the actions of minor characters were related to secondary ones. An assumption that we made was that individuals hearing this story anticipate a sequential pattern of story events associated with the behavior of *each* character in this multiple-character story that is similar to the sequential pattern posited by story grammar approaches for single-protagonist stories. Without going into detail, we first describe the primary components of the helpfulness and leadership themes, respectively, and then describe the secondary components.

The primary component of macrostructure associated with the helpfulness theme consists of the setting information, initiating event, internal reaction, attempt, and outcome related to the behavior of the lion. An individual relying on macrostructure information at this level might recount the tale as follows:

> A lion was walking (*setting*), and he got caught in a trap (*initiating event*). He wanted to get out (*internal reaction*), so he asked the animals who were there to help him (*setting and attempt*). Then some of the animals helped the lion out of the trap (*outcome*).

One would be inclined to say that the individual whose recall did not reflect an understanding of the text at this minimal level did not understand the text at all.

Upon identifying the tiger as a major character, another component of macrostructure that could be constructed would involve expectations of a sequential pattern of story events associated with the behavior of the tiger. Given that the subject has a concept of "story antagonist" (discussed later), identification of the tiger as a major character could occur immediately upon being told that the tiger had a long-term goal that conflicted with the goal of the lion. This component of macrostructure was hypothesized to be the primary component associated with the leadership theme. A subject relying on the macrostructure propositions of these *two* primary components might recount the tale as follows:

> A lion, who was King of the animals (*setting*), was walking and got caught in a trap. He wanted to get out, so he asked the animals who were there to help him (*initiating events*). The tiger wanted to be King himself (*setting*), so he wanted to

try to stop the other animals from helping the lion (*internal reaction*). The tiger asked the lion why they should bother to help him (*attempt*). He thought if he could get the animals to vote on the issue he would become King, so the tiger suggested a vote (*internal reaction and attempt*). The vote was a tie (*outcome*). Then some of the animals helped the lion out of the trap.

A third component of meaning that could be constructed might be termed "the unpacking of the helpfulness theme." This represents the hypothesis that individuals anticipate sequential patterns of problem-solving behavior for *minor* characters like they do for major characters, with the restriction that in a well-formed story the sequential patterns of events for minor characters *must* always be related to the goal of a major character. With the addition of this component of macrostructure, individuals would be expected to recall that each minor character: (1) has an internal reaction to the events surrounding the lion getting caught in the trap; (2) states a desire to help or not to help the lion; (3) votes; and (4) acts or does not act to release the lion.

Taken together, the first and third macrostructure components point to the information in the text that we hypothesize subjects considered in making similarity judgments that reflected the "helpfulness" theme. It is a theme of the first type mentioned earlier—namely, one involving a search for "prototypic" sequences of events that relate the behavior of minor characters to the goal of a major character. In many ways it is the multiple-character equivalent to the notion of theme suggested by Schank and Abelson (1977) for single-story protagonists.

An important point to note is that if the tiger is not perceived as an antagonist, he can be treated as a minor character whose actions are related to the third component of macrostructure. What gets left out by merely treating the tiger as a minor character is macrostructure information associated with the primary component of the leadership theme—that is, the component that elevates the tiger to the status of a villain who attempts to control the flow of story events.

A fourth component of macrostructure that could be constructed accounts for the location of major and minor characters on the "leadership" theme in the scaling analysis. It is also the source of our hypotheses about a second class of themes that individuals may construct as they comprehend text. We have termed this last component the "unpacking of the leadership theme." However, what is being "unpacked" is different from what has been discussed previously. We hypothesize that the "leadership" theme of the scaling analysis is a theme constructed by relating particular story events to a common conceptual idea. The concept, in this case, is "leadership." The theme is initiated by the lion's speech asking for help because he has "been a good leader," and it is developed further through events directly related to the second component of macrostructure described, dealing with the tiger's goal of becoming the leader. However, the individual processing the text may also notice both characteristics and actions of major and minor characters relevant to this theme. Thus the fourth component of the proposed macrostructure elevates to a special status text propositions that exemplify qualities or actions of characters that relate to the concept of what is or is not "leadership." The second and fourth macrostructure components point to information in the text that we hypothesize subjects considered in making similarity judgments that reflected the "leadership" theme.

This analysis of macrostructure provides a framework for hypotheses about the locus of difficulties that might arise in an individual's attempt to construct a representation for the story. Particular difficulties may be expected, depending on the knowledge available to individuals at different levels of development. Consider just two of the sources of knowledge discussed in this chapter. To say that individuals of a given age have *knowledge of the class of text* required to construct such a macrostructure implies that they are able to understand the prototypic sequences of problem-solving behavior associated with each major and minor character. Moreover, given that this story can be taken as one instance of a class of stories that focus on a goal conflict between two major characters, knowledge of relations *among* sequential patterns of characters' problem-solving behavior can be considered as a prerequisite. Thus predictions about whether children are likely to understand this story require an assessment of when they have the knowledge that allows them to understand the problem-solving behavior of a story antagonist in relation to the protagonist.

Even assuming prerequisite knowledge of the class of text, in any given story there may be *knowledge of social relations* that is prerequisite to understanding *constituent events* of these problem-solving sequences, and hence a lack of this knowledge could preclude construction of the story macrostructure. Of specific importance is the comprehender's experience with various types of goals and associated problem-solving attempts. In the present text we might contrast the age at which individuals are likely to have had experience with "needing help" and going about getting it (the lion's problem), and the age at which they are likely to have had experience with "wanting to be the leader of a group" and preventing a group of people from performing an action that is not to their advantage (the tiger's problem). In addition, construction of the second class of themes may require that the comprehender have a conceptual taxonomy complete with labels for organizing actions in the social world (e.g., "leadership," "courage," "greed") in order to drive the comprehension process.

In current theories of text comprehension and production (e.g., Carpenter & Just, Chap. 8, this volume; Kintsch & van Dijk, 1978), specification of a macrostructure is the most common way to represent the higher-order knowledge an individual must apply to understand a text. The previous analysis points to the need for a constraint on hypotheses about macrostructures: A hypothesized macrostructure for a class of text should be "developmentally tractable"; that is, it should provide a basis for hypotheses about the family of macrostructures that might be constructed by individuals with different levels of knowledge (cf. Klahr

& Siegler, 1978). An example of how this notion of tractability might illuminate developmental changes in performance can be seen in the context of the story under consideration. The results of the scaling analysis lead us to hypothesize that 7-year-olds as well as older individuals construct the components of macrostructure related to the helpfulness theme. However, construction of the primary and secondary components of macrostructure associated with the leadership theme increases with age, with the secondary component of this theme evident only in the performance of 18-year-olds. This hypothesis could be tested through analysis of eye movements or story recall (see, for example, Carpenter & Just, Chap. 8, this volume; Kintsch & van Dijk, 1978). However, even if such data were well explained by a simple and elegant addition of components consistent with this hypothesis, there would still be the question of what sources of knowledge might account for the predominant type of macrostructure constructed at a given age level. The results of the study described next indicate that the answer is far from simple.

Expectations and Levels of Understanding.   Data from a recent study by Bisanz (1980) provide some insights into the classes of knowledge that comprehenders of different ages may be capable of applying as they attempt to construct a macrostructure for this relatively simple story. The study we refer to is part of a larger project that focuses on children's and adults' abilities to understand the plots of multiple-character stories both in terms of their knowledge of social relations and their knowledge of story structure. In designing the study, it was assumed that when reading or listening to a story, individuals use prior knowledge to narrow the range of hypothetical plots and story paths within plots to a subset of probable alternatives (cf. Haber, 1978). It was also assumed that we may study the types of knowledge that subjects are capable of applying in this task by examining the expectations that they verbalize during the processing of a text (an assumption that may have differential validity at various points during development).

The overall tactic of the study was to formulate hypotheses about types of knowledge that individuals might be applying to comprehend a story with a number of characters. These hypotheses were ones that could be tested in terms of *specific* expectations that should be generated at *particular* points during the comprehension of the story. A tape-recorded version of the story described previously was played for subjects; and at designated points the tape was stopped and their expectations were elicited through a series of probe questions. Subjects were second, fourth, and sixth graders and college students.

One hypothesis, described previously, was that comprehenders are anticipating a pattern of story events associated with the behavior of *each major and minor* character that involves the occurrence of setting information, an initiating event, internal reaction, attempt, and outcome. Thus one characteristic of certain "stopping points" was that, intuitively, they were places that should have signaled the initiation of a new story category within the proposed sequential patterns. At such points, subjects were asked, "What do you think will be the very next thing to happen?" Of concern was whether subjects would generate an event consistent with the next class of events of the proposed patterns (e.g., given setting information for a character, subjects should have generated an initiating event—perhaps some type of problem arising for a character).

Over the course of 10 probes specifically intended to evaluate subjects' knowledge of these sequential patterns, the proportion of generated events that were consistent with these patterns was high, averaging over .94 for all probes. Furthermore, analyses revealed that there were no significant developmental differences in the probability of generating "pattern-consistent events." Thus these data would seem to support the idea that even children as young as 7 years of age had *knowledge of the proposed sequential patterns.*

The analyses just described resulted from a pooling of data across the various story characters. The data from probes intended to determine whether subjects would generate events that could be characterized as "attempts" (i.e., "attempt probes") were *reexamined for particular characters.* It was determined that there was a significant difference in the probabilities of generating "pattern-consistent events" for these characters. At least with respect to this story, there were no major differences in the nature of responses generated for major and minor characters. However, there were differences for characters whom subjects mentioned spontaneously as being "meek" or "selfish." Subjects indicated that it was hard to anticipate the behavior of these "weak" characters in relation to the plot compared to other characters.

The finding that there were differences in the probability of generating "pattern-consistent" responses for different characters has implications for a general theory of text comprehension. It suggests that knowledge of sequential patterns is not automatically applied and that subjects are more likely to expect such a pattern for some characters than others. The conditions of application may be associated with text-related knowledge, like the distinction between major and minor characters; however, they may also be related to subtle attributions of motive to characters whose likely source is the knowledge that individuals use to predict human behavior in everyday life.

There was even some evidence that adults were less likely than younger children to generate attempts for "weak" characters. This finding suggests that at times, these two groups of subjects may have been relying on different knowledge sources and that at points in this story, adults may have been relying more on their knowledge of human social behavior and younger children more on text-related knowledge.

Developmental differences did emerge when *social knowledge* germane to understanding constituent events of the proposed sequential patterns was considered. For example, one analysis examined whether subjects of a given age were more "accurate" in their expectations, in the sense that they were generating events more consistent with the problem-solving attempts included in the plot by the story author. The general type of attempt actually used in the story by all characters was persuasion (defined for the purposes of this experiment as a verbal or physical action initiated by a character intended to make the goals of other characters compatible with that of the initiating character). Responses were scored for consistency with this definition.

For some characters there was a high probability that the expectations of subjects at all ages would "match" the attempt included by the story author. For other characters there was a significant improvement over age in the ability to "match" the author's method. (In light of previous comments, it is interesting to note that the former group of characters included the lion and the latter group, the tiger.) Where younger subjects' expectations were less likely to be consistent with actual story events, they were inclined to anticipate a direct action by the individual character rather than a speech designed to sway the animals to achieve a goal. This was true despite the fact that the whole style of the story centered on characters giving such speeches.

The present results are relevant to Mandler and Johnson's (1977) suggestion that story schemata appropriate for simple stories change at various points in development. Failure to anticipate a story event might reduce the probability of recalling that event later, but is the locus of this recall failure attributable to differences in knowledge about sequential patterns (i.e., "story schemata"), differences in social knowledge systems like persuasion methods that are relevant to particular constituents of such patterns (e.g., "attempts"), or both?

In the case of very simple stories involving expectations about a sequential pattern of events related to the behavior of a single character, the present data would suggest that the locus is most likely to be at the level of knowledge relevant to constituent events (cf. Nezworski, Stein, & Trabasso, 1978). This seems especially likely with respect to the "attempt" category. However, the story employed in the present experiment required an ability to relate sequential patterns relevant to the behavior of several characters, and in a second experiment designed specifically to examine subjects' knowledge of methods of persuasion in relation to their ability to anticipate story events, the data seemed to favor a "both" explanation (Bisanz, 1980).

Of greater interest were analyses of responses to the "attempt probes" in terms of subjects' abilities to anticipate the goals that the author intended for various characters. These results bear on subjects' *knowledge about relations among sequential patterns*. Again, for some characters there was a high probability of subjects at all ages anticipating the goal intended by the story author. For other characters there was a significant improvement over age in the ability to anticipate a character's goal, and among these characters was the story antagonist. This latter finding deserves elaboration.

Most of the "mismatches" that occurred between second and fourth graders' expectations about the story antagonist and actual story events involved the children generating events that implied a subgoal for the antagonist that would set the plot on a course that would entirely skirt the impending goal conflict. These were actions that had the "antagonist" doing things that would help the protagonist out of his dilemma and *simultaneously* open the door to the tiger accomplishing his goal of being king. The spirit of these expectations is captured by the comment of a second grader who, when asked why she anticipated this kind of event rather than the deceitful action that occurred in the plot, remarked indignantly, "Because I thought they were nice animals." None of the oldest subjects generated an event consistent with such a subgoal.

The finding just described raises the issue of whether some of these younger children have a concept of "story antagonist." This amounts to asking whether these children are reliant on information given in the plot itself to infer probable relationships between characters' behavior or whether they have learned that there can be a special set of constraints associated with the behavior of two major characters who have incompatible main goals. The effects of recognizing that a story embodies such a goal conflict might be that higher probabilities of occurrence are automatically assigned to story paths that represent expectations of subgoals and problem-solving attempts that will result in behavioral conflict between the two characters. In other terminology we might call the anticipation of such story paths a "cognitive schema" or "script" for stories that focus on a goal conflict between characters.

Another hypothesis tested in this study was specifically intended to explore subjects' knowledge of relations among sequential patterns. In a single-protagonist story where the problem-solving attempt of the major character results in failure, one direction the plot can take within story grammars is the initiation of a new attempt by that character. The hypothesis examined in this study was that at such points in a multiple-character story, another likely story path is the initiation of a problem-solving attempt by another major character. Thus another place where the tape was stopped was the one clear point in the story where a major character's problem-solving attempt had just failed. Subjects were probed repeatedly about what they thought could happen next in the story.

Overall there was a significant increase in the number of event alternatives generated as subjects got older. And at all ages, the only individual characters mentioned with any frequency as being agents in these events were the protagonist and the antagonist of the story, thus providing support for the hypothesis in question. A rather surprising finding was that subjects of all ages attributed actions to a new character, like "a new animal" or "a hunter." However, the degree to which younger subjects' expectancies centered on a resolution of the plot through the introduction of a new character became evident by examining just the first alternative generated by subjects. Fifty percent of the second and fourth graders' first responses were related to actions by a new character, 16% to actions by the two major characters, and 33% to actions by individuals or groups of old characters. Sixth graders were the purists: None of their first responses dealt with actions by a new character; 50% dealt with actions by a major character and 50% with actions by individuals or groups of old characters. College students' first expectations were rather evenly spread throughout the range of possible actors: 25% to actions by a new character, 25% to actions by a major character; and 50% to the several categories dealing with actions by old characters. In addition, other probing revealed that college students were significantly more likely than younger subjects to anticipate sequences of character interactions that would normally signal further conflict and an extension of the plot.

Assuming that these results reflect the acquisition of knowledge relevant to understanding a given class of text, growing expertise may be reflected in: (1) the increasing number of reasonable alternatives generated with age; (2) the likelihood probabilities (indexed in terms of frequency of generations) assigned to those alternatives; and (3) the recursive nature of some alternatives. The first alternatives of the sixth graders most closely resembled the performance that would have been anticipated given the original hypothesis. Assuming that most college students are more widely read than sixth graders, the differences between these two groups suggest that knowledge (as it may be reflected by the likelihood probabilities assigned various alternatives), once learned, can be altered by experiences with more diverse classes of text. This is also to suggest that the recursive nature and broader range of first alternatives generated by the college students is in some way reflective of a greater facility in handling a wide range of texts; whether that comes at the expense of expertise in handling particular classes of text, like the simple story, is a question of interest.

Based on these data, we can sketch with uncertain hand a picture of the role that various sources of knowledge may play in the comprehension performance of different-aged subjects for stories similar to the one examined in these studies. The hallmark of sixth graders' expertise as they deal with stories that involve a goal conflict among characters seems to be that of script recognition and application. The data suggest that second and fourth graders are capable of applying knowledge of sequential patterns of behavior for *individual* characters, and thus they should be able to construct scripts for stories involving goal conflicts. However, their performance in the experimental task indicates that they may have been using information given in the plot and their knowledge of human behavior to infer probable relationships *among* the behaviors of story characters rather than making reference to a script. We would suggest that a lack of relevant social knowledge may well be a constraint on script development for them.

Not unlike the second and fourth graders, the hallmark of college students as they deal with various classes of text may be a greater reliance on "domain-related" knowledge and "strategies or procedures for understanding." By the latter, we mean methods for (1) deciding when knowledge of sequential patterns should be applied, and (2) inferring relations between sequential patterns that may rely on social knowledge, knowledge of various classes of text, knowledge of authors' styles, and so on. This is not to say that college students do not apply scriptlike knowledge appropriate to stories involving goal conflicts. Rather, we would suggest that they may supplement their knowledge of scripts with domain-related knowledge and powerful procedures for understanding. The benefits of this hybrid strategy might be a greater flexibility and facility in handling the content of the plot and the ability to "switch scripts" or shift to a greater reliance on knowledge of the relevant content domain if the initial script proves inappropriate.

This study provides some insights into the development of knowledge sources that readers may apply in constructing macrostructures for the relatively simple story that we have considered. Of course, in developmental research, the distinction between having the knowledge and *having the knowledge to apply such knowledge* has been a crucial issue in explaining performance differences over age (cf. Flavell, 1970). This is one reason why the study of "strategic knowledge for understanding" is likely to be more crucial to understanding "novice performance" where the novices are children learning about both subject-matter areas and their own memory functions than "novice adults" in a subject-matter area such as we discuss next. However, the results underscore the subtle interactions between knowledge sources and levels of knowledge acquisition that must be examined in order to understand the types of macrostructures that comprehenders can construct. We now turn to research designed primarily to explore the relationship between levels of expertise in a content domain and comprehension performance.

SUBJECT-MATTER KNOWLEDGE AND THE COMPREHENSION PROCESS

Whereas the study of children's story understanding has been focused primarily on knowledge of particular classes of text, recent research with adults has examined how knowledge of a relevant subject-matter domain influences comprehension (e.g., Spilich et al., 1979). The idea that domain-related knowledge influences our ability to understand text information is not new; a number of writers have expressed the notion that our ability to understand written or spoken text is directly related to our knowledge of the topic that is being discussed (e.g., Moore & Newell, 1974; Schank, 1975). Indeed, it seems intuitively obvious that the person who knows more about American history will be more readily able to understand the contents of a book on American history than a person with minimal knowledge of the topic. What is new, however, is that we are beginning to learn something about the mechanisms involved when a person utilizes his or her knowledge of a subject to comprehend text and acquire new information. In this section, we briefly describe some findings that illustrate this.

Subject-Matter Knowledge and Comprehension: Three Findings

Our initial work on the role of domain-related knowledge in comprehension involved the domain of baseball (Spilich et al., 1979). Two groups of individuals were delineated by a pretest, with one group high in baseball knowledge (HK) and one group low (LK). The LK individuals varied in their level of knowledge but generally were not "no knowledge." These groups were matched on reading-comprehension test performance.

With respect to comprehension, HK and LK individuals could differ in knowledge in at least three ways, but to illustrate these possible differences, some background is necessary. Baseball may be viewed as a game that consists of states and actions that produce changes in the state of the game. (It also is possible to relate the action of baseball to knowledge of physical events of the world, as Soloway [1978] has done, but for our purposes we do not consider knowledge of the physical contingencies.) Furthermore, the game states are not all of equal significance, and Spilich et al. (1979) delineated four levels of importance of states with respect to the goals of the game. At each of these levels, there are characteristic actions that produce the particular game states. Finally, we note that an account of a baseball game bears a strong resemblance to a narrative story. The "theme" in baseball is the competitive and cooperative action among the players (Soloway, 1978) as it relates to the goal of the game. As in narratives, there are successive attempts to achieve the goal and subgoals that result in success or failure, and there is a final resolution of the action sequence; namely, one team wins.

With these comments, we now turn to the three possible differences between HK and LK individuals that could produce differences in comprehension. First, there is knowledge of the baseball concepts per se, which permits the individual to understand the nature of the game actions and game states—for example, "inning," "run," "out." Second, there is knowledge of how particular game actions may produce differences in the game states—for example, how an infield ground ball may lead to a change in the number of outs. Third, there is knowledge of the possible *sequences* of game actions and state changes that permit the individual to understand the "flow" of the game. This type of knowledge especially involves relating information about what previously occurred in the game to information that is occurring (or even will occur). Because the LK individuals demonstrated on a baseball test that they had a knowledge of basic concepts, it was assumed that any performance differences of HK and LK individuals would be primarily attributable to differences in the second and third factors.

To examine how differences in knowledge could affect comprehension performance, HK and LK individuals were presented with an account of a half inning of a fictitious baseball game. They recalled the account and subsequently were given a 40-question test on the contents. For our purposes we shall consider three findings of this work. First, HK individuals recalled *more* and *qualitatively different* information than LK individuals. Quantitative differences occurred with respect to the number of propositions recalled. Regarding qualitative differences, HK individuals recalled more information of greater significance to the game when the data were scored in terms of the previously mentioned levels of importance. On the other hand, the LK individuals tended to recall more irrelevant information—for example, the weather. (The questionnaire results indicated that HK individuals often knew much of that information but did not state it in their recall protocols.) The possible reasons for these recall differences are considered in relation to the second and third findings discussed next.

The second finding relates to the processing of text information. A modified version of the Kintsch and van Dijk (1978) model was employed. As previously noted, this model is based upon the propositional structure of the contents of a passage and delineates two types of structure. Micropropositional structure refers to the coherence of propositions that are in close proximity in the text. Macropropositional structure refers to propositions that are based upon general statements of importance to the contents of the passage. In the model, recall is considered in relation to how often micropropositions are processed in working memory and in relation to macropropositional structure. In our modification, four levels of macrostructure were assumed, these levels being consonant with the four levels of the game's goal structure. We further assumed that macrostructure information could be carried over in a working memory system as a person reads or listens to the text. This carry-over would then permit previously read information to be integrated with subsequently read information. In baseball, this carry-over is important because the reader must keep track of things like the number of outs and the positions of runners, all of which were considered to be macrostructure information.

Our analysis supported the position that HK individuals were better able to carry over important information—that is, macrostructure propositions—as they were reading. This information included the score, the number of outs, the positions of the base runners, and—for a given batter—the ball–strike count. By trying a number of models, it was found that the best-fitting model for both HK and LK individuals involved the maintenance of such game-related information, but as indicated, HK individuals were able to carry over more information. Furthermore, because this finding referred to macrostructure rather than microstructure information, it was argued that some type of working memory system was required to handle macrostructure information in addition to the working memory system posited by Kintsch and van Dijk (1978) that carries over microstructure propositions. The nature of the macrostructure-related system is something of an open question. The more traditional working memory system or buffer may be involved in processing microstructure information, whereas macrostructure information may be: (1) on an active (A)-list (Anderson, 1976); (2) in a second working memory system; or (3) in some expanded version of the single system typically hypothesized. Whichever view is held, what does seem clear is that domain-related knowledge in the form of macrostructure propositions maintained in working memory facilitates the process of monitoring new information as well as comprehending it and recalling it.

The superior ability of HK individuals to carry over appropriate macrostructure information and relate it to new information was interpreted in terms of the two possible sources of HK and LK knowledge differences already mentioned. The LK individuals may have been less able to relate the actions of the game to the changes of state of the game, and/or they were less able to keep track of the sequential "flow" of the game. We would contend that the latter factor is of greater importance because the LK protocols revealed especially poor recall of sequences of actions and state changes. Furthermore, additional work has indicated that LK individuals are able to generate a logical sequence of game actions and states but subsequently are unable to recall the particular sequence with substantial accuracy, even though they themselves generaged the passage. Viewed in terms of narrative structure, the LK individuals were able to recall the setting information, the initial event, and outcomes reasonably well, but they generally were unable to recall the sequence of repeated attempts and outcomes that develop the theme of the story.

The last finding considered is that the text-processing study, as well as other research (Chiesi, Spilich, & Voss, 1979), strongly indicated that HK individuals use the context developed by antecedent textual information more than LK individuals to facilitate the recall of the passage contents. Phrased another way, HK individuals are better able to recall the sequences of information involving action and state changes because they are better able to integrate prior information with the subsequent input. The point, then, is that HK individuals are not simply better at remembering a "chain" of events, but they are better at constructing an integrated representation in terms of the meaning of the game. On the other hand, the fact that LK recall appears to be more "telegraphic," consisting of specific events that are not integrated, suggests that the LK text representations consist of discrete events rather than sequentially integrated patterns.

The important aspect of this conclusion is that differences in the representations of HK and LK individuals and differences in the relative ability to integrate sequences of information may be attributed to knowledge differences. As mentioned previously, the HK individuals have knowledge of the various sequences of actions and game state changes that are possible; the LK individuals, though not necessarily deficient in what a specific sequence may be, have considerable trouble in monitoring the sequences. The problem thus for the LK individual involves identifying and/or monitoring a particular pattern of actions and states. In a sense, this is a deficiency representative of the third broad class of knowledge we discussed in the section on children's story understanding—namely, a deficiency in procedural knowledge.

Some Current Research

The results considered thus far raised two questions that we investigated sub-sequently (Voss, Vesonder, & Spilich, 1980). First, the half-inning account we used in the previously mentioned study was generated by an HK individual. However, given that LK individuals have a less sophisticated general knowledge of the game, there is the possibility that LK individuals could construct half-inning accounts that are somehow less complex than those constructed by HK individuals. One question then is, What differences may exist in HK- and LK-generated passages? Given that there are differences in such passages, a second question is how HK and LK recall would be affected as a function of the knowledge level of the individual generating the passage. Two experiments were designed to explore these issues. In the first study, each HK and LK participant generated a half-inning account of a fictitious baseball game. Two weeks later, each person was asked to recall what he or she had generated.

Though not presenting the results in detail, the important findings were as follows. The HK-generated passages differed from the LK-generated ones in two ways. First, the former contained more fully developed descriptions of the game actions and related state changes. For example, whereas an LK individual may assert: "The batter got a hit and went to first base," the HK individual may assert: "The batter hit a ground ball between the shortstop and third baseman that went into left field for a single." Furthermore, when it was mentioned, for example, that a runner was on second base with two outs, the HK individual would specify a new game state in relation to the action of the next batter, whereas the LK would not. Thus an HK subject might say, "The batter hit a ground ball down the third baseline and beat the throw to first base. The runner advanced to third."

The second difference was that LK individuals tended to generate more irrele-vant information such as what the crowd was thinking or how the batter knew a hit was needed at this part of the game. Moreover, when HKs generated irrele-vant information, it tended to be more specific than the type of information generated by LK individuals. These two findings are similar to results described earlier dealing with passage recall.

Another finding of interest is that recall of the passage contents 2 weeks after the passages were generated produced little difference in HK and LK perfor-mance in terms of overall proportion of propositions recalled. Also, when the propositions of the originally generated text were classified in terms of the goal structure of the game of baseball, as was done in the Spilich et al. (1979) study, there was little difference in the types of propositions recalled by HK and LK individuals. However, when measures were used that provided for determining recall of the sequential "flow" of the information, performance of HK individuals was superior to that of LK individuals. This finding indicates that the LK individual had trouble recalling the sequential characteristics of the text even when he or she had generated the text. Finer-grained analyses not presented here supported this conclusion.

For the second experiment, the three "most typical" HK-generated passages and the three "most typical" LK-generated passages were selected from the passages generated in the first study. We gave these six passages to both HK and LK individuals one passage at a time, measuring recall before presenting the next passage. A significant interaction in recall was obtained; whereas HK individuals recalled HK-generated and LK-generated passages with about equal facility, LK individuals recalled LK-generated passages much better than they recalled HK-generated passages. Moreover, LK recall of LK-generated passages was not significantly different from HK recall.

The question raised by these results is, of course, how the differences in the HK- and LK-generated passages could produce the differences in recall. Although the LK-generated passages yielded a few more errors based upon "baseball logic" than the HK-generated passages, these errors seemed inconsequential.

We want to suggest that the results of both studies may be explained by two hypotheses that involve the underlying knowledge differences of HK and LK individuals. The first hypothesis involves the role of knowledge upon the encoding of text information. As previously stated, the HK individuals have a superior ability to monitor the sequences of game actions and state changes that can occur in a game; and although both HK- and LK-generated passages contained about the same number of state changes, HK individuals recalled the changes and the sequence of changes much better than LK individuals. Thus, because of their superior ability to integrate sequences of actions and state changes, HK individuals' recall is superior. In addition, the HK individuals generated more elaborated descriptions of game actions. We hypothesize that such elaborate descriptions provide a unique encoding for the particular sequences of actions and state changes, and this uniqueness facilitates subsequent retrieval.

The second hypothesis involves the role of experience. We would suggest that a major factor involved in becoming an HK individual is learning to identify particular actions and relate them to state changes and to automate this process so that sequences of actions and state changes may be readily monitored. In other words, although a person may have knowledge of specific baseball concepts while first learning about baseball, considerable experience is required for the person to develop the skill of integrating the sequences of actions and state changes. By analogy, in learning a motor skill, a person may learn fundamental components of a skill, but it requires practice for the skill to be developed in execution and performance—that is, to become automated. Likewise, this is the case with knowledge. One can learn the basic concepts of the game, but only with experience is a person able to develop the procedures that permit rapid execution of the understanding process.

An interesting theoretical issue is raised by the hypothesized differences in HK and LK performance with respect to monitoring the flow of information—namely, the relation of the present findings to those of deGroot (1966), Chase and Simon (1973), and others regarding chess players. The results on the chess work led Chase and Simon to conclude that expert chess players store thousands of patterns in memory that enable them to recall game-related patterns with extreme accuracy. This view is analogous to stating that the HK person in the baseball domain is able to recognize game states (which are far fewer in baseball than in chess). In chess, of course, state changes are marked by minimal action (picking up a piece and moving it), whereas in baseball it is the actions that produce the state changes. What we have suggested is that HK individuals, by the way they encode the actions and related state changes, are better able to integrate action–state-change sequences than LK individuals. In chess, HK individuals would likely show superior recall of sequences of state changes because they would perceive sequences of moves as an integrated attack, defense, etc. Thus, even though the integration process is in some ways different in the two domains, the underlying process is held to be essentially the same—that expertise includes the ability to integrate sequences of significant domain-related information and to recognize the particular game states and where the states fit in possible game sequences. Indeed, the integration of which experts are capable may involve integrating input information over minutes, hours, or even days. However, the novice is not nearly so capable in this skill of integration.

Before beginning the final section, a speculative point should be made about the role of domain-related knowledge in the educational process. There are two senses in which the term *understanding* is often used: first, understanding based upon the ability to comprehend the particular language; and second, understanding based upon a knowledge of the particular subject matter, which generally includes terminology and conventional expressions characteristic of the particular domain but also takes for granted a basic understanding of the language. Although it is not a major issue of this chapter, we believe that instruction in reading comprehension often has failed to distinguish between these two uses of the term *understanding,* and that it has been assumed that the first form of *understanding* is primary. The weak form of the assumption that comprehension is a function of language knowledge per se is that, to comprehend text, all one needs is a "basic grasp of English," whatever that may mean. The stronger form of the assumption is that knowledge of the language is sufficient to understand almost anything written or spoken in the language. Although knowledge of the language is necessary for comprehension, the research discussed in this section suggests that in many cases knowledge of the subject matter is also required for comprehension to occur, and there may be many "levels of understanding" for a given text, depending on how much the reader knows. In fact, we would speculate that because of the increased specialization in our technological society, understanding based upon language per se is less helpful, relatively speaking, than it was years ago. Phrased another way, it is important that individuals nowadays start to develop subject-matter knowledge and ''general procedures for understanding text'' that can make use of that knowledge relatively early in life, because of: (1) the usage of technical vocabulary and metaphorical expression that are related to specific subject-matter domains, and (2) the greater variety of texts and subject-matter areas with which the reader is confronted.

TOWARD A THEORY OF READING: SOME CONSIDERATIONS RELATED TO THE ROLE OF HIGHER-ORDER KNOWLEDGE

In this chapter we have endeavored to show that text comprehension and the related processes of text generation and recall are strongly influenced by higher-order knowledge. We have tried to point out that being able to decode each word does not guarantee that a reasonably sophisticated representation of the passage will result. Furthermore, we have noted that there are factors of importance to comprehension associated with different sources of organized semantic information and procedures that individuals apply in using that information. A number of chapters in this volume discuss the nature of lexical access, lexical search, and related processes. Although these processes are obviously a necessary part of reading, we suggest that reading needs to be treated more seriously as a hierarchical arrangement of skills that require development and practice at all levels. In this volume, this is recognized more strongly in principle than in practice. Perhaps this is because the study of higher-order knowledge systems important to comprehension can proceed relatively independent of the study of lexical access.

In this chapter, we delineated three sources of higher-order knowledge that might play a role in the comprehension process: (1) knowledge related to classes of text, such as the structure of multiple-character narratives; (2) knowledge of subject-matter areas relevant to these texts; and (3) procedures or strategies for understanding. These sources of knowledge can be viewed as data bases that the reader can draw upon in the construction of representations for texts. It was also pointed out that these types of knowledge can and usually do interact during the course of comprehension, and deficiencies in any one have the potential to lead to deficiencies in comprehension performance as a whole. Our thoughts about the nature of that interaction deserve some elaboration.

It was pointed out in an earlier section that knowledge related to classes of text in the form of scripts, and procedures for deciding when these scripts could be applied, might be a fairly general comprehension strategy. It seemed to characterize quite well the behavior of the sixth graders in the last narrative experiment described. In contrast, both the novices and experts in the baseball experiments seemed to reflect a general comprehension strategy that involved the application of heuristic procedures for selecting and directly applying aspects of one's knowledge about a content area in the construction of a representation for texts. However, these are caricatures of extremes, and it seems very likely that there are subtle interactions between these modes of applying knowledge during comprehension, dependent upon the knowledge sources available to an individual.

Examples of such interactions are evident in the behavior of the second graders and college students in the narrative experiment previously described. In that experiment, it was shown that second graders have a knowledge of story structure, in the sense of being able to apply knowledge about prototypic sequences of problem-solving behavior for single protagonists in comprehending multiple-character stories. However, many of these children did not seem to be applying ''scriptlike'' information that would readily allow them to understand the role of the story antagonist. Instead, they seemed to be relying on information given in the text and their own knowledge of human behavior to infer the probable relationships *among* the behaviors of characters in the plot. In contrast, college students in this experiment were hypothesized to be applying their knowledge of scripts *in conjunction with* their knowledge of the domain and procedures for understanding. In support of this latter hypothesis, Bisanz (1980) has evidence that college students who seem to be applying scriptlike knowledge for stories that focus on a goal conflict use their knowledge of social actions (in this case, methods of persuasion) to elaborate their hypotheses about the *form* the goal conflict will take (e.g., a conflict of direct actions vs. verbal confrontation).

It would seem that the strategy of applying general heuristics for text processing in conjunction with ''content domain'' knowledge must be the default strategy at all ages. However, such a strategy has the potential of being supplemented by special purpose ''text-related'' knowledge (i.e., scripts) after extended experience with a given class of text. As was suggested previously, one constraint on the development of this special purpose knowledge for young children with respect to narrative may be a ''sufficient'' understanding of a relevant content domain—human social relations (in the experimental story described here, knowledge of power struggles and methods of persuasion). A knowledge of this domain that is inadequate for understanding major story events may also prevent the detection of consistent sequences of behavioral interaction among story characters necessary for script development. Whether this constraint is relevant beyond the domain of narratives is an open question. Once individuals are capable of readily applying a script of a given class of text, we are proposing that further expertise may come in the simultaneous utilization of knowledge sources that maximize the comprehender's opportunities of recognizing discrepant information or handling novel input.

The discussion thus far has largely considered developmental differences in semantic knowledge systems and the interaction among such systems that might result in differential understanding of a text. The importance of procedures for understanding was made most salient in the baseball research. Most of the LK individuals, though able to generate a reasonable sequence of actions and state changes, had difficulty in integrating and recalling such sequences. Moreover, this difficulty was attributed to a lack of experience in using procedures that enable the individual to identify and differentially encode sequences of actions and game states.

One issue of theoretical import is whether the two types of content domains we have been discussing here—knowledge of human goals pertaining to the achievement of power and methods of persuasion, and rules for the game of baseball—are fundamentally similar or different in their effects on comprehension. Both deal with "goal-directed human activities" and thus may be considered subsets of that larger domain. The results we have discussed are suggestive of the fact that the effects of levels of expertise in these subdomains are similar over the age ranges we and others have examined. For example, the youngest subjects in experiments using narrative prose have the greatest ease in understanding setting, goal, and outcome information. Similarly, if a baseball text is viewed as narrative, the low-knowledge individuals recall what might be termed setting, goal information, and some of the major events, but they have difficulty recalling the equivalent of "attempts" as well as sequences of important game actions and related state changes. The common patterns in comprehension and recall found in these two types of passages may reflect a common theory of problem solving in human behavior that adult baseball "novices" and the first and second graders of narrative experiments share. If so, in cases where "scriptlike" knowledge is not being applied or is being weakly applied, the comprehension performance of "novices"—be they children over 6 years of age or adults—when they are dealing with topics that fall under the broad rubric of "goal-directed human activities" may exhibit similar performance characteristics.

Carpenter and Just (Chap. 8, this volume) have pointed to the need for a taxonomy of goals for reading. In light of the previous comment, we would point to a similar need for a taxonomy that groups the content domains that, in the agreement of individuals within a given culture, share similar "grand theories." Given such a taxonomy and knowledge about the performance of novices and experts for certain subdomains, we could readily develop, for example, hypotheses about the types of knowledge that a comprehender is capable of transferring to texts dealing with new topics that the comprehender may recognize as sharing a similar "grand theory."

In closing, we note that we began this chapter by mentioning a need to tie the study of children's story understanding to research on text processing in novices and experts within a content domain. We began this section by indicating a further need for a more integrated understanding of the role that various levels of knowledge play in reading. Given the preceding discussion, it would seem that the perspective developed throughout this chapter—that of studying the role of higher-order knowledge in reading in terms of developing and interacting knowledge sources—has the potential for providing the common framework that would allow interested researchers to address the first concern. Whether it can be used to address the second need, so apparent in the proceedings of this conference, remains to be seen.

ACKNOWLEDGMENTS

The research of this chapter was supported by the Learning Research and Development Center, supported in part as a research and development center by funds from the National Institute of Education (NIE), United States Department of Health, Education, and Welfare. The authors would like to thank Jeffrey Bisanz for his comments on parts of this manuscript.

REFERENCES

Anderson, J. R. *Language, memory and thought.* Hillsdale, N.J.: Lawrence Erlbaum Associates, 1976.

Bisanz, G. L. *A framework for developmental investigations of story comprehension: Thematic structure and author–reader communication.* Unpublished master's thesis, University of Pittsburgh, 1977.

Bisanz, G. L. *Sources of knowledge and related expectations in story comprehension: Developmental considerations.* Unpublished doctoral dissertation, University of Pittsburgh, 1980.

Bisanz, G. L., LaPorte, R. E., Vesonder, G. T., & Voss, J. F. On the representation of prose: New dimensions. *Journal of Verbal Learning and Verbal Behavior,* 1978, *77,* 337–357.

Bisanz, G. L., & Voss, J. F. *Developmental changes in understanding themes that interrelate story characters.* Paper presented at the meeting of the Midwestern Psychological Association, Chicago, May, 1978.

Botvin, G. J., & Sutton-Smith, B. The development of structural complexity in children's fantasy narratives. *Developmental Psychology,* 1977, *13,* 377–388.

Bower, G. H. Experiments on story comprehension and recall. *Discourse Processes,* 1978, *1,* 211–231.

Brown, J. B., Collins, A., & Harris, G. Artificial intelligence and learning strategies. In H. O'Neil (Ed.), *Learning strategies.* New York: Academic Press, 1978.

Chase, W. G., & Simon, H. A. Perception in chess. *Cognitive Psychology,* 1973, *4,* 55–81.

Chiesi, H. L., Spilich, G. J., & Voss, J. F. Acquisition of domain-related information in relation to high and low domain knowledge. *Journal of Verbal Learning and Verbal Behavior,* 1979, *18,* 257–274.

deGroot, A. D. Perception and memory versus thought: Some old ideas and recent findings. In B. Kleinmuntz (Ed.), *Problem solving: Research, method and theory.* New York: Wiley, 1966.

Flavell, J. Developmental studies of mediated memory. In H. W. Reese & L. P. Lipsitt (Eds.), *Advances in child development and behavior* (Vol. 5). New York: Academic Press, 1970.

Fraisse, P. *The psychology of time.* New York: Harper & Row, 1963.

Goldman, S. R. *Children's semantic knowledge systems for realistic goals.* Unpublished doctoral dissertation, University of Pittsburgh, 1978.

Haber, R. N. Visual perception. *Annual Review of Psychology*, 1978, *29*, 31–59.

Kintsch, W., & van Dijk, T. A. Toward a model of text comprehension and production. *Psychological Review*, 1978, *85*, 363–394.

Klahr, D., & Siegler, R. S. The representation of children's knowledge. In H. W. Reese & L. P. Lipsitt (Eds.), *Advances in child development and behavior* (Vol. 12). New York: Academic Press, 1978.

Mandler, J. M. A code in the node: The use of a story schema in retrieval. *Discourse Processes*, 1978, *1*, 14–35.

Mandler, J. M., & Johnson, N. S. Remembrance of things parsed: Story structure and recall. *Cognitive Psychology*, 1977, *9*, 111–151.

Miller, J. R., & Kintsch, W. *Readability and recall of short prose passages: A theoretical analysis.* Unpublished manuscript, University of Colorado, 1979.

Moore, J., & Newell, A. How can MERLIN understand? In L. W. Gregg (Ed.), *Knowledge and cognition*. Hillsdale, N.J.: Lawrence Erlbaum Associates, 1974.

Nezworski, T., Stein, N. L., & Trabasso, T. *Story structure versus content effects on children's recall and evaluative inferences.* Paper presented at the meeting of the Psychonomic Society, San Antonio, November 1978.

Piaget, J. *The language and thought of the child.* London: Routledge & Kegan Paul, 1960. (Originally published, 1926.)

Rumelhart, D. E. Notes on a schema for stories. In D. Bobrow & A. Collins (Eds.), *Representations and understanding: Studies in cognitive science*. New York: Academic Press, 1975.

Schank, R. C. The role of memory in language processing. In C. Cofer (Ed.), *The structure of human memory*. San Francisco: Freeman, 1975.

Schank, R., & Abelson, R. *Scripts, plans, goals, and understanding*. Hillsdale, N.J.: Lawrence Erlbaum Associates, 1977.

Shantz, C. U. The development of social cognition. In E. M. Hetherington (Ed.), *Review of child development research* (Vol. 5). Chicago: University of Chicago Press, 1975.

Soloway, E. M. *"Learning = Interpretation + Generalization:" A case study in knowledge-directed learning.* Unpublished doctoral dissertation, University of Massachusetts, 1978.

Spilich, G. J., Vesonder, G. T., Chiesi, H. L., & Voss, J. F. Text processing of domain-related information for individuals with high and low domain knowledge. *Journal of Verbal Learning and Verbal Behavior*, 1979, *18*, 275–290.

Stein, N. L., & Glenn, C. G. An analysis of story comprehension in elementary school children. In R. O. Freedle (Ed.), *New directions in discourse processing* (Vol. 2). Norwood, N.J.: Ablex, 1979.

Stein, N. L., & Goldman, S. Children's knowledge about social situations: From causes to consequences. In S. Asker & J. Gottman (Eds.), *The development of friendship*. Cambridge: Cambridge University Press, in press.

Thorndyke, P. W. Cognitive structures in comprehension and memory of narrative discourse. *Cognitive Psychology*, 1977, *9*, 77–110.

Voss, J. F., Vesonder, G. T., & Spilich, G. J. Text generation and recall by high knowledge and low knowledge individuals. *Journal of Verbal Learning and Verbal Behavior*, 1980, *19*, 651–667.

10 Attentional and Automatic Context Effects in Reading

Keith E. Stanovich
Oakland University

It is by now well known that throughout the 1950s and 1960s a conceptual change occurred within the field of experimental psychology (see Lachman, Lachman, & Butterfield, 1979, for one of the more thorough discussions of what has been termed the "cognitive revolution"). The rise of the information-processing framework led to a renewed interest in reading-related phenomena (Venezky, 1977). Many of the classic problems of the turn of the century that were so well described by Huey (1908/1968) are now being pursued with intensity. For example, studies of letter perception and the word superiority effect appear frequently in the experimental psychology literature. However, it is indeed surprising that until very recently, there has been little work on how word recognition is influenced by a prior sentence context. In the 1960s the seminal tachistoscopic studies of Tulving and Gold (1963) and of Morton (1964) were published, but little else. It was not until the early 1970s, when Meyer and his associates (Meyer & Schvaneveldt, 1971; Meyer, Schvaneveldt, & Ruddy, 1975; Schvaneveldt & Meyer, 1973) introduced the study of single-word priming effects using a lexical decision task, that the interest of experimental psychologists was piqued.

The lack of work on sentence context effects has recently begun to be remedied as researchers increasingly recognize that any complete theory of the reading process must account for how prior context affects ongoing word recognition. Another factor accounting for the recent interest in this research area has been the continuing popularity of theories that posit a large role for sentence context in the reading process (e.g., Goodman, 1970; Smith, 1971). For example, Smith (1971) has theorized that fluent reading is only possible when the reader uses prior context to reduce the amount of stimulus information that needs to be extracted from the word (or words) currently being fixated. Thus, some current work on sentence context effects has sought to test such theorizing, and several of the studies discussed later bear directly on the models of Smith (1971) and Goodman (1970). Finally, the study of sentence context effects is of interest to experimental psychologists, independent of its relevance to theories of reading, because the phenomena under investigation are prime examples of how perceptual recognition is the result of a complex interaction between stimulus information and prior knowledge. Developing a thorough description of the interaction between data-driven and conceptually driven processing is one of the fundamental tasks of modern cognitive psychology (Norman, 1976).

It is with this background in mind that I wish to discuss a research program on sentence context effects that Richard F. West and I initiated in the mid-1970s. The state of the art at the time has been alluded to earlier. Morton (1964) and Tulving and Gold (1963) had broken ground in this area. However, both these studies employed tachistoscopic recognition paradigms, and their relevance to the immediate processing demands and time constraints of contextual usage in actual reading was unclear. If previous contextual information does act to speed ongoing word recognition, then its effects must occur rapidly—that is, before the word can be recognized on the basis of purely visual information. Thus, tachistoscopic paradigms that allow virtually unlimited time for response may not be tapping the same processes that mediate contextual effects during ongoing reading. Fortunately, the problem of assessing the on-line processing effects of context was amenable to attack via the chronometric methods that had been spawned by the cognitive revolution. Meyer and Schvaneveldt (1971) thus employed a reaction-time method, the lexical decision task, in the study of the effects of a single-word context.

Despite the interest in single-word priming effects precipitated by the work of Meyer and associates, work on the effect of a sentence context on the speed of visual word recognition was slow getting off the ground (although it should be noted that Marslen-Wilson, 1973, 1975; Morton & Long, 1976; and others had investigated the effect of a sentence context on auditory recognition). The lexical decision task was not extended to the investigation of sentence context effects until the work of Schuberth and Eimas was published in 1977. These investigators presented subjects with sentence contexts that had their terminal word deleted. After the 1.5-sec exposure of the context, a target stimulus appeared that could either be a word that was congruous with the previous context, a word that was incongruous with the previous context, or a nonword. Compared with a control condition in which no context was presented, lexical decision times were faster when target words were preceded by a congruous context and slower when they were preceded by an incongruous context.

The basic experimental methodology of the research program that is described was very similar to that employed in the Schuberth and Eimas study. Sentences with the terminal word deleted were presented as contexts. The last word of the context was always the word *the*. Target words were presented that were either congruous or incongruous with the previous context. The control condition was one in which only the word *the* preceded the target word. There were two major differences between our methodology and that of Schuberth and Eimas. We employed a naming task rather than a lexical decision task. Thus, in our studies the subject simply had to name the target word as soon as it appeared, and a voice-activated relay measured the subject's voice onset latency. In addition, rather than present the context for a fixed period during which it was to be read silently, we had the subject read the context out loud. In our procedure the onset of the target word is initiated when the experimenter pushes a button synchronously with the subject's articulation of the word *the,* which is always the last word of the context. This procedure has the advantage of providing greater control over exactly when the subject is processing the context, and it allows the experimental manipulation of the time between the processing of the context and the onset of the target word. The inherent disadvantage of the procedure is that the experimenter's response is, of course, variable. We tried to minimize this variability by giving the experimenter extensive practice in synchronizing his button press with the subject's articulation of the word *the*. In addition, the experimenter was told to adopt a criterion that occasionally resulted in his pressing the button before or during the subject's articulation of *the,* thus aborting the trial. A rough check on whether the experimenter's criterion was constant across conditions was provided by counting the number of such mistrials in each condition.

A DEVELOPMENTAL STUDY

In our first study (West & Stanovich, 1978) we had fourth-grade, sixth-grade, and adult readers perform the task already described. The results are displayed in Fig. 10.1 and are rather easily described. All three groups of subjects showed significant contextual facilitation effects (faster reaction times in the congruous condition than in the no-context condition). However, the magnitude of the facilitation effect did not increase with age. In fact, there was a slight tendency for the facilitation effect to decrease with age, but this trend did not reach statistical significance. Consistent with this pattern was the fact that correlations between standardized reading measures and the magnitude of the facilitation effect were all significantly negative, indicating that larger facilitation effects were associated with lower reading ability. The pattern of results from the incongruous condition was somewhat different. The fourth and sixth graders displayed significant inhibition effects (slower reaction times in the incongruous condition than in the no-context condition). However, there was no hint of inhibition in the reaction times of the adults (if the unpredictable condition of an experiment reported by Perfetti and Roth, Chap. 11, this volume, is comparable to the

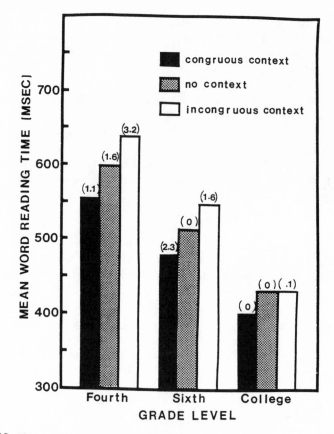

FIG. 10.1   Mean naming times as a function of grade level and context condition. Mean percentage of errors indicated in parentheses.

no-context condition of West and Stanovich, then the results of these two experiments are highly convergent).

There were two general aspects of the results of the West and Stanovich (1978) study that were surprising. First, there was no trend toward increasing contextual facilitation with increasing reading ability. In fact, there was a mild trend in the opposite direction. Most models of reading, particularly the influential theories of Smith (1971) and Goodman (1970), predict that better readers should show larger contextual effects. According to Smith (1971), fluent reading is only possible because contextual redundancy reduces the number of stimulus features that need to be extracted in order to identify a word, thus speeding word recognition. The second surprising finding was the unexpected disappearance of inhibition in the reaction times of the adults. Although this result has the appearance of a qualitative difference, there is nothing in the literature on psycholinguistics that would suggest that contextual processing changes qualitatively between sixth grade and adulthood.

THE TWO-PROCESS THEORY OF EXPECTANCY

Since general theories of the reading process were of no help in the interpretation of our results, it was fortunate that a theory of expectancy that had recently been introduced into the experimental psychology literature provided an elegant and powerful explanation. This was the two-process theory of expectancy developed by Posner and Snyder (1975a, 1975b). They proposed that semantic context affects recognition via two processes that act independently and that have different properties. The two processes are similar to the spreading activation and location-shifting models originally proposed by Meyer and Schvaneveldt (1971). The automatic activation process occurs because when stimulus information activates a memory location, some of the activation automatically spreads to semantically related memory locations that are nearby in the network (Collins & Loftus, 1975). The automatic spreading activation process is fast acting, does not use attentional capacity, and does not affect the retrieval of information from memory locations unrelated to those activated by the context (see Neely, 1977, for a fuller discussion). Thus, the automatic activation process quickly results in a contextual facilitation effect but does not cause an inhibitory effect when a word is incongruous with its preceding context. The idea of contextual facilitation due to an automatic spreading activation mechanism has received support from several studies (Davelaar & Coltheart, 1975; Fischler, 1977a; Fischler & Goodman, 1978; Neely, 1977; Swinney, Onifer, Prather, & Hirshkowitz, 1979; Tversky, Havousha, & Poller, 1979; Underwood, 1977).

The other expectancy process in the Posner–Snyder theory is a conscious-attention mechanism. This mechanism responds to a preceding context by directing the limited-capacity processor to the memory location of the expected stimulus. The conscious-attention mechanism is slow acting, utilizes attentional capacity, and inhibits the retrieval of information from unexpected locations because the limited-capacity processor must be "shifted" to a location some distance away in the memory network so that information can be read out. Posner and Snyder (1975a, 1975b) presented evidence consistent with their proposition that there are two independent processes contributing to context effects and that the two processes have different properties. Several recent studies of semantic context effects using single-word priming tasks have provided some support for the two-process theory of Posner and Snyder (Fischler, 1977a; Neely, 1977; Tweedy, Lapinski, & Schvaneveldt, 1977; Yates, 1978).

As previously mentioned, the Posner–Snyder theory provides an intriguing explanation of the developmental results of West and Stanovich (1978). According to their theory, the entire pattern of results follows from the simple empirical fact that the time to recognize words in isolation decreases as reading ability increases (Perfetti, Finger, & Hogaboam, 1978; Perfetti & Hogaboam, 1975). The pattern of inhibition in the results occurs because the isolated word recognition speed of adults is so fast that a word can be identified before the slow-acting conscious-attention mechanisms can exert its inhibitory effect. Instead, only the automatic spreading activation component of the contextual processing has time to operate before the word is recognized, thus resulting in contextual facilitation, but no corresponding inhibition in the reaction times of the adults. The word recognition processes of children, however, may be slow enough to allow the conscious-attention mechanism to have an effect, resulting in both contextual facilitation and inhibition in the reaction times of the children. Thus, rather than being the result of a discontinuous, qualitative change in processing, the disappearance of inhibition between sixth grade and adulthood is, instead, the result of the gradual increase in word recognition speed with age, resulting sometime during this age range in word recognition time that is faster than the expectancy process that is the cause of inhibition effects. The theory also explains the slight tendency for the magnitude of the facilitation effect to increase as reading ability decreases. In readers with slow word recognition speeds, there are two, rather than one, expectancy processes contributing to facilitation.

In addition to providing an explanation of the West and Stanovich (1978) data, the Posner–Snyder theory provides an account of the results of several other developmental studies of contextual facilitation that are consistent with the findings of West and Stanovich and thus, for the same reasons, cannot be accommodated by many popular theories of the reading process (see Perfetti & Roth, Chap. 11, this volume). For example, although none of the other studies have allowed the assessment of facilitation and inhibition (due to the lack of a neutral control condition), several have found that context had a greater influence on the recognition times of the poorer readers (Biemiller, 1977–1978; Perfetti, Goldman, & Hogaboam, 1979; Roth, Perfetti, & Lesgold, 1979; Schvaneveldt, Ackerman, & Semlear, 1977). As previously mentioned, the theories of reading that emphasize the importance of conceptually driven processes (sometimes termed *top-down models*) predict exactly the opposite. However, it is also the case that serial-stage models, where higher-level processes cannot initiate until the completion of lower-level processes (termed *bottom-up models*), make the same predicitons as top-down models regarding contextual facilitation effects in readers of different abilities.

This author has argued elsewhere (Stanovich, 1980) that in terms of general models of reading, only interactive models that allow for compensatory processing can account for the existing research on individual differences in contextual effects on word recognition. Interactive models (see Rumelhart, 1977, for a more complete discussion) assume that a pattern is synthesized based on information provided *simultaneously* from several knowledge sources (e.g., feature extraction, orthographic knowledge, lexical knowledge, syntactic knowledge, semantic knowledge). Whereas in top-down models, semantic processes direct lower-level processes, in interactive models, semantic processes constrain the alternatives of lower levels but are themselves constrained by lower-level analyses. Thus, each level of processing is not merely a data source for higher levels, but instead seeks to synthesize the stimulus based on its own analysis and the constraints imposed by both higher- and lower-level processes. If we add to the general interactive model the assumption that a process at *any* level can compensate for deficiencies at any other level, we now have open to us a possibility that has been inadequately explored in the reading literature—namely, that a deficiency in a lower-level process may lead to a *greater* reliance on higher-level knowledge sources. Thus, a reader with poor word recognition skills may actually rely more on contextual factors because these provide much needed additional sources of information (see Perfetti & Roth, Chap. 11, this volume, for similar arguments). It is just this phenomenon that is suggested by the growing body of research showing that the word recognition times of poorer readers are more affected by prior context (Biemiller, 1977–1978; Perfetti, Goldman, & Hogaboam, 1979; Roth, Perfetti, & Lesgold, 1979; Schvaneveldt, Ackerman, & Semlear, 1977; West & Stanovich, 1978).

Of course, interactive-compensatory models are actually a general *class* of theory. The exact nature of the compensatory trade-off remains to be specified. However, based on the research and theory previously reviewed, the Posner–Snyder theory appears to provide a valuable first step toward a more precise specification of how compensatory processing may occur at the level of word recognition. According to this theory, the actual mechanism by which the compensatory trade-off is accomplished is a simple one. When word recognition is slow, another higher-level expectancy process (the conscious-attention mechanism) has time to operate and thus provides additional facilitation due to contextual information. Thus, a deficiency at a lower level results in a higher-level knowledge source becoming more implicated in performance.

TESTS OF THE TWO-PROCESS THEORY

The success of the Posner–Snyder theory in explaining the results of the West and Stanovich (1978) experiment and, in addition, its intriguing implications regarding individual differences in contextual facilitation and compensatory processing made further tests of the model seem appropriate. Thus, in our next experiments (Stanovich & West, 1979) we attempted to test some of the strongest predictions made by the Posner–Snyder theory. An interesting prediction regarding contextual inhibition was immediately apparent. In contrast to theories that would posit some complex change in linguistic processing, the Posner–Snyder theory explains the disappearance of inhibition between sixth grade and adulthood as merely being the result of the gradual increase in word recognition speed that, sometime during this age range, becomes faster than the conscious-attention expectancy mechanism. If it is indeed the case that the disappearance of inhibition during this age range is not due to any qualitative change but is, instead, the result of changes in the relative speeds of the processes involved, then certain clear predictions follow. For example, manipulations that slow word recognition time should cause the performance of the adults to mimic that of the children. This was the logic of our first test of the Posner–Snyder theory, an experiment where we had subjects perform the contextual naming task under conditions similar to those in the West and Stanovich (1978) study and under conditions where the contrast of the target word was reduced by the use of a neutral density filter. It was thought that degrading the visual conditions of the target word would slow its recognition by a couple of hundred milliseconds and allow time for the conscious-attention expectancy mechanism to operate. Accordingly, we expected to observe an increase in contextual effects in the degraded condition. In particular, the Posner–Snyder theory predicts a marked increase in the magnitude of the inhibition effect.

The results of the experiment are displayed in Table 10.1. The normal stimulus condition replicated the results of West and Stanovich (1978). The 8-msec inhibition effect did not approach significance. However, the 15-msec facilitation effect was smaller than what we had previously observed and of marginal significance. Nevertheless, this should not be of great concern, since several demonstrations of facilitation effects by other investigators and the large facilitation effects in our subsequent experiments hardly leave their existence in doubt. The pattern of results from the degraded condition was entirely consistent with the Posner–Snyder theory. In contrast with the lack of inhibition under normal stimulus conditions, a highly significant 88-msec inhibition effect was obtained. This was the most important prediction made by the Posner–Snyder theory. Also consistent with the theory, however, was the fact that the contextual facilitation effect was larger in the degraded condition than in the normal stimulus condition (49 msec vs. 15 msec).

Although the results of this experiment were supportive of our interpretation of the Posner–Snyder theory, there is one viable alternative explanation that deserves consideration—that is, an explanation in terms of strategies of process-

TABLE 10.1
Mean Reaction Times in Milliseconds

Stimulus Condition	Congruous	No Context	Incongruous
Normal	451	466	474
Degraded	687	736	824

ing. Specifically, our explanation is based solely on the *time* available to the two expectancy processes. However, it is important to realize that the conscious-attention mechanism is just that—a conscious strategy that the subject can choose or *not* choose to employ (see Posner & Rogers, 1978, for a more complete discussion of this point). Thus, it is possible that only in difficult tasks, such as the degraded condition of the previous experiment, is the subject motivated to use the attentional mechanism to generate expectancies. According to this explanation, it is the task characteristics—specifically, the level of difficulty—rather than processing time per se, that led to the pattern of results observed in the previous experiment. Fortunately, an alternative explanation in terms of task difficulty is easily tested since there are other ways of manipulating the amount of time available to the expectancy processes. In our next experiment we orthogonally varied stimulus quality and the response–stimulus interval (RSI) (the amount of time between the response to the last word of the context and the onset of the target word). The processing-time and task-difficulty explanations make differential predictions regarding the effects of stimulus quality and RSI. The predictions involving the inhibition effect are the crucial ones. For reasons just stated, the task-difficulty explanation predicts that inhibition will be observed only under conditions where the stimulus is degraded and should be independent of RSI (which, in the range manipulated, should not affect the difficulty of target-word naming). In contrast, if it is processing time per se that is important, then the effects of RSI and stimulus degradation should mimic each other. Specifically, the processing-time explanation predicts that inhibition should be a monotonically increasing function of the interval between the response to the context and the beginning of lexical retrieval of the target word, regardless of how this interval is produced.

The results of the experiment designed to test these predictions are displayed in Table 10.2. In this experiment two levels of stimulus quality (normal and degraded) and two levels of RSI (150 msec and 750 msec) were varied orthogonally. There were highly significant facilitation effects in all four conditions. The results regarding the inhibition effects were supportive of the processing-time explanation rather than the task-difficulty explanation of the results of Experi-

TABLE 10.2
Mean Reaction Times in Milliseconds and Mean Percentages
of Errors Indicated in Parentheses

RSI	Stimulus Condition	Context Condition Congruous	Context Condition No Context	Incongruous
150	Normal	674 (0)	785 (.6)	793 (.6)
150	Degraded	827 (2.8)	951 (5.0)	967 (8.3)
750	Normal	685 (0)	738 (1.1)	769 (0)
750	Degraded	814 (1.1)	910 (6.7)	962 (6.7)

ment 1 of Stanovich and West (1979). Only the 750-RSI normal and 750-RSI degraded conditions displayed significant inhibition effects (of 31 msec and 52 msec, respectively). This finding contradicts the prediction of the task-difficulty explanation—that inhibition would only be found under degraded conditions. Instead, inhibition was a monotonically increasing function of the time delay between the reading of the context and the beginning of lexical access of the target word, regardless of how produced (i.e., by increasing the RSI, slowing the target-word encoding stage, or both).

The results of this experiment can be more clearly seen in Fig. 10.2, where facilitation and inhibition are separately plotted as a function of the interval between the articulation of the last context word and the completion of the encoding stage of target-word processing. Thus, assuming a 100-msec stimulus-encoding stage, the total interval in the 150-RSI normal condition is 250 msec. Plotted next is the 150-RSI degraded condition, where the 166-msec degradation

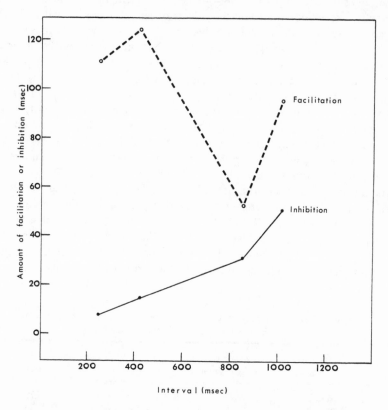

FIG. 10.2. Amount of facilitation and inhibition as a function of the interval between the articulation of the last context word and the completion of the encoding stage of target-word processing.

effect—assumed to be entirely located in the encoding stage—makes the total interval 416 msec. The interval is 850 msec in the 750-RSI normal condition and 1022 msec in the 750-RSI degraded condition. Figure 10-2 shows a steady increase in the inhibition effect as the time interval available for contextual processing increases. This is an important prediction made by the processing-time interpretation of the Posner–Snyder theory. In regard to the facilitation effect, three of the conditions show effects of a similar magnitude (about 100 msec), whereas there is a dip to 53 msec in the 750-RSI normal stimulus condition. Stanovich and West (1979) speculated that the 750-RSI normal condition falls in a range where there has been decay of the automatic activation, but not enough time for the full effect of the attentional facilitation component, which is presumably the main cause of the facilitation effect in the 750-RSI degraded condition. A similar drop in contextual facilitation was observed by Neely (1977) in a single-word priming experiment, and he offered a similar explanation.

In order to ensure that the facilitation without inhibition observed in the Stanovich and West (1979) experiments was not due to a failure to employ the conscious-attention expectancy strategy, an additional experiment was conducted. It could be argued that the previous experiments did not encourage the use of such a strategy, because only one-half of the target words were congruous with the sentence, and no recall of the sentence contexts was required of the subjects. A priori, it would seem that such an experimental situation would discourage conscious expectancy formation. Nevertheless, Stanovich and West (1979) did observe significant inhibition effects under conditions where target-word recognition was delayed. This finding suggests that conscious expectancies were being employed but that their effects were only manifest when given enough time to operate. Despite the results of the Stanovich and West (1979) study, it was thought desirable to test the alternative strategy explanation further. This is easily done since the processing-time explanation predicts that under conditions where facilitation without inhibition is observed, manipulations that affect the subject's conscious strategies should not alter the pattern of results. Thus, the next experiment was designed to induce the subjects to use conscious expectancies by increasing to 80% the proportion of trials in which the target words were congruous with the sentence. The strategy explanation predicts that significant inhibition effects should be observed under such conditions, whereas the processing-time explanation predicts that facilitation without inhibition should still be observed.

The results of the experiment are displayed in Table 10.3. The 65-msec facilitation effect was significant at the .01 level, and the 17-msec inhibition effect did not approach significance ($F < 1$). Thus, the results of this experiment seem to be more supportive of the processing-time explanation than of the conscious-strategy explanation. Although a 17-msec inhibition effect was observed, it did not approach statistical significance and was considerably smaller than the 65-msec facilitation effect. The pattern of benefit dominance was still

TABLE 10.3
Mean Reaction Times in Milliseconds
and Mean Percentages of Errors
Indicated in Parentheses

Context Condition		
Congruous	Neutral	Incongruous
608 (2.1)	673 (0.6)	690 (1.7)

apparent despite the fact that 80% of the target words were congruous with their contexts, a proportion that should have induced the subjects to form conscious expectancies.

Although the research just described has been consistently supportive of the Posner–Snyder theory, Fischler and Bloom (1979) have suggested that the pattern of results may have occurred because a naming task was employed. They questioned whether the same pattern would have emerged had a lexical decision task been employed, and further argued that the lexical decision task is more appropriate for studying the effects of context in actual reading. Although it is certainly true that word naming does not *require* lexical access, there is every reason to believe that lexical access is involved in word naming. Forster (1976) argued for the latter claim by pointing to three relevant empirical facts: Words are named faster than pronounceable nonwords; high-frequency words are named faster than low-frequency words; and semantic facilitation effects have been observed in naming tasks. In addition, although it is true that the magnitude of the effects of many important variables changes depending on whether the lexical decision or naming task is used, it is also the case that with regard to at least some variables in the word recognition literature, the two tasks converge. For example, the magnitudes of both the semantic priming and spelling-to-sound regularity effects are similar across the two tasks (see Meyer, Schvaneveldt, & Ruddy, 1975; and Stanovich & Bauer, 1978; respectively). Predictably, however, much argument has been generated by the question of which task is more appropriate for the study of reading phenomena. Rather than enter what promises to be an interminable debate, it was thought preferable to address the question empirically. Thus, the next experiment was run under conditions identical to the RSI-150 normal condition of the Stanovich and West (1979) paper. The only difference was that instead of naming the target word, the subject made a lexical decision. All the nonword fillers used in the experiment were pronounceable.

The results of the experiment are displayed in Table 10.4. The 53-msec contextual facilitation effect was significant at the .001 level, whereas the 12-msec inhibition effect did not approach significance ($F < 1$). The finding of contextual facilitation without inhibition appears to have been clearly replicated using a lexical decision task. Unfortunately, the error data are problematical. The error percentage differences across conditions are in the direction indicating an

TABLE 10.4
Mean Lexical Decision Times in
Milliseconds and Mean Percentage of
Errors Indicated in Parentheses

Context Condition		
Congruous	Neutral	Incongruous
803 (4.3)	856 (2.1)	868 (6.8)

inhibition effect, and an analysis of variance on the error percentages indicated that the effect of context condition was significant at the .05 level. Thus, the strong conclusion that this experiment clearly replicated the earlier work must be attenuated. It should be noted that reaction times in lexical decision tasks are slower than those in naming tasks due to response incompatibility. If conscious expectancies can influence a late stage of processing, such as the response decision operation, then some degree of inhibition would be expected. The relative response incompatibility in lexical decision tasks may contribute to the inhibition observed in sentence context experiments in another way. It is possible that the presence of an incongruous relationship between the context and target word primes a ''no'' response (i.e., congruity judgments affect word/nonword judgments). This might occur because in the lexical decision task, after the lexicon has been accessed, further transformation of the information is necessary in order to arrive at the response execution stage that executes a ''yes'' response (these response-decision operations are more complex in lexical decision tasks than in naming tasks, see Theois & Muise, 1977). If the incongruity can be detected while these operations are taking place, then the incongruity may have a chance to prime a ''no'' response, thus delaying response decision operations that are leading to the execution of a ''yes'' response. As a result, the response times in lexical decision tasks may be partially reflecting processes occurring *after* lexical access has been achieved. The possibility of post-lexical effects becoming involved in the response times suggests that the use of the lexical decision task to assess sentence context effects on ongoing word recognition may be problematic.

In another test of the Posner–Snyder theory, the logic was again employed that if an explanation of the West and Stanovich (1978) results in terms of the Posner–Snyder theory is correct, then it should be possible to get the performance of the adults to mimic that of the children simply by manipulating the length of time needed for target-word recognition. Rather than lengthening this time by contrast reduction, as in the previous experiments, it was thought desirable to vary target-word difficulty by manipulating natural language variables like word frequency and word length. Thus, for the next experiment a new set of sentence contexts and two target words that were congruent with each context were constructed. These sentences were, as a whole, at a higher level of difficulty than those employed in the work previously described, since the latter sentences were constructed to be read by fourth graders. In addition, for each sentence one of the targets was an easy word, and one of the targets was a difficult word. Difficult words were less frequent and contained more letters than easy words. It was thought desirable to let both of these variables—which naturally covary—define our manipulation of word difficulty, since on the basis of previous work, we knew that differences in word recognition time of over a couple of hundred milliseconds are necessary to cause different patterns of facilitation and inhibition. Manipulating word frequency by itself rarely leads to experimental effects of more than 100 msec in naming tasks.

According to the Posner–Snyder theory, there should be more time for the conscious-attention mechanism to operate when the target word is difficult, since difficult words take longer to recognize. Thus, larger contextual effects (especially inhibition effects) should be evident in the difficult-word condition. As regards the final word of a sentence, there is, of course, a tendency for easy words to be more predictable than difficult words. It was decided not to try to eliminate this natural language correlation in the materials, both for reasons of ecological validity (see Petrinovich, 1979) and because it serves to work *against* the predictions of the Posner–Snyder theory. This is especially true when we contrast the Posner–Snyder theory with other recent theoretical statements. For example, Fischler and Bloom (1979) argued that facilitation will only be found for highly predictable words. The arguments in their paper would lead one to predict that facilitation will be found only for the easy words and that performance on the difficult words will be inhibition dominant (i.e., a large inhibition effect and minimal facilitation will be observed). According to Becker's (1980) most recent version of his verification model, the easy and difficult words should display equivalent inhibition effects, and the easy words should show facilitation effects greater than, or at least equal to, those displayed by the difficult words (see Stanovich & West, in press, for a fuller discussion of the predictions of the verification model). In contrast to the predictions derived from the Fischler and Bloom (1979) paper and the verification model of Becker (1980), the Posner–Snyder theory predicts larger inhibition *and* facilitation effects for the difficult words.

In order to try to push the Posner–Snyder theory to its predictive limits, one more variable was included in the study being described. Subjects were given practice in rapidly naming one-half of the target words (equal numbers of easy and difficult words) before participating in the experiment. Practiced words should be recognized faster, and context effects should be attenuated with such words. However, there was a problem that we anticipated with the practice variable. Specifically, we questioned whether in a single session we could induce a practice effect of the same order of magnitude as the word difficulty variable. This would have been desirable since, as in the experiment where RSI and stimulus quality were manipulated, we could have observed whether the two variables had similar effects on contextual processing.

The experimental logic and design were similar to the earlier experiments. The RSI used in each condition was zero. However, the experiment was run on a different tachistoscopic apparatus. The horizontal visual angle of the words was larger, and the contrast of words was greater. Context condition, word difficulty, and practice were all orthogonally varied, within-subject variables. A pilot study in which the sentence contexts were presented to 25 college students as a cloze task produced data indicating that the difficult words were less predictable. Across all contexts the easy target word was predicted 43% of the time on the subject's first guess, whereas the difficult target word was predicted only 11% of the time on the subject's first guess.

The results of the experiment are displayed in Table 10.5. The main effects of context, word difficulty, and practice were all significant at the .001 level. Although it was statistically significant, the main effect of the practice variable was only 30 msec, not nearly enough of a time difference to lead to differential context effects. Thus, the practice variable did not interact with context condition but did interact with word difficulty. Larger practice effects were shown with the more difficult words. Fortunately, the word difficulty variable produced a healthy 108-msec main effect. The interaction between word difficulty and context condition was significant at the .025 level. The more difficult words displayed larger context effects despite the fact that they were less predictable. An important prediction made by the Posner–Snyder theory was thus confirmed. However, a glance at Table 10.5 will reveal that the greater contextual effects for the difficult words did not become apparent in precisely the manner predicted by the Posner–Snyder theory. Specifically, difficult words displayed larger facilitation effects than easy words; but there was no difference between the two in the magnitude of the inhibition effect, since neither word condition displayed any inhibition. It was expected that the increase in the contextual effect for the difficult words would be particularly apparent when inhibition effects were considered. However, it is argued here that the account of these results given by the

TABLE 10.5
Mean Reaction Times in Milliseconds and Mean Percentage
of Errors Indicated in Parentheses

Practice Condition	Word Type	Context Condition			Facilitation	Inhibition
		Congruous	Neutral	Incongruous		
Unpracticed	Easy	507 (0.4)	548 (2.1)	534 (1.4)	41	−14
Practiced	Easy	494 (0.7)	526 (1.7)	532 (1.0)	32	6
Unpracticed	Difficult	610 (4.9)	687 (6.6)	671 (3.1)	77	−16
Practiced	Difficult	566 (1.7)	635 (3.1)	623 (1.7)	69	−12

Posner–Snyder theory, though not perfect, appears to be clearly superior to that of other recent theoretical statements. For example, based on their work, Fischler and Bloom (1979) would predict that little facilitation would be observed with the difficult words because of their low predictability. Similarly, Becker's (1980) verification model fails to predict the larger facilitation found for difficult words. Given the failure of alternative conceptualizations, it would appear to be worthwhile to pursue further the question of whether the results of this experiment are really imcompatible with the Posner–Snyder theory.

The larger facilitation effects in the difficult-word conditions are clearly predicted by the Posner–Snyder theory. Since, as previously mentioned, the differential predictability of the two word sets works against this prediction, its confirmation is even more impressive. The larger facilitation effects occur because it takes longer to recognize the difficult words, leaving more time for the spreading activation and conscious-attention mechanisms to operate. However, since no inhibition was observed in the difficult-word conditions, we are forced to assume that the larger facilitation effect was entirely due to the automatic activation component. This is not a completely unfounded conclusion since Fischler and Goodman (1978), using a single-word priming paradigm, demonstrated that rather small differences in effective contextual interval were associated with significant changes in contextual effects that were entirely due to automatic spreading activation.

The other major result that must be explained is the lack of inhibition in the difficult-word conditions. This finding suggests that even though the difficult-word conditions were some 108 msec slower than the easy-word conditions, the former still did not allow enough time for the conscious-attention mechanism to become implicated in performance. Thus, the results could be summarized as indicating that manipulating the effective contextual interval by 108 msec in the range under consideration has sizable effects on the automatic activation expectancy mechanism but little effect on the conscious-attention mechanism. First of all, it should be emphasized that this conclusion is entirely consistent with the work of Fischler and Goodman (1978) on the time course of spreading activation and the work of Stanovich and West (1979) on the time course of inhibition due to conscious attention (see their Figure 1). Secondly, the RSI in the experiment was set at zero. Finally, it should be noted that the effective contextual interval in even the unpracticed difficult condition of this experiment was in a range where, based on previous research, inhibition would not be expected. This was because the experiment was run on a different apparatus with visual conditions that led to faster overall reaction times. The slowest condition in this experiment (the unpracticed difficult-word condition) had reaction times approximately 100 msec faster than the RSI-150 normal conditon of Experiment 2 in the Stanovich and West (1979) paper (where no inhibition was observed) and reaction times equal to those in the 80% congruous study reported earlier (where, also, no inhibition was observed). Thus, the speed of recognition of even the unpracticed difficult words was in a range where inhibition would not be expected. Of course, this explanation can be tested by simultaneously manipulating word difficulty and the response–stimulus interval (RSI) between the reading of the last context word and the presentation of the target word. These two variables were manipulated orthogonally in the next experiment.

The results of the final experiment in this series are displayed in Table 10.6. In this experiment, word difficulty and RSI (0 or 800 msec) were varied orthogonally, and the practice variable was dropped. The results of this experiment replicated an important finding of the previous experiment—that word difficulty interacted with context condition. Larger contextual effects were observed in difficult-word conditions even though the difficult words were less predictable. In addition, the RSI by context condition interaction replicated the data pattern observed in Experiment 2 of the Stanovich and West (1979) paper. More importantly, the explanation given earlier for the lack of inhibition in the difficult-word conditions of the previous experiment received support. There was no inhibition in the difficult-0 condition, replicating the lack of inhibition in the comparable conditions of the previous experiment. However, when the RSI was lengthened, the difficult words displayed a highly significant inhibition effect. These results are all consistent with an explanation of context effects in terms of the Posner–Snyder theory. The only outcome of this experiment that was not quite consistent with the theory was the lack of inhibition in the easy-800 condition. The 30-msec inhibition effect in that condition did not reach accepted levels of statistical significance ($p < .15$). Taken as a whole, however, the results are largely supportive of the theory.

Before turning to a final experiment that had a somewhat different purpose than the work presented thus far, a brief summary statement is perhaps warranted at this point. The two-process expectancy theory of Posner and Snyder provided an intriguing explanation of the developmental results of a study of sentence context effects conducted by West and Stanovich (1978). In six subsequent experiments designed to test the theory, the success of its predictions was moderate to high, and thus it represents the best current theoretical explanation of our work on sentence context effects. At the very least, it provides a better explana-

TABLE 10.6
Mean Reaction Times in Milliseconds and Mean Percentage
of Errors Indicated in Parentheses

Word Type	RSI	Context Condition			Facilitation	Inhibition
		Congruous	Neutral	Incongruous		
Easy	0	746 (0.0)	785 (2.6)	774 (2.6)	39	−11
Easy	800	731 (0.0)	754 (3.1)	784 (0.5)	23	30
Difficult	0	891 (2.6)	986 (4.7)	997 (6.3)	95	11
Difficult	800	864 (2.1)	930 (4.7)	1009 (6.3)	66	79

tion than other recent models of context effects, including Becker's (1980; Becker & Killion, 1977) verification model and the hypotheses of Fischler and Bloom (1979) regarding target-word predictability.

THE ISSUE OF ECOLOGICAL VALIDITY

Recently, we have begun to address the rather sticky issue of the ecological validity of studies of context effects. That is, how well are we approximating in our laboratory experiments the real magnitude of context effects that occur in the actual reading situation? A recent study by Mitchell and Green (1978) suggests that this issue deserves our attention. In order to assess whether context has an effect on processing in reading, Mitchell and Green employed a paradigm where subjects pressed a button to advance themselves through an on-line visual display of a passage three words at a time. The interresponse times were used as indices of processing difficulty. They found that the processing of a critical three-word frame was not facilitated by the presence of a syntactically predictive cue in the previous frame. A post hoc analysis did reveal a tendency for semantically selective verbs to facilitate the processing of subsequent material. However, Mitchell and Green argued that this effect was not the result of context affecting word recognition but was in fact *post*lexical. Their argument was that semantically selective verbs reduce the need for an inference to be made when the material in the following frame is integrated with previous information. Thus, semantic selectivity facilitates comprehension processes that occur after word recognition has taken place.

As a whole, the Mitchell and Green experiments offered little support for the idea that contextual information acts to speed ongoing word recognition. Since their procedure was designed to approximate the real-time constraints of actual reading, their work raises the question of just how well experiments employing single-word and single-sentence contexts are estimating the magnitude of context effects that occur in the actual reading situation. For example, in most experiments where the context is presented for a fixed time period before the target word, the interval between context and target is larger than that normally occurring in reading. To a lesser extent, this is also the case in the procedure used in the studies reported here. That procedure introduces three additional delays between the time the subject identifies the word *the* and the onset of the target word: the subject's articulation time, the experimenter's delay in pressing the button, and any RSI that has been included in that particular condition. Thus, it can still justifiably be argued (e.g., Mitchell & Green, 1978) that contextual processes (even automatic ones) operate too slowly to influence ongoing word recognition, and that the contextual effects observed by Stanovich and West (and others) were due to the presence of an unusually long interval between context and target—in short, that previous experimental paradigms overestimated the magnitude of context effects.

In the final experiment an attempt was made to eliminate the three artificial delays inherent in the procedure of Stanovich and West (1979) in order to determine whether the context effects that have previously been observed were dependent upon the presence of an unusually long context–target interval. This was accomplished by making three changes in experimental procedure. The first, and most obvious, was to set the RSI to zero. The other changes involved having the subjects read the context silently and push the target-word initiation button themselves. The subjects were given rather elaborate instructions designed to induce them to press the button as soon as they saw the last context word *the*. For example, the instructions strongly emphasized that the subject was not to read the context, delay, and then press the button. They were instructed to inform the experimenter if, by mistake, this happened, and subjects seemed reliable in reporting such errors. In summary, although this procedure is certainly no panacea, it does entirely eliminate the articulation lag, and probably markedly reduces the time between the identification of the last context word and the onset of the target word. The sentences used in the experiment were those from the Stanovich and West (1979) experiments, and in all other respects (visual conditions, etc.) the procedure was like that employed in those studies. The results of the experiment are displayed in Table 10.7. An analysis of variance indicated that the effect of context condition was significant at the .05 level. However, planned comparisons indicated that neither the 16-msec facilitation effect nor the 22-msec inhibition effect was significant by itself. (The new procedure used in this experiment renders the interpretation of facilitation and inhibition problematic, however, this is not crucial here since the focus of the experiment is on the total context effect, rather than the specific components that are attentional and automatic).

There are two outcomes that would have made the interpretation of this experiment relatively clear-cut. Had the contextual effects completely disappeared, then the hypothesis of Mitchell and Green (1978) would have received strong support. On the other hand, had the magnitude of the contextual effect

TABLE 10.7
Mean Reaction Times in Milliseconds
and Mean Percentage of Errors Indicated
in Parentheses

Context Condition		
Congruous	*Neutral*	*Incongruous*
709 (1.1)	725 (2.8)	747 (3.3)

approximated the effect found in the 150-RSI normal condition of the Stanovich and West (1979) study (119 msec), then the argument that the single-sentence context studies differ from reading in their processing requirements would lose force. The actual result was an intermediate one. A significant effect of contextual condition was observed, but the magnitude of the effect (38 msec) was considerably less than that found in the comparable condition in Experiment 2 of the Stanovich and West (1979) paper. Thus, one might conclude that the general thrust of the argument of Mitchell and Green (1978) is correct. As the interval between context and target word is brought more in line with that obtained in normal reading, contextual effects diminish. However, the present experiment suggests the possibility that a small residual effect of context still remains even when the conditions of normal reading are approximated.

There are valid arguments on both sides of the issue raised by Mitchell and Green (1978), but it appears to the present author that the moderate conclusion already stated is a reasonable summary of the currently available evidence. Consider the present state of the literature in regard to this particular issue. Both Forster (1976) and Mitchell and Green (1978) have argued the strong position that the presence of a prior sentence context has no effect on lexical access. Forster (1976) describes two experiments similar in methodology to those conducted by Stanovich and West (1979). In one experiment there was no significant contextual effect. However, in an experiment where the target word was masked and reduced in duration, a significant effect was observed. The latter result is, of course, consistent with the evidence presented and reviewed earlier. The former result is simply inconsistent with the results of Stanovich and West (1979), those of several other experiments reported in this chapter, and those of other investigators (e.g., Alford, 1979; Fischler & Bloom, 1979; Schuberth & Eimas, 1977).

The bulk of the results reported by Mitchell and Green (1978) are consistent with their hypothesis. However, in a post hoc analysis, they did find a tendency for semantically selective verbs to facilitate subsequent processing. Mitchell and Green (1978) argued against interpreting this result as indicating that context affects ongoing word recognition. Instead, they argued that it was necessary to make an extra inference in order to integrate word frames that followed non-predicitve verbs with the rest of the passage. Thus, they maintained their stance that contextual effects in reading do not act rapidly enough to influence ongoing word recognition. However, Fischler and Goodman (1978) have reported findings that appear to contradict the latter claim. In a single-word priming experiment, they observed significant semantic context effects even when the stimulus onset asynchrony was only 40 msec, indicating that semantic contexts can act rapidly enough to influence ongoing word recognition. Of course, Mitchell and Green (1978) could counter with the argument of Forster (1976)—that the constraints of a semantically related word and sentence fragment are so fundamentally different that generalizations from experiments involving the former to theories about the latter are not justified. This argument loses force, however, when one considers the experiments of Blank and Foss (1978), Morton and Long (1976), and Marslen-Wilson and Welsh (1978), who worked with full sentence contexts. Using auditory recognition paradigms, these investigators found that contextual processes do operate fast enough to affect ongoing word recognition (see also Cole & Jakimik, 1978; and Tyler & Marslen-Wilson, 1977).

In light of the preceding, an attenuated version of the Mitchell and Green (1978) hypothesis seems most consistent with all of the currently available evidence. The heart of their conjecture—that when the time constraints of the experimental situation and the ecological validity of stimulus materials more closely approximate those found in actual reading, then contextual effects on ongoing word recognition diminish—appears to be sound. This hypothesis is supported by the results of the last experiment reported earlier, the results reported by Mitchell and Green (1978) themselves, and by the recent work of Fischler and Bloom (1979) and of Alford (1979). Employing a lexical decision task, Fischler and Bloom (1979) found that only the recognition of words that were highly predictable from their previous contexts was facilitated. Alford (1979) used a naming task and selected his materials from "natural" sources, rather than choosing them for their high predictability as is done in many experiments. He observed a facilitation effect of only 19 msec, suggesting that previous experimentation may have overestimated the magnitude of context effects that occur in everyday reading (see also, the McConkie & Zola chapter in this volume).

Although the research already reviewed is supportive of the general thrust of the arguments of Mitchell and Green (1978), their strong position—that contextual effects on ongoing word recognition are totally absent—appears to be too extreme. The last experiment reported earlier suggested that a small contextual effect may still be present even when the time constraints of actual reading are approximated, a conclusion that also receives support from the work of Fischler and Goodman (1978), Marslen-Wilson and Welsh (1978), Morton and Long (1976), and Tyler and Marslen-Wilson (1977) (although it should be noted that the Marslen-Wilson & Welsh and Morton & Long experiments involved auditory recognition). This author would argue that there is a small residual effect of context on ongoing word recognition, but consistent with the results of Stanovich and West (1979) and the other experiments already reported, the time constraints of actual reading are such that the effect is due to automatic activation rather than conscious prediction. It should be noted that the results of Mitchell and Green (1978) are not entirely inconsistent with this conclusion. Recall that they found facilitation due to semantically constraining contexts but not syntactically constraining texts. Since spreading activation is usually conceived as a semantically based effect (see Collins & Loftus, 1975), the results of Mitchell and Green could be interpreted as indicating that in the fluent reader, prior context facilitates word recognition only through an automatic, semantically based spreading activation process, and that the effect is rather small.

SUMMARY AND CONCLUSIONS

Several studies from an ongoing research program on sentence context effects were presented. The initial developmental results appeared to be rather parsimoniously explained by the two-process theory of expectancy of Posner and Snyder. Further experiments that were designed to test the theory directly were largely supportive of its predictions. Although there were some discrepancies, the very least that can be said is that the Posner–Snyder theory provides a better account of the body of data than do other models. One other advantage of the Posner–Snyder theory is that it provides one explicit example of how compensatory-interactive processing might take place. A compensatory-interactive model of processing hypothesizes that a pattern is synthesized based on information provided simultaneously from all knowledge sources and that a process at *any* level can compensate for deficiencies at any other level. Compensatory-interactive models appear to be the only type of theorizing that can render certain findings in the reading literature nonparadoxical, such as the fact that poorer readers have been found to display larger contextual facilitation effects (Biemiller, 1977–1978; Perfetti, Goldman, & Hogaboam, 1979; Roth, Perfetti, & Lesgold, 1979; Samuels, Begy, & Chen, 1975–1976; Schvaneveldt, Ackerman, & Semlear, 1977; West & Stanovich, 1978). The Posner–Snyder theory provides a specification of how compensatory processing guarantees the latter finding. When word recognition is slow, another higher-level expectancy process (the conscious-attention mechanism) has time to operate and thus provides additional facilitation due to contextual information. Since poorer readers have slower word recognition times, it is more likely that this additional source of facilitation is implicated in their performance. Also consistent with this account is the fact that semantic context has a larger effect on the recognition times of fluent readers when the target word is degraded (Becker & Killion, 1977; Forster, 1976; Massaro, Jones, Lipscomb, & Scholz, 1978; Meyer, Schvaneveldt, & Ruddy, 1975; Sanford, Garrod, & Boyle, 1977; Stanovich & West, 1979).

A consideration of the way in which the two expectancy mechanisms of the Posner–Snyder theory act to compensate for slow word recognition speed suggests an interesting distinction between types of compensatory processing. This is the distinction between an optional and an obligatory compensatory trade-off. An obligatory trade-off is one that is necessitated by the structure of the processing system. For example, according to Morton's (1969, 1970) logogen model, when the processing rate is slowed, factors affecting the evidence requirements of logogens have a greater effect on performance (see Seymour, 1976). This trade-off is inherent in the structure of the system. In a similar manner, the increased facilitation produced by spreading activation when word recognition is slowed also represents an obligatory trade-off, since spreading activation is automatic (not under subject control) and is a function of the structure of the semantic memory system. In contrast, the greater facilitation due to the formation of conscious expectancies that results when word recognition is slowed is an optional compensation. Conscious expectancy formation is under the control of the subject and need not necessarily be invoked when word recognition is slow.

A reasonable account of the bulk of the literature on sentence context effects is provided when the Posner–Snyder theory is integrated with a weak version of a hypothesis advanced by Mitchell and Green (1978). Their argument is that as the stimulus materials and real-time processing constraints of the experimental situation more closely approximate the actual reading situation, contextual effects on ongoing word recognition will be attenuated. An experiment reported earlier, as well as the work of other investigators (e.g., Alford, 1979; Fischler & Bloom, 1979), appears to support this general conclusion. There does, however, appear to be a small residual effect of sentence context on word recognition, even when the processing constraints of actual reading are closely approximated. Consistent with the Posner–Snyder theory, it was argued earlier that this residual contextual effect is largely due to automatic spreading activation.

The research discussed earlier also has implications for a widely used technique in developmental investigations of context utilization—the cloze task. In this task the subject is presented with a sentence that has a word removed and is asked to produce the missing word. Accuracy is the performance measure, and the subject is under no time pressure. Obviously, performance on the cloze task is dependent on the ability to generate consciously a word consistent with the sentence. The question that is raised by the studies reviewed in this chapter is how this conscious prediction process is related to the processes that cause contextual facilitation in actual reading. If, as has been argued, the conscious-attention process is less implicated in contextual facilitation as reading proficiency develops, then performance on cloze tasks may be less indicative of actual context usage at the higher reading levels. Thus, the correlation between reading proficiency and cloze performance (e.g., Ruddell, 1965) may not be indicative of a causal relation. Older and better readers may respond more accurately on cloze tasks because of their larger store of linguistic and general knowledge. This does not necessarily mean that greater conscious contextual prediction is implicated in their more rapid reading speeds (see Perfetti & Roth, Chap. 11, this volume). In fact, if they are reading rapidly enough, it is likely that any effect of context on recognition is due to automatic spreading activation rather than conscious prediction. Reaction-time measures similar to those used in the experiments reported here are probably better indicators of context use in the actual reading situation than are cloze tasks.

A few restrictions on the conclusions already stated should, however, be mentioned. First of all, lest it appear that these conclusions are relegating sentence context effects to a position of minor importance in reading theorizing, it should be noted that the foregoing conclusions apply primarily to the *fluent* reader. The Posner–Snyder theory predicts that contextual effects become more important for readers with slower word recognition speeds, a prediction that has ample empirical confirmation. So whereas it is true that contextual effects on ongoing word recognition must be relegated to a position of minor importance in models of the fluent reading process, models that also attempt to account for the performance of the poorer reader or for the development of reading fluency will have to elevate contextual facilitation processes to a position of some importance.

The possibility and/or importance of facilitation due to spreading activation has been questioned on the grounds that sentences rarely contain words that are directly associated (Forster, 1976). Such criticisms seem to assume that spreading activation occurs within a highly simplified semantic memory network, such as the simple hierarchical structure described by Collins and Quillian (1969) for purposes of illustration. However, spreading activation resulting from the moderate and sometimes tangential relationships between the words in typical sentences would be much more likely if the structure of semantic memory was somewhat more complex. The extended Quillian model discussed by Collins and Loftus (1975) and the active structural networks described by Norman and Rumelhart (1975) are models of semantic memory where facilitation due to spreading activation from the words within sentences would be more likely to occur. The results of a study by Fischler (1977b) are consistent with this argument. He found that priming can occur for pairs of words that are not associated, as long as the words are semantically related. Thus, spreading activation appears to be extremely pervasive and not simply limited to strongly associated words. Nevertheless, the point is well taken that it would be desirable to have a more precise specification of exactly how spreading activation operates to facilitate words within the same sentence. Finally, it should be noted that neither the experiments reported here nor most of the studies reviewed have investigated the effects of contextual material occurring before the sentence containing the critical word. Such effects have been demonstrated on comprehension time (cf. Garrod & Sanford, 1977) but no studies of the effects of contextual information from prior sentences on ongoing word recognition have been reported. It is thus possible that contextual information prior to the sentence containing the critical word acts to facilitate recognition and that the effect may be attentional. Several studies that address this possibility are currently being initiated. However, in regard to single-sentence context effects, the Posner–Snyder theory—amended with the hypothesis of Mitchell and Green (1978)—appears to provide the best framework for integrating the results of the experiments reported here with other recent work on context effects.

REFERENCES

Alford, J. A. *The interaction of sentential context and stimulus quality in word recognition.* Paper presented at the annual meeting of the Midwestern Psychological Association, Chicago, May, 1979.

Becker, C. A. Semantic context effects in word recognition: An analysis of semantic strategies. *Memory & Cognition,* 1980, *8,* 493–512.

Becker, C. A., & Killion, T. H. Interaction of visual and cognitive effects in word recognition. *Journal of Experimental Psychology: Human Perception and Performance,* 1977, *3,* 389–401.

Biemiller, A. Relationships between oral reading rates for letters, words, and simple text in the development of reading achievement. *Reading Research Quarterly,* 1977-1978, *13,* 223–253.

Blank, M. A., & Foss, D. J. Semantic facilitation and lexical access during sentence processing. *Memory & Cognition,* 1978, *6,* 644–652.

Cole, R. A., & Jakimik, J. Understanding speech: How words are heard. In G. Underwood (Ed.), *Strategies of information processing.* London: Academic Press, 1978.

Collins, A. M., & Loftus, E. F. A spreading-activation theory of semantic processing. *Psychological Review,* 1975, *82,* 407–428.

Collins, A. M., & Quillian, M. R. Retrieval time from semantic memory. *Journal of Verbal Learning and Verbal Behavior,* 1969, *8,* 240–247.

Davelaar, E., & Coltheart, M. Effects of interpolated items on the association effect in lexical decision tasks. *Bulletin of the Psychonomic Society,* 1975, *6,* 269–272.

Fischler, I. Associative facilitation without expectancy in a lexical decision task. *Journal of Experimental Psychology: Human Perception and Performance,* 1977, *3,* 18–26. (a)

Fischler, I. Semantic facilitation without association in a lexical decision task. *Memory & Cognition,* 1977, *5,* 335–339. (b)

Fischler, I., & Bloom, P. A. Automatic and attentional processes in the effects of sentence contexts on word recognition. *Journal of Verbal Learning and Verbal Behavior,* 1979, *18,* 1–20.

Fischler, I., & Goodman, G. O. Latency of associative activation in memory. *Journal of Experimental Psychology: Human Perception and Performance,* 1978, *4,* 455–470.

Forster, K. I. Accessing the mental lexicon. In R. J. Wales & E. Walker (Eds.), *New approaches to language mechanisms.* Amersterdam: North-Holland, 1976.

Garrod, S., & Sanford, A. Interpreting anaphoric relations: The integration of semantic information while reading. *Journal of Verbal Learning and Verbal Behavior,* 1977, *16,* 77–90.

Goodman, K. S. Reading: A psycholinguistic guessing game. In H. Singer & R. Ruddell (Eds.), *Theoretical models and processes of reading.* Newark, Del.: International Reading Association, 1970.

Huey, E. B. *The psychology and pedagogy of reading.* New York: Macmillan, 1908. (Republished by MIT Press, Cambridge, Mass., 1968.)

Lachman, R., Lachman, J., & Butterfield, E. *Cognitive psychology and information processing: An introduction.* Hillsdale, N.J.: Lawrence Erlbaum Associates, 1979.

Marslen-Wilson, W. D. Linguistic structure and speech shadowing at very short latencies. *Nature,* 1973, *244,* 522–523.

Marslen-Wilson, W. D. Sentence perception as an interactive parallel process. *Science,* 1975, *189,* 226–228.

Marslen-Wilson, W. D., & Welsh, A. Processing interactions and lexical access during word recognition in continuous speech. *Cognitive Psychology*, 1978, *10*, 29–63.

Massaro, D. W., Jones, R. D., Lipscomb, D., & Scholz, R. Role of prior knowledge on naming and lexical decisions with good and poor stimulus information. *Journal of Experimental Psychology: Human Learning and Memory*, 1978, *4*, 498–512.

Meyer, D. E., & Schvaneveldt, R. W. Facilitation in recognizing pairs of words: Evidence of a dependence between retrieval operations. *Journal of Experimental Psychology*, 1971, *90*, 227–234.

Meyer, D. E., Schvaneveldt, R. W., & Ruddy, M. G. Loci of contextual effects on word recognition. In P. M. A. Rabbitt & S. Dornic (Eds.), *Attention and performance V*. New York: Academic Press, 1975.

Mitchell, D. C., & Green, D. W. The effects of context and content on immediate processing in reading. *Quarterly Journal of Experimental Psychology*, 1978, *30*, 609–636.

Morton, J. The effects of context on the visual duration threshold for words. *British Journal of Psychology*, 1964, *55*, 165–180.

Morton, J. The interaction of information in word recognition. *Psychological Review*, 1969, *76*, 165–178.

Morton, J. A functional model for memory. In D. A. Norman (Ed.), *Models of human memory*. New York: Academic Press, 1970.

Morton, J., & Long, J. Effect of transitional probability on phoneme identification. *Journal of Verbal Learning and Verbal Behavior*. 1976, *15*, 43–51.

Neely, J. H. Semantic priming and retrieval from lexical memory: Roles of inhibitionless spreading activation and limited-capacity attention. *Journal of Experimental Psychology: General*, 1977, *106*, 226–254.

Norman, D. A. *Memory and attention*. New York: Wiley, 1976.

Norman, D. A., & Rumelhart, D. E. *Explorations in cognition*. San Francisco: Freeman, 1975.

Perfetti, C. A., Finger, E., & Hogaboam, T. Sources of vocalization latency differences between skilled and less skilled young readers. *Journal of Educational Psychology*, 1978, *70*, 730–739.

Perfetti, C. A., Goldman, S. R., & Hogaboam, T. W. Reading skill and the identification of words in discourse context. *Memory & Cognition*, 1979, *7*, 273–282.

Perfetti, C. A., & Hogaboam, T. Relationship between single word decoding and reading comprehension skill. *Journal of Educational Psychology*, 1975, *67*, 461–469.

Petrinovich, L. Probabilistic functionalism: A conception of research method. *American Psychologist*, 1979, *34*, 373–390.

Posner, M. I., & Rogers, M. G. K. Chronometric analysis of abstraction and recognition. In W. K. Estes (Ed.), *Handbook of learning and cognitive processes* (Vol. 5). Hillsdale, N.J.: Lawrence Erlbaum Associates, 1978.

Posner, M. I., & Snyder, C. R. R. Attention and cognitive control. In R. Solso (Ed.), *Information processing and cognition: The Loyola symposium*. Hillsdale, N.J.: Lawrence Erlbaum Associates, 1975. (a)

Posner, M. I., & Snyder, C. R. R. Facilitation and inhibition in the processing of signals. In P. M. A. Rabbitt & S. Dornic (Eds.), *Attention and performance V*. New York: Academic Press, 1975. (b)

Roth, S. F., Perfetti, C. A., & Lesgold, A. M. *Reading ability and children's word identification processes*. Paper presented at the annual meeting of the Midwestern Psychological Association, Chicago, May 1979.

Ruddell, R. B. The effect of similarity of oral and written patterns of language structure on reading comprehension. *Elementary English*, 1965, *43*, 403–410.

Rumelhart, D. E. Toward an interactive model of reading. In S. Dornic (Ed.), *Attention and performance VI*. Hillsdale, N.J.: Lawrence Erlbaum Associates, 1977.

Samuels, S. J., Begy, G., & Chen, C. C. Comparison of word recognition speed and strategies of less skilled and more highly skilled readers. *Reading Research Quarterly*, 1975–1976, *11*, 72–86.

Sanford, A. J., Garrod, S., & Boyle, J. M. An independence of mechanism in the origins of reading and classification-related semantic distance effects. *Memory & Cognition,* 1977, *5,* 214–220.

Schuberth, R. E., & Eimas, P. D. Effects of context on the classification of words and nonwords. *Journal of Experimental Psychology: Human Perception and Performance,* 1977, *3,* 27–36.

Schvaneveldt, R., Ackerman, B. P., & Semlear, T. The effect of semantic context on children's word recognition. *Child Development,* 1977, *48,* 612–616.

Schvaneveldt, R. W., & Meyer, D. E. Retrieval and comparison processes in semantic memory. In S. Kornblum (Ed.), *Attention and performance IV.* New York: Academic Press, 1973.

Seymour, P. H. K. Contemporary models of the cognitive process. II. Retrieval and comparison operations in permanent memory. In V. Hamilton & M. D. Vernon (Eds.), *The development of cognitive processes.* London: Academic Press, 1976.

Smith, F. *Understanding reading.* New York: Holt, Rinehart & Winston, 1971.

Stanovich, K. E. Toward a interactive-compensatory model of individual differences in the development of reading fluency. *Reading Research Quarterly,* 1980, *16,* 32–71.

Stanovich, K. E., & Bauer, D. W. Experiments on the spelling-to-sound regularity effect in word recognition. *Memory & Cognition,* 1978, *6,* 410–415.

Stanovich, K. E., & West, R. F. Mechanisms of sentence context effects in reading: Automatic activation and conscious attention. *Memory & Cognition,* 1979, *7,* 77–85.

Stanovich, K. E., & West, R. F. The effect of sentence context on ongoing word recognition: Tests of a two-process theory. *Journal of Experimental Psychology: Human Perception and Performance,* 1981, in press.

Swinney, D. A., Onifer, W., Prather, P., & Hirshkowitz, M. Semantic facilitation across sensory modalities in the processing of individual words and sentences. *Memory & Cognition,* 1979, *7,* 159–165.

Theios, J. & Muise, J. G. The word identification process in reading. In N. Castellan, D. Pisoni, & G. Potts (Eds.), *Cognitive Theory, Vol. II,* Hillsdale, N.J.: Lawrence Erlbraum, Inc., 1977.

Tulving, E., & Gold, C. Stimulus information and contextual information as determinants of tachistoscopic recognition of words. *Journal of Experimental Psychology,* 1963, *66,* 319–327.

Tversky, B., Havousha, S., & Poller, A. Noun–modifier order in a semantic verification task. *Bulletin of the Psychonomic Society,* 1979, *13,* 31–34.

Tweedy, J. R., Lapinski, R. H., & Schvaneveldt, R. W. Semantic-context effects on word recognition: Influence of varying the proportion of items presented in an appropriate context. *Memory & Cognition,* 1977, *5,* 84–89.

Tyler, L. K., & Marslen-Wilson, W. D. The on-line effects of semantic context on syntactic processing. *Journal of Verbal Learning and Verbal Behavior,* 1977, *16,* 683–692.

Underwood, G. Contextual facilitation from attended and unattended messages. *Journal of Verbal Learning and Verbal Behavior,* 1977, *16,* 99–106.

Venezky, R. L. Research on reading processes: A historical perspective. *American Psychologist,* 1977, *32,* 339–345.

West, R. F., & Stanovich, K. E. Automatic contextual facilitation in readers of three ages. *Child Development,* 1978, *49,* 717–727.

Yates, J. Priming dominant and unusual senses of ambiguous words. *Memory & Cognition,* 1978, *6,* 636–643.

11 Some of the Interactive Processes in Reading and Their Role in Reading Skill

Charles A. Perfetti and Steven Roth
University of Pittsburgh
Learning Research and Development Center

In this chapter, we discuss some features of a model of reading that is both sensitive to individual differences and consistent with the assumption that reading processes are interactive in some interesting way.[1] We first describe how this model is interactive in a way that helps us account for individual differences in reading skill. This is followed by a discussion of some research strategies and results that make contact with the model.

At the most general level, an interactive model needs to account for processes in contact with each other. "Conceptually guided" and "data driven" are ways of talking about processes in isolation. However, the force of a serious proposal that processes are interactive is that "conceptually guided" and "data driven" refer not so much to processes as to sources of information. The interactive processes are the continuous use and updating of these information sources. Accordingly, we speak of information levels, particularly a conceptual level and a graphic level.

There are two contrasting views of reading failure that are brought into focus by an interactive framework of this kind. One view is that reading failure is often a matter of conceptually based data either not being sufficiently available or not being sufficiently used. The other view is that reading failure derives in large part from failures at fluent coding of graphically based information—that is, word

---

[1]This model, which has come to be known as the verbal efficiency model of reading skill, has developed out of collaboration with Alan Lesgold (Lesgold & Perfetti, 1978; Perfetti & Lesgold, 1977; 1979), who deserves much credit for any sensible aspects the model might contain but is blameless for the more quaint views that we promote here.

decoding and identification.[2] This is the suggestion provided by the verbal efficiency model of reading skill. The central interactive claim of this model is that the context-free verbal coding is a rate-limiting process in reading. Further, a slow verbal coding rate adversely affects not just the rate of processing but, in some cases, the asymptotic performance level. Although slow word identification typically will retard comprehension in subtle ways, it can, on occasion, severely disrupt comprehension by promoting the deactivation of recently established contexts (Lesgold & Perfetti, 1978; Perfetti & Lesgold, 1977, 1979).

This central claim can be understood as a consequence of some general assumptions concerning some of the interactive processes in reading:

1. Reading is interactive in that different processes are responsible for providing data and sharing the data with other processes. This seems to be the central characteristic of the interactive reading model described by Rumelhart (1977).

2. Relationships among processes are not exclusively stage sequential. However, they are assumed to be ordered, forward-feeding processes. (This assumption has been explored by McClelland [1979] in his cascade model.) Process 2 can begin with very little data provided by Process 1, and it can reach asymptote (complete execution) prior to the completion of Process 1. However, it cannot rise above zero—that is, begin its execution—prior to the beginning of Process 1. Influences of higher-level information sources are on the rate at which lower-level processes execute or on the asymptotic level sufficient for further processing. However, lower-level processes do not strongly depend on higher-level data.

3. A process is rate limiting to the extent that other processes depend on its data. Although any process (data source) may be rate limiting in principle, there is reason to think that some processes will be more rate limiting than others. In particular, the more other processes depend on a given data source, the more the rate of the process providing such data affects the total set of processes in question. For example, if word identification depends on letter identification at least in part, then activation (recognition) of individual letters will be a rate-limiting process in word identification. A system that recognizes letters only with difficulty will be slow at identifying words relative to a system that easily recognizes letters. Similarly, at a higher level, if semantic parsing depends on word identification, then word identification will be rate limiting for semantic representation.

4. Influences of higher-level information sources (conceptual guidance) on lower-level information sources are essentially rate-constant effects. They do not affect the dependence of higher-level processes on logically prior, lower-level

---

[2]Throughout this discussion lower-level verbal processes in general, rather than specifically graphically based ones, are potential sources of reading failure. We refer to "graphic level" only because the evidence we present here is restricted to print.

ones. For example, if word identification can be executed more quickly in context, then so can any other process that depends on word identification. The effect of conceptual data is either to make word identification easier or to make subsequent use of these data—for example, semantic parsing—more efficient.

In summary, we assume a model of reading whose processes are at once interactive and *asymmetrical*. Top-down and bottom-up data are not used in strictly reciprocal ways. An important consequence of this asymmetry is that so called bottom-up processes can carry on reasonably well without top-down processes, but not vice versa. No matter how helpful top-down processes are, they are neither definitive nor essential.[3]

Implications for an Analysis of Reading Skill

An interactive model based on such assumptions has some implications for the sources of reading failure. The key theoretical principle is the asymmetry of higher- and lower-level data sources. Because low-level processes can execute without higher-level data and because the effects of conceptually derived data are constant with respect to lower-level processes, the following general possibilities present themselves.

Type 1: Slow Coder. An individual can have a slow rate on a potentially fast rate process such as word identification. The effect of this is to limit the rate and possibly the asymptotic level of a later process such as sentence comprehension. The individual in this case can be assumed to show relationships between the rate of word identification and the rates of other subprocesses that are within the normal range. Further, his or her entire processing time to sentence comprehension is speeded up in a constant manner by the addition of conceptually derived information.

Type 2: Slow Sentence Computer. An individual can have moderately fast rates for a low-level process but slower rates on later sentence computations that partly depend on its data. That is, inefficient use is made of data from lower-level processes. This state of affairs would describe the (perhaps apocryphal) reader who can identify single words fluently but can't seem to put words together.

Type 3: Contextual Abstainer. A third possibility is that a reader may have relatively fast rates for word identification and relatively efficient slopes of later functions relative to word identification, but may fail to show the shift in all

---

[3]This claim is made without ignoring the importance of examples of ambiguity in which incorrect readings are achieved without sufficient conceptual guidance. A reader's tolerance of such sentences is probably very limited.

subprocses rates that normally derives from prior higher-level data. Such an individual may also give the impression of reading word by word. This reader differs from the slow sentence computer in that, given word identification, he or she can perform mental computation on sentences; however, neither word identification nor the processes that depend on it are much affected by conceptually derived data.

Within the framework of this model, all other possible sources of reading process failure reduce to a variant of one of the three types. However, no research that we know can forcefully distinguish among the three types. Short of doing so here, we try to make some contact between these hypothetical types and some data that have been collected.

STUDIES OF CONTEXTUAL INFLUENCES ON WORD IDENTIFICATIONS

One approach to how conceptually derived data and graphically derived data interact in reading is to affect the quality of the two data sources. For example, conceptually derived data are used to create an expectancy of the word *game* in the following sentence: *According to Goodman, reading is a psycholinguistic guessing* _____. *Game* is less expected in the sentence, *The President was afraid that he would lose the* _____. We might expect the identification of *game* to require more data-based information in the President context than in the reading context.

The opposite state of affairs is achieved by disrupting the quality of the graphic data. For example, deleting letter features will degrade the graphic quality of a word and make the identification process more dependent on conceptually based information. This, then, is the logic of some research we have carried out: Degrading the quality of conceptually based information makes processing more dependent upon data-based information. Degrading the quality of data-based information makes processing more dependent on conceptually based information. We disrupt conceptual information by presenting words not predictable from the discourse context. We disrupt data-based information by deleting letter segments from words to be identified.

The first question is whether less skilled readers are characterized by a reduced ability to use conceptually derived data to affect word identification. If subjects are measured on their speed of word identification in discourse context, Type 3 subjects should fail to show a facilitation relative to their identification of words in isolation. Type 2 subjects may or may not show a facilitation, depending on the asymptotic level of subprocesses rather than the rate. If the subprocesses dependent on word identification are slow in rate, there is some probability that comprehension of the discourse will be insufficient to guide word identification. On the other hand, if only the rate of comprehension is affected by the Type

2 syndrome and not the asymptote, then Type 2 subjects should be able to use discourse context to guide word identification provided sufficient time is allowed (with limited time, asymptote may not be reached). Thus the situation we are describing—one in which word identification is measured with and without conceptually derived data in the form of discourse context—should distinguish between Type 1 and Type 3, with Type 2 somewhat indeterminant.

A series of studies provides data on the use of context in word identification by readers of high and low skill.[4] These studies provided discourse contexts to subjects and measured the latency of identification of isolated words within the discourse.

EXPERIMENT 1

Story Discourse

The first experiment is one of three reported in Perfetti, Goldman, and Hogaboam (1979), in which discourse context was provided by a short story. Subjects read the text on a stack of cards and, after completing each card, turned their gaze to a screen for the presentation of the next word. They were to say the word as quickly as possible. Word length and word frequency were orthogonally varied with two context conditions, words seen as part of a story or in isolation. The predictability of the words within the story was assessed by having an independent sample of subjects predict the words while hearing the story read.

A major result was that less skilled readers benefited from story context at least to the same extent as did skilled readers. Indeed, there was an interaction of skill and context to suggest that less skilled readers made more use of context than skilled readers. This is illustrated in Fig. 11.1, which plots median identification latencies as a function of the predictability of the target, the latter being indexed by the percentage of subjects in an independent group who predicted a given target word in the story.

The intercept of the functions of Fig. 11.1 can be interpreted as the identification rate for an unpredictable word, whereas the slope is the gain in identification time with increasing predictability. Less skilled readers showed both higher intercepts and greater slopes. The 162-millisecond intercept difference between skilled and less skilled readers is smaller than the difference observed in the isolated presentation condition (not shown), which was over 300 milliseconds. Whereas skilled readers' isolation latencies were identical to the intercept of their

---

[4]All results discussed here apply to young readers, 8 to 10 years old, classified by a reading comprehension test as being skilled or less skilled. Skilled readers are chosen from above the 60th percentile, and less skilled readers are below the 40th percentile of the Metropolitan Achievement Reading Subtest. Less skilled readers are within the normal range on IQ tests.

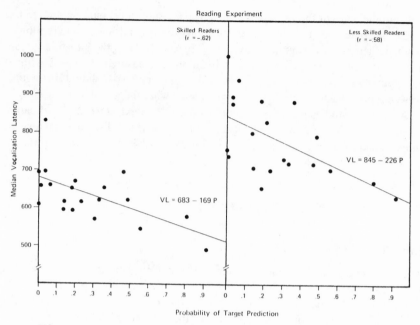

FIG. 11.1. Word identification latency as a function of target predictability (Perfetti, Goldman, & Hogaboam, 1979).

predictability function of Fig. 11.1, less skilled readers had isolation latencies of around 1 second. Thus, for less skilled readers, even a low-predictable word in context was identified faster than a word in isolation. However, for skilled readers, words in isolation were just as fast as words in context with low predictability.

There is further evidence from this study that less skilled readers are very sensitive to context. We can examine the relative facilitation provided by context for the four types of words identified. Less skilled readers typically show especially long identification latencies to long words (Hogaboam & Perfetti, 1978) and to less frequent words (Perfetti & Hogaboam, 1975). This is consistent with the verbal efficiency model's assumption that verbal codes are not quickly activated by the less skilled reader and that the more activation of the code depends on subword units, the less accessible it is. Compared with short words and very common words, longer and less common words may be accessed only after a greater activation of subword units—for example, grapheme and phoneme sequences. If less skilled readers are sensitive to context, some of the difficulty they have with long or less familiar words should disappear, because less graphic data are needed for identification.

This is essentially what happened when we examined context facilitation scores in this experiment. This facilitation score is the difference between subjects' latencies to isolated words and to words in story context. (Expressing facilitation as a ratio, which somewhat reduced floor effects, does not alter the general pattern of facilitation effects.) Two findings are worth noting: One is that skilled readers show no facilitation for short high-frequency words and only modest variable effects for other word types. This could be a floor effect, but it may be an interesting floor effect. The interesting possibility is that skilled readers' data-based processes are so quickly executed that they provide data sufficient for identification before conceptual data become useful. Some facilitation was seen for longer or less familiar words, for which slightly more time is needed to derive data sufficient for identification. In such cases conceptually derived data are helpful in reducing the amount of information needed. The top-down processes in this case have time to execute before the bottom-up processes have completed.

The second result is that less skilled readers showed very large facilitation for long low-frequency words. Processing of graphically based data is very slow for any of several reasons having to do with coding subword units. Conceptually based data, assumed to be independent of the graphic data, have ample time to provide input prior to the completion of the slower data-driven process. Just as skilled readers may be showing a small facilitation limited by the quicker of two processes, less skilled readers may be showing a large facilitation limited by the slower of the two processes.

We can consider the foregoing suggestions by reference to the processing possibilities implied by the earlier description of the model. For skilled readers, word coding is a very quickly executing process and shows a quick rise to asymptote. For less skilled readers, word coding is a more slowly executing process with a relatively slow rise to asymptote. By our assumption concerning the constant effects of conceptually derived data, these word-coding processes should be affected by context in the way illustrated in Fig. 11.2.

Figure 11.2 shows hypothetical rate functions for word identification processes. All functions are shown to reach the same asymptotic level of activation, expressed as the percentage of processing sufficient to activate a word identification decision. The question is how context affects the rise time of different word identification functions.

The top panel of Fig. 11.2 shows the effect of three different context conditions on a hypothetical fast-rise function, characteristic of a skilled reader. The bottom panel, according to the model, shows the effect of these three different context conditions on a hypothetical slow-rise function, characteristic of a less skilled reader. (Alternatively, the word-processing function of the top panel can characterize words easy to code, and the function of the bottom panel can characterize words difficult to code. More is said about this in a later section.)

The word-processing function is described generally as an exponential function of time, with a rate constant, r, for individuals or words. The ordinate is the percentage of processing completed; thus all functions reach the same asymptote. The general form of this function is:

$$P = 1 - Kt^r$$

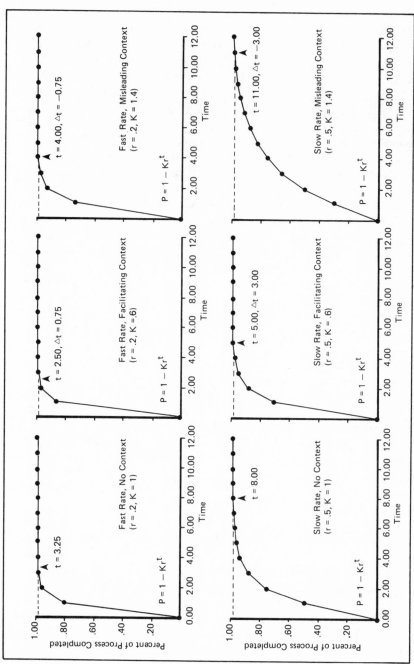

FIG. 11.2. Hypothetical word identification functions, showing percentage of process completed over units of time. The top three panels show a fast-rate, high-skill reader. The bottom three panels show a slow-rate, low-skill reader. Within each panel, the three functions from left to right show no context, facilitating context, and misleading context. The value of t in each case is the number of time units prior to reaching asymptote. The value of Δt is the increase or decrease in t with context compared with no context.

where t is time, K is the reciprocal of a constant that represents the contribution of conceptually derived data, and r is the rate constant. Each panel shows functions for three values of the context constant, K. In each panel, the first function ($K = 1$) can be thought of as an identification function for a word in isolation. The second is a faster rising function ($K < 1$) that can be thought of as an identification function in discourse context. The third function is a slow-rise ($K > 1$) identification in a misleading context.

Thus this simple activation model, which turns out to share some of the basic assumptions of Morton's (1969) logogen model, assumes that identification of a word in context is a function of the subject's basic identification rate (r) and his or her skill in use of context (k), or, equivalently, the helpfulness of the context. Such an assumption is at least consistent with the data of the experiment described earlier (Perfetti et al., 1979). In that study, an individual's isolated identification latency and ability to predict words both correlated with identification times in context.

More interesting is the assumption that the effects of context are greater for a slower executing function than for a faster executing one. That is, any arbitrarily high value of processing percentage will be achieved more quickly with context than without, but the gain due to context is a function of the time without context. This is the sense in which skilled readers may be, not less sensitive to context, but less dependent upon it.

EXPERIMENT 2

Bottom-Up Surprises

We turn now to a question of what happens when conceptually derived data fail to be useful. We have suggested that skilled readers have more quickly executing data-based processes and thus less dependence on conceptually based data. By the kind of framework we have presented, the asymmetry in the use of these two levels of data has an implication for situations in which texts are not helpful. Skilled readers should have little trouble identifying words in such texts because of their quickly executing data-based processes. Less skilled readers will show difficulties because their slower data-based processes effectively make them more context dependent. In this experiment there were three context types that differed in the predictability and sensibility afforded to a target word. One context type was highly constrained, so that the particular target word shown was predictable. A second type was moderately constrained, but the target word itself was virtually unpredictable. The third type of context was completed by a word that was not simply unpredictable but typically counterindicated by the context. The three context types are exemplified here for the target word *dump*.

1. *The garbage men had loaded as much as they could onto the truck. They would have to drop off a load at the garbage _____.*
2. *Albert didn't have the money he needed to buy the part to fix his car. Luckily, he found the part he wanted at the _____.*
3. *Phil couldn't decide whether to go to the movies or to the party. Both sounded like lots of fun, but he finally decided to go to the _____.*

Thus the target *dump* in (1) is highly predictable, in (2) is lexically unpredictable but semantically reasonable, and in (3) is both unpredictable and semantically surprising. To verify that we constructed texts with these properties, we had fifth-grade children of normal reading skill predict the final word of these texts. For the predictable contexts, the target was correctly predicted 80% of the time. (Almost all targets were predicted correctly by at least 9 or 10 subjects, but 3 of 18 targets turned out to be less predictable than planned.) The lexically unpredictable but semantically reasonable category was indeed generally unpredictable, with only 2.8% correct predictions. The semantically surprising targets were never correctly predicted. In addition, we judged whether the target produced by the subject was sensible and grammatical in the given context. Nearly all productions were judged to be both grammatical and sensible in all three contexts. Thus, the semantically surprising condition did not involve difficult contexts, only unexpected endings.

The question is, what happens when subjects are required to identify words in such contexts? The highly predictable contexts should produce very short latencies, and the unpredictable contexts should have longer ones. What of the semantically surprising contexts? By our account, skilled readers should identify words in surprising contexts at a rate whose limit is set by the data-based identification process, which is very rapidly executing. That is, they should do about as well as in contexts of low predictability. However, less skilled readers should identify words in surprising contexts at a rate limited by the contextual processes that, because of slow identification processes, have had time to execute. Since the contextually derived data are distinctly nonhelpful in this case, the graphic data will be found to be unmatched with the conceptual data, and time to analyze the graphic data further will be needed.

Table 11.1 shows that these expectations were confirmed for fourth-grade subjects. This is dramatic evidence that skilled readers can process words with little effect of context and that less skilled readers are somewhat more dependent on context.

We can refer again to Fig. 11.2 to illustrate why anomalous contexts should have the effects that they did. In Fig. 11.2 the effect of anomalous context is represented in the rightmost functions of each panel. (The context constant, K, is greater than 1 for anomalous contexts.) The fast-rise function of the skilled reader has reached asymptote without being affected by anomalous context. The slow-rise function of the less skilled reader has not reached asymptote prior to the

TABLE 11.1
Identification Latencies for Three Context Types
(Experiment 2)

Context Type	Target Predictability in Percent	Target Identification Latency	
		Skilled Readers	Less Skilled Readers
Highly predictable	80%	612	693
Unpredictable	3%	706	863
Anomalous	0%	717	967

effect of either predictable or anomalous contexts. Thus the former is greatly facilitating, and the latter is inhibiting.

It is interesting that with subjects 1 year younger, the effects shown in Table 11.1 were not obtained. For third-grade subjects, both skill groups were faster in predictable contexts and slower in surprising contexts. Although we have no basis for any strong developmental conclusions here, it is possible to conjecture that a developmental progression may be involved. As children get older and better at reading, they may move toward reduced reliance on context as a result of increased ability to use graphic data. This conclusion parallels that of West and Stanovich (1978), who found children, but not adults, affected by anomalous contexts. In contrast, Fischler and Bloom (1979) have found inhibitory effects of anomalous contexts in lexical decisions of adults—that is, skilled readers. The possible reasons for such a discrepancy are interesting but beyond our purpose.

Context Generation Experiments

One implication of the preceding discussion seems to be that the time to activate a context representation may be relatively uniform across individuals. However, this seems implausible and is certainly not implied by the verbal efficiency model. Indeed, individuals should vary in the activation of context-appropriate verbal networks. The time course of contextual activation may be separable into automatic and nonautomatic components, with the automatic activation being very rapid and very short-lived (Posner & Snyder, 1975; Stanovich & West, 1979; see also Stanovich, Chap. 10, this volume). Individual differences could occur at either or both of these components.

We do not have data that would address the rapidity of context activation, but we do have some concerning the level of performance when subjects are asked to predict words from a text. Such prediction is a comprehension task that requires building a text model and filling in the missing pieces.

In one of the experiments of Perfetti, Goldman, and Hogaboam (1979), skilled and less skilled subjects predicted the target words from the stories. Not surprisingly, skilled readers correctly predicted 32% of the words compared with 22% for less skilled readers. Since subjects were shown the target word just after predicting it and were required to identify it (say it) as quickly as possible, some comparison between identification of correctly predicted and of incorrectly predicted words was possible. Although all readers were quicker to identify a word that they had just predicted, skilled readers' latencies to unpredicted words were as low or lower than less skilled readers' latencies to predicted words. In other words, when less skilled readers had correctly predicted a word, they were about equal to skilled readers when the latter had not predicted the word. Thus, we have the result that skilled readers are at once better at using context and less dependent on it.

Why is there no evidence of this greater context sensitivity in the skilled reader's word identification? The answer is again in the relationship between K, r, and t shown in Fig. 11.2. For a reader with a fast rate, a large advantage of K is needed relative to the K for a reader with a slow rate of word processing.

In a recent study we have examined context use in short, two-sentence texts rather than in stories. Subjects heard the sentences and were given 15 seconds to produce as many words as possible that could complete the pair of sentences. Contexts were of three types in their degree of constraint—high, moderate, and low. As can be seen in Table 11.2, high-constraint contexts, by definition very constraining, produced the fewest number of responses but the most accurate prediction. Moderate- and low–constraint conditions, as expected, were more productive both in number of types and number of tokens. Also as designed, low-constraint context did not yield accurate prediction. Moderate constraint was very productive, averaging 6.52 responses per 15 seconds and yielding an average of about 28 distinct word types over 15 subjects. This compares with an average 36 distinct types by the low-constraint context.

The moderate-context condition produced predictive variability, and it is here that reader differences are seen. Skilled readers produced the target word 23.7% of the time compared with 15.2% by the less skilled readers. By contrast, in the high-constraint condition, the target was generated by 92.9% of skilled and 94.4% of less skilled readers; and in low constraint, each reader group produced the target less than 1% of the time. This means that we were successful in arranging texts that were so constraining that all subjects could produce the word and also texts that were so unconstraining that practically no subjects could predict the word. It is in the moderately constraining context that individual differences can be seen.

Accordingly, to begin to understand differences in use of context, it is useful to examine some of the individual items within the moderate-context condition. One way in which contexts differ seems to be the structure of permissible targets. For example, some structures can be characterized as relatively *horizontal*, whereas others are more *vertical*. A *horizontal* structure is one in which a number of target alternatives is possible and the alternatives do not comprise an ordered set, as in Text 4:

TABLE 11.2
Context Completion for Three Context Types:
Summary Statistics

Context Type	Mean Number of Tokens per Context	Mean Number of Types per Context	Type Token Ratio per Context	Mean Percentage Target Predictions	
				Skilled Readers	Less Skilled Readers
High constraint	58.2 (3.88)	12.39	.21	92.9	94.4
Moderate constraint	97.8 (6.52)	27.75	.28	23.7	15.2
Low constraint	85.7 (5.71)	36.44	.43	0.2	0.1

Note. Cell means of first three columns are averages of the skilled and less skilled groups, $n = 15$ for each group. The two groups did not differ in either number of types or number of tokens. Numbers in parentheses are the mean numbers of word predictions per subject. The percentages of target predictions are based on the occurrence of the target word without respect to its order.

4. *John bought a new chair, and he couldn't decide where to put it. Finally, he put it near the _____ (window).*

In Text 4, the possible targets comprise a disjunctive, horizontal set of elemenets: sofa, table, corner, piano, etc. This results in a relatively low constraint, as evidenced by the large number of different response types—32 by skilled readers and 34 by less skilled readers. Further, there was no advantage for skilled readers in predicting the exact target. In fact, more less skilled readers included the target (*window*) in their predictions than skilled readers.

By contrast, there are texts that suggest a more ordered structure in which the possible targets are related as an event sequence or a script (Schank & Abelson, 1977). The relationship among the possible target elements is implicational rather than disjunctive, as in Text 5.

5. *Lenny wanted to write a letter to his friend. He opened the drawer and looked for a _____ (stamp).*

Text 5 is more constraining than Text 4 because it suggests a word that names an object to participate in a letter-writing script. Skilled readers produced only 14 response types, whereas less skilled readers produced 21 response types, including 12 of the skilled readers' 14. However, there was a more interesting difference. Whereas all subjects began their prediction list with *pen, pencil,* or *paper,* about half of the skilled subjects eventually named *stamp,* but only two of the less skilled subjects did. One possible description of this result is that skilled readers were more likely to complete a letter-sending script than were less skilled readers. The latter were more likely to fill in only the first part.

Single examples can be misleading, as consideration of Text 6 shows.

6. *When I got home from work, I wanted to eat a fruit. I went to the re-frigerator and got a* _____ *(pear).*

Text 6, also an example of the moderate-constraint class, is clearly constraining as to semantic category but rather unconstrained beyond that. Accordingly, subjects produced words with a frequency distribution that mimics category norms (Battig & Montague, 1968): *apple, orange, pear,* and *grape* in more or less that order, a total of 16 fruits (including 2 vegetables) for skilled readers. Skilled subjects predicted *pear* 13 times (4 on the first try), compared with 8 (1 on the first try) for the less skilled subjects. The surprise is that less skilled readers, as a group, produced 26 response types compared with only 16 by the skilled group. Although they produced 14 of the 16 types produced by the skilled subjects, their total included 9 items that could not be classified either as fruits or vegetables but that did fit the refrigerator constraint (e.g., cake, pie, pizza). It was as if some less skilled subjects either forgot about the fruit constraint in the preceding sentence or quickly exhausted their fruit list and were forced to ignore the constraint. The evidence tends to favor the former description. The nonfruit responses tended to occur early in the generated list. It is possible that some individuals who would have little trouble producing instances of a semantic category do have trouble when a constraint isn't available in the sentence being currently processed or when one is presented in addition to other constraints. For such subjects, some relevant information is no longer available or at least is no longer usable. Notice that this explanation would serve Text 5 as well as Text 6. Thus the scriptal description may be superfluous.

Additionally, there are word frequency effects to consider. The skill differences in prediction were generally confined to low-frequency words. However, we believe a simple explanation in terms of context-free lexical availability or vocabulary can be ruled out. The examples examined do not encourage such an explanation, nor were the frequency effects in the right direction; it's not that less skilled readers did more poorly on low-frequency targets compared with high-frequency targets. It's rather that skilled readers did much better on low-frequency than high-frequency targets. A moment's reflection shows this to be a very sensible state of affairs. Being sensitive to context entails predicting words, not on the basis of their *general* availability in the lexicon, but on their *specific* appropriateness for a given context.

However, the nature of context-sensitivity differences remains to be determined. In some of the cases examined, such differences are consistent with the hypothesis that skilled subjects are activating a more complete script, as in the stamp example. In other cases, less skilled readers seem not to be using very simple constraints in the text, perhaps especially when the constraint is in the prior sentence. In all of this, it should be kept in mind that the difference in prediction preformance was restricted to contexts of moderate constraint. When things were highly constrained, less skilled subjects were good users of context.

The picture that emerges from these studies is that children vary in their ability to generate context-appropriate words as well as in their ability to identify words. Indeed the two abilities are correlated. For example, in Perfetti et al. (1979) the correlations between subjects' identification latencies to isolated words and number of correct target predictions in a story was − .60. Subjects who were faster at word identification tended to be subjects more accurate at predicting the next word in a story. Skilled readers thus appear to have at least two advantages. They are more efficient at context-free verbal coding and more able to use context in anticipating words. Their entire advantage due to context use does not always show up in identification latencies because, by the model presented here, gain in context is limited by the execution rate of lower-level processes. Frederiksen (1978; also Chap. 14, this volume) reports that superior young adult readers take advantage of context in word identification more than do low-skill adults, especially for low-frequency words. Apparently, at the higher level of word-coding skill characteristic of young adults, differences in context sensitivity begin to show themselves.

Experiments with Degraded Inputs

As we noted earlier, one way to examine interactive reading processes is to vary the quality of conceptually derived data and the quality of the graphically derived data together. We have already seen some effects due to the quality of the context. We turn now to studies that have simultaneously varied quality of context and quality of graphic input. The quality of the input was varied by deletion of letter segments.

There are two experiments that produced similar results. In the first, the two stories used by Perfetti, Goldman, and Hogaboam (1979) were read by a different group of subjects. The words to be identified were the same ones identified in the original study. Degrading of the words was achieved by random deletion of dots from computer-printed letters. The degree of degradation ranged from 0% (intact words) through 35% at 7% intervals.

We expected that when subjects were asked to read a story and identify words that vary in their graphic and visual quality, there would be an orderly function relating level of degradation and word identification. More interestingly, we imagined that conceptually derived data should play a large role in identification that increases as the quality of the graphic data decreases. Third, we expected the point on the degrading function at which the reader becomes very dependent on context to be higher for the skilled reader than for the less skilled reader. This follows from one assumption concerning the relationships between the use of graphically derived and conceptually derived data. Context should become useful sooner for a slowly executing word process and for one with a lower asymptote, as would be the case with a degraded word. An implication of this reasoning is that we should find a point at which the less skilled readers' word identification performance matches the skilled readers' performance. A point relatively high on the degrading function of a skilled reader should correspond to a point lower on the degrading function of a less skilled reader.

In considering the results, it is useful to examine asymptotic identification performance as well as the rate of identification. The asymptote is seldom an issue for normal reading with undegraded stimuli, but with degraded stimuli there is ample opportunity for incomplete identification. Figure 11.3 shows the identification accuracy functions for words seen in isolation and in story contexts.

One significant finding is that with a relatively modest 14% degrading, asymptotic word identification is lowered for words in isolation, even for skilled readers. However, for words in context, the asymptote holds steady until somewhere between 21% and 23% degrading. In effect, this means that the ultimate identifiability of a word is affected by its predictability: A graphic data reduction of 21% is traded off against a predictability of about 26%, which is the average predictability of words in the stories used in the experiment. It's also apparent from Fig. 11.3 that the effect of context was greater for less skilled readers. In fact, in context there is very little difference in asymptotic word identification between skilled and less skilled readers. In isolation, the picture is clearly different and consistent with the hypothesis that skilled readers require less graphically based information to achieve asymptotic identification, at least up to 35% degrading, at which point the differences may begin to disappear.

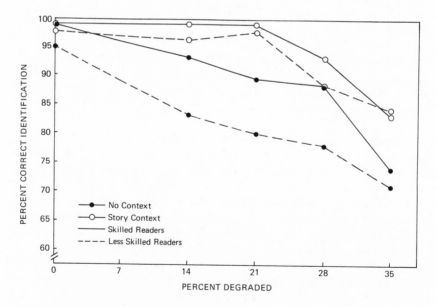

FIG. 11.3.   Percent correct word identification as a function of visual degrading for discourse context and no-context conditions.

If we look at rates instead of asymptotes, we get a similar picture as shown in the latencies of Fig. 11.4. Skilled readers are less affected by context and degrading. However, the effect of degrading was to increase the size of context effects for both groups. In addition, there is some comfort in these data for our assumption that context interactions with reading skill represent interesting floor effects—that is, floors having to do with process rate limits, rather than measurement limitations. Note that at high levels of degrading, the increased context effects for skilled readers approximate the context effects for less skilled readers for nondegraded words. In a sense, the 42% degrading caused the skilled readers to read as slowly as less skilled readers do normally, and as a result they show comparable improvement with context.

A second study of this sort was carried out to allow further analysis of context effects and to gain better control of materials. Since the first degrading study showed that performance remained fairly high even at 35%, we extended the degrading to 42% in the new study (Roth, Perfetti, & Lesgold, 1979). The texts used in this experiment were two-sentence texts of high, moderate, and low constraint, as described in a previous section of this chapter. (The high-constraint texts were completed by words that were very predictable.)

We expected that the highly constrained contexts would lead to a high asymptote unaffected by degrading. Indeed identification accuracy was nearly 100% for words in such contexts, even with 42% degrading. This was true for less skilled as well as skilled readers. If context is constraining enough, minimal graphic information is required.

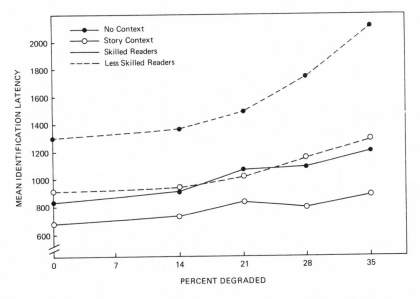

FIG. 11.4. Word identification latencies as a function of visual degrading for story context and no-context conditions.

We also expected and obtained the two-way interactions of reading skill with context and with degrading, as before. The degrading functions for skilled and less skilled readers were similar for all three conditions of sentence context. Since there was no three-way interaction, Fig. 11.5 shows the effect of context on word identification latencies for the two groups of readers combined. Notably, the highly constraining contexts produced short times for both reader groups, even at 42% degrading. Identification times were about 600 milliseconds for skilled readers and about 700 milliseconds for less skilled readers. Also of interest is that the degrading functions for moderate and low constraint diverged with degrading. Identification times were indistinguishable between these two subtly different text types until there was loss of stimulus information. With degrading, the advantage of a slightly more constraining context is more apparent for both groups of subjects.

The interactions of reading skill with degrading and with context are shown in Figs. 11.6 and 11.7, respectively. These data essentially replicate the results of the first experiment. Skilled readers are less dependent on context and less affected by degrading. These two effects appear to be independent statistically.

An important aspect of the analysis that we have been discussing is that context effects compensate for slowly executing word-level processes. An impli-

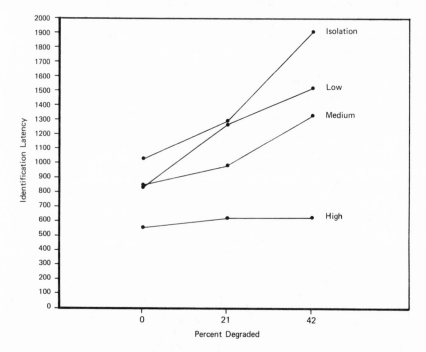

FIG. 11.5.   Word identification latencies as a function of visual degrading for four levels of contextual constraint.

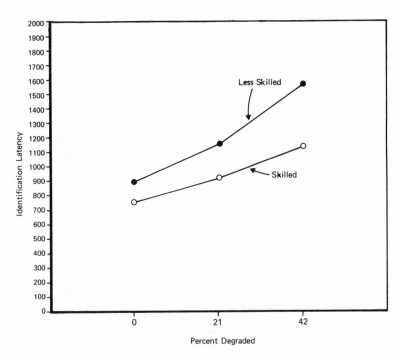

FIG. 11.6. Word identification letencies as a function of visual degrading for two levels of reading skill.

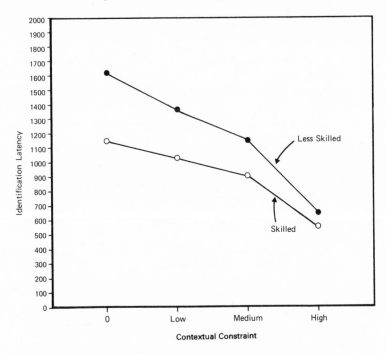

FIG. 11.7. Word identification latencies as a function of degree of contextual constraint for two levels of reading skill.

cation of this is that either a reader's typical word-level processing rate or the amount of graphic information in a word effectively produce slowed word-level processes. In either case, a slow rate can be compensated by context effects. In other words, context should be facilitative when word-level processes are slow, whether these processes are slow because of characteristics of the reader or because of characteristics of the word. This implies that if we examine amount of context facilitation as a function of isolated word identification, we should get a monotonically increasing function regardless of level of degrading and reading skill. Indeed, according to the model depicted in Fig. 11.2, this should be a linear function of the form $\Delta t = t_i - K't_i$ where Δt is the gain in context, t_i is the latency in isolation, and K' is a multiplicative constant reflecting the effect of context and the criterion P value $(K' = \log (1 - P)/\log K)$. Such functions are shown in the latencies of Fig. 11.8 for the highly constraining and moderately constraining contexts of the experiment just described.

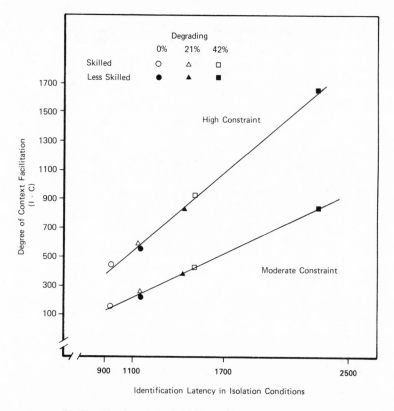

FIG. 11.8.   Degree of context facilitation as a function of isolated word identification latency for two levels of constraint. Plotted points represent group means for different degrading levels and reading skill.

The abscissa plots means for the six isolation conditions (two reading skills by three levels of degrading). The ordinate shows the context facilitation score, indexed simply by the difference between an isolation condition and its corresponding context condition. As predicted by the model, these functions illustrate that context facilitation was an increasing linear function of word-level identification processes. As these processes slow down, either because they are processes of less skilled readers or because they are processes operating on degraded word stimuli, the time saved because of context increases. For example, we can see that at 21% degrading, skilled readers had both the same context facilitation and the same isolation times as the less skilled readers at 0% degrading. Thus at 21% degrading, skilled readers were performing the same as less skilled readers without degrading.

A comparison of points along the two functions of Fig. 11.8 demonstrates how differences in the usefulness of context (and, by extension, the ability to use context) can be masked by slow word-level processes. For example, at any given level of performance in isolation, high constraint produces more facilitation than moderate constraint. However, the facilitation effect produced by moderate constraint exceeds that of high constraint when *different* levels of isolation performance are compared. This is consistent with the assumption that individual differences in prediction performance may not lead to corresponding differences in context facilitation because of larger individual differences in word coding.

Trade-Offs of Graphically-Derived and Conceptually Derived Data

Interactive processes of the sort under discussion are mutually supporting in the ordinary case. Data derived from the text allows identification of a word to be made with less data from the graphic input, and vice versa. However, the asymmetry in the relationship of these two processes allows us to examine trade-offs between them in some conditions.

One such condition is the misleading context, discussed previously. There we saw problems for the less skilled reader when the word to be identified was a surprise. A complementary condition is provided by word degrading. If context guides the reader to expect a word that doesn't occur or guides the individual to have very low expectations concerning a word, a degraded word may be misread. The misreading may be described as relaxing the criterion for graphically derived data in the face of poor graphic data and fair or good conceptual data. Of course, subjects make errors in ordinary reading, and there is a significant literature on the analysis of oral reading errors, especially of beginning readers (Biemiller, 1970; Cohen, 1974–1975; Lesgold & Curtis, Chap. 13, this volume; Weber, 1970). Although oral reading of text is a situation that strongly demands conceptually derived data, occurrence of errors is a matter of chance. By contrast, the misreading of a particular word is allowed by the experimental task that we have used. Ordinarily, failures to identify single words are too infrequent to provide sufficient data. However, such errors can be increased by showing degraded words.

In two of the experiments described previously, we were able to compare the errors made in isolation with the errors made in context. The probability of error should be greater out of context than in context, and indeed it was. More informative is the quality of the errors. When a word is seen in isolation, there are not specifiable conceptual data to constrain identification. Accordingly, identification should be governed mainly by processes that extract visual features of letters and whole words and find matches in memory. By contrast, a discourse context adds constraint. Ordinarily this constraint lowers the level of graphically derived data needed for identification. However, when the graphic data are degraded, context may provide, in a sense, too much constraint. Instead of searching the lexicon for the best match with the low-quality graphic data, the reader is forced to search a more limited lexical area for a match. If an error is made, it may be less likely to be a good match on visual features. Given two general sources of constraint, one is likely to be less satisfied, and ignoring context may be less likely than lowering the criterion for graphic features.

Errors were analyzed according to two sources of word-level data and conceptual data. For the latter, incorrect responses were evaluated for their contextual appropriateness and sorted into three levels. For the word-level data, errors were scored for the use of visual constraint and graphic constraint. Visual constraint took account of two factors—the length (in number of letters) of the response compared with the length of the target word, and the envelope or shape of the response compared with the envelope of the target word. The graphic constraint was based on overlap of letters between the target and the response. Both individual letters and letter sequences contributed to the graphic score (which was not proportionalized by number of target letters).

Since it was not our purpose to compare visual with graphic constraint, the two scores were standardized over the sample of observed errors and then linearly transformed. This gives the two scores equal means and variances and allows us to focus on changes in the use of the constraints in context compared with isolation. In order to obtain the most meaningful comparisons possible, further analysis focused on just those items that produced errors by both groups of readers. This assured a common base for the visual and graphic constraint measures. These measures are sensitive to the opportunities for visually and graphically similar responses, and such opportunities vary across words. Table 11.3 gives a summary of the sources of constraint present in these errors.

Table 11.3 shows that in context, the graphic and visual sources of constraint were less observed. Graphic overlap especially was reduced in context. (The interaction of context and constraint source is statistically marginal, $p = .09$.) In other words, when errors were made in context, the errors did not retain the

TABLE 11.3
Visual and Graphic Transformed
Overlap Scores for Errors

	Context Condition	
	Isolation	Context
Group		
Skilled	117	97
Less skilled	88	72
Source		
Visual	106	95
Graphic	118	74

Note. Context effect, $p = .08$; skill effect, $p = .02$; context × source ≤ .09.

letters of the target word to the same degree as in isolation. Instead, responses were heavily determined by context and made fairly consistent with the weak constraint provided by word shape and length. This confirms our expectation that trade-offs would occur between conceptually derived and graphically derived data.

A second expectation was confirmed—namely, that errors of skilled subjects would retain more visual and graphic features of the target than would errors of less skilled readers. Further, there was no tendency for only the visual or the graphic measure to reflect this difference. Skilled readers tended to show use of more constraint by both measures. More interesting perhaps is the lack of a skill by context interaction. The advantage of skilled readers in producing slightly more verdical errors did not increase or decrease with context. Finally, we should emphasize the fact that the visual and graphic overlap of even less skilled readers' errors was very high. It is far from the case that their responses were not based on graphic and visual input.

To examine whether the groups differed in the extent to which their errors retained contextual constraints, they were compared on the three-level contextual appropriateness measure. There was no hint of a difference. Subjects tended to give highly appropriate responses, and the occasions in which context was sacrificed were equal in number for the two groups.

In summary, the analysis of errors suggests that the asymptotic level of identification is higher for skilled readers when the features are degraded and that even the misidentifications are based on more graphic data. Whereas context raises the asymptotic level of identification (as well as the rate), it reduces the readers' ability to honor graphic constraints when identification is not achieved. The trade-off between conceptually derived and graphically derived data is equally characteristic of skilled and less skilled readers.

WORD PROCESSES

We think we have ruled out at least one of the three types of reading problems suggested at the beginning of this chapter. Children do not seem to have severe problems using context in word identification, so Type 3 seems an unlikely syndrome. That leaves two types—the reader whose use of low-level data to identify words is inefficient, and the reader who is efficient enough at word identification but less efficient in using word-level data in other processes. We haven't done the type of research that would identify this syndrome. It requires finding some children whose isolated word identification processes are indistinguishable from skilled readers and then providing them tasks sensitive to other processes. Our subjects who are less skilled in reading are typically slower in word identification. This causes us to conclude that Type 1 is fairly common, although the possibility remains that there exist significant numbers of Type 2 readers.

Although we do not suggest that only inefficient verbal processing is responsible for reading difficulty, the implied linkages between word processing, sentence processing, and standardized paragraph comprehension are reasonably well established. For example, the link between word-processing speed and performance on standardized comprehension tests has been demonstrated in studies reported in this chapter and elsewhere (e.g., Curtis, 1980; Perfetti, Finger, & Hogaboam, 1978).

The link between sentence-processing speed and paragraph comprehension can also be demonstrated. For example, skilled readers are faster at deciding the truth of universal affirmative and negative sentences (e.g., produced by the paradigm *A banana is/is not a fruit/animal*) (Perfetti & Bell, 1978). A somewhat richer example of this link comes from studies of verbal arithmetic (Perfetti, Riley, & Greeno, 1978). When verbal problems with trivial computational components and simple, uniform macrosemantic structures (Heller & Greeno, 1978) were presented for solution, less skilled readers required about 45% more time to read and respond to a three- or four-line display. Since the problems were semantically uniform, reading speed differences can plausibly be linked more to word processing than to semantic context. Further, differences in computation were not responsible for differences in reading comprehension times. When equivalent numerical problems were used, differences associated with reading skill were much smaller (15%) and not statistically significant.

In one of these verbal arithmetic studies, the problem was displayed line by line to allow sentence-processing times to be measured. This is of special interest because the second sentence of a problem clearly requires integration with the first sentence, which basically announces the initial problem state. The second sentence asserts a modification to the problem state that in some problems may imply immediate computation but more often implies only a direction in the change of state. The results of this study were a skill × sentence interaction such that less skilled readers required relatively more time on the second sentence. Mean differences in time per sentence between skilled and less skilled readers increased from .43 to .88 from the first to the second sentence. Comparisons of different problem formats tended to rule out computational processes as accounting for this result. Instead, when reading time was partitioned into components of simple sentence encoding, sentence integration, and computation, differences between skilled and less skilled readers were present for simple sentence encoding and integration but not for computation.

The link between individual-word-processing speed and sentence-processing speed is also established by these data. Subjects' word identification latencies, measured on a completely different set of words, account for about half the variance ($r = .72$) in reading times. (By contrast, the correlation of reading times with numerical computation time was .31, and with a standardized test of math concepts, it was $- .27$.)

These links are quite suggestive but not as convincing as data from a study that would simultaneously examine processing components involved in comprehension. An example of what is needed comes from a recent study of adult readers by Graesser, Hoffman, and Clark (1980). In their study, reading times were measured in sentences within passages in which variables assumed to reflect word-level and higher-level processes were embedded. For example, higher-level variables included the narrativity of the passage, the familiarity of the material, and the number of new-argument (i.e., nonanaphoric) nouns. Word- and sentence- level variables included, among others, number of words per sentence—number of propositions per sentence. Two results are especially interesting in the present context. For one, the higher-level variables, mainly narrativity, accounted for more reading-time variance than did the lower-level variables. A second result was that when the subject sample was divided according to overall reading speed, the difference between fast and slow readers was mainly in the lower-level variables of number of words and number of propositions (also within-sentence syntactic predictability). In other words, the process that was important as a determinant of average reading speed turned out not to be the same process on which fast and slow individuals differed. Thus, in this case, the use of narrative structure was important, but slow readers were sensitive to it in much the same way as fast readers. By contrast, the number of words in a sentence makes more of a difference to a slow reader than a fast reader. Although this finding is consistent with our hypothesis that word-processing rate is a greater rate-limiting process than higher-level processes, the points are more methodological. For one thing, such studies are valuable because they simultaneously examine theoretically motivated processing components. Moreover, this study demonstrates that although word-level processes may seem trivial compared with higher-level processes, they may be responsible for more individual differences than processes that are equally critical overall but less rate limiting across a given range of individual talents.

The Nature of Word-Processing Differences

Even if the case for more top-down-based problems becomes stronger, the prominent fact of word-processing differences would have to be dealt with. The nature of these differences is beyond the present scope. However, at least a point or two can be raised concerning the possibilities.

One point is whether to focus on processes or knowledge with respect to word processes. The former is less concerned with the units of identification and more concerned with the role of attention in identification. In this discussion we have been more concerned with speed than with attention. However, the same issue is involved in either case—namely, the use of graphic inofrmation and what characterizes knowledge concerning graphic data. That is, whether one describes the process of the skilled reader as attention free or as rapidly executing, the knowledge base for the process is of interest.

There is reason to think that skilled readers acquire "low-level" knowledge that is useful for rapid context-free identification. Prominent among such knowledge is knowledge concerning orthographic structure (Venezky & Massaro, 1979) and knowledge concerning positional privileges of letters (Mason, 1975). Of these two, there is evidence that orthographic structure is more important in accounting for results of experiments in which arrays of letter strings are searched for the presence of target letters (Massaro, Venezky, & Taylor, 1979). Even with orthographic knowledge identified as a particularly powerful word-processing variable, there would remain questions concerning phonological codes that can be accessed by orthography. The use of such codes may be important in some aspect of reading whether or not rapid word access depends on it.

We have some data that are suggestive but far from conclusive for some of these matters. In a series of search experiments, subjects searched visually for targets comprising *consonant pairs, pseudowords, words,* and *semantic categories.* The set size varied from one to seven items to allow data on both slopes and intercepts. Intercept differences between skilled and less skilled readers were found in the bigram and pseudoword tasks for both positive and negative trials. Since the intercept reflects components of total response time other than rate of processing, such differences are probably less informative than differences in slope, which should index the rate of processing. Slope differences were not found for consonant bigrams but were found for both words and pseudowords. This is evidence that the rate of processing bigrams was not different between high- and low-ability readers but that the rate of processing larger units was different. The important factor may be that letter strings be regular and codable—attributes of both pseudowords and real words but not of bigram strings. Whether it's the orthographic regularity or the phonemic codability is difficult to say. One implies the other. In any case, we have other evidence that suggests that skilled readers can take better advantage of pronounceable and regular nonword letter strings when the letter string is presented first, followed by a letter probe (Perfetti, 1978). It is possible that one advantage of orthographically regular strings is their codability into objects suitable for linguistic memory. Indeed there is some evidence to suggest that less skilled readers may not make as much use of phonetic codes as do skilled readers (Liberman, Shankweiler, Liberman, Fowler, & Fischer, 1977; also see chapters by Barron [12] and by Katz &Feldman [4], this volume). It is possible that one of the word processes strongly associated with reading skill is that of using the regularity of orthography as input to linguistic coding. However, there are other possibilities. The supportable point is that the processing of subword units is one of the lower-level processes of high efficiency for the skilled reader.

SUMMARY

We have assumed a general interactive-process model that allows different types of process interaction depending on rate of early executing processes and growth of later executing processes that depend on earlier processes. Total processing is also affected by conceptually derived data that affect processing rates by a constant. This description predicts that individuals who are highly skilled at lower-process will be less affected by conceptually derived data. Our research suggests that readers of lower skill are both more dependent on context, because of slow executing word-level processes, and, in some conditions, less able to use context. However, their use of context was demonstrated to be sufficient to provide significant help in word identification. By contrast, they are much affected by degraded input, a fact consistent with the model's assumption that a slower rate of processing graphic data characterizes the less skilled reader. Other research gives at least suggestive support to the linkage between word processes and comprehension.

ACKNOWLEDGMENTS

We wish to acknowledge the substantial assistance of Laura Bell with much of the research discussed in this chapter and also the help of Jim Herrmann in one of the experiments reported. The research reported herein was supported by the Learning Research and Development Center and, in part, by funds from the National Institute of Education (NIE), United States Department of Education.

REFERENCES

Battig, W. F., & Montague, W. E. *Category norms for verbal items in 56 categories*. University of Colorado, August 1968.

Biemiller, A. The development of the use of graphic and contextual information as children learn to read. *Reading Research Quarterly,* 1970, *6,* 1, 75–96.

Cohen, A. S. Oral reading errors of first grade children taught by a code emphasis approach. *Reading Research Quarterly,* 1974-1975, *10,* 4, 616-650.

Curtis, M. E. Development of components of reading skill. *Journal of Educational Psychology,* 1980, *72,* 656-669.

Fischler, I., & Bloom, P. Automatic and attentional processes in :ffects of sentence contexts on word recognition. *Journal of Verbal Learning and Verbal Behavior,* 1979, *18,* 1-20.

Frederiksen, J. R. Word recognition in the presence of semantically constraining context. Paper presented at annual meeting of the Psychonomic Society, San Antonio, Texas, November, 1978.

Graesser, A. C., Hoffman, N. L., & Clark, L. F. Structural components of reading time. *Journal of Verbal Learning and Verbal Behavior,* 1980, *19,* 135-151.

Heller, J. I., & Greeno, J. G. *Semantic processes in arithmetic word problem solving.* Paper presented at the Midwestern Psychological Association meeting, Chicago, May, 1978.

Hogaboam, T., & Perfetti, C. A. Reading skill and the role of verbal experience. *Journal of Educational Psychology,* 1978, *70,* 5, 171-729.

Lesgold, A. M., & Perfetti, C. A. Interactive processes in reading comprehension. *Discourse Processes,* 1978, *1,* 323-336.

Liberman, I. Y., Shankweiler, D., Liberman, A. M., Fowler, C., & Fischer, F. W. Phonetic segmentation and recoding in the beginning reader. In A. S. Reber & D. L. Scarborough (Eds.), *Towards a psychology of reading. The proceedings of the CUNY conference.* New York: Wiley, 1977.

Mason, M. Reading ability and letter search time: Effects of orthographic structure defined by single-letter positional frequency. *Journal of Experimental Psychology: General,* 1975, *104,* 2, 146-166.

Massaro, D. W., Venezky, R. L., & Taylor, G. A. Orthographic regularity, positional frequency, and visual processing of letter strings. *Journal of Experimental Psychology: General,* 1979, *108,* 107-124.

McClelland, J. L. On the time relations of mental processes: An examination of systems of processes in cascade. *Psychological Review,* 1979, *86,* 4, 287-330.

Morton, J. Interaction of information in word recognition. *Psychological Review,* 1969, *76,* 165-178.

Perfetti, C. A. *The verbal part of reading difficulty.* Paper presented at the Seventh World Congress on Reading, Hamburg, Germany, August, 1978.

Perfetti, C. A., & Bell, L. B. *Reading skill differences in simple comprehension.* Unpublished manuscript, 1978.

Perfetti, C. A., Finger, E., & Hogaboam, T. Sources of vocalization latency differences between skilled and less-skilled young readers. *Journal of Educational Psychology,* 1978, *70,* 5, 730-739.

Perfetti, C. A., Goldman, S. R., & Hogaboam, T. W. Reading skill and the identification of words in discourse context. *Memory & Cognition,* 1979, *7,* 273-282.

Perfetti, C. A., & Hogaboam, T. W. The relationship between single word decoding and reading comprehension skill. *Journal of Educational Psychology,* 1975, *67,* 461-469.

Perfetti, C. A., & Lesgold, A. M. Discourse comprehension and sources of individual differences. In M. Just & P. Carpenter (Eds.), *Cognitive processes in comprehension.* Hillsdale, N.J.: Lawrence Erlbaum Associates, 1977.

Perfetti, C. A., & Lesgold, A. M. Coding and comprehension in skilled reading and implications for reading instruction. In L. B. Resnick & P. Weaver (Eds.), *Theory and practice of early reading.* Hillsdale, N.J.: Lawrence Erlbaum Associates, 1979.

Perfetti, C. A., Riley, M., & Greeno, J. G. *Comprehension and computation: The role of sentence encoding in verbal arithmetic.* Paper presented at the Psychonomic Psychonomic Society meeting, San Antonio, Texas, November, 1978.

Posner, M. I., & Snyder, C. R. R. Facilitation and inhibition in the processing of signals. In P. M. A. Rabbitt & S. Dornic (Eds.), *Attention and performance V.* New York: Academic Press, 1975.

Roth, S. F., Perfetti, C. A., & Lesgold, A. M. *Reading ability and children's word identification processes.* Paper presented at the Midwestern Psychological Association meeting, Chicago, May 1979.

Rumelhart, D. Toward an interactive model of reading. In S. Dornic (Ed.), *Attention and performance VI.* Hillsdale, N.J.: Lawrence Erlbaum Associates, 1977.

Schank, R. C., & Abelson, R. P. *Scripts, plans, goals, and understanding.* Hillsdale, N.J.: Lawrence Erlbaum Associates, 1977.

Stanovich, K. E., & West, R. F. Mechanisms of sentence context effects in reading: Automatic activation and conscious attention. *Memory & Cognition,* 1979, *7,* 77–85.

Venezky, R., & Massaro, D. The role of orthographic regularity in word recognition. In L. B. Resnick & P. Weaver (Eds.), *Theory and practice of early reading.* Hillsdale, N.J.: Lawrence Erlbaum Associates, 1979.

Weber, R. M. A linguistic analysis of first grade reading errors. *Reading Research Quarterly,* 1970, *3,* 429–451.

West, R. F., & Stanovich, K. D. Automatic contextual facilitation in readers of three ages. *Child Development,* 1978, *49,* 717–727.

12 Reading Skill and Reading Strategies

Roderick W. Barron
University of Guelph, Ontario, Canada

It is possible to regard the mental lexicon as representing different sources of information about printed words. These sources include visual-orthographic, phonological, syntactic, and semantic information, and they may have different functions in the processes of reading. Syntactic information, for example, specifies the grammatical roles of words in sentences, whereas semantic information specifies the meanings of words. Visual-orthographic information may be regarded, at least in part, as an access code that functions as an interface between print and the semantic and syntactic information stored in the lexicon. Phonological information may also be regarded as an access code for semantic and syntactic information, but it may have an additional function of providing subjects with a representation that can be easily maintained in short-term memory. In this chapter, I am concerned with how differences in reading skill are related to differences in the use of visual-orthographic and phonological information in word recognition and in comprehension. I refer to the use of visual-orthographic information as a visual strategy and to the use of phonological information as a phonographic strategy.

VISUAL AND PHONOGRAPHIC STRATEGIES

A visual strategy involves matching a visual representation of a printed word with its corresponding visual-orthographic entry in the lexicon. The visual-orthographic entry for a word is assumed to contain information about an array of abstract visual letter identities and to be sufficient for accessing syntactic and semantic information. The assumption of the sufficiency of visual information is consistent with evidence indicating that readers, even when they are beginners, do not need to use phonological information in accessing the lexicon (e.g., Barron & Baron, 1977; Kleiman, 1975). Evidently, both visual and phonological information can be used (e.g., Baron, 1973; see Barron 1978a, in press, for a review of the evidence on this issue).

A phonographic strategy involves translating a visual representation of an item into a phonological representation. There are several possible ways this translation process might be carried out. One involves using grapheme-to-phoneme correspondence rules. A major difficulty with a rule-based translation process is that grapheme-to-phoneme rules do not apply to all English words, as some (e.g., *have, broad, sword*) are exceptions to the "rules" to which most words conform. It would probably be necessary to increase substantially the total number of rules in order to account for exception words, at least within currently available descriptions of English orthography (e.g., Venezky, 1970). Unfortunately, this increase would sacrifice the economy that originally motivated the formulation of the rules. Several psychological models have been proposed (e.g., Baron & Strawson, 1976; Barron, 1980; Coltheart, 1978) to account for the difference between regular words (e.g., *wade, globe, road*), which conform to grapheme-to-phoneme rules, and exception words. These models propose that two independent, parallel processes are involved in arriving at a phonological representation for an item. One process is lexical and involves using visual-orthographic information to retrieve the phonological representation of an item in the lexicon. The other process is nonlexical and involves generating a phonological representation from visual-orthographic information by applying grapheme-to-phoneme correspondence rules. Only the lexical process would be successful with exception words, whereas only the nonlexical process would be successful with nonwords (e.g., *dorch*); both processes, however, would be successful with regular words.

Although these dual-process models would appear to account for how print is translated into sound, they have limitations in several areas. First, it is difficult to see how grapheme-to-phoneme rules can be applied without consulting the lexicon, as it is often necessary to use morphemic information to segment an item into its constituent units before applying the rules. It appears necessary, for example, to determine whether or not certain letter clusters span a morphemic boundary before grapheme-to-phoneme rules can be applied correctly (e.g., *ph* spans a morphemic boundary in *shepherd*, but not in *graphic*). In fact, it is possible that morphemic information is involved in segmenting nonwords as well as words (e.g., Marcel, 1980). Second, Glushko (1979; also see Chap. 3, this volume) has reported evidence that appears to be inconsistent with the predictions of dual-process models and that challenges the regular–exception word distinction. Glushko centered his experiments around the finding that subjects are faster at reading aloud regular words than exception words (e.g., Baron & Strawson, 1976; Glushko, 1979; Gough & Cosky, 1977; Stanovich & Bauer,

1978). A dual-process interpretation of these results involves the idea that regular words are faster because both the lexical and nonlexical processes would be likely to come up with the same phonological representation. Conflicting representations would be likely with exception words, however, because the nonlexical process uses grapheme-to-phoneme rules, and they would generate incorrect phonological representations. This conflict between the two processes would slow response time (rather than just produce errors) if a mechanism were available for resolving the conflict, such as a spelling check process (e.g., Barron, 1980; Coltheart, Davelaar, Jonasson, & Besner, 1977).

Glushko (1979) proposed an activation–synthesis model in order to account for why regular words are read aloud more rapidly than exception words. According to his model, both visual-orthographic and phonological information is activated by a word when subjects attempt to read it aloud. However, Glushko (1979) proposed that this activated information originates from two sources: the word itself and the word's orthographic neighbors (e.g., words that have similar spelling patterns). The generation of an articulatory program for pronouncing a word would involve an attempt to synthesize the phonological information activated by the word with that activated by its neighbors. According to the activation–synthesis model, exception words would be slower than regular words because, on the average, exception words may be more likely to activate phonological information that is inconsistent with that activated by their orthographic neighbors. The exception word *broad*, for example, would activate orthographic neighbors (e.g., *road*, *toad*, *load*) that have phonological representations that are inconsistent with the representation for *broad*. As a result, the synthesis process would be expected to take longer and be more error prone than for a regular word (e.g., *wade*) that did not have inconsistent neighbors (e.g., *fade*, *made*, *jade*).

Glushko (1979) used the activation–synthesis model to predict that subjects would be slower on items that activated inconsistent rather than consistent phonological information regardless of whether they were exception words, regular words, or nonwords. This prediction would not be made by dual-process models for at least two reasons. First, regular words should not produce inconsistent information as these items can be read aloud by retrieving their corresponding pronunciations from lexical memory or by applying grapheme-to-phoneme rules. Second, dual-process models do not include the possibility that information about an item's orthographic neighbors is activated along with information about the item itself. Glushko (1979) found that subjects were slower on regular words, such as *wave*, which is likely to activate an inconsistent neighbor like the exception word *have*, than on regular words like *wade*, which is not as likely to have inconsistent neighbors. Similarly, he found that subjects were slower on nonwords like *bint*, which is likely to activate an inconsistent exception word neighbor like *pint*, than on nonwords like *bink*, which is not as likely to have inconsistent neighbors. These results suggest that it may be possible to account for the pronunciation of regular and exception words, and even nonwords, by a single-process model that uses the same mechanisms (activation and synthesis) and the same knowledge sources (visual-orthographic and phonological) with all three types of items. There does not appear to be much merit in the dual-process proposal of different mechanisms and knowledge sources for different types of items. The results further suggest that the regular–exception distinction may not be as useful as the consistent–inconsistent distinction in accounting for differences in the speed and accuracy with which words can be read aloud. Finally, the results suggest that subjects use specific stored knowledge about visual-orthographic letter patterns and their associated phonological representations in reading words aloud. This conclusion does not imply that grapheme-to-phoneme rules are not used at all—only that there may be alternative ways of characterizing how print is translated into sound that are more comprehensive than the rule-based characterizations that are currently available.[1]

Although Glushko's (1979) activation-synthesis model appears to provide a more adequate account of phonographic translation than is provided by dual-process models, the fact that it is a single-process model suggests that it might conflict with the distinctions made earlier between visual and phonographic strategies in reading. I think, however, that these two strategies can be incorporated into the framework provided by the activation–synthesis model without sacrificing its single-process characteristics, by considering the following factors. First, activation of phonological information depends upon prior activation of at least some visual-orthographic information. As a result, it may take more time for phonological than visual-orthographic information to become activated enough that it can influence synthesis processes, response decision processes, or be used as an access code to semantic and syntactic information. Second, as already mentioned, visual-orthographic and phonological information may have different functions in reading, and it is possible that these functions are related, at least in part, to differences in the speed with which the two types of information can be activated. Since visual-orthographic information is sufficient for accessing syntactic and semantic information, it may be used alone when rapid word recognition is possible—for example, with relatively familiar words and when semantic and syntactic information have been activated by prior sentence context. Phonological information may be used when visual-orthographic information is relatively slow in specifying accurately the identity of a word (e.g., with unfamiliar words). It may also be used when it is necessary to form a representation of a word that can be maintained in short-term memory (e.g., an auditory image or an articulatory representation for purposes of comprehen-

---

[1]Baron (1979), Brooks (1978), and Marsh, Friedman, Welch, and Desberg (in press) have also proposed alternatives to rule-based characterizations of how print is translated into sound. Their proposals (e.g., use of analogies) are similar to the activation–synthesis model, as they argue that subjects use orthographic neighbor information in the translation process.

sion). These factors suggest that it may be possible to preserve the distinction between visual and phonographic strategies in reading within the framework provided by the activation–synthesis model.

Reading Skill Differences in the Use of Visual and Phonographic Strategies

One source of evidence on the use of visual and phonographic strategies comes from studies of differences in reading skill. In the remainder of this chapter, I discuss this evidence. In addition, I present two experiments, one on word recognition (Experiment 1) and one on comprehension (Experiment 2), which are designed to examine the relationships between reading skill and the ability to use visual and phonographic strategies.

Boder (1971, 1973) investigated the use of these two strategies by a group of children identified as having severe developmental dyslexia. She showed that 63% of the children appeared to be impaired in their ability to use a phonographic strategy in word recognition. They seemed to be specifically deficient in their ability to translate print into sound, as they had a great deal of difficulty reading aloud words that were visually unfamiliar. Boder referred to these children as being dysphonetic and contrasted them with a very small group of children (10% of her sample of dyslexic children) whom she referred to as being dyseidetic. These latter children seemed to have some ability to translate visually unfamiliar words into phonological representations, but they appeared to be specifically deficient in their ability to retain the visual representations of printed words. These dyseidetic children could be regarded as being impaired in the use of a visual strategy.

Parallel evidence of individual differences in the ability to use visual and phonographic strategies is suggested by studies of acquired dyslexia. Investigators (e.g., Marshall & Newcombe, 1973; Patterson & Marcel, 1977; Shallice & Warrington, 1975) have shown that deep dyslexics are deficient in their ability to use a phonographic strategy, as they are virtually unable to read aloud nonwords but are able to pronounce words that are visually familiar, even when the words are printed in alternating type case (e.g., rEaD; Saffran & Marin, 1977). Surface dyslexics (see Marshall & Newcombe, 1973), on the other hand, seem to be impaired in their ability to use a visual strategy since they appear to be reliant upon a phonographic strategy, although they do not use that strategy very efficiently (e.g., they may read words aloud incorrectly and/or fail to comprehend words they do read aloud correctly).

Although these examples of developmental and acquired dyslexia suggest that specific forms of reading disability may be associated with impairments in visual or phonographic strategies, most of the evidence on children with reading difficulties suggests that the majority of them may be more impaired in the use of a phonographic strategy than a visual strategy (e.g., Jorm, 1979). Severe impairments in the use of a visual strategy seem to be restricted to small subgroups of children (e.g., Boder's dyseidetic children). Furthermore, Vellutino (1977, 1978) has argued that most children with reading problems do not appear to be impaired in visual processing of nonlinguistic material, at least when memory demands are low (e.g., Arnett & DiLollo, 1979; Ellis & Miles, 1978; Morrison, Giordani, & Nagy, 1977; but see Lovegrove, Bowling, Badcock & Blackwood, 1980, for contrary evidence). On the other hand, the evidence on visual processing of linguistic material appears to be mixed. For example, Katz and Wicklund (1972) found no effect of reading skill when subjects searched for a letter in a string of letters. When the ability to use visual-orthographic structure was assessed in visual search tasks, however, Mason (1975) showed an advantage for skilled over less skilled readers, whereas Stanovich and West (1979) did not. One of the major sources of evidence on impairments in the use of a phonographic strategy is that less skilled readers are slower and less accurate than skilled readers in reading aloud nonwords (e.g., Barron, 1978b, 1980; Firth, 1972; Frederiksen, 1978; Hogaboam & Perfetti, 1978; Perfetti, Finger, & Hogaboam, 1978; Perfetti & Hogaboam, 1975) and low-frequency words (Perfetti & Hogaboam, 1975). Less skilled readers do not, however, differ very much from skilled readers in reading aloud highly frequent words (e.g., Perfetti & Hogaboam, 1975). These results suggest that children who differ in reading skill also differ in their ability to activate phonological representations of printed words and/or to articulate them.

Reading skill differences in the use of a phonographic strategy have also been obtained with a lexical decision task in which subjects are required to decide whether or not an item is a word. This task differs from reading aloud since overt articulation is not necessary. Furthermore, the logic of the task requires consultation of the lexicon, and semantic priming effects have been obtained with it (e.g., Meyer & Schvaneveldt, 1971; Neely, 1977; Shulman & Davison, 1977). Using a lexical decision task, several investigators (e.g., Coltheart et al., 1977; Rubenstein, Lewis, & Rubenstein, 1971) have shown that subjects are slower at responding to nonwords like *mone,* which sound like words (i.e., pseudohomophones), than to nonwords like *moke,* which do not. This pseudohomophone effect suggests that subjects use a phonographic strategy. Considered within the framework of an activation–synthesis model, a pseudohomophone effect might arise because the nonword *mone,* for example, activates a phonological representation that is associated with semantic information for a word in the lexicon (e.g., *moan*). Activation of visual-orthographic information, on the other hand, would indicate that *mone* was not a word, as semantic information would not be associated with that specific pattern of letters. However, extra visual-orthographic processing time may be required to determine that the item does not have a semantic identity. As a result, conflicting information derived from the more slowly activating phonological information (i.e., *mone* does have a semantic identity) may influence response decision processes and may slow response time. The control item *moke*, on the other hand, is less likely to produce conflicting information because it does not have semantic information associated with either its visual-orthographic or phonological representations.[2]

If phonological activation is slower than visual-orthographic activation and if less skilled readers are particularly slow at phonological activation (e.g., it may not be well automated for them), then less skilled readers might not be as likely to show a pseudohomophone effect as skilled readers. This prediction was supported by the results of Barron (1978b), who found that skilled readers were significantly slower on pseudohomophones than control items, whereas less skilled readers did not differ significantly in response time on the two types of items, although they did make more errors on the pseudohomophones (the readers were fifth and sixth graders who differed in reading comprehension but not in nonverbal IQ). These results are consistent with the reading aloud results since they suggest that skilled readers are better able to use a phonographic strategy than less skilled readers.

Lexical decision times for regular and exception words were compared in a subsequent experiment (Barron, 1980, Experiment 1). According to the activation–synthesis model, subjects should be faster on regular than on exception words because exception words are more likely to activate phonological neighbors that are inconsistent with the presented word (assuming that regular words are chosen that are unlikely to activate inconsistent phonological neighbors). The inconsistent activations from the exception words may disrupt synthesis processes involved in the formation of a phonological representation. If the less skilled readers are slower in activating phonological information than the skilled readers, then phonological information (and accompanying synthesis processes) would be less likely to influence word recognition. As a result, they should be less likely than skilled readers to be faster on regular than exception words.

The predicted inability of the less skilled readers to use effectively a phonographic strategy suggests that they may be more reliant upon a visual strategy in a lexical decision task than the skilled readers. In order to explore subjects' ability to use a visual strategy, half of the exception and regular words had high summed single-letter and bigram positional-frequency values (Mayzner & Tresselt, 1965), whereas the other half had low values. These frequency counts provide gross measures of visual-orthographic structure, and they appear to influence the visual processing of printed words (e.g., Gibson, Yonas, & Shurcliff, 1970;

---

[2]The control item *moke* is not completely innocent of providing conflicting information to response decision processes; it could activate orthographic neighbors (e.g., *woke, make, more*) that have semantic identities. Activation of orthographic neighbors by nonwords is discussed more fully in Experiment 1.

Mason, 1975; Massaro, Venezky, & Taylor, 1979; McClelland & Johnston, 1977). Subjects should be faster on high- than low-positional-frequency items to the extent that they rely upon a visual strategy.

Sixth-grade children who differed in reading comprehension, but not in non-verbal IQ, were used as subjects. The results indicated that skilled readers were significantly faster and more accurate on regular (also generally consistent) words than on exception words; whereas the less skilled readers did not differ significantly on these items in response time, although they did make more errors on the exception words. Less skilled readers, on the other hand, were significantly faster on the high- than the low-positional-frequency words, whereas the skilled readers did not show a significant positional frequency effect. There were not any error differences for either group. These results provide further evidence that the skilled readers may be better able to use a phonographic strategy than the less skilled readers. Although the absence of a regular–exception word effect for the less skilled readers suggests that they were more reliant upon a visual strategy than the skilled readers, the positional frequency effect indicates that they were able to use a visual strategy fairly effectively. The absence of a positional frequency effect for the skilled readers is somewhat puzzling, but it should not be interpreted as indicating that they were deficient in using a visual strategy. Perhaps the skilled readers' ability to use phonological information reduced their reliance upon visual-orthographic information in the lexical decision task.

EXPERIMENT 1

Although the evidence presented thus far indicates that skilled readers are better able than less skilled readers to use a phonographic strategy in a lexical decision task, it is possible that some characteristic of the lexical decision task itself reduced the likelihood of less skilled readers activating rapidly phonological information and showing a regular–exception word effect. One possible characteristic of the task is the relationship between the words and nonwords. In Barron (1980), the nonwords (e.g., *helt*) were derived from the words (e.g., *felt*) by changing only one letter. The fact that the nonwords tended to be orthographically regular, as well as sharing spelling patterns with the words, makes it very likely that the nonwords would activate orthographic neighbors (e.g., *helt* might activate *felt, heel, belt, hilt, melt,* etc.). Regardless of whether or not the neighbors were in the list of regular and exception words the subjects were given, they could be a source of conflicting information for response decision processes involved in determining whether or not the item was a word. The neighbors activated by the nonword may access semantic and syntactic information, thus indicating that a word rather than a nonword had been presented and that a yes rather than a no response was appropriate. Activation of phonological information under these circumstances might only increase the confusion between the words and nonwords, because the neighbors of nonwords would be provided with an additional access code for semantic information. Consequently, it is possible that subjects actually tried to reduce their use of a phonographic strategy in the Barron (1980) experiment. In fact, the regular–exception word effect was not very large (29 milliseconds), and its existence may reflect the greater degree to which phonological activation is automated for the skilled than for the less skilled readers. Furthermore, the evidence is mixed on regular–exception word effects in lexical decision tasks involving adult readers: Stanovich and Bauer (1978, Experiment 2) obtained a small but reliable effect, whereas Coltheart, Besner, Jonasson, and Davelaar (1979) did not obtain a reliable effect. Orthographically regular nonwords were used in both of these investigations.

If the activation of orthographic neighbors of nonwords decreases the likelihood that subjects will use a phonographic strategy, then reducing the number of nonword neighbors might be expected to increase the use of that strategy. One way of reducing the number of nonword neighbors is to use random letter strings (e.g., *tspma*) rather than orthographically regular nonwords, since random letter strings are unlikely to activate many orthographic neighbors. Use of a phonographic strategy might be more likely with random letter strings for there would be fewer nonword neighbors available that could use phonological information to access semantic information and produce response conflict. In order to determine if using letter strings as nonwords increases the likelihood of subjects using a phonographic stragegy in a lexical decision task, and to examine further the use of a visual strategy, an experiment similar to that reported by Barron (1980) was carried out with skilled and less skilled readers.

Method

Thirty-two skilled and 32 less skilled readers were chosen from a larger group (180) of fifth- and sixth-grade children (10 to 12 years old) on the basis of their scores on the nonverbal section of the Canadian Lorge–Thorndike Intelligence Test and on the comprehension subsection of the Gates–MacGinitie Reading Test. The two groups had the same average nonverbal IQs (106) but differed in average reading comprehension by more than one standard deviation ($SD = 10$). The skilled readers' average comprehension score was 60; the less skilled readers' was 43; and they differed significantly, $t(62) = 14.31, p < .001$. These children were very similar in age, IQ, and reading comprehension to those used in Barron (1980) and identical to those used in Barron (1978b). None of the children had been identified by their schools as having severe reading or learning disabilities.

Eighty exception words were selected on the basis of being members of a small group of words that did not conform to grapheme-to-phoneme generalizations or "rules" identified by Venezky (1970). The exception word *flood,* for example, is one of the few words in which the *oo* digraph is pronounced as a [ə] rather than a [u]. Eighty regular words were chosen so as to conform with Venezky's (1970) grapheme-to-phoneme rules, which had a large number of examples. Relatively few of the regular words were inconsistent in the sense of having highly frequent, orthographic neighbors that were exception words. One-half of the regular words and exception words had high single-letter and bigram positional-frequency values (Mayzner & Tresselt, 1965), whereas the other half had low values on that measure of visual-orthographic structure. The four categories of words (regular–high positional frequency, exception–high positional frequency, regular–low positional frequency, exception–low positional frequency) were very similar in average word frequency (Carroll, Davies, & Richman, 1971; average of the Grade 5 and 6 norms), number of letters and syllables, and in parts of speech. The words are listed in Table 12.1, and their average statistical characteristics are presented in Table 12.2. The nonwords (e.g., *imxk, tmpsa, joztbh, bxdaqhz*) were very difficult to pronounce, were orthographically irregular, and did not share any letters with their corresponding word, although they did have the same number of letters. They were simply strings of consonants with one randomly placed vowel, and their average summed single-letter (722) and bigram (3) positional-frequency values were relatively low. Finally, only 1 of the 160 nonwords had any orthographic neighbors

TABLE 12.1
Words Used in Experiment 1

Regular–High Positional Frequency		Exception–High Positional Frequency		Regular–Low Positional Frequency		Exception–Low Positional Frequency	
dive	chase	pint	prove	puff	merry	debt	align
fuse	press	wool	build	dull	escape	bury	liquor
pine	tribe	shoe	grass	gull	follow	view	engine
cape	plate	foot	shove	hull	attack	heir	pigeon
nice	smoke	whom	aisle	yell	rubber	pier	debris
cave	bitter	cafe	marine	cell	coffin	busy	island
fill	batter	tour	heifer	bell	commit	echo	junior
crime	hammer	chalk	police	kiss	bubble	calf	tongue
whale	matter	suede	castle	arrow	invite	broad	trough
shade	winner	choir	recipe	skull	cannon	cough	rhythm
trade	barrel	sword	senior	stuff	bottom	laugh	eighth
scale	barren	canoe	subtle	offer	copper	yacht	honour
blame	butter	tough	friend	blade	ribbon	flood	asthma
brace	correct	sweat	soldier	cliff	flannel	onion	circuit
prone	chatter	gauge	machine	bluff	express	ocean	biscuit
slave	compile	whose	receipt	stiff	discuss	dough	ancient
brave	reptile	doubt	foreign	staff	imitate	sugar	whistle
snake	connect	worse	colonel	funny	sparrow	depot	freight
glide	possess	suite	routine	drill	clipper	cello	dungeon
crane	spatter	chaos	service	skill	dispose	break	massage

TABLE 12.2
Word Length and Frequency Characteristics of the Words in Experiment 1

| Word Type | Mean Summed Letter Positional Frequency | | Mean Word Frequency | Mean Number of Letters per Word |
	Single-Letter	Bigram		
Regular–high positional frequency	1801	204	27	5.4
Exception–high positional frequency	1789	191	26	5.4
Regular–low positional frequency	1071	144	26	5.5
Exception–low positional frequency	1080	93	28	5.5

where an orthographic neighbor is defined as a word in the Kučera and Francis (1967) word list that shares all but one letter with a nonword.

Procedure and Apparatus

The words were presented individually on slides in lowercase type. The children were instructed to press a button when they were ready to see a word. This resulted in a projector shutter opening, a timer starting, and a single word being displayed (maximum horizontal visual angle = 2.50 degrees). If an item was a word, the children responded by moving a small lever horizontally toward the word *yes* printed on the desk at which they were seated. If it was not a word, they moved the lever in the opposite direction toward the word *no* printed on the desk. The children were tested individually and were given about 20 practice trials in order to acquaint them with the procedure and apparatus. The words and nonwords were presented in random order with the constraint that no more than four instances of one type of item could appear in succession. Finally, when the children made an error on an item, the item was displayed again, and they were asked to read it aloud and to indicate again whether or not it was a word. This interrogation process was carried out without any time pressure to respond.

Results

A reader (skilled, less skilled) × positional frequency (high, low) × word type (regular, exception) analysis of variance was carried out on the median correct response times to the words for each subject in each condition. The major finding was a significant interaction among the three variables, $F(1,62) = 6.67$, $p <$ .025. The means of the median response times making up this interaction are presented in Table 12.3. This table shows that the less skilled readers were faster on regular than exception words and that the size of this difference was about the same in the high- and low-positional-frequency conditions. The difference between high- and low-positional-frequency items was very small in both the regular and exception word conditions. These observations were supported in a separate analysis of the less skilled readers; the main effect of word type was significant, $F(1,31) = 5.13$, $p < .05$, but the main effect of positional frequency and the interaction of the two variables were not, $Fs(31) < 1$. These results indicate that the less skilled readers can use a phonographic strategy when the nonwords are strings of letters. Like the skilled readers in Barron (1980), they appeared to reduce their reliance upon visual-orthographic information for they did not show a positional frequency effect.

Table 12.3 also shows that the skilled readers were faster on the regular than the exception words in both the high-, $t(31) = 3.40$, $p < .01$, and low-, $t(31) = 5.10$, $p < .001$, positional-frequency conditions. However, the size of the regular–exception word difference was much larger in the low-than the high-positional-frequency condition, as indicated by a significant positional frequency × word type interaction, $F(1,31) = 18.36$, $p < .001$. The positional frequency effect was significant for the exception, $t(31) = 3.33$, $p < .01$, but not for the regular words, $t(31) = 1.68$, $p > .10$. These results are consistent with Barron (1980), as they indicate that skilled readers use a phonographic strategy. The results also indicate that when positional frequency is high, skilled readers are less likely to use a phonographic strategy than when it is low.

The children's errors were divided into two categories based upon how they responded during the interrogation that followed an incorrect response. An error was called a "knowledge" error if the children failed to classify or pronounce the item correctly. An error was called an "other" error if the children could classify

TABLE 12.3
Means of Median Response Times in Milliseconds to the High-
and Low-Positional-Frequency, Regular and Exception Words
Presented in Experiment 1 (Percentage of "Other" Errors are in Parentheses)

| | *High Positional Frequency* | | | *Low Positional Frequency* | | |
	Regular	*Exception*	*Diff.*	*Regular*	*Exception*	*Diff.*
Less skilled	886	936	−50	895	938	−43
readers	(2.03)	(2.19)	(−0.16)	(2.50)	(2.50)	(0.00)
Skilled	819	860	−41	805	909	−104
readers	(0.63)	(2.19)	(−1.56)	(2.03)	(4.69)	(−2.66)

and pronounce the item correctly. The other errors are the most informative for the present experiment because they, along with the response-time data, provide an indication of how children who differ in reading skill process regular and exception words that they know. The knowledge errors, on the other hand, represent errors that arise from not knowing a word and provide little information about how it was processed. It is possible that other and knowledge errors have not been distinguished in response-time experiments, particularly those involving adults, because it was assumed that the subjects had lexical entries for all the words they were given and could pronounce them correctly (i.e., it was assumed that all the errors were other errors).

Overall, an average of 5.64% of the subjects' responses to the words were incorrect; 3.29% of the subjects' responses were classified as knowledge errors, and the remaining 2.35% were classified as other errors. An analysis of variance on the knowledge errors indicated that the skilled readers (2.23%) made fewer errors than the less skilled readers (4.34%), $F(1,62) = 6.67$, $p < .025$. The subjects made more knowledge errors on the exception words (6.33%) than on the regular words (0.24%), $F(1,62) = 53.74$, $p < .001$; and on the low- (3.79%) than on the high- (2.77%) positional-frequency words, $F(1,62) = 4.73$, $p < .05$. Reading skill interacted with word type, $F(1,62) = 5.52$, $p < .025$, and with positional frequency, $F(1,62) = 5.92$, $p < .025$, indicating that the less skilled readers had somewhat larger regular–exception and positional frequency differences than the skilled readers. There was no evidence that either the skilled or less skilled readers sacrificed their accuracy in order to increase their speed, since the knowledge errors were either positively correlated or not significantly negatively correlated with response time in all conditions ($ps > .10$). These results indicate that although less than 6% of the subjects' responses to the words were incorrect, almost 60% of those incorrect responses were based upon deficiencies in lexical or pronunciation knowledge. These knowledge errors tended to be more prevalent for less skilled than skilled readers and for exception and low-positional-frequency words than for regular and high-positional-frequency words.

The other errors are presented in Table 12.3. An analysis of variance indicated that the subjects made more other errors on exception than regular words, $F(1,62) = 5.09$, $p < .05$, and on low- than high-positional-frequency words, $F(1,62) = 6.07$, $p < .025$. The main effect of reading skill was not significant, $F(1,62) < 1$, but reading skill interacted with word type, $F(1,62) = 4.39$, $p < .05$. This interaction can be seen in Table 12.3. The skilled readers made more errors on the exception than on the regular words in both the high-, $t(31) = 2.06$, $p < .05$, and low-, $t(31) = 2.58$, $p < .025$, positional-frequency conditions, but the difference between the two types of words was not significant for the less skilled readers in either positional frequency condition, $ts(31) < 1$. There was no evidence that the skilled or less skilled readers sacrificed their accuracy in order to increase their speed; response time was either positively correlated or not significantly negatively correlated with the other errors ($ps > .10$) in all conditions.

Finally, 1.21% of the skilled readers and 2.11% of the less skilled readers' responses to the nonwords were incorrect. None of these errors were classified as knowledge errors. The skilled readers made more other errors on the words than on the nonwords, $t(31) = 2.70$, $p < .025$, whereas the difference between the two types of items was not significant for the less skilled readers, $t(31) < 1$. The response time to the words and nonwords did not differ for either group of readers, $ts(31) < 1$.

Discussion

The results indicate that both the skilled and the less skilled readers can use a phonographic strategy in a lexical decision task when the nonwords do not have any orthographic neighbors. These results are consistent with the possibility that subjects (particularly the less skilled readers) were less likely to use a phonographic strategy in the Barron (1980) study because the nonwords in that experiment increased response conflict by accessing semantic information through their visual-orthographic and phonological neighbors. Considering the Barron (1980) experiment and Experiment 1 together, the results indicate that both groups of readers can exercise some control over the information they use in word recognition, since they appeared to shift their strategies as a function of the characteristics of the nonwords. The skilled readers, however, seem able to use efficiently a phonographic stragegy in a wider variety of task situations than the less skilled readers, possibly because they can activate phonological information more rapidly. In addition, the fact that the regular–exception word effect was smaller for the skilled readers when the words had high positional frequency values suggests the possibility that they may be somewhat more flexible than the less skilled readers in using both visual and phonographic strategies.

Although it has been argued that the regular–exception word effect arises because the exception words are more likely to activate inconsistent phonological information than the regular words, another interpretation of the effect is possible. Exception words may be more likely to be "one-of-a-kind" words than regular words in the sense that they have fewer orthographic neighbors than regular words. It is possible that a word with a large neighborhood (e.g., *fill*) will be responded to more rapidly than one with a small neighborhood (e.g., *debt*). This possibility involves the assumption that the speed with which a word can be activated is based on some combination of the activation values of the item and its corresponding neighbors. If the regular words in Experiment 1 have more orthographic neighbors than the exception words, then it might be possible to attribute the regular–exception word effect to a difference in the amount of activation contributed by the neighbors of the two types of words. This hypothesized neighborhood-size effect would occur even if visual-orthographic information were the only information activated. Furthermore, the effect might be more likely to occur in a lexical decision task, since that task does require that an item be given a specific, overt response.

In order to determine if the results of Experiment 1 could be attributed to orthographic neighborhood size, the Kučera and Francis (1967) word list was used to determine the number of words (i.e., neighbors) that shared all but one letter with each of the words used in Experiment 1. Since it was very likely that the frequency of the neighbors (Kučera & Francis, 1967), as well as their total number, might contribute to the activation level for an item, the sum of the log frequencies of the neighbors for each item was determined. Table 12.4 shows that the average value of this measure was somewhat higher for the regular than for the exception words in both the high-, $t(78) = 2.27$, $p < .05$, and low-, $t(78) = 2.36$, $p < .05$, positional-frequency conditions. The effect of positional frequency was not significant for either the regular, $t(78) = 1.38$, $p > .10$, or exception, $t(78) = 1.93$, $p > .05$, words; nor was the positional frequency $\times$ word type interaction significant, $F(1,156) < 1$.

Although this analysis suggests that the difference between regular and exception words might be attributed to differences in the frequency and number of their orthographic neighbors, an examination of the values for individual words indicated that the neighbors of four of the regular words in each of the two positional frequency conditions (*cave, fill, pine, cape, yell, cell, bell, dull*) had considerably higher summed log frequency values than the other words (the average of the eight items was 21.6784). When these eight items were deleted and the neighborhood analyses repeated, the regular–exception word differences was no longer significant in the high-, $t(74) = 1.04$, $p > .10$, or low-, $t(74) = 1.21$, $p > .10$, positional-frequency conditions. In order to determine if the eight items with high neighborhood values influenced subjects' performance, the median correct response times and percent of other error scores for each subject in each condition were recomputed with those items deleted. An analysis of the response times indicated that the reader $\times$ positional frequency $\times$ word type interaction remained significant, $F(1,62) = 4.51$, $p < .05$. A separate analysis of the skilled

Table 12.4
Average Values of the Sum of the Log
Frequencies of the Orthographic
Neighbors of the High- and Low-
Positional-Frequency, Regular and
Exception Words in Experiment 1

| Positional | Spelling Regularity | |
Frequency	Regular	Exception
High	6.7536	3.8138
Low	4.7418	2.3770

readers indicated that the positional frequency × word type interaction was again significant, $F(1,31) = 13.14$, $p < .001$, and that the difference between the regular and exception words remained significant in both the high-, $t(31) = 2.82$, $p < .01$, and low-, $t(31) = 4.68$, $p < .001$, positional-frequency conditions. A separate analysis of the less skilled readers, however, indicated that the main effect of word type was no longer significant, $F(1,31) = 3.28$, $p > .05$, and that the effects of positional frequency and the interaction of word type and positional frequency remained nonsignificant, $Fs(31) < 1$. The percent of other error analyses was not changed by the deletion of the high neighborhood value items. The skilled readers did not make any errors on the deleted items. Although the less skilled readers made a few errors on these items, the difference between the regular and exception words remained nonsignificant, $ts(31) < 1$. Again, errors and response times were positively correlated or not significantly negatively correlated ($ps > .10$).

These analyses of the effects of orthographic neighborhood size and frequency suggest that the regular–exception word effect cannot be attributed to a possible difference in the amount of activation contributed by the orthographic neighbors of the regular and exception words in Experiment 1, at least for the skilled readers. The results are consistent with the possibility that the regular–exception word effect for these readers arises from the activation of inconsistent phonological information by an exception word and its neighbors. The less skilled readers, on the other hand, may be using the possible difference in activation level between regular and exception words, since regular words were not significantly faster than exception words when the words with very high neighborhood values were deleted. These results are consistent with the earlier conclusion (e.g., Barron, 1978b, 1980) that the less skilled readers are not as able as the skilled readers to use a phonographic strategy effectively.

The fact that the less skilled readers showed a regular–exception word effect for knowledge, but not other, errors suggests an interpretation of why the less skilled readers in the Barron (1980) experiment made more errors on exception than regular words, even though there was no difference in response time. It is possible that many of their errors were knowledge errors, particularly on the exception words. They may not have made more other errors on the exception than the regular words. Unfortunately, other and knowledge errors were not distinguished in Barron (1980); hence it is not possible to provide evidence for this interpretation of the error results in that experiment.

Finally, the results of Experiment 1 appear to be inconsistent with those of Shulman, Hornak, and Sanders (1978). These investigators used a lexical decision task involving priming in which adult subjects were required to respond yes if two simultaneously displayed items were both words. A no response was required if either one or both of the items were nonwords. Like Meyer, Schvaneveldt, and Ruddy (1974), Shulman et al. (1978) found that adult subjects were faster on pairs of words that rhymed and had similar spelling patterns (e.g., *bribe, tribe*) than on corresponding control items (*bribe, freak*). Subjects were slower on pairs of items that had similar spelling patterns but did not rhyme (e.g., *freak, break*) than on corresponding control items (e.g., *tribe, break*). These results suggest that subjects were using a phonographic strategy. Contrary to the results of Experiment 1, however, evidence for the use of a phonographic strategy (i.e., the *freak, break* condition) disappeared when the nonwords in Shulman et al.'s (1978) experiment were random letter strings rather than pseudowords. Subjects were faster on both *bribe/tribe* and *freak/break* pairs than on the corresponding control pairs. Although the results of the Shulman et al. (1978) experiment are difficult to interpret within an activation–synthesis framework, it is possible that using letter strings to eliminate competing nonword neighbors increased the effectiveness of visual priming among items with similar spelling patterns as well as the likelihood of using phonological information. The increased visual priming may have allowed visual-orthographic information to be activated so rapidly that the phonological information did not have time to influence word recognition. Consistent with the possibility that phonological effects in word recognition can be reduced by increasing the speed of visual-orthographic activation, Stanovich and Bauer (1978) found that the regular–exception word difference can be eliminated in a lexical decision task if adult subjects are allowed to sacrifice their accuracy in order to increase their response speed. Singer (1980) has obtained similar results with items constructed from artificial letters.

EXPERIMENT 2

In addition to functioning as an access code in word recognition, phonological information may also have a function in comprehension. It may provide subjects with access to speech codes (e.g., articulatory, auditory imagery) that can be used to retain segments of text in short-term memory during the processes of comprehension. If readers are deficient in their ability to use phonological information, they may have problems in comprehending text, particularly when the material is difficult and information has to be held briefly in short-term memory before it can be completely integrated into ongoing semantic and syntactic analyses of text.

There is evidence that children who differ in reading skill also differ in their ability to use phonological information in memory tasks. Liberman, Shankweiler, and their colleagues, for example, have shown that skilled readers are more likely than less skilled readers to be affected by the phonological similarity of items in recall and recognition tasks. These investigators (Liberman, Shankweiler, Liberman, Fowler, & Fischer, 1977) used a task developed by Conrad (1963) and showed that skilled readers were less accurate in recalling lists of phonologically confusable consonants than lists of consonants that were not phonologically confusable. The recall accuracy of the less skilled readers, on the other hand, did not differ as much between the two types of lists. Mark, Shankweiler, Liberman, and Fowler (1977) obtained a similar pattern of results with phonologically similar and dissimilar word pairs in a recognition task, suggesting that the recall results were not due to the two groups of readers using different rehearsal strategies. Finally, Shankweiler, Liberman, Mark, Fowler, and Fischer (1979) have shown that the reading skill differences they found in the recall of phonologically confusable letters can be obtained when the items are presented auditorily as well as visually. Similarly, Byrne and Shea (1979) found that less skilled readers made fewer phonological confusion errors than skilled readers in a recognition task when the items were presented auditorily.

Taken together, these experiments on memory are consistent with the word recognition results discussed earlier, as they suggest that skilled readers are better able than less skilled readers to use a phonographic strategy. It is not clear, however, whether the smaller phonological confusion effects for less skilled readers arise from slow phonological activation, from formation of inadequate phonological representations, or from the use of alternative coding schemes, (e.g., visual-orthographic). In addition, the Shankweiler et al. (1979) and Byrne and Shea (1979) results suggest that the less skilled readers may have difficulty using phonological information regardless of the modality of the input. Unfortuantely, these memory experiments may have limited generality since they have not employed tasks that provide information about how phonologically based memory codes are used during comprehension. Levy (1975, 1977, 1978a, 1978b, Chap. 1, this volume), however, has developed a task in which it may be possible to obtain this information.

Subjects in Levy's task were presented with a series of study sentences that were followed by a test sentence. The test sentence was either identical or changed from one of the previously presented study sentences, and subjects were required to detect whether or not it had been changed. Although Levy changed the test sentences in a variety of ways, the basic results can be illustrated in her semantic condition. In that condition, a changed test sentence was one in which the subject and object nouns were reversed from a study sentence. If, for example, subjects were presented with the sentence "The serious jury addressed the confused judge," then that sentence would be rendered nonidentical by changing it to "The serious *judge* addressed the confused *jury*." Levy presented the sentences either auditorily or visually. On half of the study sentence trials, the subjects were also required to perform simultaneously a vocalization task of repeatedly counting aloud from 1 to 10 as fast as possible. Levy found that vocalization suppressed subjects' recognition accuracy substantially in reading but did not appear to suppress it in listening. These results did not depend on the amount of practice, the rate of presentation, or whether the subjects could control their reading rate.

Levy's results can be interpreted as indicating that vocalization interfered with a phonologically based memory representation of the study sentences during reading. Unfortunately, Levy's results do not provide much information about what aspects of a phonologically based representation actually conflicted with vocalization (e.g., articulation, auditory imagery). A recent experiment by Perfetti and McCutchen (1979), however, suggests that vocalization may interfere, at least in part, with articulatory information in memory. They required subjects to vocalize one sentence while simultaneously reading another sentence for meaning. They found that subjects sacrificed their fluency on the vocalization task in order to maintain their performance on the reading task when the words making up the sentences in both tasks began with consonants having the same place of articulation (alveolar). It is not clear why vocalization failed to suppress performance as much in the auditory as in the visual presentation condition in Levy's task. One interpretation is that reading is more difficult than listening, possibly because the process of activating phonological information and accessing, for example, articulatory information is more complicated in reading than in listening. As a result, reading may require more processing capacity than listening. It is also possible that auditory presentation may allow more immediate access to syntactic information, which may be used as an organizational device in memory.

Although Levy's suppression task only approximates "real" reading or listening, it has the virtue of making considerable memory demands upon the subject while also requiring comprehension. As a result, Mirc and Barron (1979) used the task to investigate differences in the ability of skilled and less skilled readers to use a phonographic strategy for purposes of remembering information during the processes of comprehension. If skilled readers are better able to use a phonographic strategy in remembering than less skilled readers (e.g., Liberman et al., 1977; Mark et al., 1977), then vocalization might produce a larger suppression effect for the skilled than for the less skilled readers in the reading task. Furthermore, the results of Shankweiler et al. (1979) and Byrne and Shea (1979) suggest that a similar pattern of results might be expected in the listening task.

Method

The subjects in the Mirc and Barron (1979) study were fifth- and sixth-grade children (10 to 12 years of age) and were chosen in a manner very similar to how the children used in Experiment 1 and in Barron (1978b, 1980) were selected. The 32 skilled and 32 less skilled readers had identical average IQs (102) on the nonverbal section of the Canadian Lorge–Thorndike Intelligence Test, but differed significantly ($t(62) = 11.60$, $p < .001$) on the reading comprehension subtest of the Gates–MacGinitie Reading Test. The average reading comprehension score of the skilled readers was 58, and the average for the less skilled readers was 43. As in the earlier experiments, these children had not been identified by their schools as having severe reading or learning problems.

Materials

The study and test sentences were seven words long and were constructed according to the article/adjective/noun/verb/article/adjective/noun format used by Levy. The words were taken from fifth- and sixth-grade-level spelling books in order to make them appropriate to the children's reading level. Two study sentences were used, and the test sentences were changed by reversing the subject and object nouns (as in the semantic condition of Levy's experiments). A third of the test sentences were filler items involving reversals in the adjectives or changes in the verb. They were used in order to increase the likelihood that subjects would comprehend the study sentences as well as remember their wording.

Procedure and Design

In the reading condition, the children saw the two study sentences for 7 seconds each. These sentences were followed immediately by the test sentence (also available for 7 seconds), and the children were required to decide whether or not it was identical to one of the two study sentences. The sentences in the listening task were presented for the same duration as those in the reading task in order to equate the two tasks in the amount of time the information was available to the children. A vocalization task of counting repeatedly from 1 to 10 was required on half the study trials in both listening and reading. The children's rate of vocalization was monitored, and they appeared to have no difficulty in maintaining a consistently high rate of counting across the conditions.

Results

The data were converted into probability-of-a-hit (H) and probability-of-a-false-alarm (FA) values for each subject. Following Levy, an attempt was made to correct for the effects of response bias on sentence recognition by subtracting the false-alarm from the hit scores for each subject (H − FA). In addition, d' scores were computed, and they produced the same pattern of results as the H − FA scores. A task (reading, listening) × vocalization (yes, no) × serial position of the study sentences (1, 2) × reading skill (skilled, less skilled) analysis of variance was carried out on H − FA scores (Task, Vocalization, and Serial Position were within-subject factors, and Reading Skill was a between-subjects factor). The average values of the scores making up this analysis are presented in Table 12.5.

The first thing to note about the data in Table 12.5 is that vocalization suppressed recognition accuracy, particularly for the most recently presented

TABLE 12.5
Mean Hit Minus False-Alarm Scores for the Skilled and Less Skilled
Readers in the Task, Vocalization, and Sentence Position
Conditions in Experiment 2

	Serial Position of Study Sentence					
	1			*2*		
	No			*No*		
Task-Reader	Vocalization	Vocalization	Diff.	Vocalization	Vocalization	Diff.
Reading–skilled	.66	.58	.08	.86	.53	.33
Reading–less skilled	.57	.41	.16	.69	.34	.35
Listening–skilled	.66	.55	.11	.88	.71	.17
Listening–less skilled	.46	.35	.11	.77	.69	.08

study sentence (Serial Position 2) in the reading task. However, the size of the vocalization effect was virtually the same for the skilled and less skilled readers in all conditions of the experiment. This observation is supported by the fact that the main effect of vocalization was significant, $F(1, 62) = 72.88$, $p < .001$, but that vocalization did not interact with reading skill anywhere in the analysis of variance ($ps > .50$). Contrary to expectations, these results suggest that both groups of readers were equally able to use a phonographic strategy in Levy's task.

There were two significant second-order interactions. The first was among the reading skill, task, and serial position variables, $F(1,62) = 6.15$, $p < .025$. A separate analysis of the data for Serial Position 2 produced a significant reading skill $\times$ task interaction, $F(1,62) = 5.24$, $p < .05$, that indicated that the two groups of readers differed in reading, $t(62) = 3.63$, $p < .01$, but not in listening, $t(62) = 1.52$, $p > .10$. When the data in Serial Position 1 were analyzed, however, the skilled readers were more accurate than the less skilled readers in both tasks, as only the main effect of reading skill was significant, $F(1,62) = 12.13$, $p < .01$. These results indicate that the skilled and less skilled readers differ in reading but not listening when subjects were required to recognize a sentence immediately after it had been presented (Serial Position 2). However, when the recognition test was delayed by 7 seconds (Serial Position 1), the skilled readers were more accurate than the less skilled readers in both reading and listening.

Serial position also interacted with the vocalization and task variables, $F(1,62) = 6.95$, $p < .025$. A separate analysis of the data in Serial Position 2 indicated that significant vocalization effects were obtained in both the reading, $t(31) = 8.29$, $p < .001$, and listening, $t(31) = 3.74$, $p < .01$, tasks. However, the size of the vocalization effect was much larger in reading than listening, as indicated by a significant vocalization $\times$ task interaction, $F(1,31) = 18.50$, $p < .001$. These results are consistent with Levy's findings, for they indicate that vocalization produced greater suppression effects in reading than in listening. The results in Serial Position 1, however, are inconsistent with Levy's findings. They indicate that the suppression effect was the same size for both reading and listening, since only the main effect of vocalization was significant, $F(1,31) = 12.42$, $p < .01$.

Discussion

Contrary to the predictions, the results of Experiment 2 (Mirc & Barron, 1979) indicate that vocalization suppressed the recognition accuracy of the skilled and less skilled readers by about the same amount, indicating that the two groups of readers were equally able to use a phonographic strategy in Levy's task. These results are inconsistent with those reported by Liberman, Shankweiler, and their colleagues in which the phonological confusability of items had a greater effect upon the recognition and recall accuracy of skilled readers than less skilled readers.

It is difficult to determine why the suppression effect was not greater for the skilled than for the less skilled readers. It does not appear that there were floor or ceiling effects, since the skilled readers were below perfect performance (1.00), and the less skilled readers were well above chance (0.00) performance. In addition, the results of Experiment 2 closely parallel those obtained by Levy in her semantic condition, at least for the sentences presented in Serial Position 2. It is possible that some characteristic or combination of characteristics in the Levy task prevented a reading skill × vocalization interaction from emerging. The requirement to vocalize may have encouraged the skilled readers to avoid using a phonographic strategy, as it impaired their performance. Less skilled readers, on the other hand, may have tried to use a phonographic strategy in order to overcome the memory demands of Levy's task. These hypothesized trade-offs in the use of a phonographic stragegy as a function of reading skill could have produced the present results. It is also possible that counting from 1 to 10 does not provide a sufficiently specific form of articulatory interference with the memorial representations of the sentences, assuming that the representations involve articulatory information (e.g., Perfetti & McCutchen, 1979). As a result, counting may only have functioned to tie up general processing capacity, and the amount of that capacity might not differ with regard to reading skill in Levy's task. Unfortunately, there does not appear to be any evidence that could be used to distinguish among these possible interpretations.

Finally, the results of Experiment 2 indicated that the skilled and less skilled readers had similar listening performance when memory demands were relatively low. However, when the memory demands were increased, the performance of the less skilled readers declined substantially, so that the two groups differed in both reading and listening. These results are consistent with Byrne and Shea (1979) and Shankweiler et al. (1979), as they suggest that deficiencies in auditory language processing may appear in less skilled readers when their memory capabilities are taxed.

CONCLUSIONS AND IMPLICATIONS

The arguments and evidence presented in this chapter suggest that children who differ on a standard test of reading comprehension also differ in the strategies they use in recognizing printed words. One of the strategies involves using visual-orthographic information to access semantic and syntactic information in the lexicon. This visual strategy is considered sufficient for lexical access and can be carried out relatively rapidly. A phonographic strategy involves using phonological information to access semantic and syntactic information. This stragegy is also sufficient for lexical access, but it is slower than the visual strategy since it is based on prior activation of visual-orthographic information.

The available evidence suggests that the less skilled readers used in Experiments 1 and 2 and in Barron (1978b, 1980) are primarily deficient in their use of a phonographic strategy. There are several possible reasons for this deficiency. First, less skilled readers may not be able to activate phonological information as rapidly as skilled readers. For example, they are not as likely to show pseudohomophone and regular–exception word effects as skilled readers, possibly because these effects may arise from rapidly activating conflicting or inconsistent phonological information. Second, the less skilled readers may also be more likely to produce inadequate phonological representations than the skilled readers. There is not much evidence for this possibility in Experiment 1, as the less skilled readers made only slightly fewer other errors than the skilled readers, and there were no effects of reading skill ($ps > .10$) when the pronunciation errors on the incorrect words were analyzed separately. Nevertheless, the adequacy of phonological representations, as well as the speed of their activation, may be a factor in the inability of more seriously impaired readers than those in the present experiments to use a phonographic strategy. Third, less skilled readers may not be as able as skilled readers to use phonological information, regardless of whether the input is auditory or visual. The results of Byrne and Shea (1979), Shankweiler et al. (1979), and the first serial position data from Experiment 2 are consistent with this possibility, at least for tasks in which demands are placed upon memory. Fourth, it is possible that successful use of a phonographic strategy is based upon short-term memory ''capacity,'' and the less skilled readers may have a smaller capacity (Jorm, 1979). Although this possibility might be regarded as being consistent with the results of Byrne and Shea (1979) and Liberman, Shankweiler, and their colleagues, their experiments do not allow capacity differences to be distinguished from differences in phonological coding ability (assuming they could be distinguished). Furthermore, the skilled and less skilled readers did not differ in listening performance in Experiment 2 under immediate memory conditions (i.e., the second serial position). Accordingly, differences in short-term memory capacity per se may not account for reading skill differences in the use of a phonographic strategy.

Although there appear to be several reasons why less skilled readers might be deficient in using a phonographic strategy, it is not clear why this deficiency is related to differences in reading comprehension ability. After all, visual-orthographic information is sufficient for lexical access, and phonological information is activated more slowly than visual-orthographic information. One possible reason why reading comprehension ability is related to the use of a phonographic strategy is that the strategy provides an alternative means of accessing semantic and syntactic information particularly when a visual strategy may be relatively inadequate (e.g., with unfamiliar words). Stanovich (1980, Chap. 10, this volume) has pointed out that less skilled readers are more likely than skilled readers to rely upon sentence context to facilitate word recognition. This reliance may be based, at least in part, upon the difficulty that less skilled readers have in rapidly activating phonological information and using it to access semantic and syntactic information. Although context may facilitate word recognition, a rapidly activated phonological code may provide access to more precise information about the syntactic and semantic identity of a word than is provided by context, and it may provide access to that information without sacrificing much processing speed.

Use of a phonographic strategy may also be related to reading comprehension skill because it provides an effective means of maintaining information in short-term memory. Unfortunately, the results of Experiment 2 are inconsistent with this function of a phonographic strategy insofar as the use of the strategy distinguishes skilled and less skilled readers. There appear, however, to be several possible reasons why Levy's vocalization task did not distinguish the two groups of readers; hence it may be premature to dismiss the memory function of a phonographic strategy. Indeed, the results of Liberman et al. (1977) and Mark et al. (1977) suggest that the skilled and less skilled readers may differ in their ability to use a phonographic strategy in memory tasks.

In summary, the ability to use a phonographic strategy may be related to reading comprehension skill for two reasons. First, it may influence the speed and precision with which the syntactic and semantic identities of words can be accessed. Second, it may provide a memory representation for information during comprehension. These conclusions are consistent with the fact that differences in the speed and precision of lexical access and differences in the ability to retain information during comprehension are regarded as being very important in accounting for differences in reading comprehension skill in some interactive models of reading (e.g., Lesgold & Perfetti, 1978; Perfetti & Lesgold, 1978, 1980; Perfetti and Roth, Chap. 11, this volume).

The possibility that skilled and less skilled readers may differ in their use of a visual as well as a phonographic strategy has not been considered in any detail in this chapter. The results of Barron (1980) indicated that the less skilled readers were sensitive to differences in visual-orthographic structure when it may have been relatively difficult for them to use a phonographic strategy. On the other hand, the skilled readers in Experiment 1 seemed to use effectively both visual-orthographic and phonological information. It is possible that the ability to use a phonographic strategy is related to the ability to use a visual strategy even though visual-orthographic information is activated prior to phonological information. This influence may arise in learning to read, since the process of acquiring a phonographic strategy may encourage children to attend to the sequential and positional constraints on individual letters in words. This process may be encouraged in programs that take a relatively analytic approach to word learning, such as phonics (e.g., Venezky & Massaro, 1979). Indeed, the relative success of phonics-based approaches (e.g., Chall, 1967) may be due, in part, to the possibility that they help children to learn both visual and phonographic strategies.

Finally, there are both advantages and disadvantages to using Glushko's (1979, Chap. 3, this volume) activation–synthesis model as a framework for examining reading skill differences in the use of visual and phonographic strategies. One advantage is that it allows the two strategies to be viewed as involving the same mechanisms (activation and synthesis), but having sources of knowledge (visual-orthographic and phonological) that are available at different times in the process of word recognition. In addition, the concept of an orthographic neighborhood is attractive because it suggests the possibility that speed and accuracy of word recognition may depend upon relationships between the to-be-recognized word and other words in the lexicon. The major disadvantage of the model is that it has not been worked out in detail (see, however, Rumelhart and McClelland, Chap. 2, this volume). Consequently, it is difficult to determine, for example, how conflicting phonological information is actually synthesized or what kinds of top-down and bottom-up constraints are imposed upon the activation process. Furthermore, it appears necessary for the model to provide a detailed account of pheomena that appear to involve the use of rules and the learning of rules. Nevertheless, the activation–synthesis model appears to offer a unique perspective on the processes of word recognition, and it appears to provide a more adequate account of the available data than dual-process models.

ACKNOWLEDGMENTS

This research was supported by a grant from the National Sciences and Engineering Research Council of Canada (A9782). Portions of the paper were written while I was on sabbatical leave at the Department of Experimental Psychology, University of Oxford. I thank the department for the use of their facilities and the Social Sciences and Humanities Research Council of Canada Leave Fellowship program for support. I gratefully acknowledge the assistance of Brenda Chipperfield, Juha Kumpunen, and Colleen MacFadden in collecting and analyzing the data and the cooperation of the children as well as their principals, teachers, and parents. Finally, I thank Betty Ann Levy for comments on an earlier version of this chapter and Bob Glushko for discussions on phonography and for carrying out the analyses of the orthographic neighbors of the words used in Experiment 1.

REFERENCES

Arnett, J. L., & DiLollo, V. Visual information processing in relation to age and reading ability. *Journal of Experimental Child Psychology*, 1979, *27*, 143–152.

Baron, J. Phonemic stage not necessary for reading. *Quarterly Journal of Experimental Psychology*, 1973, *25*, 241–246.

Baron, J. Orthographic and word-specific mechanisms in children's reading of words. *Child Development*, 1979, *50*, 60–72.

Baron, J., & Strawson, C. Use of orthographic and word-specific knowledge in reading words aloud. *Journal of Experimental Psychology: Human Perception and Performance*, 1976, *4*, 207–214.

Barron, R. W. Access to the meanings of printed words: Some implications for reading and learning to read. In F. B. Murray (Ed.), *The recognition of words: IRA series on the development of the reading process*. Newark, Del: International Reading Association, 1978. (a)

Barron, R. W. Reading skill and phonological coding in lexical access. In M. M. Gruneberg, R. N. Sykes, & P. E. Morris (Eds.), *Practical aspects of memory*. London: Academic Press, 1978. (b)

Barron, R. W. Visual and phonological strategies in reading and spelling. In U. Frith (Ed.), *Cognitive processes in spelling*. London: Academic Press, 1980.

Barron, R. W. Development of visual word recognition: A Review. In T. G. Waller & G. E. MacKinnon (Eds.), *Reading research: Advances in theory and practice* (Vol. 3). New York: Academic Press, in press.

Barron, R. W., & Baron, J. How children get meaning from printed words. *Child Development*, 1977, *48*, 587–594.

Boder, E. Developmental dyslexia: Prevailing diagnostic concepts and a new diagnostic approach. In H. R. Myklebust (Ed.), *Progress in learning disabilities* (Vol. 2). New York: Grune & Stratton, 1971.

Boder, E. Developmental dyslexia: A diagnostic approach based on three atypical reading–spelling patterns. *Developmental Medicine and Child Neurology*, 1973, *15*, 663–687.

Brooks, L. Non-analytic correspondences and pattern in word pronunciation. In J. Requin (Ed.), *Attention and performance VII*. Hillsdale, N.J.: Lawrence Erlbaum Associates, 1978.

Byrne, B., & Shea, P. Semantic and phonetic memory codes in beginning readers. *Memory & Cognition*, 1979, *7*, 333–338.

Carroll, J. B., Davies, P., & Richman, B. *The word frequency book*. Boston: Houghton Mifflin, 1971.

Chall, J. *Learning to read. The great debate*. New York: McGraw-Hill, 1967.

Coltheart, M. Lexical access in simple reading tasks. In G. Underwood (Ed.), *Strategies of information processing*. London: Academic Press, 1978.

Coltheart, M., Besner, D., Jonasson, J. T., & Davelaar, E. Phonological recoding in the lexical decision task. *Quarterly Journal of Experimental Psychology*, 1979, *31*, 489–507.

Coltheart, M., Davelaar, E., Jonasson, J. T., & Besner, D. Access to the internal lexicon. In S. Dornic (Ed.), *Attention and performance VI*. Hillsdale, N.J.: Lawrence Erlbaum Associates, 1977.

Conrad, R. Acoustic confusions and memory span for words. *Nature*, 1963, *197*, 1029–1030.

Ellis, N. C., & Miles, T. R. Visual information processing in dyslexic children. In M. M. Gruneberg, R. N. Sykes, & P. E. Morris (Eds.), *Practical aspects of memory*. London: Academic Press, 1978.

Firth, I. *Components of reading disability.* Unpublished doctoral dissertation, University of New South Wales, 1972.

Frederiksen, J. R. Assessment of perceptual, decoding and lexical skills and their relation to reading proficiency. In A. M. Lesgold, J. W. Pellegrino, S. D. Fokkema, & R. Glaser (Eds.), *Cognitive psychology and instruction.* New York: Plenum Press, 1978.

Gibson, E. J., Shurcliff, A., & Yonas, A. Utilization of spelling patterns by deaf and hearing subjects. In H. Levin & J. Williams (Eds.), *Basic studies on reading.* New York: Basic Books, 1970.

Glushko, R. J. The organization and activation of orthographic knowledge in reading aloud. *Journal of Experimental Psychology: Human Perception and Performance,* 1979, *5,* 674–691.

Gough, P., & Cosky, M. One second of reading again. In N. Castellan, D. Pisoni, & G. Potts (Eds.), *Cognitive theory* (Vol. 2). Hillsdale, N.J.: Lawrence Erlbaum Associates, 1977.

Hogaboam, T. W., & Perfetti, C. A. Reading skill and the role of verbal experience in decoding. *Journal of Educational Psychology,* 1978, *70,* 717–729.

Jorm, A. F. The cognitive and neurological bases of developmental dyslexia: A theoretical framework and review. *Cognition,* 1979, *7,* 19–33.

Katz, L., & Wicklund, D. A. Letter scanning rate for good and poor readers in grades two and six. *Journal of Educational Psychology,* 1972, *63,* 363–367.

Kleiman, G. M. Speech recoding and reading. *Journal of Verbal Learning and Verbal Behavior,* 1975, *14,* 323–339.

Kučera, H., & Francis, W. N. *Computational analysis of present-day American English.* Providence, R.I.: Brown University Press, 1967.

Lesgold, A. M., & Perfetti, C. A. Interactive processes in reading comprehension. *Discourse Processes,* 1978, *1,* 323–336.

Levy, B. A. Vocalization and suppression effects in sentence memory. *Journal of Verbal Learning and Verbal Behavior,* 1975, *14,* 304–316.

Levy, B. A. Reading: Speech and meaning processes. *Journal of Verbal Learning and Verbal Behavior,* 1977, *16,* 623–638.

Levy, B. A. Speech analysis during sentence processing. *Visible Language,* 1978, *12,* 81–101. (a)

Levy, B. A. Speech processing during reading. In A. M. Lesgold, J. W. Pellegrino, S. D. Fokkema, & R. Glaser (Eds.), *Cognitive psychology and instruction.* New York: Plenum Press, 1978. (b)

Liberman, I. Y., Shankweiler, D., Liberman, A. M., Fowler, C., & Fischer, W. F. Phonetic segmentation and recoding in the beginning reader. In A. S. Reber & D. L. Scarborough (Eds.), *Toward a psychology of reading.* Hillsdale, N.J.: Lawrence Erlbaum Associates, 1977.

Lovegrove, W. J., Bowling, A., Badcock, D., & Blackwood, M. Specific reading disability: Differences in contrast sensitivity as a function of spatial frequency. *Science,* 1980, *210,* 439–440.

Marcel, A. J. Surface dyslexia and beginning reading: A revised hypothesis of the pronunciation of print and its impairments. In M. Coltheart, K. E. Patterson, & J. C. Marshall (Eds.), *Deep dyslexia.* London: Routledge & Kegan Paul, 1980.

Mark, L. S., Shankweiler, D., Liberman, I. Y., & Fowler, C. A. Phonetic recoding and reading difficulty in beginning readers. *Memory & Cognition,* 1977, *5,* 529–539.

Marsh, G., Friedman, M. P., Welch, V., & Desberg, P. A cognitive-developmental approach to reading acquisition. In T. G. Waller & G. E. MacKinnon (Eds.), *Reading research: Advances in theory and practice.* (Vol. 3). New York: Academic Press, in press.

Marshall, J. C., & Newcombe, F. Patterns of paralexia: A psycholinquistic approach. *Journal of Psycholinguistic Research,* 1973, *2,* 175–199.

Mason, M. Reading ability and letter search time: Effects of orthographic structure defined by single letter positional frequency. *Journal of Experimental Psychology: General,* 1975, *104,* 146–166.

Massaro, D. W., Venezky, R. L., & Taylor, G. A. Orthographic regularity, positional frequency, and visual processing of letter strings. *Journal of Experimental Psychology: General,* 1979, *108,* 107–124.

Mayzner, M. S., & Tresselt, M. E. Tables of single-letter and digram frequency counts for various word length and letter position combinations. *Psychonomic Science Monograph Supplements,* 1965, *1,* 13–32.

McClelland, J. L., & Johnston, J. C. The role of familiar units in the perception of words and nonwords. *Perception & Psychophysics,* 1977, *22,* 249–261.

Meyer, D. E., & Schvaneveldt, R. W. Facilitation in recognizing pairs of words: Evidence of dependence between retrieval operations. *Journal of Experimental Psychology,* 1971, *90,* 227–234.

Meyer, D. E., Schvaneveldt, R. W., & Ruddy, M. G. Functions of graphemic and phonemic codes in visual word recognition. *Memory & Cognition,* 1974, *2,* 309–321.

Mirc, E. E., & Barron, R. W. *Effects of concurrent vocalization upon reading and listening comprehension of good and poor readers.* Paper presented at the Society for Research in Child Development meetings, San Francisco, March, 1979.

Morrison, F. J., Giordani, B., & Nagy, J. Reading disability: An information processing analysis. *Science,* 1977, *196,* 77–79.

Neely, J. H. Semantic priming and retrieval from lexical memory: Roles of inhibitionless spreading activation and limited capacity attention. *Journal of Experimental Psychology: General,* 1977, *106,* 226–254.

Patterson, K. E., & Marcel, A. J. Aphasia, dyslexia and the phonological coding of written words. *Quarterly Journal of Experimental Psychology,* 1977, *29,* 307–318.

Perfetti, C. A., Finger, E., & Hogaboam, T. W. Sources of vocalization latency differences between skilled and less skilled readers. *Journal of Educational Psychology,* 1978, *70,* 730–739.

Perfetti, C. A., & Hogaboam, T. Relationships between single word decoding and reading comprehension skill. *Journal of Educational Psychology,* 1975, *67,* 461–469.

Perfetti, C. A., & Lesgold, A. M. Discourse comprehension and sources of individual differences. In P. A. Carpenter & M. Just (Eds.), *Cognitive processes in comprehension.* Hillsdale, N.J.: Lawrence Erlbaum Associates, 1978.

Perfetti, C. A., & Lesgold, A. M. Coding and comprehension in skilled reading. In L. B. Resnick & P. A. Weaver (Eds.), *Theory and practice of early reading.* Hillsdale, N.J.: Lawrence Erlbaum Associates, 1979.

Perfetti, C. A., & McCutchen, D. *Phonological codes in reading.* Paper presented at the Psychonomic Society meetings, Phoenix, Arizona, November 1979.

Rubenstein, H., Lewis, S. S., & Rubenstein, M. A. Evidence for phonemic recoding in visual word recognition. *Journal of Verbal Learning and Verbal Behavior,* 1971, *10,* 645–657.

Saffran, E. M., & Marin, O. S. M. Reading without phonology: Evidence from aphasia. *Quarterly Journal of Experimental Psychology,* 1977, *29,* 515–526.

Shallice, T., & Warrington, E. Word recognition in a phonemic dyslexic patient. *Quarterly Journal of Experimental Psychology,* 1975, *27,* 148–160.

Shankweiler, D., Liberman, I. Y., Mark, L. S., Fowler, C. A., & Fischer, F. W. The speech code and learning to read. *Journal of Experimental Psychology: Human Learning and Memory,* 1979, *5,* 531–545.

Shulman, H. G., & Davison, T. C. B. Control properties of semantic coding in a lexical decision task. *Journal of Verbal Learning and Verbal Behavior,* 1977, *16,* 91–98.

Shulman, H. G., Hornak, R., & Sanders, E. The effects of graphemic, phonetic and semantic relationships on access to lexical structures. *Memory & Cognition,* 1978, *6,* 115–123.

Singer, M. H. The primacy of visual information in the analysis of letter strings. *Perception & Psychophysics,* 1980, *27,* 153–162.

Stanovich, K., & Bauer, D. Experiments on the spelling to sound regularity effect in word recognition. *Memory & Cognition,* 1978, *6,* 410–415.

Stanovich, K. E. Toward an interactive-compensatory model of individual differences in the development of reading fluency. *Reading Research Quarterly,* 1980, *16,* 32–71.

Stanovich, K. E., & West, R. F. The effect of orthographic structure on the word search performance of good and poor readers. *Journal of Experimental Child Psychology,* 1979, *28,* 258–267.

Vellutino, F. R. Alternative conceptualization of dyslexia: Evidence in support of a verbal-deficit hypothesis. *Harvard Educational Review,* 1977, *47,* 334–354.

Vellutino, F. R. Toward an understanding of dyslexia: Psychological factors in specific reading disability. In A. L. Benton & D. Pearl (Eds.), *Dyslexia: An appraisal of current knowledge.* New York: Oxford University Press, 1978.

Venezky, R. L. *The structure of English orthography.* The Hague: Mouton, 1970.

Venezky, R. L., & Massaro, D. W. The role of orthographic regularity in word recognition. In L. B. Resnick & P. A. Weaver (Eds.), *Theory and practice of early reading.* Hillsdale, N.J.: Lawrence Erlbaum Associates, 1979.

13 Learning to Read Words Efficiently

Alan M. Lesgold and Mary E. Curtis
Learning Research and Development Center
University of Pittsburgh

INTRODUCTION

Recent contributions to the instructional psychology of reading have tended toward a consensus that poor readers are deficient in some portion of the processing involved in accessing phonological codes from memory (Frederiksen, 1978a; Jackson & McClelland, 1979; Jorm, 1979; Perfetti & Lesgold, 1977; Vellutino, 1977; and others). This deficiency is increasingly well documented, but there has yet to emerge a clear picture of what it means. Perfetti and Lesgold (1977; Lesgold & Perfetti, 1978) have proposed that the efficiency of the reading process depends critically on the efficiency of phonological code access, but this is only one of the possibilities. The work described in this chapter is the first part of an attempt to study the development of both overall reading ability and verbal encoding efficiency in an effort to see how the two are related.

The structure of this chapter is as follows: First, we present some foundations for a theory of the types of prerequisite relationships that can exist between cognitive competences. Second, we use this theory as a basis for understanding the nature of the observed correlation between phonological or articulatory proficiency and reading achievement, and show how this concern motivated the longitudinal study of beginning reading now in progress. Finally, we present a considerable amount of preliminary data and discuss their implications for the issues raised earlier.

NOTES TOWARD A THEORY OF PREREQUISITES

The notion of prerequisites for instruction is as old as formal instruction itself. Today, it is taken for granted that there are certain components of a curriculum that must precede others. As each new approach to education or to the psychology of education has developed, there have been implicit or explicit reinterpretations of the meaning of prerequisite relationships within that new approach. However, there has not been such a reinterpretation to correspond to the full emergence of the use of cognitive process models as a major tool of cognitive psychology.

Current views of prerequisite relationships between skills tend to derive from the work on learning hierarchies (Gagne, 1962, 1965). This work is based upon a combination of an expansion of verbal learning into the cognitive realm (Gagne, 1965) and rational task analysis (cf. Resnick, 1973). The basic idea that has evolved is that if one wishes to teach a complex skill, one should analyze that skill into component subskills, which should be taught first. This "working backwards" approach is applied recursively to build an overall map of the dependency relations between progressively more complex subskills (see, as an example, Resnick, Wang, & Kaplan, 1973).

Empirical approaches have been suggested for the validation of hierarchies. Most of them call for verifying that if a particular sequence of skills has the property that each skill in the sequence is a prerequisite for the next, then test items that measure performance on this sequence should form a Guttman scale (i.e., no one should correctly answer an item that measures Skill B but fail to pass an item that measures Skill A if Skill A is prerequisite to Skill B). Although there have been attempts to specify the nature of prerequisite relationships with greater rigor (e.g., Gagne, 1968), a common weakness of these approaches is that they use rational analyses of *final performance* to order the course of instruction. This point leads us to consider two sets of candidate definitions for prerequisite relationships: one set that is based upon the extent to which a prerequisite skill is necessary for *performance of a target skill,* and a corresponding set that is based upon the necessity of a skill for learning *a target skill.* We list several types of prerequisites next and then comment on them.

Prerequisite Relationships in Skill Performance

1. Performance of the target skill always includes performance of the prerequisite skill. For example, adding three-digit numbers requires adding one-digit numbers.

2. Performance of the target skill usually, but not necessarily, includes performance of the prerequisite skill. An example of such a prerequisite skill would be use of a foot pedal as a prerequisite for driving. Performance of the target skill of driving includes the use of foot pedals as control devices. However, here the relationship is not one of necessity, since it is possible to drive by using an alternative control device, as amputees, in fact, do.

3. Efficiency of the prerequisite skill is a limiting factor on performance of the target skill. That is, efficiency of the prerequisite skill is not *required* for

performance of the target skill but will represent an *advantage* in its performance. For example, being a poor reader limits one's ability to be a chef (it would be handy to be able to read cookbooks), so we can think of reading as an efficiency prerequisite to chef duties.

Prerequisite Relationships in Skill Learning

4. Skill A is prerequisite to Skill B if the performances involved in learning the target skill, *B*, necessarily include performances of the prerequisite skill, *A*. For example, if it is impossible to learn how to add without being able to count, then counting would be a necessary prerequisite to *learning* to add, even though it would not be a *performance* prerequisite.

5. The prerequisite skill is usually required in order for learning the target skill to take place. For example, knowledge of decimal arithmetic is usually required in learning statistics, but one could imagine teaching statistics to people who knew the arithmetic operations with fractions but not with decimals. Once they knew statistics, they could use computer programs to do their computations. Here, then, is a case where one skill can be substituted for another during *learning* without necessarily detracting from final *performance*.

6. Finally, one might speak of one skill being prerequisite to another if efficiency of the prerequisite skill affects the *rate at which the target skill is learned*. For example, reading fluency is prerequisite to learning a number of skills in the sense that those skills are learned more efficiently if one can easily read certain instructional material. The *performances* of the target skills, though, may involve no reading.

Given the foregoing ways of characterizing prerequisite skills, we can now specify the task of this chapter as exploring the nature and extent of the prerequisite relationship between efficient phonological-articulatory skills and the learning and performance of reading skills. The merits of each type of prerequisite relationship in explaining the correlation between phonological-articulatory coding and reading achievement are examined next.

The first relationship is clearly ruled out, since we know that skilled reading sometimes proceeds without access to phonological codes (e.g., Bradshaw, 1975). Similarly, the fourth type must be eliminated, since it is not the case that less skilled readers are unable to access and use phonological information (Barron, Chap. 12, this volume). The second and fifth types are more plausible, particularly since words can be recognized via both access to phonological codes and direct access of visual representations (Wernicke, 1874, 1966). Furthermore, it appears that skilled readers tend to use a phonological strategy in word identification whereas less skilled readers rely more on their visual memories for words (Barron, 1978). In terms of our theory of prerequisites, the correlation between phonological coding and a reading skill could be due to either: (1) failure of less skilled readers to compensate fully for slow phonological access by increased use of the visual route (Relationship 2); or (2) failure of reading instruction to teach poor phonological coders to rely more on "direct access" in reading (Relationship 5). There is, however, evidence that causes us to question whether these relationships are the appropriate description of the data on differences between skilled and less skilled readers. There is considerable doubt: (1) that visual access and phonological access are independent processes (Barron, Chap. 12, this volume); and (2) that all reading can proceed without access to phonological codes (Lesgold & Perfetti, 1978; Perfetti & Lesgold, 1979). Thus, we question the possibility that visual access can always be substituted for phonological access without detracting from final performance.

This leaves us with Relationships 3 and 6, which suggest that differences in phonological coding are the cause of either less effective reading or less effective learning of reading skills. Ignoring time constraints and motivational issues, if Relationship 3 holds between phonological coding and reading performance, then improving encoding should improve overall reading. Of course, this assumes that poor readers can in fact be brought to a high enough level of phonological encoding efficiency. As it turns out, there has been considerable research in recent years that purports to show that verbal processing deficiencies are enduring qualities of at least some less skilled readers. In the next sections, we briefly review two threads of this work—one showing that poor readers have some differences in visual evoked potentials over the parietal lobes, and the other showing that verbal memory access and processing speeds are slower in poor readers at all age levels.

Electroencephalographic Evidence.   In a recent paper, Jorm (1979) argues that poor readers have a "genetically-based dysfunction of the inferior parietal lobule [p. 19]" and suggests that such children should be taught by methods that assume they will never have the level of verbal processing efficiency and capacity that normal readers have. To buttress this theory, Jorm points out that the structures of the inferior parietal lobe of the brain are important in the kinds of performances that less skilled readers are unable to do well. The critical evidence is that which purports to show that less skilled readers have a dysfunction of the inferior parietal lobe. Here, Jorm cites four studies (Connors, 1970; Preston, Guthrie, & Childs, 1974; Preston, Guthrie, Kirsch, Gertman, & Childs, 1977; and Symann-Louett, Gascon, Matsumiya, & Lombroso, 1977) that show lower levels of evoked response from the parietal lobes, particularly the left, in response to word stimuli and perhaps also to light-flash stimuli.

The question is whether these studies provide adequate evidence for Jorm's claim that evoked response differences are direct manifestations of structural differences that cause low reading achievement. Although the inferior parietal lobe of the left hemisphere is an important locus of verbal processing, including some of the processing less skilled readers are less able to perform, the evoked potential differences may simply be an indication that the processing we know to be different in effect is also different in the electrical phenomena it produces near

the parietal lobe. Or if not merely an epiphenomenon of verbal processing differences, the evoked response differences may be the result of verbal processing
experience differences.

That is, a control group equivalent in reading achievement to a dyslexic group
may have had more learning experience with simple word-processing tasks—and
we are dealing here with evoked responses to single words!! Also, the dyslexic
groups in these studies were drawn from special classrooms and may have more
substantial problems than one would find, say, in an urban public school
classroom. Thus, although there seems to be some evidence here that at least
some of the differences between normal readers and poor readers are quite
enduring and pervasive, there is no evidence that this difference is either the
major cause of reading problems in more normal children or that it is the same as
the more specific speed-of-vocalization difference upon which we are concentrat-
ing.

*Does Phonological Coding Speed Distinguish Normal from Poor Readers at
All Age Levels?*   Differences in verbal processing efficiency have been observed
in less skilled readers at several age levels, leading to the conclusion that at least
some of the slower access to verbal codes that less skilled readers show may be
unaffected by practice. In children, there have been clear demonstrations that
elementary-school poor readers are slower in saying words and pseudowords
than good readers, especially when the word to be vocalized is low in frequency
or multisyllabic (Hogaboam & Perfetti, 1978; Perfetti & Hogaboam, 1975).
Frederiksen (1978b) looked at a number of performances in high school children
who were split into four groups on the basis of their scores on the Nelson–
Denney reading test. Children in the lowest quartiles (based upon national
norms) were slower in vocalization of low-frequency words and pseudowords
and also required more time per syllable than better readers to make a lexicality
judgment on a multisyllable letter string.

To summarize, clear evidence exists that poor readers, in both elementary
school and high school, are slower at tasks that involve retrieving a verbal/
phonological code in response to a visual stimulus. There is some evidence that
this difference persists into adulthood, but this evidence involves above-average
versus average readers and different tasks. This may mean that phonological
coding speed is necessary for efficient reading performance (Relationship 3).
However, it may also mean that phonological coding speed is needed to *learn* to
read and, for that reason only, stays correlated with subsequent reading performance (Relationship 6). There is one extensive study that can be interpreted as
offering evidence for the latter claim that the verbal processing speed differences
that are pervasive over age are correlationally, but not causally, related to overall
reading ability differences. This is a study by Curtis (1980) in which poor readers
in third and fifth grades were compared to children of equivalent age but average
reading ability and to an ability-matched group of younger children of average
reading ability for their age.

Using high-frequency words and pseudowords, Curtis found the expected phonological coding deficits for the poorer readers at both age levels, but she also found that the predictive power of phonological coding speed tended to decrease with increasing reading ability—relative to the predictive power of listening comprehension. This result is not inconsistent with the claim that verbal memory access stays slow in poor readers over age, but it may also suggest that verbal memory access speed is a less critical need in higher levels of reading.

This may indeed be the case, but there are at least two alternative possibilities. First, tests of listening comprehension may themselves involve more verbal memory retrieval in later grades. More generally, different performances were required in the listening comprehension tests at different grade levels (at least in the sense that subject variability involved different items), whereas the same words were used at all levels of the vocalization latency measurement. Presumably, if progressively harder words were used for the vocalization task at higher grade levels, that task might have retained its relative predictive power. This issue is discussed again near the end of this chapter. Another possibility is that to some extent, poor readers come to use alternative strategies to get around their verbal memory access problems, permitting a partial approximation to good performance. If this is the case, the direct deleterious effect of slow code access would decrease over grade levels.

To conclude, it would be useful to have data on the changes in children's verbal memory access speed and in their reading speed and overall reading ability as they progress through school. This would permit at least some further precision in understanding whether phonological coding abilities are needed to learn to read but are not, in fact, necessary in skilled reading per se.[1] In the next two sections, we describe the methodology and initial results of a longitudinal study designed to provide this additional information.

METHOD

The Mastery-Referenced Developmental Design

Ordinarily, developmental studies produce data in which various dependent measures are plotted as a function of age. In the present study, we have chosen a

---

[1]We cannot, thus far, separate this theory from an alternative that the phonological processing efficiency correlation with reading is due to a general limit on memory function that shows itself most strongly in phonological processing. For example, a slowness in retrieving any verbal code (the name of something) would show up most when the input is weak. Bouma and Legein (1977) have shown reader differences in accuracy of perception of letters from parafoveal, laterally masked displays. However, we have yet to formulate a test to distinguish the general memory access speed hypothesis from the specific phonological deficiency hypothesis. Some of the data presented next partially disentangle these two hypotheses.

somewhat different strategy. We test children when they complete various portions of the reading curriculum. This means that our basic data consist of plots of the dependent measures against level of progress or mastery through the reading curriculum. Of course, it is also possible to plot the data against age or number of days of schooling, just as might be done in a more traditional study. However, the approach we have taken allows us to separate easily three kinds of developmental effects: (1) skills that are not directly affected by the reading instruction; (2) skills affected by the instruction but that are equal over different children at points of equal mastery; and (3) skills that the curriculum does not teach equally to all children.

The second type of skill would be one that, through individualization of rate of progress through the curriculum, is successfully taught to all children. For such a skill, performance data plotted against progress through the curriculum would show no differences between children scoring high on annual reading achievement tests and those scoring lower, even though the slower children took longer to get to each test point. The third type of skill would be one for which even our mastery-referenced data plots show differences between high- and low-achievement children. Here, too, though, there are several possibilities. For example, both high- and low-ability groups may be moving toward the same performance asymptotes. In this case, we would feel that the curriculum is doing the right kind of instruction but that its mastery tests do not capture mastery of the particular performances we are studying. A more interesting alternative would be the finding that children of different achievement levels are moving to different performance asymptotes. This would suggest that current practices (and perhaps any possible teaching approach) cannot bring all children to the same levels of efficiency in that particular skill.

Design Details

We have been testing several groups, or *cohorts,* of children in this study. We present, in this report, data from Cohort A, begun in 1976, and Cohort B, begun in 1977.

The children in both cohorts were from a racially balanced urban school that used the NRS beginning reading curriculum (see Beck & Mitroff, 1972, for more information about NRS). Cohort A began with 49 children and Cohort B, with 53 children. By June of 1979, 19 of the students in Cohort A and 17 of those in B had moved or changed schools and were lost from the sample. Means of the standardized test scores available for the remaining children are shown in Table 13.1.

NRS is an individualized reading program that emphasizes both phonics and comprehension skills. The program is organized into 14 major units of more or less equal size called "levels." An average child takes about 2.5 years to get through all 14 levels. Each child was tested as soon as possible (ordinarily within

TABLE 13.1
Sample Size and Mean Achievement Scores: Cohorts A and B

| | | | Level | | | | | Letters | Phonemes | Test Scores | |
	2	4	6	8	10	12	14			Vocabulary	Comprehension
Cohort A											
Grade 1 ('76–'77)	38	38	16	—	—	—	—	42[a]	37[a]	1.7[b]	1.5[b]
Grade 2 ('77–'78)	32	32	32	28	21	17	9	—	—	2.1[b]	2.2[b]
Grade 3 ('78–'79)	30	30	30	30	28	26	21	—	—	3.0[c]	3.3[c]
Cohort B											
Grade 1 ('77–'78)	49	30	12	—	—	—	—	1.6[d]	—	—	—
Grade 2 ('78–'79)	36	36	31	23	15	9	1	—	—	2.0[b]	2.1[b]

[a]Raw scores means on Murphy Durrell Test.
[b]Grade equivalent means on Stanford Achievement Test, Primary 1.
[c]Grade equivalent means on Stanford Achievement Test, Primary 2.
[d]Grade equivalent mean on Stanford Early School Achievement Test.

a few weeks) after finishing each even-numbered unit. The numbers of children who had been tested at each level by the end of each year are also shown in Table 13.1.

We have used two basic categories of tasks: oral reading and speed of verbal processing. The oral reading material for each level of Cohort A is of two types. First, there are familiar passages, adapted with minimal change from the children's workbooks and other NRS materials. Second, there are transfer passages, which include sentences that are different from those in the curricular materials. The individual words had generally been included in the curriculum, but with lower frequency of occurrence.

In Cohort B, a subset of the familiar and transfer passages from Cohort A are used again. In addition, Cohort B children also read one familiar test passage from the next test point. Using passages that contain words to which the children have not yet been exposed in the curriculum provides measures of both the degree of reading skill acquisition outside NRS and the degree of improvement on the same passage between levels of NRS. The passages are of differing lengths over levels, reflecting the children's increasing skills. The numbers of words in each level are shown in Table 13.2.

Both oral reading speed and number of reading errors are recorded. In addition, the reading errors are qualitatively analyzed, following the procedure of Hood (1975–76). When possible, errors are also classified according to their graphemic similarity and their contextual appropriateness to the passage words. (In order for an error to be scored on these measures, it has to be an error of commission that can vary on the dimension being measured. Thus, for example, the error of skipping a word cannot be classified for graphemic similarity or contextual appropriateness, and a nonsense error would not be scored for contextual appropriateness but would be scored for graphemic similarity.) These qualitative scoring categories are shown in more detail in Table 13.3.

In addition to oral reading, testing at each level in Cohort A also includes three types of verbal processing tasks: visual, word, and category matching. In

TABLE 13.2
Mean Oral Reading Selection Lengths (Words)

| | Cohort A | | Cohort B | | |
	Familiar	Transfer	Familiar	Transfer	Next Level
Level 2	14 ($n = 4$)	20 ($n = 4$)	13 ($n = 2$)	19 ($n = 2$)	19 ($n = 1$)
4	28 ($n = 4$)	24 ($n = 4$)	29 ($n = 2$)	27 ($n = 2$)	58 ($n = 1$)
6	65 ($n = 4$)	32 ($n = 4$)	58 ($n = 1$)	62 ($n = 1$)	150 ($n = 1$)
8	75 ($n = 2$)	86 ($n = 2$)	150 ($n = 1$)	90 ($n = 1$)	145 ($n = 1$)
10	145 ($n = 1$)	106 ($n = 1$)	145 ($n = 1$)	106 ($n = 1$)	115 ($n = 1$)
12	115 ($n = 1$)	132 ($n = 1$)	115 ($n = 1$)	132 ($n = 1$)	106 ($n = 1$)
14	106 ($n = 1$)	142 ($n = 1$)	106 ($n = 1$)	142 ($n = 1$)	—

TABLE 13.3
Scoring Categories in Oral Reading Error Analysis

Error Type		
0:	*Stop*	—Child makes no response to word in 5 seconds.
1:	*Order*	—Child changes word order ("that man" for *man that*).
2:	*Reversal*	—Change of letters with a word ("was" for *saw*).
3:	*Stem*	—Correct stem, wrong ending ("bats" for *batting*).
4:	*Affix*	—Correct ending, wrong stem ("hitting" for *batting*).
5:	*Substitution*	—Word substituted for another ("hit" for *bat*).
6:	*Insertion*	—Insertion of extra word.
7:	*Omit*	—Word omitted unintentionally.
8:	*Skip*	—Word skipped intentionally.
9:	*Nonsense*	—Nonword said instead of word.

Graphemic Similarity (Applies if error type is 3, 4, 5, or 9)
0: No letters the same between error and word.
1: One letter overlaps.
2: More than one letter but less than 50%.
3: 50% or more letters overlap.

Contextual Appropriateness (Applies if error type is 2, 3, 4, or 5)
0: Error word is totally inappropriate to context.
1: Error word appropriate only in preceding context.
2: Error word appropriate in current sentence only.
3: Error word preserves meaning of text.

visual matching, two letter strings are displayed simultaneously. The upper left corner of the display always contains a word from the vocabulary of the last two levels that the child has completed; the lower right corner displays a string that is either the same or contains two changed letters. When these changes are made, they involve substitution of letters with the same basic shape as the ones being replaced to form a nonword.

In the word-matching task, the experimenter first pronounces a word. The child is then shown a word. The child's task is to decide whether the two words are the same or not. The category-matching task is similar except that the child has to decide whether a visually presented word (e.g., *horse*) is an instance of a category (e.g., *animal*) spoken by the experimenter. The words for both these tasks are chosen from the vocabulary of the last two levels the child has completed.

Each of the matching tasks has 28 trials. Fourteen words are used in each task, each word appearing once in the yes and once in the no conditions. The same words, in different orders, are used in the word and category tasks; a different set is used for the visual task. Six practice trials precede each task. A summary of the verbal processing tasks used in this cohort is shown in Table 13.4.

There are four measures of verbal processing speed in Cohort B: simple reaction time (RT), scanning RT, vocalization latency, and category-matching RT. In the simple RT task, either the word *yes* or the word *no* appears on the

TABLE 13.4
Summary of Verbal Processing Speed Tasks

Task	Yes	No	Cohort
Visual Matching	action–action	action–acfuon	A
Word Matching	"square"–square	"square"–thread	A
Category Matching	"Is this an animal?" horse	"Would you see this in the sky?" horse	A,B
Scanning	n–barn	h–barn	B
Vocalization			B
Simple RT			B

screen, and the child's task is to push the appropriate button as quickly as possible. In the scanning RT task, a letter appears on the screen, and the experimenter names it. Following this, a word replaces the letter on the screen, and the child's task is to decide whether the letter was contained in that word or not. On yes trials, the position of the letter in the word is varied. In the vocalization task, a word appears on the screen, and the child's task is to say that word out loud as quickly as possible. The category-matching RT task is the same as that described for Cohort A. Table 13.4 contains a summary of the verbal processing tasks used in this cohort.

The simple, scanning, and category-matching RT tasks each have 30 trials—15 yes and 15 no—whereas the vocalization task has 15 trials. Six practice trials precede each task. The same 15 words are used in the word RT tasks, each word appearing once each in the yes and no conditions in scanning and category matching. There are three types of words used: 5 from the last two levels of NRS that the child has just completed (familiar words); 5 that the child has either learned decoding rules for or learned as sightwords (transfer words); and 5 from the next two levels in NRS that the child would be starting (next-level words). The next-level words at each test session are always the familiar words at the next test point.

Procedure

Testing is conducted in two sessions on different days except for Levels 8–14 in Cohort A, for which all tasks can usually be given the same day. The oral reading passages are typed in the same type style as was used in the readers for the levels being tested.[2] In the reaction-time tasks, the stimuli are photographed for slides and are projected on a rear projection screen, appearing black against a white background. The opening of the projector's shutter starts a digital clock that stops when the child presses either a yes or no button. Timing is measured to the

---

[2]NRS starts with large, "primary-grades type" and switches to gradually smaller fonts.

nearest millisecond, with estimated overall precision of ±5 msec. The children are instructed to respond as quickly and as accurately as they can.

RESULTS

Changes in Basic Measures Across Levels

The means of the oral reading and verbal processing measures at each level of testing are shown in Table 13.5 (Cohort A) and Table 13.6 (Cohort B).

Oral Reading Speed and Error Rate. As indicated in these tables, both oral reading speed and error rate change as the child advances through the curriculum. Since the level of difficulty of the passages is held relatively constant across test sessions (i.e., the passages contain information that has been introduced only in the latest portion of the curriculum that has been completed), these decreases in reading time and error rate reflect the child's increasing skill in reading.

Within a given level of testing, the type of passage read also affects both oral reading measures. Passages that contain unfamiliar wording (transfer passages) are read with more difficulty than passages containing wording from the curriculum. It is interesting to note that the next-level passages—those that contain words that have not yet been introduced at the time of testing—are not any more difficult than the transfer passages. This may be a function of the design of the NRS curriculum; that is, rules of decoding that will be necessary for learning

TABLE 13.5
Means of Basic Measures at Each Level in Cohort A

| | | | | Level | | | |
	2	4	6	8	10	12	14
n	30	30	29	26	24	24	20
Familiar Passages							
WPM	34	56	73	92	75	96	96
% errors	12%	6%	7%	4%	8%	6%	4%
Transfer Passages							
WPM	24	27	48	49	56	53	76
% errors	18%	18%	13%	10%	9%	10%	9%
Visual Match							
RT	3.23	3.77	2.88	2.52	2.63	2.23	2.09
% errors	6%	9%	6%	3%	6%	2%	9%
Word Match							
RT	2.86	2.57	1.88	1.74	1.83	1.65	1.51
% errors	5%	7%	4%	4%	8%	4%	4%
Category Match							
RT	3.91	3.30	2.68	2.43	2.50	2.13	2.09
% errors	13%	11%	6%	8%	11%	8%	17%

TABLE 13.6
Means of Basic Measures at Each Level in Cohort B

	Level					
	2	4	6	8	10	12
n	36	34	28	20	15	9
Familiar Passages						
WPM	32	65	84	104	84	111
% errors	17%	6%	6%	4%	9%	5%
Transfer Passages						
WPM	29	27	54	66	65	65
% errors	17%	18%	13%	9%	10%	11%
Next-Level Passages						
WPM	30	43	62	60	81	89
% errors	28%	22%	7%	12%	5%	10%
Scanning						
RT	2.24	2.20	2.16	2.01	2.31	2.14
% errors	12%	10%	10%	5%	5%	3%
Category Match						
RT	4.26	3.58	2.96	2.42	2.48	2.52
% errors	24%	24%	22%	16%	21%	26%
Simple						
RT	1.16	.96	.92	.79	.88	.86
% errors	6%	3%	1%	1%	0%	1%
Vocalization						
RT	3.60	2.88	2.63	1.96	2.25	2.28
% errors	23%	32%	38%	18%	23%	32%

words at the next level may be stressed more than those that are not. In any case, a comparison of more interest to the goals of the present study is between the next-level passages at a given level with the familiar passages at the next level (see Table 13.6). Since these materials are the same (e.g., the next-level passage at Level 8 becomes the familiar passage at Level 10), the observed decrease in both reading time and error rate is a good indication of the rapid changes that are occurring in reading skill during the first few years of instruction.

Verbal Processing Speed Measures. Tables 13.5 and 13.6 indicate that whereas accuracy on most of these tasks is quite high, category matching and vocalization in Cohort B are more difficult than the other tasks. Further analyses of these two tasks, breaking them down by the different types of words used (i.e., familiar, transfer, and next level), are being conducted. So far, these analyses show no major pattern differences for different word types, though transfer words are generally harder (i.e., slower RTs and lower accuracy) than familiar and next-level words.

The mean reaction times in Tables 13.5 and 13.6 are for correct responses only and are averaged across yes and no trials. Inspection of these means indicates that processing speed increases across levels on all tasks but two—simple reaction time and scanning. That differences are not found on these tasks is important for several reasons. First, it confirms that changes across levels on the other tasks are not due to global changes in speed of responding. Second, it reassures us that the pattern across levels is not due to the particular words tested, since the same words are used in scanning, category matching, and vocalization within a level in Cohort B; but different words are used in each level. Finally, it indicates that changes in speed of word processing that occur as skill in reading develops are not related to changes in speed of letter processing, since the scanning task would have been sensitive to this factor. This last finding has implications that we consider near the end of this chapter.

Oral Reading Error Analysis. In addition to reading times and error rate, the oral reading task allows us to classify reading errors according to their type and their similarity to the correct word in the passage. This qualitative error classification has been highly reliable: Trained independent scorers agree on error type for 95% of the errors in a sample, on graphemic similarity for 99%, and on contextual appropriateness for 85%.

The mean proportions of errors classified as each type at each level for Cohort A are shown in Table 13.7. In spite of the fact that error rate decreases as

TABLE 13.7
Mean Proportion of Oral Reading Error Types at Each Level in Cohort A

				Level			
	2	*4*	*6*	*8*	*10*	*12*	*14*
Error Type:							
Stop	.17	.14	.02	.09	.02	.06	.07
Order	.02	.00	.00	.00	.01	.00	.01
Reversal	.00	.00	.00	.02	.02	.00	.01
Stem	.11	.09	.12	.11	.21	.27	.07
Affix	.04	.03	.04	.07	.04	.02	.02
Substitution	.47	.61	.54	.47	.46	.41	.49
Insertion	.04	.02	.05	.05	.05	.06	.06
Omit	.07	.03	.10	.09	.06	.10	.09
Skip	.01	.01	.01	.01	.00	.01	.01
Nonsense	.08	.07	.13	.09	.13	.07	.18
Graphemic Similarity:							
None	.07	.13	.20	.14	.17	.08	.10
One Letter	.18	.14	.18	.13	.08	.08	.17
Less than 50%	.04	.09	.13	.15	.07	.06	.04
50% or more	.71	.64	.49	.59	.68	.77	.68
Contextual Appropriateness:							
None	.27	.21	.19	.13	.10	.13	.11
Preceding only	.31	.25	.43	.47	.48	.35	.38
Sentence	.14	.13	.09	.13	.14	.17	.19
Meaning preserved	.28	.41	.30	.27	.28	.36	.33

children progress through the curriculum, the distributions of the types of errors occurring at each level remain quite constant in both cohorts. Substitution of a word that differs from the one in the passage accounts for approximately 50% of the errors made at each level. Order, reversal, and intentional skip errors occur very rarely. The high frequency of substitution errors may be inflated somewhat by the fact that we make no attempt to judge whether the child actually knows the word that is substituted; if the child's utterance is known to be an English word, it is scored as a substitution rather than a nonsense error.

The proportion of errors falling within each category of graphemic similarity seems also to be invariant with test level in both cohorts. The majority of errors made are, from the beginning, very similar visually to the word that appeared in the text. In terms of contextual appropriateness, only one category seems to be affected by level in the curriculum: The proportion of errors that are totally inappropriate to the meaning of the passage decreases as skill in reading increases.

Achievement-Related Differences in Basic Measures Across Levels

Although discussion of the results up to this point has focused on changes that take place in children's oral reading and verbal processing skills as they learn to read, we have also been concerned with finding out whether there are any differences on these measures among children who vary in their later achievement in reading. As a preliminary attempt at addressing this question, we have used the children's most recent reading achievement scores as a basis for classification into three groups—low, medium, and high achievers—and we have looked at the performance of these groups across levels. The achievement scores for Cohort A are from the beginning of third grade, with the following group-mean grade levels in reading: low = 2.2 ($n = 11$); medium = 3.2 ($n = 9$); high = 4.0 ($n = 8$). Scores from the beginning of second grade were used in Cohort B, since these children had not yet had their third-grade tests; and the groups' mean grade levels were : low = 1.5 ($n = 11$); medium = 2.2 ($n = 12$); high = 3.4 ($n = 11$).

Oral Reading Speed and Error Rate.   The means of familiar, transfer, and next-level reading speed across levels for the three ability groups are shown in the left panels of Figs. 13.1 through 13.5. As these figures indicate, reading speed differs widely among the three groups in both cohorts. Also, since error rate in reading and reading speed are not orthogonal factors, similar ability-group differences are found in the proportion of oral reading errors made across levels on each type of passage.

In order to get a better understanding of what these differences in oral reading speed among the ability groups mean, we performed asymptotic regression

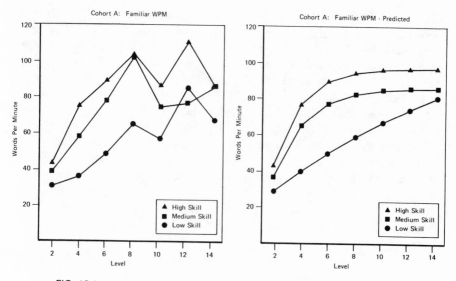

FIG. 13.1.   Actual and predicted means on familiar reading speed by levels and ability groups in Cohort A.

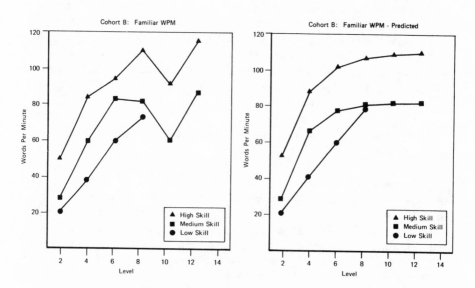

FIG. 13.2.   Actual and predicted means on familiar reading speed by levels and ability groups in Cohort B.

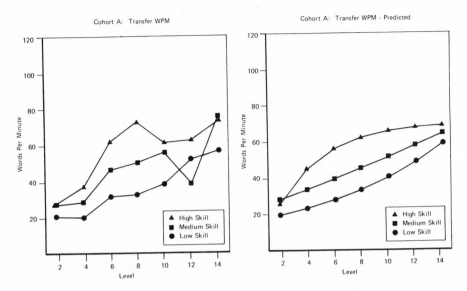

FIG. 13.3. Actual and predicted means on transfer reading speed by levels and ability groups in Cohort A.

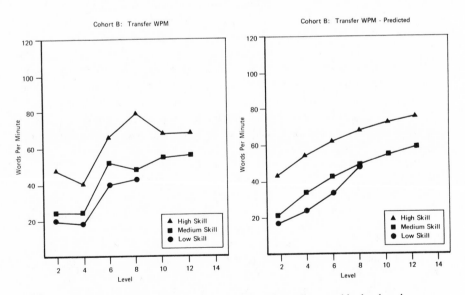

FIG. 13.4. Actual and predicted means on transfer reading speed by levels and ability groups in Cohort B.

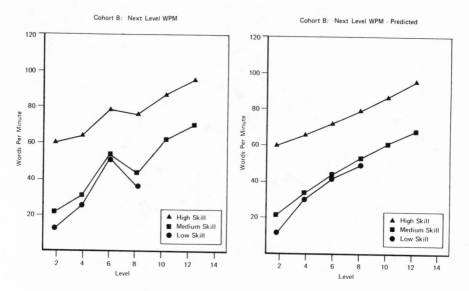

FIG. 13.5.   Actual and predicted means on next-level reading speed by levels and ability groups in Cohort B.

analyses that predicted each group's reading speed (y) at each level (x) by estimating the parameters a, b, and k for the equation $y = a \times bk^x$ (see Suppes, Macken, & Zanotti, 1978, for a related application of this model). The least-squares fits of the regression functions are significant in all cases (ps $< .03$), and the plots of the predicted means at each level for each ability group are shown in the right panels of Figs. 13.1 through 13.5.

The patterns for predicted means on familiar reading speed are strikingly similar in the two cohorts: For low readers, speed increases linearly as the children move through the curriculum ($1.0 > k > .9$), whereas in the medium and high groups, asymptote is reached by the last few levels of testing ($.4 > k > .3$). For transfer passages, low readers in both cohorts continue to make greater gains at each successive level ($1.5 > k > 1.2$), whereas the medium readers show a more linear increase ($1.0 > k > .8$), and the high readers may be showing decreasing gains at later levels ($.7 > k > .6$). Finally, on the next-level passages, both the medium and high readers appear to increase their reading speed in a linear fashion ($1.1 > k > .9$), whereas the low readers are beginning to show decreasing gains between later levels ($k = .6$).

In general, these analyses reveal several interesting differences among the groups. In quantitative terms, oral reading speed during the 1st year of reading instruction has been shown to be predictive of later reading achievement. High-ability readers are faster than medium and low readers initially, and they remain faster throughout their period of primary reading instruction. In fact, this difference in initial rate of processing rather than rate of increase in processing speed seems to be the major difference between medium- and high-skill groups.

In qualitative terms, differences are found between the low-ability group and the medium and high readers. On familiar and transfer passages, although the low group remains slower than the other two, low-skill readers make greater gains in reading speed at later levels of the curriculum than medium and high readers. This is in contrast to the next level of passages, where the gains in reading speed are more similar among the three groups, though the high-ability children are faster at all levels. This suggests that instruction in reading may be

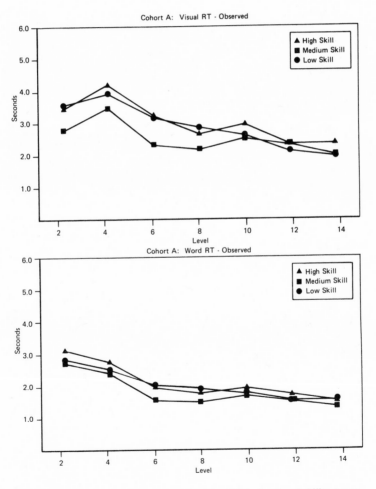

FIG. 13.6.   Means on visual and word-matching RTs by levels and ability groups in Cohort A.

having a differential effect upon the three groups: Whereas it raises oral reading speed to its asymptotic level for medium and high readers at each level, it maintains the rate of gain in reading speed for the low readers, who do not reach asymptote during the period for which we have data.

Verbal Processing Speed Measures.   The means for the reaction-time tasks across levels for the three ability groups are shown in Figs. 13.6 through 13.9. In contrast to the oral reading measures, there is only one task on which processing speed is related to later achievement differences among the groups: vocalization latency. Looking across the various measures, we see all three developmental

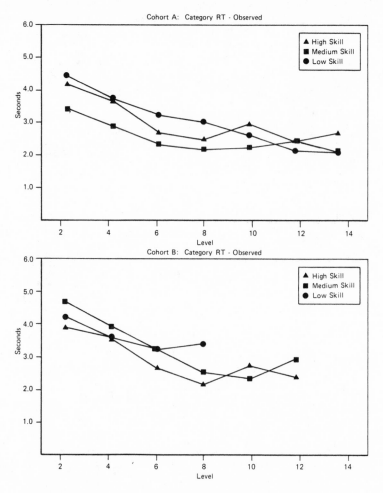

FIG. 13.7.   Means on category-matching RT by levels and ability groups in Cohorts A and B.

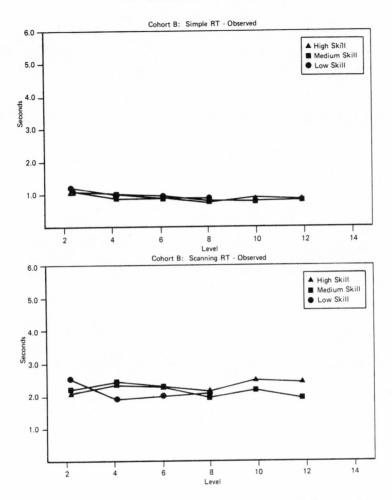

FIG. 13.8. Means on simple and scanning RTs by levels and ability groups in Cohort B.

patterns mentioned in the beginning of the "Method" section. The simple RT and scanning RT tasks (both in Cohort B) show no change over levels. Presumably, these tasks measure performance abilities unaffected by the reading instruction these children received. The visual RT task of Cohort A falls in between this pattern and a second pattern, shown by the word RT task of Cohort A and the category RT task (both cohorts), which show improvement over the course of instruction but no achievement-related differences once level in the curriculum is held constant. Finally, vocalization latency (Cohort B) shows differences that remain even after we allow for differences in rate of progress through the reading curriculum.

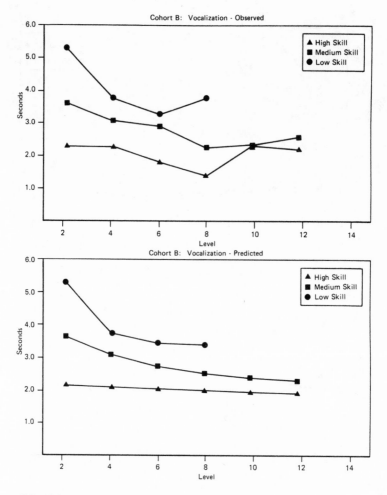

FIG. 13.9. Actual and predicted means on vocalization latency by levels and ability groups in Cohort B.

Asymptotic regression was used again to predict each group's vocalization latency at each level, and the predicted means are shown in Fig. 13.9. Although both initial processing speed and the rate of increase in this speed discriminates among the groups, a more interesting aspect of these data is the fact that all the groups appear to be approaching asymptote by Level 4. The role that instruction plays in the components of reading measured by this task seems confined to maintaining (over progressively larger reading vocabularies) rather than increasing rate of processing.

TABLE 13.8
Mean Proportions of Oral Reading Error Types by Ability Groups

| | Cohort A[a] | | | Cohort B[b] | | |
	Low	Medium	High	Low	Medium	High
Error Type:						
Stop	.08	.05	.09	.09	.11	.10
Order	.00	.00	.01	.00	.01	.00
Reversal	.01	.00	.01	.01	.01	.01
Stem	.11	.16	.12	.07	.09	.10
Affix	.05	.05	.05	.04	.05	.08
Substitution	.52	.53	.46	.48	.50	.53
Insertion	.03	.05	.05	.01	.02	.02
Omit	.04	.07	.16	.03	.02	.04
Skip	.02	.01	.00	.14	.08	.05
Nonsense	.14	.07	.06	.13	.11	.06
Graphemic Similarity:						
None	.13	.12	.16	.09	.08	.12
One Letter	.15	.12	.14	.17	.14	.10
Less than 50%	.11	.09	.04	.06	.05	.01
50% or more	.61	.67	.66	.68	.73	.78
Contextual Appropriateness:						
None	.24	.17	.03	.27	.20	.12
Preceding only	.39	.36	.41	.42	.41	.42
Sentence	.13	.11	.13	.20	.21	.19
Meaning preserved	.24	.36	.43	.11	.18	.27

[a]Collapsed across Levels 2–10.
[b]Collapsed across Levels 2–6.

Oral Reading Error Analysis. The mean proportions of oral reading error types for each ability group are shown in Table 13.8. The pattern of errors across skill groups is similar to that found across levels: Substitution errors are the most frequently occurring errors in all skill groups, and the majority of errors are graphemically similar to the words in the passage. As with successive levels in the curriculum, however, there is a difference among the groups in terms of the categories of contextual appropriateness: As reading level increases, the proportion of errors that preserve the meaning of the text increases, and the proportion of errors that are totally inappropriate to the meaning decreases.

DISCUSSION

In this section, we address a number of issues to which the data just presented are relevant. First, we consider whether the data clarify the nature of the skill(s) that poor readers lack. Then we attempt to specify the specific prerequisite relationship we have observed between those skills and overall reading achievement. Third, we examine the effects of practice for higher- and lower-skilled individuals on word decoding. Fourth, we consider the extent to which there are differences in top-down aspects of processing between higher- and lower-reading-ability children. Finally, we discuss our future plans for the study and some of the developmental issues it raises.

What Differentiates Less Skilled Readers?

A review of the data we just presented shows that less skilled readers are not distinguished from their more skilled fellows by simple choice reaction time or performance on the scanning RT task. On the word RT, category RT, and perhaps the visual RT tasks, the differences between different reading achievement groups are accommodated by their different rates of progress through the reading curriculum. That is, a slower learner shows the same performance on these tasks at a given level as was shown by a faster colleague on that level (some time earlier) on the category-matching task. In contrast, there are substantial differences on the vocalization latency measure and on measures of oral reading speed. There are also differences in the extent to which the oral reading errors of less skilled readers give evidence of contextual constraint on word identification.

Oral Reading Speed.   The oral reading speed analyses merit more detailed consideration. Basically, there is a difference in the shape of the learning curves for the different ability groups. The high and middle groups show the classical learning curve. They experience negatively accelerated growth in reading speed, with major gains from the beginning. The low group shows a much more constant, incremental improvement. One interpretation of the strongly negatively accelerated curve is that there is only a specific, easily learned skill separating the (expected-to-be) average and above-average children from reading facility. When they are taught this skill—specific word recognition rules—they integrate it with other language skills that they already have, and they are then reading with facility.

The poorer readers, in this explanation, show less transfer between learning to read one word and learning to read another. Thus, their progress in acquiring the enabling skill of word recognition is slow and incremental. They do not seem to get a ''critical (apperceptive) mass'' of word recognitions that could allow them to burst into reading expertise. This viewpoint is consistent with soft data on the use of the NRS curriculum with learning-disabled samples (Beck, 1978). There it was found that LD children progress nicely through the individualized program, achieving the specific skills taught and tested by NRS, at a slower but reasonable pace. However, these children do not show the same level of transfer to non-NRS words and sentence forms that normal children would show at the same points in the curriculum.

There is an alternative to the hypothesis that the low group learns much more slowly and with less transfer. This alternative is brought to mind by the classic study of learning in retardates by Zeaman and House (1963). They found that whereas group data showed a lower-than-normal learning rate for the retardates, each individual retardate showed a pattern closer to no learning for a variable number of trials followed by normal learning thereafter. Zeaman and House suggested that the retardates took much longer to notice relevant dimensions of the stimuli, but that once they learned where to focus their attention, they learned at a normal rate. In the same way, it is possible that all of our children show equally rapid reading progress *once they have achieved certain prerequisite skills*. Prior to that point, there would be the appearance of little or no progress in such measures as oral reading speed. Assuming different points in different children for passing the critical hurdle, the slower children, viewed through averaged data, would show about the pattern we have seen. The question is whether the averaging obscures a Zeaman–House type of pattern in some or all of the individual children.

We have examined the individual subject data from Cohort A, where we have 3 years worth of data. The patterns are mixed. Some children show long periods of no progress, followed by normal learning. Others show continual slow learning. Once we have adequate data from Cohort B (where we have the vocalization latency measure), we can examine that data for individual patterns and even see if the point of departure for children with the Zeaman–House pattern is predicted by reaching a particular level of vocalization latency performance.

Vocalization Latency.   Another issue we must consider is the nature of the differences between the more and less successful reading students in the shapes of their "learning curves" for vocalization latency. Comparing the fitted asymptotic curves of Fig. 13.9, it appears that the high-skill subgroup starts out at a fast (i.e., short RT) asymptote or at least gets there very quickly. The middle group also reaches asymptote after a few levels. The low group, however, appears to be heading toward a much different asymptote, not nearly as fast. This result is particularly striking when one realizes that the horizontal axis of the figure is in units of "levels completed," not time. When the data are plotted against "days in school," the effect is to stretch out the low curve relative to the others; that is, the less skilled readers show not only the apparently less proficient asymptotic performance but also move more slowly toward that asymptote. We consider this result in more detail in the section on practice that follows.

How Is Word Recognition Prerequisite to Reading?

The results for vocalization latency and its relationship with reading achievement help to clarify the nature of word recognition as a prerequisite for reading. As discussed earlier, we are not dealing with word recognition as a prerequisite in the sense of needing to be able to recognize words at all. Rather, we need to ask the question: What aspects of reading or of learning how to read work better when access to phonological codes is rapid and efficient?[3]

This leaves us two basic alternatives to consider. One is that some portion of the word vocalization performance will, if slow, make reading difficult. The other is that this performance inefficiency retards the process of *learning to read* but does not render reading itself that difficult once it is learned. The data, at this point, are not yet complete enough to make a final decision about which interpretation is most reasonable. If it should continue to appear that the low-skill children asymptote at a slower vocalization speed but do eventually develop normal reading speed for some materials (e.g., the familiar set), then we would have to say that slow phonological access/processing retards the *acquisition,* but not necessarily the *performance,* of oral reading of text. On the other hand, by definition, the low-skill group is subnormal *after instruction* on whatever it takes to do well on a standard reading achievement test. Consequently, we might argue that children with slow phonological processes are less expert in *performance* of some of the skills tapped by reading achievement tests.

Even this statement requires some hedging. This is because reading achievement tests often include, in their primary grades versions, a number of items that do not measure reading per se, but rather a set of component or prerequisite skills (according to the implicit reading theory of the test designer). We have not yet ruled out the possibility that our low-reading-achievement-score group is low because of specific failures on more artificial phonological code access tasks. However, none of the items in the tests we used were prima facie phonological code access tasks, and we do not—on the basis of anecdotal data—believe that low scorers are low primarily because they are too slow to get to all the items. Ultimate removal of this hedge, though, will depend upon finding, as we accumulate more years of data on the present cohorts, that vocalization latency predicts reading achievement even on levels of the test that include only reading comprehension items.

Issues of Practice

In our study, the words used for RT tasks at each testing point are selected to be in one of three categories (for Cohort A, no "next" words were used). Some are words that are introduced specifically in the last two levels ("familiar" words); some are words that contain symbol–sound correspondences taught in the last two levels ("transfer words"); and some are words that will be introduced in the

---

[3]As there were a significant number of errors by less skilled readers (*inter alia*) on the word vocalization task, it may seem unreasonable for us to claim that even the less skilled readers can do word recognition but just can't do it quickly. However, few of the errors, if any, after Level 2 were associated with *not knowing* a word. Rather, they were produced by the speeded nature of the task.

next level the child enters ("next words"). Significantly, none are words that have been known to the child (assuming that he or she learns the words at school) as reading vocabulary for very long. Thus, we are testing, at every level, words the child has not yet practiced to any great extent.

This creates two plausible situations. One is that we are really giving a variety of transfer task when we give the vocalization latency task. That is, a significant amount of the speed of performance we see in a child may be determined by how much transfer that child experienced from earlier words to the learning of the relatively new words in the test set. The other possibility is that the better readers have amassed more practice on the words being tested and that this is why they are more familiar. This second possibility is depreciated somewhat by the fact that the groups do not differ on the other word-processing RT tasks that use the same words: scanning, visual matching, audiovisual matching, and category matching. Thus, we tentatively conclude that part of the differences we see between higher- and lower-reading-ability children on vocalization latency may reflect transfer of training on earlier words.

It would be interesting also to have data in which a common word set was used at each test occasion, so that scores would be *relatively* uninfluenced by transfer effects. We have something of this sort in the data reported by Curtis (1980). The same words were used at the second-, third-, and fifth-grade levels. Here, then, we have nonlongitudinal data, at mostly higher grade levels, but that speak in part to the issue at hand. Table 13.9 shows the correlations found between various vocalization measures and standardized reading-comprehension test scores (Spache Diagnostic Reading Scales) for different subsets of the Curtis sample.

The most striking finding in the table is that across age levels, word and pseudoword vocalization latencies correlate best with reading comprehension achievement for children whose reading achievement is normal for their grade level, whereas vocalization speeds for real words and even for letters are the best correlates of the three for below-average readers. Here we see some evidence of the nature of the "transfer" effects for better readers. They have acquired word pronunciation knowledge that can be applied even to meaningless letter strings. Presumably, this knowledge facilitates acquisition of new reading vocabulary as well. For the below-average readers, these generative subword pronunciation skills appear not to develop to significant levels. We take the high correlations of letter and real-word vocalization with reading to indicate that below-average readers need to practice and overlearn recognition of all words they are likely to read. The faster they get on familiar material, presumably, the better they will do.

Another finding in the Curtis (1980) data helps us address again the issue of the nature of prerequisites to reading achievement. She performed commonality analyses on the correlations of her various measures with reading comprehension. For both average and below-average readers, the various measures could

TABLE 13.9
Correlations of Reading Comprehension Achievement Test Scores
with Vocalization Latency
(Retabulated from Curtis, 1980)

	Correlation of Reading Comprehension with:		
Subsample	Letter Vocalization	Word Vocalization	Pseudoword Vocalization
Second graders			
(average ability)	.51**	.78**	.54**
Third graders			
(average and below average)	.20	.53**	.44**
Fifth graders			
(average and below average)	.26*	.45**	.47**
Average			
(second and third grades)	.39**	.71**	.56**
Average			
(third and fifth grades)	.26*	.37**	.52**
Below average			
(third and fifth grades)	.66**	.50**	.19

*$p < .05$.
**$p < .01$.

account for about 67% of the variance in the reading scores. However, the patterns of correlation varied. For the below-average readers, word-matching speed, letter vocalization, and listening comprehension uniquely accounted for 0% to 3% each of the reading comprehension variance. Sixty percent was accounted for by variance common to all the tasks. For the third- and fifth-grade average readers, listening comprehension and pseudoword vocalization uniquely accounted for 28% and 7%, respectively, and commonly accounted for another 33%.

The appearance is of a diffuse general factor underlying the performance of the less successful readers, with general comprehension skills (measured in the listening task) and generative decoding/phonological access skills (measured by pseudoword vocalization latency) making very little independent contribution. All of these findings, of course, will benefit from additional data, such as a 3- or 4-year pattern in individual children on the growth of efficient word access skills.

Are Good Readers Playing a Better Guessing Game?

We turn now to the data on oral reading error patterns. Turning again to Table 13.8, we see that children in our three ability groups did not differ in the extent to which their oral reading errors betrayed sensitivity to the letter patterns in the words they were reading. On the other hand, they did differ in the extent to which their error words fit the context in which they were inserted. It is part of the lore of reading instruction that poor readers in phonics curricula have too much of their attention drawn to the graphemic nature of words and consequently ignore meaning. The present results are only partly consistent with that claim and suggest an alternative viewpoint.

If the less skilled readers were paying excessive attention to the specific visual input at the cost of context information, we would expect to see them being *more* sensitive than skilled readers to graphemic content. That is, they would err by missing one or two graphemes of a word, perhaps even ending up with a nonsense utterance. However, when we look at Table 13.8, we do not find this happening. The poor readers do not show significantly more sensitivity to graphemic information. Nor are there ability group differences in nonsense errors after Level 2. Also, the children are showing sensitivity to context in 75% of their errors.

This means that after the first half of first grade, there is no evidence to substantiate any strong claim that children having trouble learning to read will, if taught in a phonics-loaded program, become "word callers." If the less skilled children were paying *excessive* attention to graphemics at the expense of semantics, they would, presumably, be more likely to call out nonsense syllables while decoding; but they are not, after the first months of school, and they never have nonsense rates of even 20%. The data, as a whole, are much more supportive of the claim that slow decoding means that more cognitive capacity is *required* for words to be recognized, not that poor readers *choose* to allocate more capacity to this task (Perfetti & Roth, Chap. 11, this volume).

Future Plans for This Study

We have recently added two more cohorts to this study in hopes of further clarifying the trade-off between inefficient decoding and sensitivity to context. In one cohort, we are testing children in a curriculum with less phonics emphasis—that is, a standard basal series. They are receiving the same type of testing as Cohort B, though they started first grade a year later. We have matched a new set of test materials to their curriculum so that both cohorts have equivalence in the frequency and recency of test words in the child's in-school reading experience. Thus, in another year, we will be able to answer the comparative question: Does a less phonics-oriented curriculum produce less naive word calling and/or greater sensitivity to context in the less able children?

More important, the cross-curricular comparisons allow us to understand better the data relating phonological access speed to reading ability. The vocalization task, after all, is pretty similar to some of the activities one might observe in a phonics classroom. It could be that the ability differences reflect differences in a skill that is prerequisite only to learning how to read in such a curriculum. On the other hand, if effects of similar pattern and magnitude are found in a very different curriculum, we will have greater reason to believe that phonological processing speed is not a curriculum-specific prerequisite for becoming a good reader.

Our other new cohort contains NRS children who, in addition to being tested on the same tasks as in Cohort B, are tested on sentence and paragraph comprehension tasks. In the sentence task the child has to read a sentence and decide whether it answered a question that has just been asked by the experimenter. The paragraph task is similar except that the child has to read a three-sentence paragraph and decide whether it answers the question.

The sentences and paragraphs contain words from the levels that are being tested, and their structure is derived from Kintsch's (1974) propositional system (see Turner & Greene, 1977). In particular, each sentence in both tasks consists of a single proposition that expresses a case, quality, or locative relation. The questions are similarly structured except that an interrogative is used in place of one of the concepts. On yes trials in both tasks, the concepts in both the question and a sentence are the same, and the interrogative can be replaced by the extra concept in the sentence. On no trials, the concepts in the questions and sentence(s) are not the same. If, as Perfetti and Lesgold (1979) claim, inefficient, attention-demanding decoding skills destroy part of the top-down aspects of reading, performance on these tasks should be highly correlated with performance on the vocalization task.

Developmental Issues.   There are two major developmental issues that still need further study—and further data. First, there is the question of the exact nature of the developmental trajectories at which the present data hint. We need to see how completely the curriculum continues to produce equal performance, at different rates, on all but the vocalization latency word-processing task. More important, we need to verify that the apparent asymptote difference in vocalization latency between high- and low-reading achievers is sustained when children are classified on higher-grade reading tests (with a larger comprehension component) and when more data are available for the later levels of the curriculum.

The second issue to be undertaken in the future is the extent to which our stratified but still group data accurately reflect the progress and prospects of the individual children in the various ability groups. We have hinted at one sort of individual variability. Another that appears to be present on very cursory examination involves visual tasks (scanning and visual matching) in comparison to verbal tasks (category and word matching). There is a subgroup of children for whom the general pattern of similar RTs on the two task types does not hold. These children start out with slow visual processing, which approaches the verbal processing rate in later testings. We have yet to verify the extent or meaning of these findings. More generally, we have yet to examine, on a child-by-child basis, the relationship between time at which facility on speeded tasks is reached and the shape of the oral reading trajectories. Thus, we have a substantial task left before the results hinted at in this chapter are complete and verified.

ACKNOWLEDGMENTS

This chapter reports a project in which we have collaborated at length with Isabel Beck and Lauren Resnick. In addition, Deborah Silberblatt, Hope Cordonier, Steven Roth, Andrea Mudd-Rudolph, Albert Petrush, and Harriet Baum have played active roles in this work. Finally, the schools in which we conducted the study, though anonymous in this report, deserve our gratitude for their extreme cooperation. The work was funded by the Learning Research and Development Center through funds granted by the National Institute of Education, which does not necessarily endorse the content of this report.

REFERENCES

Barron, R. W. Reading skill and phonological coding in lexical access. In M. M. Gruneberg, P. E. Morris, & R. N. Sykes (Eds.), *Practical aspects of memory*. London: Academic Press, 1978.

Beck, I. L. Personal communication, 1978.

Beck, I. L., & Mitroff, D. D. *The rationale and design of a primary grades reading system for an individualized classroom*. (Technical Report 1972/4) Pittsburgh, Pa.: University of Pittsburgh, Learning Research and Development Center, 1972.

Bouma, H., & Legein, C. P. Foveal and parafoveal recognition of letters and words by dyslexics and by average readers. *Neuropsychologia*, 1977, *15*, 69–80.

Bradshaw, J. L. Three interrelated problems in reading: A review. *Memory & Cognition*, 1975, *3*, 123–134.

Connors, C. K. Cortical visual evoked response in children with learning disorders. *Psychophysiology*, 1970, *7*, 418–428.

Curtis, M. E. Development of components of reading skill. *Journal of Educational Psychology*, 1980, *72*, 656–669.

Frederiksen, J. R. Assessment of perceptual, decoding, and lexical skills and their relation to reading proficiency. In A. M. Lesgold, J. W. Pellegrino, S. D. Fokkema, & R. Glaser (Eds.), *Cognitive psychology and instruction*. New York: Plenum, 1978. (a).

Frederiksen, J. R. *A chronometric study of component skills in reading* (Tech. Rep. 2). Cambridge, Mass.: Bolt, Beranek, and Newman, 1978. (b)

Gagne, R. M. The acquisition of knowledge. *Psychological Review*. 1962, *69*, 355–365.

Gagne, R. M. *The conditions of learning*. New York: Holt, Rinehart & Winston, 1965.

Gagne, R. M. Learning hierarchies. *Educational Psychologist*, 1968, *6*, 1–9.

Hogaboam, T., & Perfetti, C. A. Reading skill and the role of verbal experience. *Journal of Educational Psychology*, 1978, *70*, 5, 717–729.

Hood, J. Qualitative analysis of oral reading errors: The inter-judge reliability of scores. *Reading Research Quarterly*, 1975-76, *11*, 577–598.

Jackson, M. D., & McClelland, J. J. Processing determinants of reading speed. *Journal of Experimental Psychology: General*, 1979, *108*, 151–181.

Jorm, A. F. The cognitive and neurological bases of developmental dyslexia: A theoretical framework and review. *Cognition*, 1979, *7*, 19–33.

Kintsch, W. *The representation of meaning in memory*. Hillsdale, N.J.: Lawrence Erlbaum Associates, 1974.

Lesgold, A. M., & Perfetti, C. A. Interactive processes in reading comprehension. *Discourse Processes*, 1978, *1*, 323–336.

Perfetti, C. A., & Hogaboam, T. W. The relationship between single word decoding and reading comprehension skill. *Journal of Educational Psychology*, 1975, *67*, 4, 461–469.

Perfetti, C. A., & Lesgold, A. M. Discourse comprehension and sources of individual differences.

In M. Just & P. Carpenter (Eds.), *Cognitive processes in comprehension.* Hillsdale, N.J.: Lawrence Erlbaum Associates, 1977.

Perfetti, C. A., & Lesgold, A. M. Coding and comprehension in skilled early reading. In L. B. Resnick & P. Weaver (Eds.), *Theory and practice in early reading.* Hillsdale, N.J.: Lawrence Erlbaum Associates, 1979.

Preston, M. S., Guthrie, J. T., & Childs, B. Visual evoked responses (VERs) in normal and disabled readers. *Psychophysiology,* 1974, *11,* 452–457.

Preston, M. S., Guthrie, J. T., Kirsch, I., Gertman, D., & Childs, B. VERs in normal and disabled adult readers. *Psychophysiology,* 1977, *146,* 8–14.

Resnick, L. B. Hierarchies in children's learning: A symposium. *Instructional Science,* 1973, *2,* 311–362.

Resnick, L. B., Wang, M. C., & Kaplan, J. Task analysis and curriculum design: A hierarchically sequenced introductory mathematics curriculum. *Journal of Applied Behavior Analysis,* 1973, *6,* 679–710.

Suppes, P., Macken, E., & Zanotti, M. The role of global psychological models in instructional psychology. In R. Glaser (Ed.), *Advances in instructional psychology* (Vol. 1). Hillsdale, N.J.: Lawrence Erlbaum Associates, 1978.

Symann-Louett, N., Gascon, G. G., Matsumiya, Y., & Lombroso, C. T. Wave form difference in visual evoked responses between normal and reading disabled children. *Neuropsychologica,* 1977, *27,* 156–159.

Turner, A., & Greene, E. *The construction and use of propositional text base.* (Tech. Rep. 63). Boulder, Colo.: Institute for the Study of Intellectual Behavior, University of Colorado, 1977.

Vellutino, F. R. Alternative conceptualizations of dyslexia: Evidence in support of a verbal-deficit hypothesis. *Harvard Educational Review,* 1977, *47,* 334–354.

Wernicke, C. *Der aphasische symptomenkomplex.* Breslau: Cohn and Wiegert, 1874.

Wernicke, C. The symptom complex of aphasia. In R. S. Cohen & M. W. Wartofsky (Eds.), *Boston studies in the philosophy of science* (Vol. 4). Dordrecht: Reidel, 1966.

Zeaman, D., & House, B. J. The role of attention in retardate discrimination learning. In N. R. Ellis (Ed.), *Handbook of mental deficiency: Psychological theory and research.* New York: McGraw-Hill, 1963.

14   Sources of Process Interactions in Reading

John R. Frederiksen
Bolt Beranek and Newman Inc.

Readers process and decode words and phrases in context, not in isolation. They interpret words as lexical units that are referentially related to earlier text elements. They build propositional structures for sentences in the light of previous structures they have built in reading earlier text. They are sensitive to the cohesive elements of a text and are influenced by the author's staging of references to one idea or another.

This rendition of reading is a statement of an interactionist theory of reading (cf. Rumelhart, 1977). It assumes that decoding of orthographic forms and interpretation of lexical categories take place under the control of a discourse context. The "bottom-up" processing of information from the printed page is integrated with the "top-down" processing that proceeds from prior meaning to the discovery of future meaning. We undertake an analysis of how such processes interact once our general view of components of reading has been presented.

The view of reading ability we espouse is a pluralistic one: Skilled reading is, we believe, a result of the successful acquisition of a number of highly automatic, component processes that operate together in an integrated and mutually facilitative manner. If the human central nervous system has any one salient characteristic, it is an extremely large capacity for storing information—and procedures for processing information. Yet a second, all too familiar characteristic of human cognition is the limitation in processing capacity that is revealed whenever one is required to perform two or more information-processing tasks simultaneously. Studies of dual-task performance have shown, however, that with practice, a controlled, resource-limited process can become in effect an automatic, data-limited process (Norman & Bobrow, 1975; Shiffrin &

Schneider, 1977). Moreover, such an automatic process does not degrade performance on some other task with which it is performed concurrently. Given the large storage capacity available, there is clearly great potential for a learner to develop automatic skills for handling a variety of information-processing tasks. And these automated skills will enable the learner, with practice, to meet the simultaneous processing demands of complex tasks, such as reading, that draw upon those skills. Skilled reading may, in effect, represent the culmination point in the development of a powerful multiprocessor that can simultaneously analyze word structure, make lexical identifications, and process discourse structures and do all this in an integrated fashion.

The ONR-sponsored research project on which I report represents our attempt to identify component skills involved in reading. The domain of our inquiry includes processing of information that takes place: (1) in decoding the printed word, (2) in analyzing and comprehending text (or discourse), and (3) in integrating contextual and perceptual information in encoding words and phrases (see Fig. 14.1). Within these three general domains of processing, sets of component processes are distinguished: *Word analysis processes* deal with the perception of multiletter "chunks" (such as *sh, ou, able, ing,*), with the translation of graphemic units to the phonological units of speech, and with the retrieval of appropriate lexical categories. *Discourse analysis processes* are those employed in retrieving and integrating word meanings, in comprehending the basic propositions underlying sentences, in tying concepts in a given sentence with those in previous sentences, and in inferring additional facts or events that are not explicitly presented in a text but that are nonetheless a part of the underlying meaning to be comprehended. *Integrative processes* are those that permit a reader to use information from perceptual sources in conjunction with information derived from comprehension of prior text to encode subsequent words and phrases efficiently. Integrative processes operate on two conceptually distinct data bases (e.g., the orthographic and semantic/conceptual bases) that are themselves developed as a result of prior (or concurrent) information processing (e.g., word analysis or discourse processing). Their effect is: (1) to reduce the level of word analysis required for lexical retrieval; and (2) when successful, to increase confidence in the text model that is providing the basis for extrapolations to upcoming text.

Within the framework of the componential analysis of reading, three types of process interaction are discussed:

1. Botton-Up Processing Interactions. The manner of, or efficiency in, processing information at one level may influence processing of information at a higher level. Illustrations include effects of perceptual skills on manner of orthographic decoding and lexical retrieval.

2. Top-Down Processing Interactions. Availability of information concerning discourse context influences the depth and character of word analysis (decod-

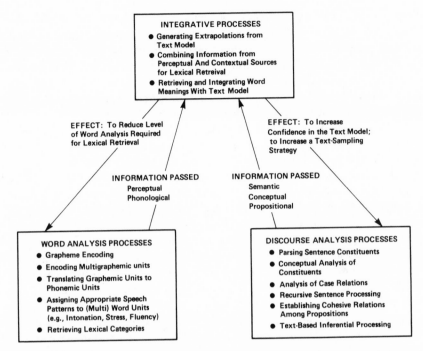

FIG. 14.1.   Categories of reading processes and the nature of their interactions.

ing), methods for lexical retrieval, and size of units in encoding text. A second example (which is not discussed here) might be the effects of macropropositions or text schema on the manner in which propositions are encoded from individual sentences within a text (cf. Anderson, Reynolds, Schallert, & Goetz, 1976).

3. Sequential Interactions in Text Processing.   Although it is obvious that processing of prior text conditions the conceptual analysis of subsequent text, the investigation of rules used by readers in understanding the various cohesive forms of English is in its infancy. Studies of the effects of staging, topicalization, syntactic form, number of available referents, and other text variables on subjects' performance in comprehending anaphoric reference, which have led to a tentative set of rules that appear to be used by readers in assigning text referents, are presented.

PERCEPTUAL SKILLS AND LEXICAL RETRIEVAL

Rather than treating word identification as a unitary skill having a single, measurable level of automaticity, we have attempted to identify separate components representing perceptual and linguistic subprocesses (Frederiksen, 1977,

1979). The linguistic process—phonemic translation of orthographic information—is measured by studying subjects' vocalization latencies in pronouncing pseudowords—that is, orthographically regular nonwords that vary in complexity (length, syllabic structure, types of vowels, etc.). To identify the perceptual component of word analysis, we have endeavored to show that good and poor readers differ in their ability to encode letter patterns that are orthographically regular in English, but that may have a relatively low frequency of occurrence (Frederiksen, 1978).

The task we employed allowed us to measure the relative processing times a reader requires in encoding common letter pairs (such as *sh*) and less common letter pairs (such as *lk*), all of which actually occur within English words. In the bigram identification task, the subject was shown a four-letter array that was preceded and followed by a four-character masking pattern. The actual stimulus array varied from trial to trial: On a third of the trials, the stimulus items were familiar English words, whereas on the remaining trials, the items were presented with two letters continuously masked so that only a single pair of adjacent letters (a bigram) was visible (e.g., *sh, ab,* or *th*). The bigrams were chosen so as to differ in location within the item and in their frequency of occurrence in English prose (Mayzner & Tresselt, 1965). In all cases, the subject's task was to report all the letters that he or she could see, as quickly and accurately as possible. This task was a perceptually difficult one, since the stimulus exposure allowed only 90 to 100 msec prior to the onset of the masking stimulus. The subjects were 48 high school students, divided into subclasses on the basis of scores on the Nelson–Denny Reading Test. The Nelson–Denny test consists of three sections: a vocabulary test, a timed reading passage, and a series of passages followed by comprehension questions. The total score is determined by adding together the vocabulary and comprehension scores. Four subclasses were defined on the basis of total scores. These were: (1) ≤ 40th percentile; (2) 41–85th percentile; (3) 86–97th percentile; and (4) 98 and 99th percentiles. There were 12 subjects in each group.

The results show us that subjects of high and low reading ability differ in their sensitivity to redundancy built into an orthographic array. Subjects' response times in encoding low- and high-frequency bigrams are shown in Fig. 14.2. We are particularly interested in the increment in RT as we go from high-frequency to low-frequency bigram units. The magnitude of this RT difference is greater for the poorest readers than for the proficient readers, and falls at intermediate levels for the middle groups of readers. Thus, whereas high-ability readers are capable of efficiently processing orthographically regular letter groups that occur in English, whatever their actual frequency of occurrence, low-ability readers' efficiency in identifying such letter groups is limited to only those letter groups that frequently occur within the words of the language.

A second task we have studied allowed us to corroborate our identification of this perceptual skill component. In this task subjects were presented with a

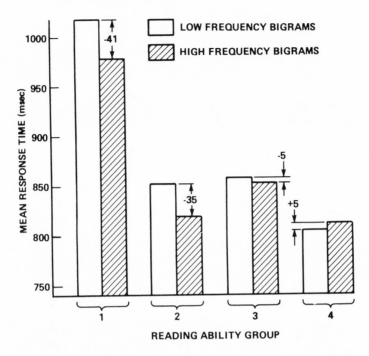

FIG. 14.2.   Mean response latency for reporting bigrams that vary in their frequency of occurrence within English words. Results are plotted for each of four reading ability groups.

briefly exposed four-letter stimulus array, followed by a masking field.[1] Stimuli were either high-frequency words such as *salt* or *this*, pseudowords such as *etma* or *vige*, or unpronounceable nonword anagrams such as *rtnu* or *tbda*. Stimuli were presented for durations ranging from 6 to 50 msec, and for each subject, we measured the number of correctly reported letters for each exposure duration and stimulus type. The subjects were 20 high school students, classified according to reading ability as before, this time with 5 subjects per group. The results for a typical subject are shown in Fig. 14.3. A logit transformation of Pr(correct) yields a linear plot (a logistic function) with two parameters: a location parameter—representing the duration required to get 50% correct; and a slope parameter—representing the rate of growth in encoded information (measured in logit units per unit time). Interestingly, though there were no differences among groups of good and poor readers in the values of the location parameter, there were marked differences in the values of the slope parameter. These differences in slopes for pseudowords and nonword anagrams are shown in Fig. 14.4. Of

---

[1]This experiment was carried out in collaboration with Marilyn Adams.

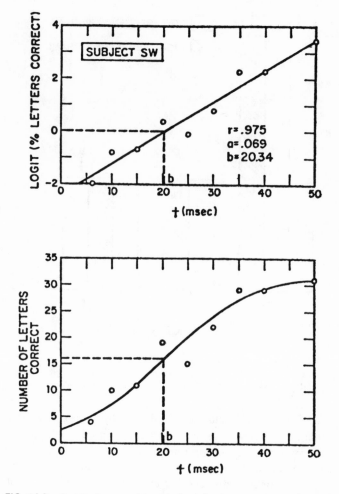

FIG. 14.3. Results for one subject obtained for the anagram experiment. Raw numbers of letters correct are plotted at the bottom for each exposure time. The logit transformations for the same data are shown at the top, along with least-squares estimates of the slope (*a*) and *x*-intercept (*b*). The correlation (*r*) here was .975.

particular importance here is the degree to which good and poor readers are, in their perceptual encoding, sensitive to the presence of orthographically regular multiletter units of which pseudowords are composed. Good readers showed an increase in encoding rate of .032 logits/msec when pseudowords were substituted for nonword anagrams, whereas poor readers showed an increase of only .010 logits/msec. Thus, only the better readers showed an ability to profit from orthographic regularity in encoding sets of letters. These were also the readers, we

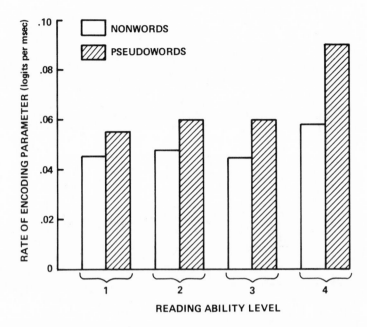

FIG. 14.4.   Mean values of the slope (rate of encoding) parameter for nonword anagrams and pseudowords, plotted separately for four reading ability groups.

have seen, who showed an ability to recognize efficiently multiletter units covering a wide band of frequencies, including presumably those of which our pseudowords were composed.

Having established that there are good–poor reader differences in encoding of multiletter perceptual units, the question at issue is: What are the effects of this perceptual skill on a reader's subsequent decoding of orthographically regular words or pseudowords? We assume, as we have illustrated in Fig. 14.5, that word analysis processes operate in a cascading fashion (McClelland, 1978), with higher-level processes of phonemic decoding and lexical retrieval operating, from the outset, with the information available to them. As information pertaining to the presence of multiletter orthographic units becomes available, decoding can proceed on the basis of those units; if such units are not identified, decoding must be carried out on the basis of single-letter patterns. Likewise, lexical retrieval can be based upon visual feature characterizations, encoded letters or multiletter units, or phonological representations, depending on the speed with which the earlier encoding processes are carried out and on the accessibility of the lexical category in memory. Here we have an example of process interaction by virtue of interlocking data bases. The operation of one process (perceptual encoding) alters the data base for a second process (translation) and may render it more (or less) efficient.

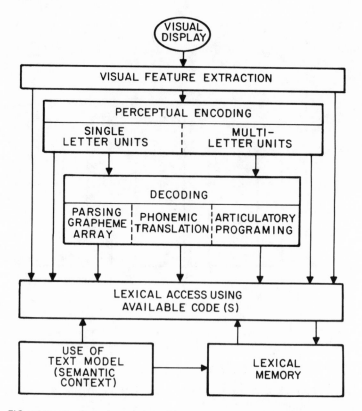

FIG. 14.5. A schematic rendering of the processing model representing component skills in reading. The diagram is meant to illustrate the notion of parallel inputs from lower-level to higher-level processes and from higher levels to lower levels of analysis.

The conception of a series of cascading processing stages allows us to make specific predictions about skill interactions among components. Decoding from single letters involves a complex series of rules acquired over several years of initial reading instruction (cf. Venezky, 1970). Decoding based upon a set of multiletter units that have relatively invariant pronunciations involves much simpler rules and can proceed more quickly. Our first prediction, then, is that good readers, who are proficient at perceiving multiletter units, will not only decode pseudowords more quickly but will also show smaller increments in decoding time as difficulty of decoding is increased. This prediction received support. In Fig. 14.6 we have plotted, for pseudowords, the mean decoding times for 12 readers in each of 4 ability groups (the total number of subjects was, in this case, 48) along with their increments in decoding times when stimuli were lengthened from four to six letters. In each case, low-ability readers show less efficient decoding than do high-ability readers. The association between decoding effi-

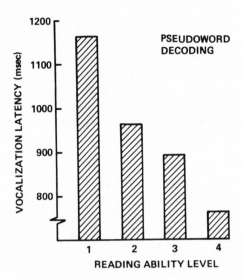

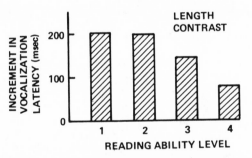

FIG. 14.6. Measures of decoding efficiency are plotted here for subjects representing four reading ability levels. The measure plotted at the top is the mean pseudoword vocalization latency; at the bottom is plotted the mean increment in vocalization latency as pseudoword length is increased from four to six letters.

ciency and the perceptual ability to encode multiletter units can be evaluated by looking at intercorrelations between length effects in decoding pseudowords, reading ability level, and skill in perceiving multiletter units, as measured in the bigram experiment. The correlation between the perceptual ability (the bigram effect) and decoding efficiency (the increment in latency for each added letter) was significant ($r = .27$, $p < .05$). And the correlation did not drop appreciably when general reading ability was partialed out ($r = .21$ in that case). Thus, decoding appears to proceed more efficiently when the perceptual units are letter groups rather than individual letters.

A second prediction from our conception of a series of cascading processes deals with the accessibility of words in the internal lexicon. The most salient variable indicative of lexical accessibility is, of course, word frequency. Our prediction is that orthographic decoding, as indexed by the predictability of vocalization latencies for words from those for pseudowords having comparable orthographic form, will be more in evidence for low-frequency words, which are less accessible and thus processed to greater depth, than for high-frequency words, which are more accessible and thus processed to lesser depth. For each subject, we correlated pseudoword-decoding latencies with those for words that were matched in orthographic form (length, syllabic structure, vowel type, and initial phoneme). The mean correlations are shown in Fig. 14.7 for two reading ability groups (Levels 1 and 4). The evidence shows that all groups of readers do utilize processes of orthographic analysis in recognizing words as well as in pronouncing pseudowords; the mean correlation for words and pseudowords matched in orthographic form was .37 and was significant ($p < .001$). However, it is only the high-ability readers who were able to reduce substantially their degree of word analysis processing when the stimulus word was of high frequency. These data show us how differences in the involvement of the higher-level word analysis processes are determined, for skilled readers, by differences in the accessibility of lexical items in memory.

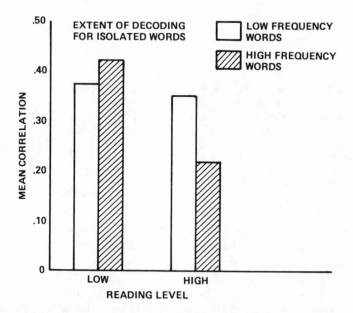

FIG. 14.7.   A measure of the extent of decoding for isolated words is plotted for readers in the bottom and top ability groups. The depth of decoding measure is the correlation of pseudoword vocalization latencies (for pseudowords varying in length, syllabic structure, and type of vowel) with latencies for words having matching orthographic structure.

CONTEXT EFFECTS ON LEXICAL DECODING AND RETRIEVAL

The next experiment (Frederiksen, 1978) I describe was aimed at uncovering the characteristic ways in which readers integrate information derived from context with that from the printed page as they identify words in a text. Readers of high and low ability were asked to pronounce target words that were either tightly or loosely constrained by a prior context sentence. Consider, for example, the following sentence in which the final word has been omitted:

1. I reminded her gently that this was something that she really should not
_____.

This sentence provides a context for a target word, which could be any one of a number of possibilities: *buy, do, take, see, read, tell*, etc. Look now at a second sentence:

2. Grandmother called the children over to the sofa because she had quite a story to _____.

Here, there are only a few words that might fit the sentence: *tell, relate, present*, and the like. In our experiment, we were interested in how readers use the weak context (as in the first sentence) or the strong context (as in the second) in decoding and identifying a final target word. The constraining power of a context was scaled by presenting sentences such as (1) and (2) as free-response cloze items. Subjects read each sentence stem and wrote down all the words they could think of that fit the sentence context. We then counted the total number of separate words that the subjects as a group were able to generate for each context; we termed this value the *domain size*. Domain sizes were approximately 15 items for the weak contexts and 8 for the strong contexts.

The subjects in this experiment were 20 high school students chosen to represent a wide range of reading ability levels. As before, readers were classified into 4 groups of 5 on the basis of scores on the Nelson–Denny Reading Test. The subjects first read a context sentence. They then pressed a button and were shown the target word, which they were required to pronounce. Our response measure was their latency in pronouncing the target word, measured from the onset of the target. The priming effect of context was then the RT for reading words in context subtracted from that for similar words presented in isolation. Some of the key findings are presented in Fig. 14.8, in which we have plotted the decrease in vocalization latency from a no-context control condition when strongly or weakly constraining contexts were provided. Data are plotted here for the top and bottom reading ability groups.

All subjects showed a large priming effect for highly constraining contexts (shown at the top), with a smaller priming effect for weakly constraining contexts (shown at the bottom). However, it is the differential effect of context for high- and low-frequency test words that provides the most information about processes for context utilization. Low-ability readers appeared to employ a controlled, serial process for generating contextually relevant lexical items to test against perceptual evidence when the final word appeared. Their performance improved

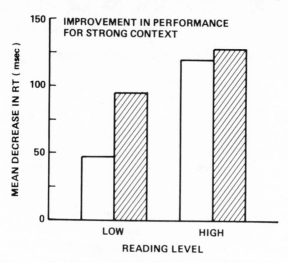

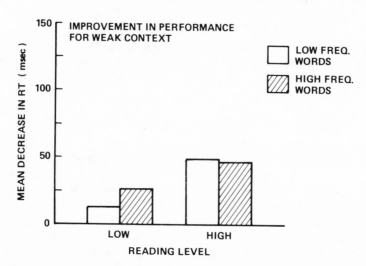

FIG. 14.8.   Effects of sentence context on word-naming latencies. Contexts varied in degree of constraint, and target words varied in frequency. Results are presented for readers in the bottom and top ability groups.

with the addition of a context sentence, but only when the context was strongly constraining. Even then, the only extensive improvement was when the target word was a high-probability word (such as *back*) that was the first one they would be likely to guess. Context was of little help to this group of readers when the target item was an uncommon word, such as *buns,* and higher-probability options existed for them, such as *rolls.* "Good" readers, on the other hand, appeared to have available a parallel, automatic process for facilitating the identification of contextually relevant lexical items. This process operated for them even when the context pointed to a large set or domain of items, and the degree of facilitation due to context was no different for high- or low-probability words within the context-relevant domain. We note that Stanovich and West (in press) have manipulated ease of word decoding and found evidence for a rapid, automatic, spreading activation process for contextual facilitation that leads to a priming of contextually relevant words, with no inhibitory effects on contextually inappropriate words. When the stimulus was degraded and recognition times increased, there was evidence for a controlled, attentional process for memory search (cf. Posner & Snyder, 1975a, 1975b) that had, as well as a facilitative effect, an inhibitory effect on recognition of contextually inappropriate, unexpected words. Our results show that when one examines separately the performance of good and poor readers, similar differences are found in the processing of high- and low-frequency words. Good and poor readers appear to differ in the extent to which the automatic, spreading activation mechanism has supplanted the controlled search process as the mechanism for contextual influence. We note also that it is the existence of an automatic process that allows for substantial effects of context in good readers, even when the context is a weak one.

In addition to evaluating the overall ability of readers to utilize context in recognizing words, we were interested in how readers would reduce their reliance on bottom-up word analysis processes when they were reading words as part of a sentence. To this end, we employed our measure of the depth or degree of orthographic decoding in reading. As before, we used the subjects' onset RTs in pronouncing pseudowords made up of a variety of orthographic forms (varying in length, number of syllables, type of vowel, etc.) as a measure of their difficulty in decoding those forms. Reading times for words (having the same variety of forms) were then correlated for each individual subject with decoding times for the corresponding pseudowords. Our notion was that if decoding activity continues in the processing of words in context, we would find this to be a high correlation, since whether it is dealing with words or pseudowords, the decoder will have the same degree of difficulty with each of the orthographic forms it is processing. If decoding is not employed, then we could expect to find a correlation of zero.

In Fig. 14.9 we have plotted the means of these individual correlations for each context condition. The provision of context brings about a reduction in depth of processing, and this is particularly evident when the context sentence

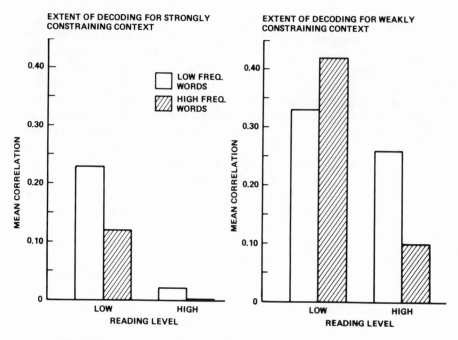

FIG. 14.9.   Measures of the extent of decoding when words are presented in strongly or weakly constraining context. The depth of decoding measure is described under Fig. 14.7.

strongly constrains the missing word. Here, word analysis can be said to proceed to lesser depth, or perhaps to the same depth on fewer occasions. The poor readers, who show the lowest skill levels in decoding, are also the ones who appear to be the least able to reduce their dependence on their inefficient decoding skills when context is provided. For the strong readers, however, contextual information is traded off against effort expended at orthographic analysis. Indeed, when these readers are presented high-frequency words in a highly constraining context, they appear to be able to circumvent completely the use of a decoder ($r = 0.$). The reader differences we have found in depth of decoding in the presence of context are similar to those postulated by Perfetti and Roth, in this volume, for their third hypothetical individual.

In summary, then, readers—depending on their ability—appear to be capable of reducing their reliance on orthographic decoding processes when contextual information—along with visual information—is available for making lexical identifications. The general finding that information pertaining to likelihood (frequency) of a lexical category and that derived from context both influence recognition latencies is compatible with either a logogen theory (Morton, 1969) or a spreading activation theory (Collins & Loftus, 1975). However, neither of these views represents fully the differences between good and poor readers in the lexical domain (or scope) of context effects. Neither view gives adequate consideration to the differences shown by these groups of readers in what we have called automaticity of context effects. And neither viewpoint fully captures the effect of integrative processes on depth of orthographic decoding. These latter findings are more consistent with the notion of concurrent—and interacting—top-down and bottom-up processes suggested by Rumelhart (1977) and with the distinction between automatic and controlled processes for using context suggested by Posner and Snyder (1975a, 1975b) and by Stanovich and West (in press).

SOLVING PROBLEMS OF TEXT REFERENCE

The final experiment I describe represents a first attempt at explicating the kinds of sequential interactions that occur in text processing. The experiment was concerned particularly with the use of knowledge derived from text in assigning referents for words that follow. Although the range of cohesive forms in English includes more subtle forms of lexical reference that are also of interest (e.g., synonyms, superordinates, properties, collocational expressions, etc.; cf. Halliday & Hasan, 1976), the experiments we have carried out to date have concentrated on a much less subtle form of text reference—pronominal reference. Pronouns are referential words; instead of being interpreted semantically in their own right, they make reference to something else for their interpretation. The referential relation is thus explicitly marked in the case of pronouns, whereas it is not generally marked in other cases of lexical reference.

Our purpose was to identify text characteristics that influence a reader's difficulty in resolving problems of pronominal reference. In the process, we hoped to draw inferences about the rules used by readers in searching for and selecting referents from prior text at the time a pronoun is encountered. Table 14.1 illustrates some of the text characteristics that we have explored. For example, in Sentence A, the number of potential referents for a pronoun has been varied. *He* could potentially refer to either *engineer* or *fireman*, whereas *it* can only refer to the *brake level*. In B, we have manipulated the distance in the text between referent and pronoun. A sentence intervenes between the pronoun *they* in the final sentence and its referent, *Arnold and Raymond*, in the initial sentence of the set. In C, we have a set where an intervening sentence uses the pronoun *she* in the same way as does the final sentence, to refer to *Alice*. (This would not be the case if the alternative intervening sentence, beginning "The sun had..." had been used.) The sentences in Pair D allow us to study the topicalizing effect of placing a referent noun phrase in the subject position. In D, both the referent *modern advertising* and pronoun *it* are subjects of their respective sentences. If the paraphrase of the first sentences printed at the bottom were used instead, this would not have been the case. In E, we illustrate how texts can be constructed to

TABLE 14.1
Discourse Processing: Finding Referents for Pronouns

A. *Number of Potential Referents*
The engineer told the fireman to pull the brake lever, but *he* said *it* was stuck.
B. *Number of Intervening Sentences*
Arnold asked Raymond to play ball.
But unfortunately it started to rain.
So *they* waited for *it* to stop.
C. *Mediated Versus Nonmediated Intervening Sentences*
Alice rubbed her eyes and looked again.
She couldn't make out what had happened at all.
Was *she* in a shop?

The sun had just set, and there was little light.
D. *Topicalizing the Referent*
Modern advertising does not, as a rule, seek to demonstrate the superior quality of the product.
It plays up to the desire of Americans to conform, to be like the Joneses.

The superior quality of the product is not, as a rule, what modern advertising seeks to demonstrate.
E. *Foregrounding an Incorrect Referent*
The congressman's early struggles were a subject he reminisced about in two candid interviews.
The interviews were filmed in the spacious corner office that he had occupied for the past 30 years.
They were pieces of a past that was still clearly alive and very much part of the current picture.
F. *Lexical Reference*
The 19th century was a period in which numerous immigrants came to America.
At first, people came from England, Ireland, Germany, and Sweden.

---

manipulate the staging of references to alternative noun phrases. In E, following the initial sentence there is an intervening sentence that brings to the foreground an "incorrect" potential referent (*interviews*) and thus places the correct referent for the target pronoun—*struggles*—in the background. Finally, in F we illustrate another form of reference that we have explored—what Halliday and Hasan term "lexical reference." The lexical term *people* in Sentence 2 is semantically related to *immigrants* in Sentence 1, and by virtue of that relation, it serves to reference the earlier concept. Each of these text variables has been explored in the present research.

The subjects were 44 high school students who varied, as before, in reading ability. In the experiment, the subject reads a text, sentence by sentence. From time to time, an underscore appears beneath a word (pronoun) in a current sentence, and the subject must at that time supply (vocally) the correct referent for the pronoun. However, the primary data obtained are the reading times per syllable for each sentence in the text.

Some of our most important findings are presented in Figs. 14.10 through 14.14. We first asked if there was an increase in reading time when a pronoun was substituted for its referent noun phrase. The relevant data are shown in Fig. 14.10. We found an increase in reading time when the referential relationship was pronominal compared with that when a lexical category was simply repeated. Reading times for finding pronoun referents were as large as those for reading sentences that contain no direct references but include other forms of lexical reference—particularly use of collocational expressions (see F in Table

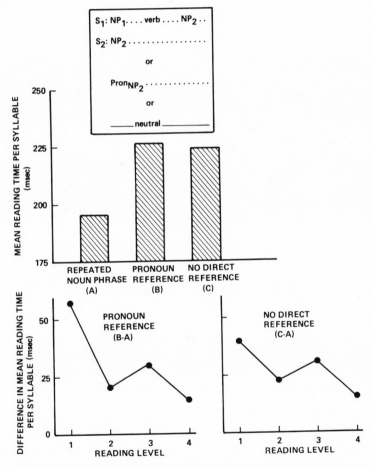

FIG. 14.10.   Mean reading time for reading sentences containing: (A) a repeated noun phrase; (B) a pronoun substituted for the repeated noun phrase; and (C) no direct reference but containing lexical references. Differences among reading ability groups for selected contrasts are shown at the bottom of the figure.

14.1). Finally, the bottom of Fig. 14.10 shows that increments in reading times for these conditions were larger for the poorer readers.

These analyses show that readers require time to analyze the coherent features of a text. The time they require is greater when a reference problem must be solved. When reference is by pronoun, a search of previous text and selection of a referent noun phrase is involved, whereas when reference is by lexical collocation, semantic distinctions must be evaluated to establish referential relationships. Note that the patterns of reader differences for these two types of cohesion were highly similar despite the processing differences that are likely to differentiate these two types of cohesion.

The second question we dealt with concerned the nature of processing that takes place when a pronoun is encountered. A pronoun marks a need to establish a reference to earlier text. Beyond this marking function, readers might "reinstate" or "reconsider" the set of potential referent noun phrases that are available in the prior text and make a selection from among them as soon as semantic constraints within the sentence will allow such a selection. Or, on the other hand, the pronoun might merely serve a marking function, with retrieval of the appropriate referent awaiting the occurrence of adequate semantic constraints within the sentence containing the pronoun. To investigate these possibilities, we analyzed the effect of varying the number of antecedent noun phrases that agree with the pronoun in gender and number. We noted also that our final (target) sentences were constructed so that the pronoun occurred at or near the beginning, ahead of its disambiguating semantic context. This feature of our target sentences should maximize the possibility of reinstatement of multiple antecedents. Our results, shown in Fig. 14.11, support the reinstatement theory. There were increases in reading times when the initial sentences were rewritten to contain a second noun phrase that agreed in gender and number with the referenced noun phrase, even though it was not referenced by the pronoun and was not semantically compatible with the context provided for the pronoun in the final sentence.

Additional evidence supporting the reinstatement theory was obtained by introducing another set of experimental conditions. For each text, we constructed an alternative final sentence in which the pronoun could refer to either of the antecedent noun phrases of Sentence 1. For example, an alternate for D in Table 14.1 is: "It is seldom presented with any view toward educating the public about possible uses or abuses." Here *it* can refer either to *modern advertising* or to the *product,* whereas in the sentence it replaced, semantic constraints allowed the pronoun to refer only to the former noun phrase. If readers select only a single antecedent noun phrase as a trial referent for the pronoun, whatever antecedent they select will fit the context of the ambiguous target sentence. This will not be the case for the unambiguous target sentence. If both antecedents are initially selected as the reinstatement theory prescribes, then a selection among them must be made on the basis of the semantic context of the target sentence, and this selection should be more difficult—and time-consuming—when the sentence is

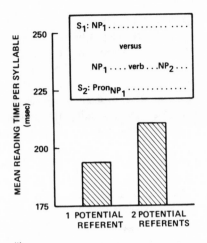

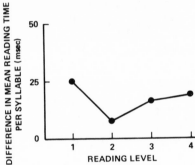

FIG. 14.11.   Effect on reading time for sentences containing a pronoun brought about by varying the number of available, potential referent noun phrases in the initial sentence of a two-sentence paragraph. Differences among readers are shown at the bottom of the figure.

ambiguous. Our results again clearly supported the latter hypothesis. Reading times for ambiguous target sentences were 277 msec/syllable, but they were only 208 msec/syllable for the unambiguous target sentences. Thus there was an increase in reading time when the target sentence was semantically compatible with either of two prior text referents over that when only one referent was sensible—even though both referents, in principle, constituted a correct response. Our general conclusion is that when they encounter pronouns, good and poor readers both appear to retrieve all of the alternative referents that are available for a pronoun (i.e., nouns that agree in gender and number) and then select from among them the referent that fits the semantic constraints of the sentence in which it occurred.

Our third purpose in the experiment was to study the effects of text characteristics on rules or priorities used by subjects in assigning referents to pronouns. Our notion here is that an author can manipulate the topicalization of particular referent noun phrases through the use of stylistic devices that emphasize one or another noun phrase (Grimes, 1975). Emphasized or topicalized noun phrases may be more readily assignable as referents than noun phrases that are relegated to the background. One device used to establish a topic is the placement of a noun phrase in the subject position of a sentence. Accordingly, we studied the effect of varying the position of the referenced noun phrase within the initial sentence. Our results are shown in Fig. 14.12. It illustrates that readers, particularly the poorer readers, appear to use a strategy of selecting the grammatical subject of an initial sentence as the preferred referent for a pronoun occurring in a following sentence. Their reading times were faster when the referent for a pronoun in the target sentence was the subject of the prior sentence than when it was placed in the predicate. Note that this result is at variance with proposals such as that of Kintsch and van Dijk (1978), who suggest that subjects develop a

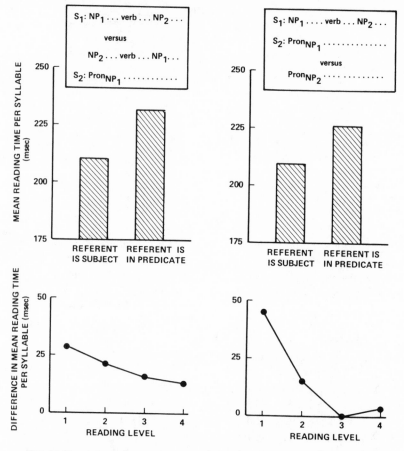

FIG. 14.12.   Effects on reading times for sentences containing pronouns brought about by foregrounding the referent noun phrase (making it the subject of the initial sentence). Differences among reader groups are shown at the bottom of the figure.

propositional base for each sentence as they progress through a text, with the resulting propositional representation serving as the sole basis for analyzing cohesive ties among sentences.

The topical status of a concept introduced by a noun phrase in Sentence 1 can be manipulated by varying the manner in which it is referenced in other, intervening sentences. Referring to a noun phrase within an intervening sentence can serve to increase its topical status if the pronoun used to reference it is also the subject of the intervening sentence. Data relevant to this prediction are shown in Fig. 14.13. A prior pronominal reference to the target noun within the intervening sentence reduced the time needed to find the appropriate referent for the pronoun when reading the final sentence. However, this facilitating effect of an earlier pronominal reference to the target was only found when the referring pronoun was the subject of the intervening sentence. Put another way, referring to the target noun phrase through a pronoun in the predicate of the intervening sentence appears to have demoted its topical status, probably at the expense of an increase in the topical value of whatever alternative noun phrase is the subject of the intervening sentence.

This last observation led us to investigate a final set of staging features of text that could influence priorities in assigning pronoun referents. Our idea was to

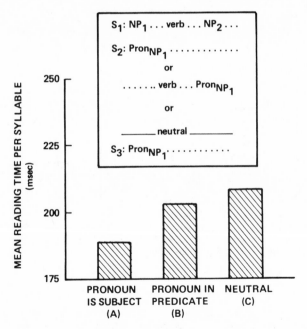

FIG. 14.13.   Effect on reading times for sentences containing pronouns brought about by prior use of the same pronoun within a mediating sentence, in subject or predicate position.

introduce an intervening sentence that began with the alternative noun phrase of Sentence 1—the one that was not to be referenced in the final sentence. By introducing a sentence that stresses the alternative noun phrase, we would be reducing the topical status of the original subject noun phrase and increasing the time needed to find it when it is referred to in the target sentence. Results of this text manipulation are given in Fig. 14.14. It is evident that bringing the alternative noun phrase to the foreground within an intervening sentence (as in Condition B) lengthened the time for finding the correct referent for a pronoun occurring subsequently over that obtained when the intervening sentence was "neutral" and did not contain a direct reference to either noun phrase (Condition A).

There is another interesting finding in Fig. 14.14. When a pronoun was substituted for the lexically repeated NP^2 in the second sentence (Condition C),

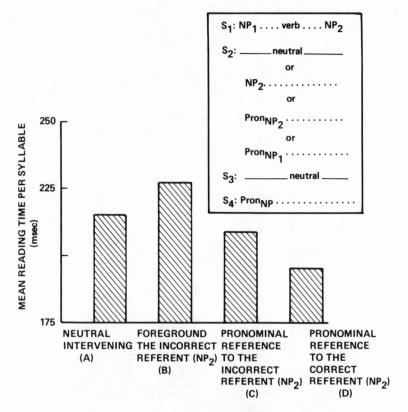

FIG. 14.14.   Effect on reading times for sentences containing pronouns brought about by foregrounding an incorrect referent by (B) lexical repetition or (C) pronominal reference. The reading time for the case where an intervening sentence refers pronominally to the correct referent is shown for comparison. (This value, taken from the previous figure, has been increased by 8 msec to adjust for the effect of adding an additional neutral intervening sentence.)

not only was there no increase in time needed to process the final sentence comparable to that for Condition B but actually a small decrease in reading time below that obtained when a neutral sentence replaced the referencing intervening sentence. Moreover, the mean reading time for Condition C was only 11 msec longer than that found when the pronoun in the intervening sentence referred to the same referent as the pronoun in the final sentence (Condition D in Fig. 14.14). We can conclude from this rather surprising finding that: (1) referring to a referent pronominally does not have as large an effect on topical status as does the actual repetition of the referent noun phrase as the subject of a sentence; and (2) the use of a pronoun in an intervening sentence to refer to one noun phrase does not increase difficulty in later using the same pronoun to refer to another referent noun phrase; it actually has a small priming effect. This last result is consistent with the reinstatement theory, since processing of the first pronoun reinstates both NP^1 and NP^2 to working memory until the point at which a selection can be made of NP^2 on semantic grounds. Thus, paradoxically, in the processing of the intervening sentence, the nonreferenced noun phrase has been "primed" as well as the noun phrase actually referred to.

In summary, when we manipulated a number of text variables thought to alter difficulty of resolving problems of anaphoric reference in a text, we found a consistent pattern of differences among readers of varying abilities, suggesting that there are differences in the automaticity of skills employed in dealing with this problem. Readers appear to be sensitive to surface grammatical structure of the text in selecting the proper referents for pronouns. Text variables that emphasize the importance of a particular noun phrase simultaneously serve to make that noun phrase more readily available as a referent for a pronoun. Poor readers appear to be more dependent on topical status in finding pronominal referents than good readers. This suggests that their search of memory for prior discourse may be less automatic and more attention demanding, as it was found to be in the earlier study of context utilization. Incidentally, Lesgold, Curtis, and Gallagher, in an unpublished study reported by Perfetti and Lesgold (1977), found similar differences in sensitivity to prior discourse for skilled and less skilled readers in their study of direct and indirect antecedents. The substitution of an indirect antecedent such as *grass* in Sentence 1:

Jane likes the smell of freshly cut *grass*. The grass was wet.

for a direct antecedent such as *grass* in the following alternative to Sentence 1 produced an increase in reading time of 238 msec for less skilled readers when reading Sentence 2, but only 57 msec for the highly skilled readers.

Jane decided not to sit on the *grass*. This result is typical of many of the good–poor reader differences we have observed. When the complexity of processing is increased, the resulting processing-time increments are greatest for readers who lack automatic processes for performing the routine functions of text referencing and lexical retrieval that occur in reading connected discourse.

GENERAL DISCUSSION

In studies of representative skills in the domains of word analysis, discourse analysis, and integrative processes, we have identified differences in the processing characteristics of highly skilled and poorly skilled high-school-age readers. A number of generalizations can be drawn from the results we have accumulated. First, young adult readers who differ widely in skill as measured by a standard test of reading comprehension do not differ in their ability to decode orthographic forms successfully, find referents for pronouns, or perform any of the other tasks we have used to analyze the components of reading. Rates of errors do not as a rule distinguish groups of high- and low-ability readers. Rather, it is the chronometric aspect of processing that consistently provides a basis for distinguishing levels of expertise in this subject population. Second, we can say that performance differences within the various components we have investigated typically take the same form: When test materials are increased in difficulty, a larger price in processing time is paid by poorer readers than by the stronger readers. Third, this distinction in the efficiency or automaticity of components appears to extend to all three of the processing domains we have explored. And fourth, we have found evidence that less efficient processes are of an attention-demanding nature. They behave like serial processes, and this restricts their usefulness to only the most regular and predictable circumstances of application—to the most frequent letter patterns, to the most predictable words, to the most salient topics in a discourse, and so forth.

Prompted in part by unpublished remarks of Perfetti at a 1979 APA symposium, I would like now to indulge in a little speculation about the role of an executive in controlling and coordinating the component processes that are active in reading. I believe that when skill is low and attention-demanding mechanisms are involved in performing the subprocesses of reading, an executive of a sort may be involved in allocating the processing resource to the various processing components, albeit inefficiently. I am persuaded of this as much as anything by Perfetti and Lesgold's (1977) interesting depiction of hysteresis problems that plague poorer or younger readers. The role of an executive in the "normal" reading of skilled readers is, I believe, another matter. If such readers have developed component processes that are highly automatic and that interact primarily by virtue of the common memory stores on which they act (cf. Rumelhart, 1977), then there is little need for an executive processor. Perhaps we are too much influenced by the control problems inherent in cognitive systems viewed as single-processer devices. In reading, as in other studies of skilled human performance in dual- (or multi-) task environments (Hawkins, Church, & de Lemos, 1978), we may increasingly come to view a skilled performer as the beneficiary of a system of integrated, automatic processing components. Such components, I believe, will be found to interact by virtue of interlocking data bases, or on account of skill interactions whereby expertise in one processing component alters the character of processing for some other component. Only in less skilled readers, whose processing is typified by its controlled, attention-demanding character, will we expect process interactions to be introduced due to competition for a limited processing resource. An adequate conception of interactive processes in reading must, I believe, recognize that the mechanisms for process interaction may differ for expert and nonexpert readers.

We have characterized the mechanism for process interactions in skilled readers as due primarily to the joint effects of automated component processes on a common memory store. The notion that integration of processes in reading can be achieved in this way without an executive scheduler must, however, be qualified. It is very likely that in less routine reading tasks that involve reading for the purposes of solving particular problems, a strategic component is introduced. Skimming for the gist, locating main ideas, finding text that is informative about a particular topic, and even the careful following of a difficult argument all involve nonautomatic skills and the executive control of reading components in the service of particular reading goals. Interactions between processes involved in these goal-directed reading activities and the more automatic components of reading remain to be explored and are a worthy topic for future research.

ACKNOWLEDGMENT

The research described herein was supported primarily by the Personnel and Training Research Programs, Psychological Sciences Division, Office of Naval Research, under Contract No. N00014-76-C-0461, Contract Authority Identification No. NR-154-386, and also by the National Institute of Education under Contract No. US-NIE-C-400-76-0116. The support and encouragement of Marshall Farr and Henry Halff, are gratefully acknowledged. I would like to thank Richard Pew for fruitful discussions during the many phases of the work, Marilyn Adams with whom I collaborated in the Anagram Experiment, and Barbara Freeman and Jessica Kurzon, who implemented the experimental design.

REFERENCES

Anderson, R. C., Reynolds, R. E., Schallert, D. L., & Goetz, E. T. *Frameworks for comprehending discourse* (Tech. Rep. No. 12). Urbana, Ill.: University of Illinois, Laboratory for Cognitive Studies in Education, 1976.

Collins, A. M., & Loftus, E. F. A spreading-activation theory of semantic processing. *Psychological Review*, 1975, *82*, 407–428.

Frederiksen, J. R. Assessment of perceptual, decoding, and lexical skills and their relation to reading proficiency. In A. M. Lesgold, J. W. Pellegrino, S. Fokkema, & R. Glaser (Eds.), *Cognitive psychology and instruction*. New York: Plenum, 1977.

Frederiksen, J. R. *Word recognition in the presence of semantically constraining context*. Paper presented at the annual meetings of the Psycholonic Society, San Antonio, Texas, November 11, 1978.

Frederiksen, J. R. Component skills in reading: Measurement of individual differences through chronometric analysis. In R. R. Snow, P.-A. Federico, & W. E. Montague (Eds.), *Aptitude, learning, and instruction: Cognitive process analysis*. Hillsdale, N.J.: Lawrence Erlbaum Associates, 1979.

Grimes, J. *The thread of discourse*. The Hague: Mouton, 1975.

Halliday, M. A. K., & Hasan, R. *Cohesion in English*. London: Longman, 1976.

Hawkins, H. L., Church, M., & de Lemos, S. *Time-sharing is not a unitary ability* (Tech. Rep. No. 2). Eugene, Oreg.: University of Oregon, Center for Cognitive and Perceptual Research, 1978.

Kintsch, W., & van Dijk, T. A. Towards a model of text comprehension and production. *Psychological Review*. 1978, *85*, 363–394.

Mayzner, M. S., & Tresselt, M. E. Tables of single-letter and digram frequency counts for various word-length and letter position combinations. *Psychonomic Monograph Supplements*, 1965, *1*, 13–32.

McClelland, J. *On the time relations of mental processes: A framework for analyzing processes in cascade* (Report No. 77). La Jolla, Calif.: University of California at San Diego, Center for Human Information Processing, 1978.

Morton, J. Interaction of information in word recognition. *Psychological Review*, 1969, *76*, 165–178.

Norman, D. A., & Bobrow, D. G. On data-limited and resource-limited processes. *Cognitive Psychology*, 1975, *7*, 44–64.

Perfetti, C. A., & Lesgold, A. M. Discourse comprehension and sources of individual differences. In M. A. Just & P. A. Carpenter (Eds.), *Cognitive processes in comprehension*. Hillsdale, N.J.: Lawrence Erlbaum Associates, 1977.

Posner, M. I., & Snyder, C. R. R. Attention and cognitive control. In R. L. Solso (Ed.), *Information processing and cognition: The Loyola symposium*. Hillsdale, N.J.: Lawrence Erlbaum Associates, 1975. (a)

Posner, M. I., & Snyder, C. R. R. Facilitation and inhibition in the processing of signals. In P. M. A. Rabbitt & S. Dornic (Eds.), *Attention and performance V*. New York: Academic Press, 1975. (b)

Rumelhart, D. E. Toward an interactive model of reading. In S. Dornic (Ed.), *Attention and performance VI*. Hillsdale, N.J.: Lawrence Erlbaum Associates, 1977.

Shiffrin, R. M., & Schneider, W. Controlled and automatic human information processing: II. Perceptual learning, automatic attending and a general theory. *Psychological Review*, 1977, *84*, 127–190.

Stanovich, K. E., & West, R. F. Mechanisms of sentence context effects in reading: Automatic activation and conscious attention. *Memory & Cognition*, in press.

Venezky, R. L. *The structure of English orthography*. The Hague: Mouton, 1970.

15 Interactive Processes in Reading: Where Do We Stand?

Alan M. Lesgold and Charles A. Perfetti
Learning Research and Development Center

When we first planned the conference that gave rise to this book, we had three sources of motivation for such an effort. First, the variety of efforts being made by the authors of these chapters, the general improvement in psychological theory building, and the overall spirit of the times in cognitive psychology gave us some confidence that theories could be developed to connect the work on discourse comprehension and the work on word recognition aspects of reading. It was our further hope that such work would lead to improved understanding of the problems that some children have in learning to read. Finally, we were hoping that the interactive-processes account of reading that we had previously offered (Lesgold & Perfetti, 1979; Perfetti & Lesgold, 1977) could be replaced by a richer theory of the role of phonological encoding of words, which we had seen as central to the reading process.

In part, our hopes have been realized. The chapters of this book, combined with the general trends in cognitive psychology and cognitive science, show that we are progressing toward understanding how lower-level automated recognition processes work in tandem with higher-level inference processes, both general and specific, to produce effective understanding of text. On the other hand, a clear explanation of the role of phonological codes in reading remains elusive—there is an apparent mystery requiring further investigation and insight. In this postscript chapter, we explore our reasons for feeling that major new tools now exist for understanding the component interactions within a complex process like reading and that these tools can lead to better understanding of reading dysfunction. Then we briefly discuss the issue of phonological codes in reading, attempting to indicate where the issue currently stands.

PROGRESS IN THEORIZING ABOUT THE READING PROCESS

It has long been evident that reading is a very complex activity, but only recently has the necessary set of tools for directly understanding that complexity begun to appear. Until a few years ago, the best we could do was to attack each aspect of the reading process as a separate research problem, more or less as the proverbial set of blind men tried to understand the elephant. This often entailed a need for many different blind men—that is, a large number of different (but still over-simplified) research approaches—in order to gain any useful knowledge. Unfortunately, each simplistic approach manufactured its own theories of reading dysfunction, and there proliferated a complex typology of reading disorders. Since the mechanism that does the reading and the experience base that results in learning to read are both complex, it was possible to isolate apparent examples of each of these disorders; and the blind-man approach has proven to be quite useful to the special education field, aiding in understanding of many ways in which the verbal processing apparatus can fail.

However, the majority of inadequate readers do not, we suspect, have rare or exotic problems that are well suited to analysis via a complex typology. To understand why these children and adults cannot read well, we need to understand the overall reading process well enough to be able to identify its points of vulnerability, those components that must work efficiently for effective reading to occur. The positive message of portions of this book and other recent work is that we are closing in on a major portion of that goal. In the pages that follow, we offer some suggestions about why we think progress in this area has accelerated and what we think needs to be done next.

Recent Influences on Reading Research

We believe that much of the current work has been aided by a few seminal contributions of the past decade or two. These developments have come from overlapping movements in experimental psychology known as information-processing psychology, cognitive psychology, and cognitive science. The information-processing movement, born in vigilance and attention work that began during World War II, has contributed three important ideas that appear in the work reported in this volume: Morton's logogen theory (1969), the idea of a limit on the amount of conscious mental processing in which a person can engage at one time (Atkinson & Shiffrin, 1968; Kahneman, 1973; Newell & Simon,

1972), and the cascade theory of McClelland (1979) that has heavily influenced a number of the chapters in this volume. Somewhat separately, there has developed a methodology of trying to understand acquisition of a skill by studying differences between people of greater and lesser expertise (e.g., Chase & Simon, 1973). This work complemented a long tradition in reading research (comparing "good" and "poor" readers) by suggesting specific knowledge sources as responsible for expertise. Finally, the newly emerging cognitive science movement, an integration of cognitive psychology with the artificial intelligence domain, has contributed ideas derived from the work on speech understanding (Erman & Lesser, 1978) and the distinction between event-driven and goal-driven (or bottom-up vs. top-down) processing (Bobrow & Norman, 1975). We consider each of these areas in turn.

Logogen Theory. The neuron has been an influential metaphor for understanding many higher-level aspects of cognition (see, for example, McCulloch & Pitts, 1943). An important theoretical program that derives from this metaphor is the logogen theory of John Morton (1964/1968, 1969). Morton proposed that for each word one is able to recognize, there is a response unit, called a *logogen,* that is sensitive to the set of auditory, visual, and semantic features associated with that word. When the number of features that are currently active (i.e., being looked at or recently thought about) exceeds the logogen's threshold, that unit is automatically activated, and all the features are made available to the rest of the cognitive apparatus. Because logogen activation is automatic and does not require attention, the logogen theory is a theoretical forerunner of automaticity theories of reading. Indeed, Morton and Long (1976) have presented data that suggest that logogens are not subject to the capacity limitations that characterize higher levels of cognitive processing (see next section).

Morton's contributions go further than we can consider in this chapter. For one thing, the logogen is not only an embodiment of an automated recognizer for a word; it also has a natural extension to accommodate contextual processes (cf. Morton, 1969). Context is simply the set of active or recently active semantic features. Thus, a top-down or contextual influence is nothing but the activation of semantic information patterns to which the logogen is sensitive. The problem with the logogen formulation is that it leaves unanswered the question of what a *feature* is. Although an answer to this question is important for any substantial theory of semantic processes, it seemed less critical in the formulation of how a word recognizer might use information in a general way without regard to semantic structure.

Basically, the Morton logogen is similar to certain aspects of one of the recent speech-understanding models discussed later—HARPY. By having an automatic recognition response whenever a threshold number of critical "features" is activated, a theory can account for such phenomena in reading as speed–accuracy trade-offs, word frequency effects, context effects, etc. On the other hand, although logogen theory is an important precursor of more recent work, it (at least in its earlier-published versions) does not tell us enough about the overall structure of the word recognition process as it relates to reading. Further, the logogen seems to be an appropriate model only for the automated level of performance in word processing. We still need to learn how more complex, inferential, semantically driven conscious processes become "compiled" into logogens.

A Limitation on Processing Capacity.   One way to describe the inability of a person to perform some function is to say that he or she has limited capacity. Such a statement, by itself, is a nonexplanatory restatement of that person's inability. However, if it is possible to specify the nature of the capacity limitation in some detail, then a limited-capacity account becomes a more useful explanation. In the case of reading, less skilled readers have sometimes (e.g., LaBerge & Samuels, 1974; Perfetti & Lesgold, 1977) been characterized as having problems that involve a capacity limitation. The argument has been that less practiced components of word recognition require a substantial allocation of processing capacity that otherwise could be used for higher-level aspects of the reading process. It is necessary, however, to specify better what processing capacity is, in order for this sort of argument to be a contribution.

Several approaches to characterizing this limited-supply commodity have been proposed. Newell (1980) has suggested an interpretation based upon production system models of cognition. A production is a conditional mental operation; it is performed only when its specified conditions are satisfied. Any computational model of cognition can be specified as a memory structure combined with a set of productions and a discipline (set of rules) that specifies the order of execution when the conditions of several productions are simultaneously satisfied. The conditions of productions consist of patterns to be matched against active portions of memory. Some patterns are very specific, whereas others are more flexible, containing free variables (essentially, "wild cards") as part of the pattern to be matched. This flexibility means that parts of the pattern to be matched are not completely specified (e.g., "*If* someone *has a sister, that* someone *is a brother or sister*"; as opposed to "*if* John *has a sister, then* he *is a brother or sister*"). When such a pattern is matched to active memory, the free variables must be *bound* to the specific parts of the pattern for which they are to stand. Newell has proposed that there is a limitation on the instantiation, binding, and use of such variables. That is, there is a limit on the speed at which conditions of productions containing variables can be tested (i.e., it takes time to match *someone* to a specific person).

Within this approach to limited capacity, a more expert reader would presumably be modeled as one whose competence consists in having a very rich set of specific productions rather than only a smaller set of vague, nonspecific productions. The approach argues that one trades off generality for execution speed. A general production (e.g., "If the word starts with *ca*, its first syllable may have the sound /kae/) contains unbound variables in its condition, whereas a more specific one does not (e.g., *cattle* is pronounced /kaetel/). Since variable binding is a bottleneck in the system, it will be performed only if the number of productions that fit to the point of variable binding is not too large. A specific production that recognizes a situation exactly will not be impeded by this bottleneck.

In the early stages of reading, it is necessary to teach children some productions with unbound variables. These include the phonics principles that permit children to sound out words they haven't seen and the rules for recognizing familiar word stems with common affixes. Some theories of cognitive learning, such as Anderson's ACT (1976), postulate a second source of productions with unbound variables; they assert that productions with variables in their conditions are generalized from more specific productions that are the result of specific experiences. For example, experience with the word *cat* may lead to a temporary behavior of treating any word that starts with *ca* as *cat*. Such a generalization mechanism is the basis for any adaptive performance. However, in the case of word recognition, it may be counterproductive. In ACT, simple trial and error will, with practice, tend to compensate for excessive generalization by strengthening successful productions and weakening those that are too general.

To summarize, one approach to theorizing about the limitations on thinking ability is to characterize the limit as an inability to match the conditions of productions very quickly when they contain unbound variables. Children acquire productions with unbound variables through instruction, such as phonics rules and stem + affix rules, and also through overgeneralization that is adjusted with practice. Thus, children should show limited-capacity effects once they have learned the barest rudiments of reading, and these effects should persist until removed by extended practice. No one has addressed the issue of whether it is possible to design instruction to minimize the formation of, or need for, productions with unbound variables, but this would seem like a sensible issue for future work.

Another aspect of limited capacity is the limited duration of those memories that are "partial products" of cognition. Originally, psychologists spoke of long-term memory and short-term memory, with the short-term memory being extremely limited (Miller, 1956). More recently, it has become apparent that cognition requires a considerable amount of what Hunt (1973) has called "working memory." Several forms of evidence suggest that the contents of one's recent experience are temporarily available for further cognitive processing. For example, when one reads a sentence in a discourse, one usually can retrieve enough of the prior sentence(s) to resolve anaphoric references, even when those references are quite vague or indirect. If there have been intervening context changes, this retrieval becomes harder or impossible (cf. Lesgold, Roth, & Curtis, 1979).

There are several possible mechanisms for working memory loss. The simplest is to assume that working memory decays after a certain amount of time. Such an assumption is compatible with most global models of reader disability. One assumes that poor readers do too much slow (attention-demanding) processing. Thus, their working memories will decay before they are needed, at least some of the time. Unfortunately, a model of this sort cannot explain why working memory availability is diminished by shifts in the topic or context of a discourse. Consequently, it may be worthwhile to consider a more elaborate theory of working memory—one in which there is the possibility for more specific differences in working memory between better and less skilled readers.

One such theory would be that all working memory is simply a manifestation of episodic (Tulving, 1972) memory. Episodic memory can be thought of as a content-addressable trace of ongoing cognitive experience. When part of the content of an experience is used as a retrieval cue, the rest is returned, with a noise level that decreases as the input more closely matches the total cognitive activity under way during that experience. Some of the content of any such episodic memory is irrelevant but variable "system noise." Such noise will be more of a problem as the time between storage and retrieval increases (the components of the noise can be thought of as undergoing random walk; Landauer's model [1975], is a specific variation on this theme). Thus, there will tend to be a trade-off between the recency of storage for an episodic trace and the amount of partial content needed to retrieve the rest of the trace, because the number of irrelevant matching features will decrease as time passes between storage and attempted retrieval. Context shifts would also tend to decrease the match between the current ambiance of features and that of the prior context.

One might add the assumption that memory nodes matched by conditions of an executing production are automatically stored as part of episodic traces if they are matched by bound variables. If matched by free variables, their storage into episodic memory is assumed to be not as complete. Such an episodic working memory would have the property of being "bigger" for people who have a rich array of specific productions than for people who have learned only very general productions (containing many unbound variables). That is, a bigger proportion of the content of relevant episodic traces will be task relevant for the expert than for the novice, since more of the content will have been generated by the expert's own specific *procedural knowledge* and less by temporary variables. As a result, the information will be retrieved more reliably.

To summarize this section, we note that capacity limitations have been a popular way of talking about why some children don't read well. In recent years, both the empirical work on reading ability differences and the work on cognitive simulations of reading have allowed enough specification of detail for this approach to become valuable. In contrast to the earliest work on reading ability differences, it is currently more likely that a theory of ability differences will talk about the interaction of cognitive software of different types with the general bottlenecks in the human information-processing system than about possible differences in system hardware, although some level of hardware differences may be present.

Cascade Theory.   The measurement of reaction time has been the dominant empirical technique of the information-processing tradition in psychology. There are several reasons for this. First, time is a primitive unit of physical measurement. Consequently, the early psychophysics work that spawned psychology chose response time as a suitably rigorous dependent variable. Second, Saul Sternberg (1969) developed a class of experimental designs using reaction time to test theories of cognitive processing in which component processes execute in strict linear sequence. Finally, there has often been no other measure with fine enough grain to capture the level of theorizing in current research. The data of earlier psychological work, such as overall proportions of correct responses, etc., are quite overdetermined by today's theories of mental processing and thus are inadequate for testing theoretical validity. Within current paradigms, one thing that is true of even the smallest mental process is that it takes time.

Even with this impressive history, the methodologies for reaction-time analysis have generally been inadequate. This is because the basic approach was to assume that treatment manipulations could be found that would independently affect only one component of a process and that *reaction-time changes produced by such manipulations were completely due to changes in the function of the target component.* When components are assumed to interact while they are operating or when the speed at which they operate depends upon the quality of data they receive from lower-level components, the existing methodologies are not wholly adequate.

More recently, McClelland (1979) proposed a new type of relationship between components of a mental process to augment the prior model of purely sequential and noninteractive components. This new relationship is the basis for his *cascade theory.* McClelland developed in considerable detail a basis for reaction-time designs that test cascade models, and it is likely that such models will be useful alternatives for theorizing about specific mental functions, including reading. The assumptions underlying cascade theory are a somewhat generalized version of the assumptions presented in the Perfetti and Roth chapter (11) in this volume, and we do not consider all of them here. However, we should briefly review what a cascade model is.

According to McClelland, a cascade model is one in which there are two or more levels of processing that have several properties. First, each component at a given level operates continuously on outputs of components at the next lower level. Second, each component is continually outputting, with some time lag, the current state of its computations based upon the input levels it has been receiving. Finally, there is no direct transmission of data from higher to lower levels. The efficiency of each component is determined by the rate at which it responds to input. The output quality of each component is determined by the asymptotic activation level for the component (the clarity and completeness of the output it can generate given sufficient time).

The McClelland model is more restricted than some current theoretical approaches, such as the Rumelhart interactive model (1977), which does not define a strict directionality of relationships between different levels of processing. (Note also that the directionality assumption is not followed in the Rumelhart and McClelland chapter [2] for this volume.) On the other hand, there are only a few indications that the less restricted approaches require strong bidirectionality to account for available data. Perhaps this is because our theorizing sophistication is still ahead of our empirical capabilities. In any event, we can view the McClelland work as an important extension of our ability to identify theory with data closely, even if it turns out to be too restrictive as an overall model.

McClelland raised some important points in his article that deserve some discussion here. For example, he demonstrated that the same data can have a different interpretation and even multiple interpretations under the cascade theory assumptions. In the case of multifactor RT experiments, for instance, a statistical interaction of two treatment factors no longer means that the two types of manipulations must be affecting the same process component. Under the assumptions of cascade theory, any one of the following three possibilities could produce an interaction: (1) The two manipulations affect the efficiency of the same process component; or (2) the two manipulations affect the asymptotic level of output from the same component (i.e., output quality); or (3) one manipulation affects the rate (efficiency) of a component whose rate is a limitation on overall system efficiency while the other manipulation affects the asymptotic activation level (output quality) of some other component. Further, the lack of an interaction effect does not rule out the possibility that two manipulations might affect the same component.

McClelland's contribution goes beyond pointing out a set of alternative models with which current data may be consistent. He presented examples of such alternative models that appear to have great potential. For example, he commented in his (1979) article on the interaction in word recognition of attentional variation and different levels of word frequency. A cascade model that he proposed for this relationship would have the rate at which word recognition components respond be determined by the level of attention allocated to recognition and the asymptotic level of activation for the demon that recognizes a word determined by that word's frequency. Thus, low-frequency words would be recognized more slowly and less accurately than high-frequency words, especially when attention was diverted to other components than word recognition. An obvious extension of the model would state that practice using a particular word will improve its asymptotic level, perhaps with different improvement rates for different children.

Although such a model is quite appealing (especially to authors who have publicly stated hypotheses that are less precise variations on this theme), it is important to consider whether the greater precision can lead to greater possibilities for empirical validation of such hypotheses. The techniques McClelland cited, unfortunately, seem better suited to experimentation with competent (probably adult) readers than with children and seem especially unsuited to experimentation on children who read poorly. The problem is that the primitives of a cascade theory, from which more complex predictions are generated, are functions that show individual process component output as a function of processing time. Directly gathering the data for estimating those functions seems to require complex techniques, as most reading process components execute in a few hundred milliseconds or less.

The two methods that have been used thus far for such measurements are deadline tasks and response-signal tasks. In a deadline task, the subject must respond by a particular deadline, a fixed number of milliseconds after the stimulus is presented. By varying the deadline, it is possible to construct a speed-by-accuracy plot, which is the operating characteristic function that we need for directly testing a cascade model. An alternative approach requires that the subject respond as quickly as possible after a response signal. By varying the latency from stimulus onset to response signal, one can generate the operating characteristic function.

Both methods impose an additional processing load on the subject. Further, it is unlikely that a small child can understand the response-signal task in the context of a response requirement that always seems faster than normal. Children may not understand what it means to be as accurate as possible but to take no more than, say, half a second. Even adults require training on such methods (Wickelgren, 1977). Thus, the experimental procedures suggested by McClelland will not work in studies of children's reading problems. It remains to be seen whether techniques such as making more refined use of the density function for correct and error RTs from simpler tasks (for an example, see Grice, Nullmeyer, & Spiker, 1977) can get around this problem.

This does not mean that the cascade theory will not be important and useful. It has begun to deal with the problems of directly verifying interactive component theories of processing with reaction-time measures. Further, the specific cascade proposal is one of a class of models that can account for process interaction data such as reported by Perfetti and Roth in Chapter 11 of this volume. Nonetheless, the increasing specificity and complexity of theories such as McClelland's highlight the problem we wish to address next.

Issues of Methodology.   For a variety of reasons, empirical work in the study of reading skill acquisition has lagged behind theoretical work in recent years. In large part, this is because the artificial intelligence discipline has recently become strong enough to foster work in other areas. This work has given us not only metaphors for our own theories but also simulation methodologies for exploring the implications of our theoretical work. Unfortunately, methods for empirical verification of our richer and more detailed theories have not emerged as quickly, though there are hopeful signs that this is changing.

The basic problem is that children do not provide rich enough behaviors in a laboratory setting. Further, there is considerable "error variance" in their responses (some of which should be accounted for by theories and some of which are perhaps best characterized as attentional variability). Thus, even though children, and especially less skilled children, produce less complex behaviors and have less tolerance for experimental tasks, they also require more experimental trials in order to produce stable data. We are left with many degrees of freedom in our models but little detail in our data. The problem becomes even more severe when models of *learning* to read are being tested.

Four general approaches have emerged that we wish to discuss. First, whereas responses must be kept simple, stimuli can be varied in complex ways. Second, a large battery of different tasks can be used. Third, several sophisticated forms of data analysis have been applied to this problem. Finally, techniques of developmental psychology are being adapted to the study of long-term learning. We briefly explore several examples of these four approaches.

The sophisticated manipulation of stimuli is perhaps best illustrated by some of the experiments reported by Rumelhart and McClelland in Chapter 2, this volume. They had simple tasks, such as identifying single letters within words (although they used adult subjects, children can also do such tasks). What was varied was the asynchrony between the time that the target letter was presented and the time that other letters of the word were shown. These time differences were of millisecond magnitude, a very subtle manipulation; yet they produced data adequate to the testing of a rather broad and important principle.

A second example is found in the work of Frederiksen (1978a, Chapter 14, this volume). Frederiksen has combined the use of a large number of tasks with theoretically relevant stimulus variations within tasks. This permits very specific tests of complex hypotheses about the sources of reading inadequacy in his high school subjects. Frederiksen has also pioneered the use of structural analyses of correlational data to verify complex theories (1978b; personal communication, 1980). With appropriate care, it is possible to gather considerable detailed data about children's reading performances using both natural and laboratory tasks. What is difficult, if not impossible, is to gather rich enough data in true experiments (in which all relevant independent variables are manipulated directly by the experimenter).

One way around this is to use recent structural equations modeling techniques (e.g., Joreskog & Sorbom, 1978) to test complex hypotheses against correlational data. Such tests allow one to specify the hypothesized set of skills that are present in each of a battery of tests and also to verify hypotheses about the extent to which one component skill of reading enables improvement in another. A recent dissertation (Lomax, 1980) nicely demonstrates this technique and shows the verification of a "bootstrapping" model in which word recognition skill enables improved reading speed, which in turn enables even better word recognition. It also provides a guide to the relatively complex details of the technique.

A final empirical approach has been the application to reading acquisition of the developmental techniques of cross-sectional (e.g., Curtis, in press; Doehring, 1976) and longitudinal (Calfee, 1980; Lesgold & Curtis, Chap. 13, this volume) comparison. In essence, these techniques expand the Frederiksen type of approach to include multiple testings over the course of learning to read (in either the same or different subjects). When combined with the causal modeling techniques just discussed, it should be possible to generate the learning trajectories of a variety of very specific subskills for both more and less successful readers and to verify hypotheses about the sources of overall reading skill. In particular, we expect that longitudinal data, when analyzed using the Joreskog structural equations approach, will permit both specification of the components of skill at successive levels of reading expertise and the understanding of the mechanisms whereby children of different aptitude levels improve their skills. This leads us to our next topic—comparisons of experts and less skilled people.

Expert–Novice Comparisons. One approach to studying the problems children have in learning to read has been the comparison of children of differing levels of skill. This approach has a long history in reading research but has recently been most prominent in studies of high versus low achievers in the reading curriculum (e.g., Curtis, in press; Frederiksen, 1978b, Chap. 14, this volume; Perfetti & Lesgold, 1977). Such work has been largely empirical and is, for the most part, discussed elsewhere in this chapter. Our purpose at this point is to suggest that another form of contrastive research be given more attention. This is the building of empirically verified models of children's reading performance at different levels of expertise as a means of better understanding how learning to read happens.

This general approach has been analyzed into three steps by Glaser (1976). First, one must construct a model of skilled performance. Second, procedures must be developed for specifying the status of the learner's skills at instructionally relevant points in the course of learning. Finally, procedures for producing transitions from one skill level to the next need to be specified. This is essentially a means–ends approach to the problem of instruction that does not by itself represent a major breakthrough. The important breakthrough comes from the realization that specific simulation models of the different stages of reading expertise may be possible, and that it may even be possible to test instructional hypotheses by seeing if they produce transitions of a less expert model into a more expert one. At the time this chapter was written, there were a number of projects under way using variations on this approach to specify learning mechanisms for physics (Larkin, 1980), arithmetic (Brown & Van Lehn, 1980), geometry (Anderson, Greeno, Kline, & Neves, 1980), and computer programming (Polson, Atwood, Jeffries, & Turner, 1980). In the future, we expect to see similar efforts for reading. Hopefully, such modeling will be done in tandem with some of the more sophisticated empirical procedures already discussed.

Contributions from the Speech-Understanding Work.   Another major source of guidance for interactive models of reading is the work stimulated by a major Defense Advanced Research Projects Agency (DARPA) effort in the early 1970s to develop speech-understanding systems (Department of Computer Science, Carnegie-Mellon University, 1977). DARPA conducted a competition among several institutions to produce a speech-understanding system with a certain level of skill and efficiency by 1976. The goals were set very high, and it appeared that none of the projects would meet them. Two very different programs developed at Carnegie-Mellon ended up coming very close to meeting the requirements. One of them, HEARSAY-II, differed from the other efforts primarily in having a looser control structure and many different levels of relatively independent decision processes. The other, HARPY, had a more tightly structured control flow and was compiled, or optimized, in ways that precluded easy modification.

It is becoming increasingly clear that there are a number of rather elegant principles embedded within the HEARSAY effort that may be quite useful to our task of modeling another difficult, multiprocess understanding activity—namely, reading. In this section, we explore some of these principles and also consider the thesis that HEARSAY is a good step toward modeling relatively novice performances, whereas other approaches to speech understanding, such as HARPY, are better but less complete characterizations of expert performances.

One interesting comment can be made about the expert–novice difference as characterized by intelligent systems such as HEARSAY-II and HARPY. In contrast to the suggestions of some reading researchers, the expert models are more "bottom-up" than the novice models. That is, models such as HARPY do not have a central high-level strategy mechanism controlling which components are allocated attention, at least not to the extent that models such as HEARSAY-II do. Hence, the progression is from top-down novices to bottom-up experts (just as in chess; Chase & Simon, 1973). This suggests that we will want to be extremely careful in theorizing about the top-down aspects of reading. Mature readers most likely accomplish the recognition of words in a relatively bottom-up manner, as some of the chapters in this book have suggested. Presumably, they behave in a more top-down manner in making sense of the sentences they are reading, especially if they are reading in a domain for which they have little expertise.

We begin by reviewing some of the properties of the HEARSAY system, relying upon the Carnegie-Mellon summary reports (Department of Computer Science, 1977). All of the candidate speech-understanding systems are multilevel systems; that is, they contain interacting knowledge structures operating at several different levels of analysis. Although a multilevel structure is important any time complex recognition is required, it is almost an absolute necessity in speech processing because of the ambiguity of the speech signal. The very same sound sequence can have different meanings in different sound contexts. Much of this ambiguity escapes our everyday experience because we have developed multiple levels of processing. In reading, there is less ambiguity of input, but the complexity of recognition and comprehension mandates a multilevel model nonetheless.

At each of the levels of processing in HEARSAY, there are relatively independent *knowledge structures* that are activated when specific conditions are satisfied in the course of processing and that act by making certain computed results available for examination by other knowledge structures. The structures look a lot like the logogens of Morton (1964/1968), but they exist at levels lower and higher than the word level. Knowledge structures communicate via a message center or *blackboard,* a sort of unrestrained short-term memory. The basic idea is that the speech signal triggers certain low-level knowledge structures. Low-level output, combined with the original signal information, triggers more knowledge structures at higher levels, and this process continues until a high-level structure generates an overall interpretation in which it has great confidence.

Such a system, if totally unconstrained, will suffer from combinatorial explosion of the set of triggered knowledge structures. That is, each knowledge structure will execute when it can and can trigger additional knowledge structures with its actions. If there is considerable ambiguity in the signal, this will produce a mushrooming effect with more and more knowledge structures ready to execute. As a result, processing resources are overtaxed, and a correct interpretation is likely to be obscured by the chaos. To avoid these problems, there must be a discipline imposed on the system that permits only some of the triggered knowledge structures to execute. The specific discipline chosen will substantially determine the nature and effectiveness of the system.

The HEARSAY-II discipline is important for two reasons. First, it provides a lesson about how allocation of processing capacity might take place in a multicomponent system. Second, the experience of the HEARSAY project in trying out different levels at which to concentrate decisions about the allocation of resources may be instructive. Within HEARSAY, there are a number of levels of knowledge structures. Any scheme to decide which of the potentially applicable structures should execute must look at the current blackboard contents and decide how the probable effects of a particular knowledge structure will contribute toward selection of the best overall interpretation of the utterance being processed.

The problems faced by a speech-understanding system and by a text-understanding system are rather similar. The system can look at a hypothesis for the entire utterance and see which word and subword hypotheses would confirm it further, for example. Alternatively, it can select the strongest phoneme hypotheses and activate word and subword hypotheses based upon them. A number of other schemes are also possible, but any optimization scheme must take into account the results of processing done thus far and must be able to predict, at least in part, what any given knowledge structure is likely to accomplish if attention is directed toward it.

In HEARSAY, there is a component of every knowledge structure called a "response frame," which provides this prediction. Even though it seems a bit difficult to propose that we need to know what we are going to do before we do it, one might argue that it is exactly this property that characterizes successful performance of any complex activity, including human thinking activity. For example, if we have a medical problem, we decide on a specialist without knowing exactly what diagnosis he or she will make. Within psychology, there is a long tradition—going back to James and Pillsbury, among others—of positing two levels of awareness (or allocation of attention). More recently, MacKay (1973) has demonstrated that unattended information, though not being consciously noticed, can sometimes be shown to have had some influence on understanding. Thus, it is not unreasonable to think of a psychological model that functions by having relatively independent knowledge structures that are able to do a little bit of processing automatically but that require conscious attention in order to complete their work. The lesson from HEARSAY is that such models can be very effective as understanders. We expect them to become more prevalent in the future.

The issue of the level at which most attentional allocation decisions should occur is raised by the HEARSAY work but perhaps is not resolved for tasks other than the processing of sentence-level spoken utterances. HEARSAY seemed to work best when it attempted to allocate attention to knowledge structures directed at confirming word and subword hypotheses that might extend hypothesized multiword sequences. That is, hypotheses, at all levels, that would have the effect of expanding highly weighted hypotheses of two or three consecutive words in a sentence by incorporating an additional word or two were selectively favored. It remains to be seen whether the word and phrase level is critical in the meeting of top-down and bottom-up aspects of processing in reading, also; but it is a fact that for speech understanding, certain levels worked better as control levels for HEARSAY-II than did others.

One final comment might be made about the speech-understanding models in particular and intelligent systems in general. Some models seem to be better theories of expert processing, whereas others seem to be better theories of novice levels of skill. This does not mean that the expertlike models are more intelligent or more successful—many are very inadequate attempts at simulating expert behavior. Rather, it means that the style of the expertlike models is similar to the style of human experts as they have appeared in psychological studies of expertise.

To understand what an expert model is like, it may be useful to review what HEARSAY, which we consider a successful novice model, is like. HEARSAY has a very fresh mind. There are no constraints on short-term memory structure; the results of any mental process are available on the blackboard. Decisions are made in a conscious, hypothesis-testing mode that is optimized by attending first to more promising leads. The execution discipline, which decides how processing capacity (attention) is to be allocated, is extremely important to the success of HEARSAY for this reason. Finally, it is very flexible. New knowledge can be incorporated by simply adding additional knowledge structures.

In contrast, another Carnegie-Mellon model, HARPY, is more expertlike. It has automatic, clearly differentiated, short-term knowledge pathways rather than an amorphous blackboard. The flow of control is managed by the components currently executing, with each component passing off control to the appropriate successor without the (conscious) intervention of a central strategy. Knowledge structures are larger and have more extensive output. Also, HARPY tends to prune from further consideration all but the most highly weighted of hypotheses currently being considered. Finally, because HARPY is finely tuned (compiled and optimized, in computer terms), it is less easily changed than programs such as HEARSAY-II.

The contrast between HARPY and HEARSAY-II shows both the strengths and weaknesses of the two as models of expert and novice behavior. HARPY is more efficient in large part because it quickly and accurately classifies the input and brings just the right knowledge structures to bear on it. On the other hand, it is less able to handle unexpected mutations of the input and less able to learn; yet we continue to feel that experts, at least expert readers, have the flexibilities that HARPY lacks. Nonetheless, we have learned a lot from the two models and expect that their influence on improved theories of the reading process has been and will be substantial.

THE ELUSIVENESS OF PHONOLOGICAL PROCESSES

One of the process interactions of major theoretical and practical importance involves speech-based processes. In this volume, there are four chapters that have something direct to say about speech processes in reading (Baddeley & Lewis, Chap. 5; Levy, Chap. 1; Katz & Feldman, Chap. 4; and Barron, Chap. 12).

A striking fact is that evidence for speech-based processes in skilled adult reading is fairly elusive. In a conference paper presented in 1976 but only recently published (Perfetti & Lesgold, 1979), we reviewed some issues concerning speech processes in reading, including experiments with lexical access and/or comprehension, and concluded that speech processes played an important role in supporting comprehension. Certainly, this was not an idiosyncratic conclusion, supported as it was by the research of Kleiman (1975) and Levy (1975), which appeared to demonstrate an immediate memory role for speech-based processes. More contentious was our conclusion that then-available experiments could not "be used to build a strong case against phonological coding [p. 73]" as a necessary aspect of word recognition in readinglike situations. That conclusion seems not to stand well in the face of more careful research since then, especially that of Coltheart (Coltheart, Besner, Jonasson, & Davelaar, 1979; Davelaar, Coltheart, Besner, & Jonasson, 1978) on lexical access. There seems little reason to doubt that access to a word *can* occur without phonemic recoding. If so, the question becomes whether lexical access normally, rather than necessarily, involves some speech process. The focus shifts from whether access requires recoding to the conditions of reading that promote phonetic processes and to what function, if any, is served by such processes.

One reason for maintaining an interest in these questions is that children seem to rely heavily on speech processes while learning to read. There is indirect evidence for this in the fact that young readers who are relatively skilled show their most marked advantage over unskilled readers in tasks involving production (naming) of words. Lesgold and Curtis (Chap. 13, this volume) make this point for children just learning to read and note that this difference persists at least through the elementary grades. Also, Hogaboam and Perfetti (1978) report bigger differences between skilled and less skilled readers in vocalization latency than in word matching, in agreement with Lesgold and Curtis. More direct evidence relating early reading skill to speech processes comes from Liberman, Shankweiler, Liberman, Fowler, and Fischer (1977), who report greater phonemic interference effects for skilled readers in a short-term memory task. Barron (Chap. 12, this volume) suggests not only a phonemic memory factor but a phonemic lexical access factor that may favor skilled readers.

There is thus a mild paradox. Speech processes appear to be unnecessary for skilled reading, yet they are characteristic of beginning reading, especially for those who learn quickly. A reasonable way out of this paradox is to suggest a skill acquisition model based on differences between expert adult readers and novice children. Speech processes are important for beginning reading because the child must learn to map print to speech sounds. However, achieving an expert level of skill in reading involves learning to bypass the print-to-speech connection by acquiring a print-to-meaning connection (Wernicke [1874, 1966] would have been happy with this sort of model). With extended practice at lexical access, attention to phonemic correspondences of letters drops out, and perception of letter patterns automatically activates word concepts. The transition from novice to expert probably requires extensive practice, just as in other areas of intellectual skill, such as chess. The result of this practice can be described as the replacement of generalized phonemic-based production sequences with specific, unified, word recognition productions.

However, there remain a few questions with this solution. The major question is whether phonemic codes continue to serve some role subsequent to lexical access. It seemed reasonable to conclude that even if phonemic codes are un-necessary for lexical access, they are still useful for later memory and com-prehension. If so, it is reasonable to suppose that phonemic codes are activated during lexical access. A system would be rather inefficient if it postponed phonemic code access until required by comprehension blockage. What would be used to reaccess the code? Since the visual input would be gone, the only alternative other than reexamining the word(s) in question would be to reaccess the phonemic code via the semantic code. That could be a problem. At a minimum, it would be inefficient insofar as information from a semantic code is connected to a phonemic code more strongly in the *name*-to-*meaning* than in the *meaning*-to-*name* direction. Hence, retrieving a name given meaning would be more time-consuming than the converse.

Perhaps more critical is that semantic information may underdetermine phonemic information. If so, accuracy as well as efficiency becomes a problem. For example, suppose in reading an American history text, the reader encounters the sentence, ''Fillmore appeared to have enough influence to forge a com-promise in the Senate.'' If the reader's code for the ''meaning'' of Fillmore is something like [+Name, U.S. President, 19th Century], he or she does not have the information sufficient for reaccess to the name. There's nothing to keep the reader from accessing Jackson, Pierce, Harrison, or Tyler, instead.

There are two possible solutions to this problem. One is to assume that a reference-securing process uniquely determines the name. For example, the foregoing example might be supplemented with a reference-securing code such as *the one who was president 1850–1853,* or *the one nobody remembers,* or *the one whose name is the same as that of a linguist.* The reference-securing codes would uniquely determine the name needed. The advantage of this is that it relieves the reader from having to hold on to a name code. It allows an ''abstract'' meaning-reference code that reaccesses the name when necessary.

The problem with the reference-securing code lies in accounting for words without securable references. In the sentence example, one can imagine secure references for Fillmore easily enough. However, *appeared, to, have, enough,* and *influence* seem to resist reference securing. It is possible, in context, to secure reference for the entire phrase *enough influence to forge a compromise—* something like [the X sufficient to cause Y to agree to Z]. In general, phrases are more reference secured than words. Thus, the reference-securing hypothesis seems to suggest that whereas ''lexical access'' may describe an early stage of reading comprehension, the semantic processes necessary for securing reference—and hence necessary for keeping retrieval probability high—will op-erate over multiword phrases. There seems to be no reason to disallow such processes.

The second possibility that allows for postlexical name access is that phonetic (or phonemic) fragments are available. Consider the American history example again. Suppose the reader's code included [+Name, U.S. President, 19th Cen-tury, +/f—/]. The difference is that the code includes information concerning the initial phoneme. The probability of reaccessing the name is obviously greatly increased by this assumption. Name accessibility is increased even more by additional phonemic information such as other phonemes or even number of syllables. This alternative is actually a different form of the phonemic recoding hypothesis, with a built-in functional assumption. It assumes that some phonemic information is accessed with other lexical information and that at least some of it is kept available for consultation.

This version of the phonemic recoding assumption reveals a possibility of phonemic recoding that is often ignored. The code need not contain all the phonemic information needed to produce the word. It can be abbreviated or partial. This possibility is reflected neither in experiments on lexical access nor in those on sentence processing. The assumptions of existing studies seem to be that the complete sound of the word, the whole acoustic pattern, is what is involved. For example, experiments involving rhyme judgments in sentence processing (Kleiman, 1975) and pseudohomophone effects in lexical decision (e.g., Coltheart et al., 1979; Davelaar et al., 1978) have to assume that phonemic codes are similar to acoustic patterns of some sort. It's not clear that evidence from such research rules out phonemic recoding that is less complete.

In any case, the main point is that phonemic codes are useful for name access because name codes are needed to secure reference. However, if only those words with reference-securing potential (e.g., content words) need to be available, then a generalized phonemic coding procedure for all words would not be necessary. Instead, only reference-securable words would be name accessed. Syntactic words, for example, could be reconstructed.

The reason for assuming a name-accessible memory code is the usefulness of such information in comprehension and memory. Whether name codes are activated during ordinary comprehension or only during verbatim memory situations remains an issue. Baddeley and Lewis (Chap. 5, this volume) and Levy (Chap. 1, this volume) conclude that memory demands recoding but comprehension does not. If so, then we might conclude that lexical access will activate name codes just in case the reader's strategy is to have it so.

This would be a comfortable conclusion. Expert readers are good decoders and flexible word recognizers. When they need them, they generate and use name codes along with meaning codes. It might be necessary to expand this flexibility so that name code access could precede semantic access (difficult and rare words) or could follow it (high memory demands and comprehension obstacles). The problem with this is that it suggests a complex strategic component to reading when a simpler nonstrategic process would serve as well.

A less awkward model would assume that lexical access always activates phonemic codes. The only relevant strategic factor is whether a reader recodes in subword units and then uses that code to consult meaning and to place it in the text representation. The attractive feature of this proposal is that the activated phonemic code is available for later memory scanning. A name code is thus available for securing reference. By this proposal, reading skill includes the rapid activation of all lexical information, including phonemic information. In any given situation, activation of phonemic information may precede or follow activation of semantic information depending upon the depth of semantic analysis required and the familiarity of the word. The issue then turns from whether speech recoding occurs to consideration of factors that control the activation time course of lexical properties.

SUMMARY

In this chapter we have tried to point to some general issues that seem important for understanding reading and reading skill in terms of interactive processes. Interactive processes are required by the complexities of the reading task and the inevitable use by the reader of knowledge relevant to this task. However, what counts as an adequate characterization of this interactive system is still an important issue. The theoretical possibilities range from systems that require significant communication between levels to systems that use all these levels but without communication between them. All are consistent with the core of observations that require postulating an interactive system. Choices about theoretical models can be promoted by developments in other areas, such as speech-understanding systems. On the other hand, decisive choices based on convincing experimental work may await richer methodologies, which are only beginning to appear. Nonetheless, attempts to understand skill differences in reading are possible without this decisiveness. We continue to suggest that expert readers are especially characterized by highly refined lower-level procedures for handling words. Finally, we suggest that the basic questions about speech processes in reading change from deciding whether such codes are necessary to determining what kind of codes they are and to identifying the conditions of reading that promote their activation.

ACKNOWLEDGMENT

Writing of this chapter was supported by an institutional grant to the Learning Research and Development Center from the National Institute of Education, U.S. Department of Education.

REFERENCES

Anderson, J. R. *Language, congition and thought.* Hillsdale, N.J.: Lawrence Elrbaum Associates, 1976.
Anderson, J. R., Greeno, J. G., Kline, P. J., & Neves, D. M. *Learning to plan in geometry.* Paper presented at 16th Annual Carnegie Symposium on Cognition, Pittsburgh, Pennsylvannia, 1980.

Atkinson, R. C., & Shiffrin, R. M. Human memory: A proposed system and its control processes. In G. H. Bower (Ed.), *The psychology of learning and motivation* (Vol. 2). New York: Academic Press, 1968.

Bobrow, D. G., & Norman, D. A. Some principles of memory schemata. In D. G. Bobrow & A. Collins (Eds.), *Representation and understanding: Studies in cognitive science.* New York: Academic Press, 1975.

Brown, J. S., & Van Lehn, K. *Learning a procedural skill through exception conditions.* Paper presented at 16th Annual Carnegie Symposium on Cognition, Pittsburgh, Pennsylvania, 1980.

Calfee, R. C. *A design for examining pattern differences in reading abilities.* Paper presented at American Educational Research Association annual meeting, Boston, Massachusetts, 1980.

Chase, W. G., & Simon, H. A. Perception in chess. *Cognitive Psychology,* 1973, *4,* 55–81.

Coltheart, M., Besner, D., Jonasson, J. T., & Davelaar, E. Phonological encodings in the lexical decision task. *Quarterly Journal of Experimental Psychology,* 1979, *31,* 489–507.

Curtis, M. E. Development of components of reading skill. *Journal of Educational Psychology,* in press.

Davelaar, E., Coltheart, M., Besner, D., & Jonasson, J. T. Phonological recoding and lexical access. *Memory & Cognition,* 1978, *6,* 391–402.

Department of Computer Science, Carnegie-Mellon University. *Speech understanding systems: Summary of results of the five-year research effort at Carnegie-Mellon University,* August, 1977.

Doehring, D. G. Acquisition of rapid reading responses. *Monographs of the Society for Research in Child Development,* 1976, *41*(2, Serial No. 165).

Erman, L. D., & Lesser, V. R. HEARSAY-II: Tutorial introduction and retrospective view (Tech. Rep. No. CMU-CS-78-117). Pittsburgh: Carnegie-Mellon University, Department of Computer Science, 1978.

Frederiksen, J. R. Assessment of perceptual, decoding, and lexical skills and their relation to reading proficiency. In A. M. Lesgold, J. W. Pellegrino, S. D. Fokkema, & R. Glaser (Eds.), *Cognitive psychology and instruction.* New York: Plenum, 1978. (a)

Frederiksen, J. R. *A chronometric study of component skills in reading* (Tech. Rep. 2). Cambridge, Mass.: Bolt, Beranek, and Newman, 1978. (b)

Glaser, R. Components of a psychology of instruction. *Review of Educational Research,* 1976, *46,* 1–23.

Grice, G. R., Nullmeyer, R., & Spiker, V. A. Application of variable criterion theory to choice reaction time. *Perception & Psychophysics,* 1977, *22,* 431–449.

Hogaboam, T., & Perfetti, C. A. Reading skill and the role of verbal experience in decoding. *Journal of Educational Psychology,* 1978, *70,* (5), 717–729.

Hunt, E. The memory we must have. In R. C. Shank & K. M. Colby, (Eds.), *Computer models of thought and language.* San Francisco: Freeman, 1973.

Joreskog, K. G., & Sorbom, D. *LISREL: Analysis of linear structural relationships by the method of maximum likelihood* (Users Guide, Version IV, Release 2). Chicago: International Education Services, 1978.

Kahneman, D. *Attention and effort.* Englewood Cliffs, N.J.: Prentice-Hall, 1973.

Kleiman, G. M. Speech recoding in reading. *Journal of Verbal Learning and Verbal Behavior,* 1975, *14,* 323–339.

LaBerge, D., & Samuels, S. J. Toward a theory of automatic information processing in reading. *Cognitive Psychology,* 1974, *6,* 293–323.

Landauer, T. K. Memory without organization: Properties of a model with random storage and undirected retrieval. *Cognitive Psychology,* 1975, *7,* 495–531.

Larkin, J. H. *Enriching formal knowledge: A model for learning to solve problems in physics.* Paper presented at 16th Annual Carnegie Symposium on Cognition, Pittsburgh, Pennsylvania, 1980.

Lesgold, A. M., & Perfetti, C. A. Interactive processes in reading comprehension. *Discourse Processes,* 1979, *1,* 323–336.

Lesgold, A. M., Roth, S. F., & Curtis, M. E. Foregrounding effects in discourse comprehension. *Journal of Verbal Learning and Verbal Behavior, 1979, 18,* 291–308.

Levy, B. A. Vocalization and suppression effects in sentence memory. *Journal of Verbal Learning and Verbal Behavior,* 1975, *14,* 304–316.

Liberman, I. Y., Shankweiler, D., Liberman, A. M., Fowler, C., & Fischer, F. W. Phonetic segmentation and recoding in the beginning reader. In A. S. Reber & D. L. Scarborough (Eds.), *Towards a psychology of reading: The proceedings of the CUNY conference.* New York: Wiley, 1977.

Lomax, R. G. *Testing a component processes model of reading comprehension development through linear structural equation modeling.* Unpublished dissertation, University of Pittsburgh, 1980.

MacKay, D. G. Aspects of the theory of comprehension, memory and attention. *Quarterly Journal of Experimental Psychology,* 1973, *25,* 22–40.

McClelland, James L. On the time relations of mental processes: An examination of systems of processes in cascade. *Psychological Review, 1979, 86,* 287–330.

McCulloch, W. S., & Pitts, W. H. A logical calculus of the ideas immanent in nervous activity. *Bulletin of Mathematical Biophysics,* 1943, *5,* 115–133.

Miller, G. A. The magical number seven plus or minus two: Some limits on our capacity for processing information. *Psychological Review,* 1956, *63,* 81–97.

Morton, J. A preliminary model for language behavior. In R. C. Oldfield & J. C. Marshall (Eds.), *Language.* Baltimore: Penguin, 1968. (Reprinted from *International Audiology,* 1964, *3,* 216–225.)

Morton, J. Interaction of information in word recognition. *Psychological Review,* 1969, *76,* 165–178.

Morton, J., & Long, J. Effect of word transitional probability on phoneme identification. *Journal of Verbal Learning and Verbal Behavior,* 1976, *15,* 43–52.

Newell, A. HARPY, production systems, and human cognition. In R. Cole (Ed.), *Perception and production of fluent speech.* Hillsdale, N.J.: Lawrence Erlbaum Associates, 1980.

Newell, A., & Simon, H. *Human problem solving.* Englewood Cliffs, N.J.: Prentice-Hall, 1972.

Perfetti, C. A., & Lesgold, A. M. Discourse comprehension and sources of individual differences. In M. Just & P. Carpenter (Eds.), *Cognitive processes in comprehension.* Hillsdale, N.J.: Lawrence Erlbaum Associates, 1977.

Perfetti, C. A., & Lesgold, A. M. Coding and comprehension in skilled reading and implications for reading instruction. In L. B. Resnick & P. Weaver (Eds.), *Theory and practice of early reading.* Hillsdale, N.J.: Lawrence Erlbaum Associates, 1979.

Polson, P., Atwood, M. E., Jeffries, R., & Turner, A. *The processes involved in designing software.* Paper presented at 16th Annual Carnegie Symposium on Cognition, Pittsburgh, Pennsylvania, 1980.

Rumelhart, D. E. Toward an interactive model of reading. In S. Dornic (Ed.), *Attention and performance VI: Proceedings of the Sixth International Symposium on Attention and Performance, Stockholm, Sweden, July 28–August 1, 1975.* Hillsdale, N.J.: Lawrence Erlbaum Associates, 1977.

Sternberg, S. Memory-scanning: Mental processes revealed by reaction-time experiments. *American Scientist,* 1969, *57,* 421–455.

Tulving, E., & Donaldson, W. *Organization of memory.* New York: Academic Press, 1972.

Wernicke, C. *Der aphasische Symptomenkomplex.* Breslau: Cohn und Weigart, 1874.

Wernicke, C. The symptom complex of aphasia. In R. S. Cohen & M. Wartofsky (Eds.), *Boston studies in the philosophy of science* (Vol. 4). Dordrecht: Reidel, 1966.

Wickelgren, W. Speed–accuracy tradeoff and information processing dynamics. *Acta Psychologica,* 1977, *41,* 67–85.

Author Index

Numbers in *italics* refer to the pages on which the complete references are listed.

409

Subject Index

DATE DUE